Preface

This book of case studies originated with the papers submitted to the 2nd Annual Conference on *Managing in Enterprise Contexts*, jointly organised by the Sheffield Business School and the School of Financial Studies and Law at the Sheffield Hallam University and kindly sponsored by the Sheffield Training and Enterprise Council. Subsequently, a number of additional papers were gathered together from other sources on related topics, and assembled into a book of case studies on the general theme of the public sector in transition.

The book is concerned primarily with managing the transition between a wholly public sector context and a context of quasi-private markets. It spans a wide range of institutions, including further and higher education, local authorities, the health service and also the church which faces related problems. However, there are also a number of case studies of privatisation in foreign countries which deal broadly with asset sales as well as internal issues of management.

What all of the papers have in common is a desire to shed some light on the enormous difficulties which have had to be addressed as public sector organisations face up to an increasingly changeable environment which requires them to take on board in varying degrees the methods and culture of the private sector. As the cases show, some have succeeded better than others in meeting this challenge, but all have made significant progress.

Whilst most of the papers have been written by academics, they are not mere exercises in theory but are strongly rooted in addressing practicalities. They should accordingly be of interest to practitioners as well as to teachers. It should be noted that all of the papers have been refereed and a substantial amount of editorial work has been undertaken. The effort extended has undoubtedly paid dividends in terms of the quality of submissions, some of which are adaptations of material published in refereed journals. In this context Bill Richardson, Sonny Nwankwo and Luiz Montanheiro acknowledge the particularly important contribution of Peter Curwen in his role as lead editor.

The editors wish to thank all those who have contributed to the assembling of this book, whether as conference attendees, contributors of papers or in other supportive roles. We would also wish to record our thanks to our colleagues at PAVIC Publications and the sterling effort of the Graphics Unit at Sheffield Hallam University in creating such an excellent end-product. The continuing support of the Sheffield Training and Enterprise Council is also gratefully acknowledged.

Peter Curwen
Bill Richardson
Sonny Nwankwo
Luiz Montanheiro
October 1994

P636
1500
QAT M
(Cur)

THE PUBLIC SECTOR IN TRANSITION:
Case Studies in the Management of Change.

Edited by   re

Bill Richardson

Sonny Nwankwo

Luiz Montanheiro

086 339 4590.

Published by   PAVIC Publications
                                Library and Learning Resources
                                Sheffield Hallam University

Design and Typesetting by   Graphics Unit
                                Library and Learning Resources
                                Sheffield Hallam University

Printed by   Print Unit
                                Sheffield Hallam University

PAVIC Publications
Library and Learning Resources

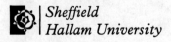 Sheffield
Hallam University

ISBN 0 86339 4590
© 1994

Contents

THE ROLE OF TQM IN FURTHER EDUCATION

Professors Dave Morris and Bob Haigh, Sheffield Business School

Introduction

It is always perilous to generalise. Such an assertion, whilst itself a generalisation, nevertheless has some validity. Generalisations which are too broad in scope lack analytical and explanatory capacity, whilst those which are too narrow in scope are open to refutation by reference to specific cases. In considering the significance of philosophy and system in Total Quality management, this paper seeks to steer a middle course between the two extremes of generalisation, the overly broad and the overly narrow. It also seeks to explore the relationship between the two concepts of philosophy and system and, finally, affords an empirical example illustration of their integration in the implementation of Total Quality management within the Student Service Department of a college of Further Education in the UK.

Philosophy

All philosophies differ in content, but all can be held to contain certain common elements. This commonality may be depicted as follows:

- a challenge to the status quo: a critique of the past and present.
- a set of values.
- a vehicle for change: which facilitates the movement from the status quo towards
- a future desired state.

Such a schema facilitates both a comparison between differing philosophies and an analysis of any one philosophy.[1] It is in this latter form that the schema will be utilised. When specifically applied to the approach to management designated by the term Total Quality management, the schema reveals the emergence of the following scenario:

1

- *a challenge to the status quo:* Konosuke Matsushita adequately summarised the more radical challenge presented to the managerial status quo existing in Europe and North America when he stated that:[2]

> We are going to win and the industrial West is going to lose out: there's nothing you can do about it because the reasons for your failure are within yourselves.
>
> Your firms are built on the Taylor model; even worse so are you heads, with the bosses doing the thinking while the workers wield the screwdrivers. You're convinced, deep down, that this is the right way to run a business.
>
> For you, the essence of management is getting the ideas out of the heads of the bosses into the hands of labour.
>
> We are beyond the Taylor model: business, we know, is now so complex and difficult, the survival of firms so hazardous in an environment increasingly unpredictable, competitive and fraught with danger, that their continued existence depends on the day-to-day mobilisation of every ounce of intelligence.
>
> For us, the core of management is precisely the art of mobilising and pulling together the intellectual resources of all employees in the service of the firm. Only be drawing on the combined brainpower of all of its employees can a firm face up to the turbulence and constraints of today's environment.
>
> This is why our large companies give their employees three to four times more training than yours. This is why they foster within the firm such intensive exchange and communication. This is why they seek constantly everybody's suggestions and why they demand from the educational system increasing numbers of graduates as well as bright and well-educated generalists: these people are the life blood of industry. Your socially minded bosses, often full of good intentions, believe their duty is to protect the people in their firms.
>
> We, on the other hand, are realists and consider it our duty to get our people to defend their firms which will pay them back a hundredfold for their dedication. By doing this, we end up being more social than you.

The radical critique which Matsushita offers of management practice in the Western manufacturing sector has equal applicability to the Western service sector and, in particular, to the educational system. After all, was it no less a person than Deming who observed that service workers have a product; service?

A somewhat less radical, but no less challenging, critique of the status quo is afforded by Lowe and McBean, who represent the deficiencies of current management practice in diagrammatical form.[3]

In both cases the message is clear. The philosophy of TQM has its origin in a critique of the status quo.

- *a set of values*: the service sector, in general, and the education areas, in particular, is favoured by the work of Parasuraman *et al*.[4] They provide a comprehensive coverage of the expectations that customers may entertain of any service, including education, and the features which they expect that service to exhibit:

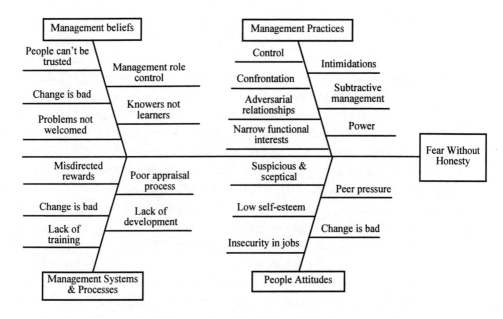

Figure 1

Source: Lowe and McBean (1989)

- *access*: involves *approachability* and ease of contact.
- *communication*: means keeping the customers *informed* in language which they can understand and *listening* to them.
- *competence*: means *possession* by the organisation's personnel of the required skills and knowledge to perform the service.
- *courtesy*: includes *politeness, respect, consideration* and *friendliness* of the organisation's personnel.
- *reliability*: involves *consistency* of performance and *dependability*.
- *responsiveness*: involves the *willingness, readiness* of employees to provide service.
- *security*: is *freedom* from danger, risk and doubt.
- *tangibles*: include the physical evidence of the quality of service provision.
- *understanding/knowing the customer*: involves making the effort to understand the customer's needs and expectations.

All the above can be said to be values which, if manifested by an organisation's personnel, will serve to meet the needs and expectations of customers in the service area of which education is a significant part.

- *a vehicle for change*: TQM through its effective implementation, is perceived as the agent of change which will sweep away the old management practices characteristic of the status quo and herald a new era. Whilst the 'Gurus' might differ somewhat in their

3

prescriptions for the implementation of TQM, there is sufficient of a consensus for it to be possible to discern a number of agreed features of TQM as a vehicle for change.

- *the customer is king*: Feinenbaum states in his analysis that the first and most important characteristic of TQM is that it "...start(s) with the customer's requirements and end(s) successfully only when the customer is satisfied with the way the product or service of the enterprise meets those requirements."[5]

- *everyone participates in TQM*: "initially, total quality participation extended only to the company president, directors, middle management, staff, foremen, line workers and salesmen. But, in recent years, the definition has been expanded to include subcontractors, distribution systems and affiliated companies."[6]

- *quality measurement is essential*: "It is necessary to determine the status of quality throughout the company. Quality measurements for each area of activity must be established where they don't exist and reviewed where they do."[7]

- *align corporate systems to support quality*: "Do the existing systems and corporate structures support the fulfilment of such goals as quality, cost and scheduling? If they are found inappropriate for meeting the cross functioning goals, is top management prepared to make the necessary changes in such areas as organisational structure, planning and control and even in personnel practices, including reallocation?"[8]

- *constantly strive for quality improvement*: "Improve constantly and forever the system of production and service, to improve quality and productivity, and thus to constantly decrease costs."[9]

- *a future desired state*: the goal that is being sought, through the critique of the status quo, through the espousing of values which are customer focused and through rigorous and effective implementation of TQM as a vehicle of change, can be graphically displayed as follows:

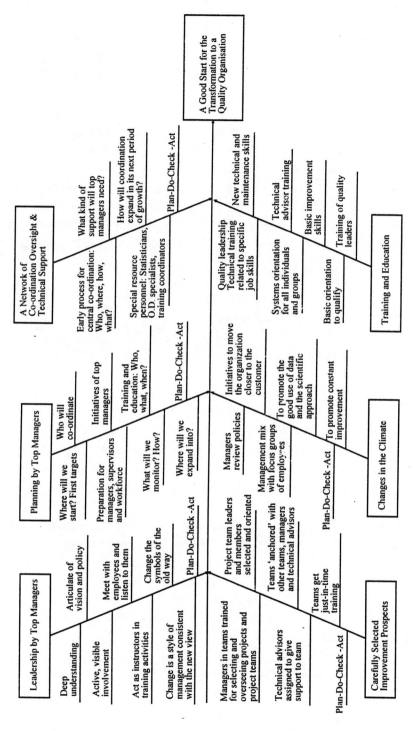

Figure 2

5

System

In recent years the term 'system' in TQM has become closely associated with documenting internal organisational processes which are repeatedly performed in such a way as to gain accreditation from an external validating body. Here reference is made to such 'systems' as ISO 9000 and BS 5750. But the term 'system' has another broader connotation, a connotation which found favour during the development of TQM. It is upon 'system' in this wider, original meaning that emphasis is now placed.

The origin of a system approach can be traced to the analogy drawn between the human body and simple, human society. The initial use made of the concept of system in social anthropology was further developed in sociology by such writers as Talcott Parsons before making its appearance in management writings. In its most basic form, a system can be portrayed thus:

INPUT ⟶ THROUGHPUT (transformation) ⟶ OUTPUT

To add complexity, a feedback loop can be added to link output to input and thus to reactivate the system into another cycle.

It is important to note that a system approach contains a set of assumptions which are inherent within the model. The message is simple: use the model, accept the assumptions. The assumptions can be stated as follows:

- a number of more or less *interrelated elements* each of which contributes to the maintenance of the total system.
- synergy, in that the totality of the system is greater than the sum of its component elements.
- a boundary, which delineates the system and which may be open, partially open or closed in relation to exchanges between the system and its environment.
- sub systems, comprising interrelations between particular elements within the total system and which themselves have the characteristics of a system.
- a flow or process throughout the system.
- feedback, which serves to keep the system in a state of dynamic equilibrium with respect to its environment.

The system approach in this wider, original sense and its application to the productive process can, for example, be seen in Deming's work.[10]

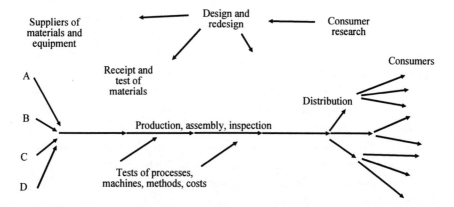

Figure 3

Source: Deming

Indeed, it is feasible to contend that it was through the utilisation of a system model that Deming's contribution to the development of TQM was born and permitted the delineation of the Deming Cycle of "PLAN, DO, CHECK, ACT"[11]

Synthesis

If a synthesis is attempted of the philosophical and system components of TQM with a view to the development of a model of implementation which encapsulates both of those key aspects, then the following is offered as one way in which that might be brought to fruition:

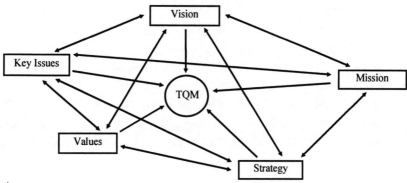

Figure 4

Some explanation is required of the terms used in the above model:

- *vision*: refers to the future desired state, the situation which is being sought, to which the organisation and its personnel are committed. It provides a central focus against which the managerial process of planning, leading, organising and controlling can be co-ordinated. Its acceptance serves to give purpose to day-to-day actions and activities at all organisational levels and to all organisational functions.
- *mission*: represents a series of statements of discrete objectives, allied to vision, the attainment of all of which will ensure the attainment of the future desired state which is itself the vision.
- *strategy*: comprises the sequencing and added specificity of the mission statements to provide a set of objectives which the organisation has pledged itself to attain.
- *values*: serve as a source of unity and cohesion between the members of the organisation and also serve to ensure congruence between organisational actions and external customer demands and expectations. Without such congruence no organisation can expect to attain efficiency, effectiveness and economy let alone ensure its long-term survival.
- *key issues*: these are issues which must be addressed in pursuit of the quality which is demanded by customers to meet their needs and expectations. A key issue can be characterised as one which is:[12]

  Important to the customer

  Creating substantial cost arising from poor quality

  Happening frequently

  Having substantial impact upon the organisation

  Creating substantial delay in the delivery of a service

Practice

It was Alexander Pope who wrote,

> For forms of government let fools contest.

> What ere is best administered is best.

With this piece of sound advice in mind, the adoption of the above model is applied to the Student Services Department of a College of Further Education.

Colleges of Further Education provide courses, largely of a vocational nature, to a primarily 16-19 age group in the UK. In so doing, they are in competition with Secondary Schools and Six Form Colleges which, whilst offering less vocationally oriented courses, draw upon 16-18 year olds. The colleges are also in competition with universities, which offer both non-vocational and vocational courses to 18 year olds and upwards. Since 1 April 1993, the Colleges of Further Education have been parted from one of their traditional paymasters, local government. Whilst still in receipt of monies from central government, this source of income has become far more tightly constrained and increasingly the colleges have found themselves obliged to compete for student generated income against their institutional rivals. For the colleges, money now follows the student. This has meant that the quality of the educational experience offered to students has become of central importance to the colleges' future. Monitoring by the governmental inspectorate means that failure to recruit and retain students will imperil the colleges' future by limiting their income and capacity for growth.

For the colleges, such changes have been significant. They have led to a questioning of the old ways of management and the search for new ways of meeting the demands placed upon them. The college which provides the basis for this case study in the implementation of TQM using the synthesised model described above, is one which has consciously chosen to make quality improvements, both in the courses it offers and the way in which they are managed, its route to survival and growth. In so doing, it deliberately chose not to emphasise quality control through the narrow use of the term system as implied by BS 5750, but sought to use the broader approach to quality as embodied in the philosophy of TQM. Such a decision was taken on an assessment of cost and effectiveness, but the telling factor was the prospect of continuous quality improvement contained within the TQM approach.

Student Service Departments within the Colleges have a brief ranging from the enrolment of students - covering counselling, medical and personal social services, student finance and accommodation - through to career guidance. They are at the forefront in providing much of the context within which students assess their educational experience. The same context is one which the governmentally appointed inspectorate also examines and upon which it makes recommendations as to the future level of funding that the colleges will receive.

In Stockman College of Further Education, the College which furnishes this example, the staff of the Student Service Department worked together to develop a vision[13]. In doing so, their deliberations were aided and informed by the knowledge which they had gained through a questionnaire of the perceived needs of both their internal and external customers. The vision statement that all of the personnel felt best reflected their aspirations for their Department and met the broader expectations of their customers was stated as:

> To continuous improve the quality of all the services
> which we offer to all of our customers.

To need to bring the vision to reality led to the development of a series of mission statements:

Statement 1: To ease the transition into Further and Higher Education for students new to the College, including those from overseas, by enabling them to make appropriate choice of course, mode of attendance, funding and other means of support, so that they are able to make the best use of their time at College.

Statement 2: To provide a high quality Counselling Service to students and staff and a welfare service to students who are experiencing practical, financial, educational or personal problems, in order to support them and enhance their educational performance.

Statement 3: To provide support for tutors and their students on an individual group or course basis in areas related to student support and work closely with others in the College in providing in-service staff development related to student support.

Statement 4: To maintain proactive and productive links with the Students Union, the College Medical Service and College faculties in developmental and preventative work for the benefit of the College community as a whole.

Statement 5: To maintain proactive links with external agencies that maintain and enhance the professional delivery and development of Student Services.

Having reached a consensus upon their vision and the mission statements necessary to its fulfilments, the staff of the Student Services Department felt that there was sufficient evidence in the feedback received in the answers to their customer questionnaire to warrant acceptance of the values to be found in the work of Parasuraman. On this basis, they next addressed the question of the strategy demanded by each of the mission statements.

Strategy Demanded for Achieving Each Mission Statement

MS 1: Initial guidance, financial advice and accreditation of prior learning and achievement (APLA).
Participation in open evenings/future events/careers event.
Individual Learning Contracts.
Accommodation Service.
Nursery Provision.

MS 2: Welfare Service.
Counselling Service.
Access Funds.

Student Loans.

Chaplaincy.

MS 3: Implementation of Equal Opportunities Policy, Student Grievance Procedures and Student Disability Procedures.

Provision of Careers Guidance for students.

Contribution to student induction courses.

Direct consultation with course tutors.

Working with Staff Development Officer to provide staff development at College and faculty levels.

Provision of work experience for students.

MS 4: Representation on College committees and working groups.

Working with the College medical staff to promote health.

Development of close links with formal staff and student groups.

MS 5: Working with specified external organisations and groups on a regular basis.

With the vision established and accepted, with the values agreed, with the mission statements codified and with the resulting, supportive strategies having been discerned, the staff of the Student Service Department moved to the identification of key issues. This paper does not permit a detailed coverage of all of the key issues which were identified and the action which was taken, but an example of how the key issue of student accommodation was addressed is detailed below(figure 5).

Conclusion

This paper has sought to show how it is possible to integrate two key elements of TQM and how the emerging synthesis can provide the basis of a model of implementation which will, itself, facilitate the attainment of continuous quality improvement.

The example is not without inherent limitations. For example, the staff of the Student Service Department of the College will undoubtedly encounter, and have to resolve, problems arising from the necessity to match the needs and expectations of both their internal and external customers with their own capability and capacity to deliver services at the level of quality demanded by those customers.

For the present, however, the staff have taken the first crucial step along the continuous quality improvement. They have put in place an infrastructure which goes some way to constituting an answer to those most difficult of questions whenever the claim to be

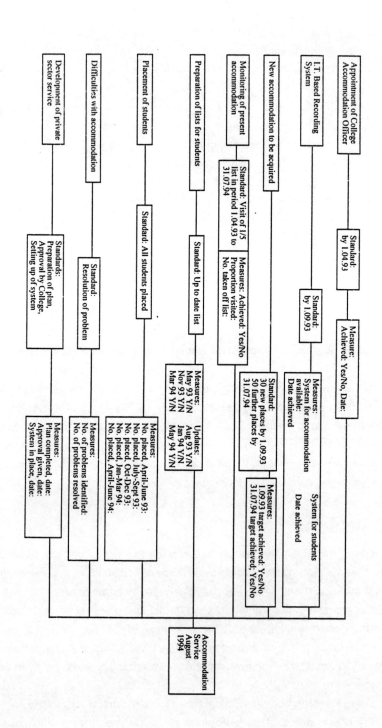

Figure 5

12

delivering quality is made, namely, 'By what means?' and 'Can you prove it?' The staff have discerned the means, they have sought to establish standards and measures by which to prove that they are delivering a quality service. Only the future will reveal whether or not the initial promise shown will be maintained and developed.

Footnotes and References

1. Clearly, the interrelationship between the four elements differs in different philosophies, with some being far more rigidly internally integrated than others.
2. Matsushita, K. Executive Director, Matsushita Electric.
3. Lowe, T.A. & McBean, G.M. (1989) 'Honesty Without Fear', *Proceedings of the 43rd Annual Quality Congress* (Toronto: ASQC) p.177.
4. Parasuraman, A., Zeitham, I.V. & Berry, L (1985) 'A Conceptual Model of Service Quality and its Implications for Future Research', *Journal of Marketing, 49* (Fall) pp. 41-50.
5. Feigenbaum, A.V. (1983) *Total Quality Control* (McGraw-Hill) 3rd ed, p.85.
6. Ishikawa, K. (1985) *What Is Total Quality Control?* (Prentice-Hall) p.91.
7. Crosby, P. (1979) *Quality Is Free* (McGraw-Hill) P.113.
8. Imai, M. (1986) *Kaizen - The Key to Japan's Competitive Success* (Random House Business Division) pp.222-23.
9. Deming, W.E. (1986) *Out of the Crisis* (MIT Center for Advanced Engineering Study) p.23.
10. Neave, H. (1990) *The Deming Dimension* (SPC Press) p.247.
11. This idea was developed by Deming from the work of Shewart.
12. Smith, A.K. Unpublished paper from the Department of Motor Vehicles, Sacramento, California.
13. The name of the College of Further Education used in this example has been altered in order to ensure its anonymity.

STRATEGIC MANAGEMENT WITHIN UNIVERSITIES: SCENARIOS OF THE FUTURE

Geoff Archer, University of York

Introduction

Strategic management is the process of making and implementing strategic decisions. Critically, it involves making a match between the resources available to an organisation and the threats and opportunities created by the external environment. The resulting strategy links what the organisation wants to achieve - its objectives - with the policies adopted to guide its activities (Bowman & Asch, 1987).

The above description of strategic management centres around the presence of an organisation, the structure of which will depend upon the expectations of the stakeholders as well as the task(s) they perform and the environment(s) in which they operate (Mintzberg, 1979). Not only can structure be affected by strategy, but the structure of an organisation can also influence the strategic decision-making process.

Universities in the 1990's operate in an environment which is changing, perhaps as rapidly as at any time in their history. This paper aims to investigate these changes and suggest how universities may respond to them. These changes are analysed by examining firstly the expectations of stakeholders and secondly changes in the external environment. A short discussion of the interaction between structure and strategy is followed by a selection of scenarios which describe some of the possible futures for a university.

University Stakeholders and Their Expectations

In trying to understand what forces drive change within the university sector, it important to understand what the expectations of these stakeholders currently are, and how these might change in response to environmental changes.

Governments

(i) National

The 1980's have seen a sharp increase in the number of students attending university, and until recently numbers were expected to continue rising throughout the 1990's. The current economic recession and the associated rise in the Public Sector Borrowing Requirement (PSBR) have severely restricted central government's ability to fund this expansion. Perhaps because of this, student loans have been introduced and subsequently accelerated. As will be argued later, the extra financial contribution borne by students (and their parents) has the potential to alter significantly the provision of higher education (HE).

In common with many other public enterprises, universities have had a large number of changes imposed upon them by government, either directly or through research councils. Examples include the reporting of key financial ratios, financial plans and publication records. The general thrust of these changes appears to have been an attempt to achieve three main objectives:

(i) To increase numbers entering HE.

(ii) To encourage the teaching of science, engineering and applied social science.

(iii) To increase the selectivity with which central government funds research.

All of these objectives are being pursued under the constraints imposed by the government's priority objective, namely reducing the PSBR.

(ii) European Union

With the increasing involvement of the European Union (EU) in funding higher education teaching and research, it is no longer sufficient for universities to seek to satisfy only the national government's expectations. There exist important funding opportunities from the EU for those establishments which possess the organisational skills required to compete successfully in the FRAMEWORK research programmes. One of the important expectations of the EU in funding such work is the building up of the technological infrastructure in its less-developed member states.

Employees

Ackoff, in a lecture entitled 'Beyond Total Quality Management' (1992), warned against the over-concentration upon satisfying customer expectations at the expense of those of employees. In a university, 'core' academic and some 'peripheral' research staff, most notably research fellows (Atkinson, 1985), hold positions that are vertically enlarged (Mintzberg, 1979). As a result, there is a strong sense of self-perceived professionalism and strong resistance to the imposition of change by other stakeholders.

Amongst lecturers in universities, particularly those with active research functions, very few are appointed because of special skills in their teaching role. Appointment is largely made on research and grant-winning ability. Indeed, the attraction to many is not the teaching role, but the prospects of a career structure not afforded to many solely within a research capacity. The expectations of this key section of university employees may become more important and more problematic if work pressures continue to rise for those who are currently active in both roles. Choices will need to be made if current trends towards greater numbers of students and increased selectivity of research fundholders continue.

Industry

Industry requires three main things from HE establishments:

(i)   The supply of a graduate workforce with general problem solving, communication and organisational skills. These skills are required regardless of any specific vocational or subject oriented skills.
(ii) The provision of courses which assist industry to continue to train and develop its human resources.
(iii) Research expertise which generates solutions to problems or provides market opportunities. These may be sought at the pre-competitive research stage, for example DTI-sponsored LINK schemes or via confidential arrangements with selected research groups.

Each of these requirements creates opportunities for HE establishments. However, it is clear that each may require different organisational structures, strategies and human resources skills. The early recognition of this within certain universities may provide them with a competitive advantage over those that attempt to be all-rounders.

Students

Students entering HE in the 1990's have to choose between an increasing number of universities offering more course options than ever before. Any demand forecast for universities needs to answer two main questions; who buys? and why do they buy?

In marketing terms, consumers are thought to buy benefits not products. Put into a university context, this implies that many students come to university and study a course not primarily because of the course subject itself, but to gain the benefits that accrue from their studies, qualifications, better career prospects and so forth. Understanding this is sometimes difficult for an academic who derives satisfaction from the exploration and understanding of a subject.

Many students choose universities and discount others on the basis of whether the university fits in with their chosen 'lifestyle' (Featherstone, 1987). Oxford and Cambridge do not, despite their obvious attractions in terms of improved career prospects for graduates, prestige etc, have the highest applications to places ratios. This may suggest that many potential Oxbridge students feel that their perception of Oxbridge life is not on their 'lifestyle shopping list'. This observation may have important implications for those universities which are attempting to widen the socio-economic background from which they obtain their students.

As the financial contribution borne by students and their parents increases, it is likely that their influence may increase in matters such as course design, accommodation and recreational facilities.

Local Populations

Many factors which students take into account when choosing a university are not under the direct control of the university, for example location, accommodation costs and transport facilities. The fact that a university cannot control these factors directly highlights the fact that universities need to understand the expectations of local populations and their representatives.

These expectations include employment opportunities, sporting and cultural facilities and, increasingly, educational facilities for the community. Where these local expectations are not satisfied, there is an increased risk of 'Town vs. Gown' hostility. In extreme cases, this hostility has led some universities to resemble fortresses as they have attempted to ensure the personal security of staff and students.

The External Environment

In the management strategy literature, the external environment has been broken down into four (STEP) domains:

- Social
- Technological
- Economic
- Political

These categories have been used in this paper as a framework for identifying the key drivers of University-sector change (Fahey & Narayanan, 1986) in the next 10 to 15 years. Fuller analysis is included for reference in the appendix which also includes personal values and environmental trends. Those STEP factors considered to be most important have been prioritised using an importance vs. predictability matrix and are shown in this way in Figure 1. Of these factors, governmental policies and related funding and technology are addressed in detail below.

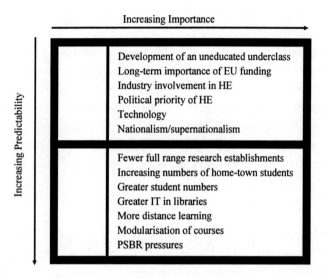

Figure 1
Important STEP factors

Political Trends and Governmental Funding

In the university system, the most important single driver is the level of overall funding. Given a governmental priority of reducing the PSBR, it seems likely that HE funding will come under further pressure. This is manifesting itself in two important trends:

- Lower units of resource for teaching costs.
- Greater selectivity in the funding of teaching and research.

The targeting of funding towards subjects which are considered to be national priorities, or at least away from the Arts, comes at a time when the numbers applying to study many Arts subjects is increasing. One of the challenges facing universities hoping to continue teaching the Arts is to find a way of ensuring that this does not financially compromise the university as a whole. The problem is especially acute for those universities which are committed to limiting class sizes.

In the political domain the emphasis has been, and is likely to continue to be, for universities to provide better value for money. The recent White Paper (Anon, 1993) has highlighted the fact that HE, and in particular the scientific sector, plays a vital role in the quest to achieve national and supra-national goals. In this sector there has been an important shift in emphasis by the government away from a laissez-faire attitude and towards non-defence related research.

Important issues raised in the White Paper include:

- Favouring the M.Sc route to a Ph.D.
- Fewer fixed-term research staff.
- Greater research funding selectivity (person NOT proposed project).

These three issues in particular may combine to create a 'triple whammy' affecting those research establishments active in both teaching and research. The need for high-quality and high-level teaching for M.Sc students means that fewer fixed-term research staff will be the norm and fewer research staff are likely to succeed in attracting research council funding. One of the most significant political factors will be the influence of EU law and directives, which are currently affecting the research decisions of industrial and governmental stakeholders.

Technological Trends

Of the technological drivers identified, the most important is likely to be the role of IT. For example, an important IT-based development is the way information is stored and delivered to universities, resulting in the substituting of electronic databases for the subscription to paper-text Journals to be held within the central library. Since the technical infrastructure is already in place in most departments and at the British Library, a switch to databases together with e-Mail access to documents, would be both technology- and demand-led. The biggest obstacle to this switch continues to be the human resource implications, and the political will and capital resources of the British and university libraries to extend the current pilot scheme (being implemented at Nottingham University) to the entire University network.

In the context of technological developments, however, perhaps even more important in the long term will be the development of interactive computer aided learning (CAL) programs - *Max Headroom* prototypes (Waistell, 1993). These are starting to be developed in many subjects backed by national funding (Dempster, 1993). As the conflicting time demands of both teaching and market-driven research rise, the relative advantages (Rogers, 1983) of CAL-based learning approaches over conventional teaching methods will start to be recognised. When neural network-based computing power is more widely available (present applications are mainly being developed for industry (Ryman-Tubb, 1993)), CAL devices will be able to modify their questions and style of tutorship to suit the individual student's ability as judged by previous responses obtained in working with the programme. Technology of this form will be feasible within the next 10-15 years.

20

In the home, TV has helped to change many routines in family life and the remote control has changed TV viewing patterns. CAL programs, if truly interactive, could change learning patterns, allowing individual students to learn at their own pace. Learning could take place whenever it was most convenient. Students could have the opportunity to switch between topics, fast-forward, rewind and explore in detail areas of particular interest. The computer tutor would probe and question in a similar manner to a conventional tutor.

Different rates of adoption of such technology could lead to universities diverging markedly in character in the future. Forecasting which universities will be at the forefront of this type of IT-based learning is difficult. However, pressure on those academics and institutions with dual-roles (teaching and research) will undoubtedly lead to the introduction of such teaching techniques in order to stabilise teaching loads. Clearly, success or failure in the use of this technology depends upon its acceptability to the user and the other stakeholders outlined earlier in this paper.

Structure and Strategy

Mintzberg (1979) describes six basic co-ordinating mechanisms which to a greater or lesser extent are all used within my University:

- Mutual adjustment.
- Direct supervision.
- Standardisation of work processes, outputs, skills and norms.

Following Mintzberg, depending upon the relative importance of these co-ordinating mechanisms, the overall organisation will tend towards one of several configurations. The dominant configuration for most UK universities has been that of the professional bureaucracy. The environment has been stable yet complex, the pull to professionalise has dominated. The core academic and senior research staff hold very vertically enlarged positions. Their tasks may be either relatively specialised in the case of a research fellow (horizontally specialised), or varied in the case of an academic who is active in both teaching, research and bureaucratic and marketing duties (horizontally enlarged).

How will changes in the environment affect this structure? In the light of the discussion in the previous section it seems likely that many of the changes in the external environment are likely to increase the pull to divisionalise the functions of universities into teaching and research functions and/or into commercially and non-commercially funded teaching or research. Given the importance that many academics place upon the symbiotic nature of teaching and research, it is unlikely that the first-mentioned type of structural change will be easily made without opposition.

Just as strategy and the environment tend to pull universities into particular structures, the structures adopted will affect strategic management processes and the strategies adopted.

The analysis and choice elements of strategic management in many universities, particularly the more traditional ones, can involve a large number of individuals in a committee with many working parties. With a weak line management structure to implement any decisions made, compromise (satisficing) rather that optimisation is the usual decision-making outcome. It is no surprise, therefore, that some universities find it difficult to generate strategies which can meet the expectations of external stakeholders. The absence of external stakeholders in the strategic decision-making process can lead to 'groupthink' (Janis, 1972) and strategies which do not truly either identify or address the strategic challenges facing universities in general and the university in particular.

To date, university strategies can be interpreted using the generic strategy approach of Porter (1985). He identifies four generic strategies corresponding to the four quadrants of the matrix below:

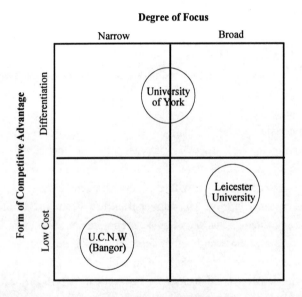

Strategic developments presently emerging might also be viewed from this generic strategy perspective. For example, rapid and substantial growth can be considered as being analogous to a low-cost generic strategy. Student:staff ratios would be increased, thereby spreading fixed costs over a greater teaching revenue base and minimising future cuts in fully-funded teaching revenues by attracting additional fees-only students.

Example of universities appearing to take this approach are Leicester and Bangor (the latter having more than doubled student numbers in the last three years). The other option, concentration upon research performance with restrained growth in student numbers, can be considered as being a differentiated generic strategy. The option to reduce the burden of fixed costs significantly by increasing student:staff ratios is not possible.

Porter highlights the point that an organisation needs to identify its key sustainable competitive advantage is and to devote its management effort towards developing that advantage. The structures currently adopted by many universities make this difficult.

Scenarios

Currently, the future of the university system is being discussed as an entity similar to the football league. In other words, there is a perceived distinction between the Super-league and the rest. One scenario being mooted divides the English university system into three parts: the first will consist of roughly six universities which will continue to both research and teach at the highest level and across a wide range of subjects; the second will contain a further dozen or so universities which will continue to both teach and research but with fewer departments fulfilling both functions; the remaining universities will be primarily teaching organisations.

The scenarios put forward below are most likely to be relevant for those universities outside the super-league. However, some features may apply for individual departments within super-league universities. The technique used to generate these scenarios is based on that described by Loveridge (1993).

These scenarios have been developed to explore possible futures for the University of York, although some of the 'event strings' described may have relevance for many other universities. They have been written in order to amplify, if not caricature, current trends and to stimulate discussion of strategic options facing universities. As such, they are the author's personal view of some of the possible futures for the university. They do not necessarily reflect the views of the University of York.

Pay-as-you-learn

Event Strings

1. In response to increasing pressure for places on several courses including Computer Science, English and Music, the university introduces additional fees, (initially means-tested) payable by students, intended to provide funding for both central and departmental facilities.
2. Increasing use of electronic document retrieval facilities by several large departments leads to pressure for a radical restructuring of existing facilities.

3. Changes in research council funding policy lead to reduced numbers of academics capable of securing research funding from SERC, NERC etc.
4. Key academic staff from strong departments are reappointed on contracts which offer significantly higher salaries and better non-financial rewards in return for long-term commitment.
5. 'Max Headroom' style interactive learning aids are introduced as optional resource components in several departments. Their popularity, with students more familiar with the computer A/V medium than traditional written sources, makes their widespread adoption appear likely.

The Times "Good University Guide" (of the Year 2010)

University of York

Size: 6,500 (4,500 undergraduate, 2,000 postgraduate).
Additional Course Fees: £1,500 - £5,000 p.a. dependent upon subject. Currently, a number of full scholarships are available each year to exceptional students from disadvantaged socio-economic and ethnic backgrounds.

Entrance requirements: Expect to have to achieve 'A' level equivalents of AAA for English, ABB for Economics and other Social Science departments and BBB-BCC for Science and Electronic Engineering departments.

Teaching Methods: The teaching system comprises:
Lectures: Largely given by teaching-only staff, supplemented by mid-course lectures by specialist (internal and external) research staff with current expertise of the subject area.
Tutorials: York's traditional small group tutorials are given by active research staff.
Multi-media: Interactive Computer Aided Learning (CAL) programs are available in most subjects. The computers are situated throughout campus and via digital telecommunication links.

Departmental strengths: Traditionally strong in English, Economics, Computer Science and Psychology, York has extended its renowned departments to include Chemistry, Biology and Environmental Economics and Management.

IT facilities: Electronic Inter-library loans and access to electronic document archives are a feature of the new library. Access is via the same routes as the CAL programs.

Accredited research personnel: York has one of the highest ratios of research personnel accredited with funding councils per student of any University.

Accommodation: First-year students are entitled to campus accommodation. Thereafter students have to find accommodation in the City of York. York suffers from a shortage of rental accommodation and many students choose to purchase property.

Graduate employment record: Subject for subject, York graduates enjoy employment prospects substantially better than other non-Oxbridge graduates. A significant number of graduates undertake higher degrees either at York or at the institutions of their 'guest' academic researchers.

'Look and feel': Gradually the 1960's-style buildings on campus are being replaced by light brick buildings which are landscaped into the lake surroundings. Student societies reflect the background of their members who are largely affluent, middle class and privately educated. Comments by recent graduates suggest that the campus atmosphere has altered significantly since the introduction of the CAL devices, with students preferring to spend time using them to gain knowledge and practise their intellectual skills rather than drink in the bars. Tutors are expressing some concern that personal communication skills may start to suffer as a result.

Security: Following several serious assaults upon students and staff by members of the local population, York has introduced better lighting and regular security patrols on and around the campus. These measures provide a safe atmosphere on campus but the underlying resentment of student lifestyle by the local population is still present. Students living off campus tend to come onto campus for classes only, preferring to work at home in the evening.

(taken from *The Times* (November 5th, 2010.)

Made-to-order! (in the 21st Century)

Event Strings:

1. Continued recession in the UK economy in the 1990's leads to even stricter controls on public spending on HE and research funding than those outlined in previously described Pay as You Learn (P.A.Y.L.) scenario.
2. York, having adopted a quality rather than quantity attitude to teaching, finds that it cannot support this policy with a research policy based mainly around research council support. Research council funding committees were dominated by academics from older universities and when faced with tough spending choices tended to favour their own institutions at the expense of others.
3. York finds its ageing academic community difficult to replace with suitable staff as first choices go to universities with better funding prospects.
4. Competition for industrial funding from both older universities with facilities funded by research councils and 'new' universities focused exclusively on commercial research activities and related funding sources leaves York 'stuck in the middle'.
5. A motion to introduce extra fees for courses is defeated by senate on ethical grounds.
6. As industry contracts out more of its non-core functions, demand increases for:
   - short, intensive courses.
   - 'get away and think' facilities.
   - distance learning facilities.
7. The changing emphasis of the UK economy (manufacturing/services) and changes in NHS and education provision lead to increased research and teaching opportunities in applied social sciences. These are areas in which York has strong young departments.
8. Increasingly, foreign companies and governments see some UK universities as good value for money providers of higher education in the English language medium. Accordingly, many departments are effectively funded by overseas companies and other foreign funding bodies. The benefits of an overseas educational experience are highly valued by these organisations.

'Made-to-order'

(University of York in the year 2010)

An extract from the introduction of a speech given by the Vice Chancellor in the SONY 'Technology in Music' lecture theatre (November 5th, 2010)

The University of York has developed over the last decade into a multi-cultural organisation which benefits from the experience brought to it by students and staff from nations throughout the world. Originally attracted by our expertise in the emerging applied social science arena, these individuals and their sponsoring bodies are now starting to shape the way the University views its external environment and its place in it.

The biggest changes have been in the way York looks at its courses and their content. No longer are the contents decided by US and delivered in a style convenient to US. Course content and delivery method are now designed in partnership with those organisations which fund the University directly through departmental support and indirectly through tuition fees.

The benefits of this approach to York are derived from the relative independence from central government that this brings. The major benefit for our supporting organisations is through the customisation of courses made possible by long-term educational partnerships. That this relationship has largely originated from overseas is entirely in keeping with the City of York's welcoming attitude to visitors from all parts of the world.

Instead of the rather snobbish image many predicted, in the early 1990s, for the University, York has benefitted from the fact that many of our students now come to York to study for short periods of time before returning to put what they have studied to use in their organisations. The modular nature of our courses has opened up the experience of University life to sections of the working population who previously could only have experienced higher education through distance learning.

Some comments have been made in the press regarding York's decision to research only in those areas where we can obtain support from sections of the business community. We believe that this is the only way that our output can be truly innovative and operate in the long-term interests of the University. Too many good ideas remained simply ideas in the old University system. Trying to wear two hats -pure research and applied teaching OR applied research and pure teaching is stifling to innovation on either front.

With the approach outlined above, we have avoided the trap of increasing the throughput of students simply in order to decrease cost per student. Our quality standards are as high as ever, if the steady path of organisations wishing to develop courses and facilities at York is any measure.

References

Ackoff, R.L. (1992) 'Beyond Total Quality Management', A lecture given at the University of Hull, 18th September 1992.

Anon, (1993) *Realising Our Potential - A Strategy for Science, Engineering and Technology* (London: HMSO) pp.62-64.

Atkinson, J. (1984) 'Manpower Strategies for Flexible Organisations', *Personnel Management*.

Bowman, C. and Asch, D. (1987) *Strategic Management* (London: Macmillan) p.4.

Dempster, J. (1993) 'Meeting Report CTI Swedish Forum', *Life Sciences Educational Computing* (July) pp.11-13.

Fahey, L. and Narayanan, V.K. (1986) *Macroenvironmental Analysis for Strategic Management* (St. Paul: West Publishing Company) pp.28-34.

Featherstone, M. (1987) 'Lifestyle and Consumer Culture' in D. Mercer (ed.) *Managing the External Environment: A Strategic Perspective* (London: Sage Publications) pp.188-193.

Loveridge, D.L (1993) in *Open University (B885) The Challenge of the External Environment*. Supplementary Reading Book 1, p.48.

Mintzberg, H. (1979) *The Structuring of Organisations* (Englewood Cliffs: Prentice-Hall).

Porter, M.E. (1985) *Competitive Advantage: Creating and Sustaining Superior Performance* (New York: Free Press) pp. 36-39.

Rogers, E.M. (1983) *Diffusion of Innovation* (New York: Free Press).

Ryman-Tubb, N. (1993) 'Neural Nets and Sensors: Technology and Future Prospects', in *UK Sensors Group Newletter* (December) p.3.

Waistell, R.C. (1993) in *Open University (B885) The Challenge of the External Environment*. Computer Based Learning Contribution #13 (CoSy Conference ad2000-01/1).

Appendix

	Short-Medium Term	**Long Term**
Sociological	-wider variety of student backgrounds -greater student members in HE -increasing numbers of students studying at local universities	-net N to S migration -increase in elderly state dependants -drug related crime creating social pressures and an uneducated underclass
Technological	-IT in library facilities -wider use of PC networking rather than central computer services depts. -wider use of computer modelling in science and social science subjects -increasingly multidisciplinary science and social science research	-enabling technology for fully interactive distance learning -greater systems thinking skills levels for the next generation of researchers as traditional research skills are automated -de/re-skilling of many employment areas
Economic	-reduction of the PSBR -exchange rate adjustments making UK university research good value overseas	-greater economic influence of industry in HE (teaching and research)
Environmental	-increase in demand for course/options with a high environmental science/management content.	-greater demand for distance learning as a way of reducing traffic or campus accommodation costs (particularly for universities in large conurbations)
Political	-degree of priority attached to HE by government amidst competition from other 'spending' depts. -expansion/disintegration of EU -science and technology white paper -HE education to mask unemployment -concentration of research in fewer institutions	-political concerns over the influence of technology upon society, particularly in areas of artificial intelligence, gene cloning and computer fraud -political nationalism of technology as the means to economic wealth generation -consolidation of political superpower blocks based around EU and East Europe, NAFTA, and the Far East, China? Effect of technology transfer
Personal Values	-moves towards part time degree courses to fit around other more vocational training	-demand for self-actualising courses option driven initially by early retirement beneficiaries

29

EVOLVING MARKETING MANAGEMENT IN HIGHER EDUCATION: TRAPPINGS OR SUBSTANCE?

Richard Varey, Sheffield Business School

Introduction

More than 20 years ago Charles Ames published an influential article in the *Harvard Business Review* in which he attempted to explain the apparent failings of the marketing concept. At that time industrial companies had copied marketing as a management tool from consumer good companies, but complained at its lack of success. Ames suggested that they had failed to understand the substance of the marketing concept and had merely adopted some of its superficial trappings, and in some cases had merely changed the name of their 'sales' activities to 'marketing'.

Currently the word 'marketing' is being widely voiced in connection with the new 'management' emphasis in higher education provision. After two decades will we see a repeat of the same mistakes as universities attempt to apply consumer marketing ideas to the special context of public service provision? Or is it possible that the considerable advances in marketing application ideas can provide a more appropriate framework for enlightened action?

The author has no time for a discussion as to whether or not we must adopt the marketing concept in higher education. Indeed, most institutions are actively engaged in the practice of marketing. They offer certain services and not others, they target certain students and not others and they package and promote their 'product' for a fee. Many administrators may not be conscious that this activity constitutes marketing. However, we must develop the application of the marketing philosophy with an appropriate emphasis for the special context of higher education. Conscious, informed decision-making as part of a systematic, rational, planned approach to marketing is more likely to yield desirable results than an ad-hoc, unco-ordinated approach.

There is a considerable body of marketing theory and practice which should be consulted by higher education managers as they develop and execute their marketing plans. Whilst many general principles, as well as specific lessons from service industries in particular, can be useful, it should not be forgotten that higher education is a unique industry and a few marketing principles unique to it await discovery and application.

Public Enterprise, Management and Marketing

In recent years a more rigorous approach to education management has been developed. Until 1987 and the publication of the government White Paper *Higher Education - Meeting the Challenge*, higher education institutions were seen as havens of academia, of educated people, abstract theory and educational ideas. The reforms have led to a change in the structure and funding of institutions and the development of more entrepreneurial skills and attitudes in order to respond to the changing needs of the country, in addition to performing the traditional vocational education role. The university is now expected to undertake more venturesome activities based on individual initiative to attract external funding. We have been cast into a competitive environment which requires the development of competitive strategies which will attract and satisfy customers. Suddenly, the marketing concept is relevant to the higher education sector.

Marketing: concept, philosophy and function - or selling by another name?

Marketing provides a match between the organisation's human, financial and physical resources and the wants of its customers. It must do this against the background of the dynamic characteristics of the environment in which the organisation operates. This includes direct and indirect competition, economic uncertainties, legal and political constraints, cultural and social trends, technological change and institutional patterns. The matching is achieved by planning, co-ordinating and controlling the product or service offered, the price that is charged, the style of promotion and the place where it is to be made available. The marketer is concerned with the interactive effects of these four elements of marketing activity, now well known as the 'four Ps' or the 'marketing mix' (Wills *et al*, 1983). Put another way 'the purpose of marketing is to create value for customers so that they will buy a company's product' (Keegan *et al*, 1992, p.6).

Marketing has its origins in the thrusting consumer products industries of 1950s North America. Increased postwar wealth and security led to a massive increase in consumer spending and demand for 'luxury' goods, and manufacturers sought a way to sell their own products in the face of rapidly increasing levels of competition. The growth of the US advertising and PR industry is testament to the early development of consumer marketing. Herein lies the origins of the notion of marketing as advertising and selling. In the 1960s and 1970s, industrial companies sought the same degree of success they had witnessed elsewhere by attempting to adopt marketing ideas. This was not always successful, and it was increasingly recognised that techniques were not always transferable to the different context. The 1980s saw a further shift in economic activity away from manufacturing of products towards a services-based economy and the notion of services marketing was developed. In recent years concern for greater social responsibility toward society has led to efforts to compete in order to maintain or improve consumer and social well-being, and not just to make a profit.

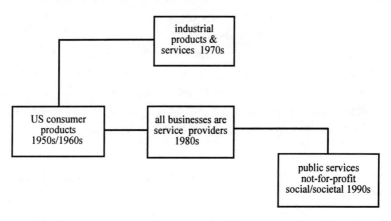

Figure 1
Evolution of Marketing Applications

Thus the marketing concept is a corporate orientation that focuses on consumer needs and wants and integrates marketing into every other corporate function. It is, simply stated, a corporate philosophy for a way of conducting business.

Marketing is often misinterpreted. It is still common, despite decades of marketing education, to hear the term 'marketing' used to mean taking a product to the market. Thus when a product is 'marketed' it is a given to be promoted and sold, but the meaning does not include design and production to meet customer needs, and is therefore too narrow to be strategic and is little more than a selling orientation. In this sense marketing is nothing more than trading activity and is certainly not a business philosophy or management technology. King (1985) identified four ways in which marketing is applied inappropriately:

- *thrust marketing* ignores what the customer wants and emphasises the selling of what can be made and price and cost cutting. Fitness for purpose, quality and value for money are not considered.
- *marketing department marketing* is a minor improvement over the establishment of a 'customer service' function but is based only on existing products and customers. There is no significant innovation, although some improvement in understanding customers can result. A specialised department is 'bolted-on' to the organisation and this relieves every one else from concerning themselves with customer needs.
- *accountants' marketing* concentrates on short-term returns and neglects long-run survival, especially in terms of R&D, quality and marketing. This approach is prevalent where executive officers are financial specialists and have no direct experience of selling or marketing.
- formula marketing is a risk-averse strategy which sees control as more important than innovation. Information is seen as important in applying tried and tested methods but is often historical and fails to give adequate attention to the future. King felt that 'real' marketing requires a strong customer focus, a long-run perspective, full use of all of the organisation's resources and innovation.

Marketing Management in Higher Education: a special case

Much of the literature on marketing in the public or not-for-profit sector fails to recognise the diversity of organisations represented. Smith (1987) has labelled the education provider as a 'social non-profit-making' organisation. His taxonomy for discriminating differences in the non-profit sector considers internal mission and the degree of competition in the external environment. Education is classed as having social objectives in a (relatively) non-competitive environment. The reforms in the UK higher education sector have markedly increased competition for the recruitment of students, whilst financial constraints have been imposed causing institutions to compete for government funding and to seek other sources of revenue such as full-cost courses and sponsorship. Universities have reacted by changing their 'product', including major updates on 'corporate' identities, in order to respond to the objectives of the *Further and Higher Education Bill* which calls for greater opportunity, choice and flexibility for those seeking post-16 education. What was once a sellers' market is now a buyers' market. This demonstrates marketing's dual function. Marketers must identify opportunities and threats and design offerings and communications with their chosen market(s).

The marketing concept envisions a mutually-satisfying exchange process between supplier and customer. The supplier then understands the needs and wants of customers and adapts its operations to deliver goods and services effectively and efficiently. This ensures a competitive advantage for the organisation. But how does the concept of exchange apply in higher education? There is real difficulty in clearly defining the 'product' and the 'customer' in higher education (Conway and Yorke, 1991).

Kotler and Levy (1969) have suggested a broader concept of marketing which is helpful in describing goods, services, organisations, people and ideas as elements which can be exchanged. Higher education provides services, has goods (for example, publications and distance learning materials) on offer to customers and institutions are long-surviving and have developed character, atmosphere and reputation which have some value (prestige and image rather than educational value). In addition, many of its employees have individual reputations and many interact directly with customers (many would argue that the university *is* the people), and research and teaching produce educated people by producing and transferring educational ideas. A variety of benefits in different forms are provided to a diverse range of 'beneficiaries'. This range of possible customers presents a problem, and marketing's job is to facilitate and realise exchanges with selected customer groups which may include school leavers, mature students (including adult returners (Pye, 1991)), potential academic staff, local and national politicians, foreign students and their governments, industry, academic staff, administrators and support staff, sponsors, parents and the local community in general. Each group represents a set of different needs and the marketer's tool of segmentation (see Saunders and Lancaster (1980) for a discussion of 'student benefit segments') is useful and can be developed as part of an overall marketing plan which should establish priorities based on continuously updated knowledge of needs, customer selection criteria, and the nature of competitive forces and other external opportunities and threats.

What is the primary objective of higher education and how is this best met? I believe that the purpose of a university is to discover, consolidate and communicate new knowledge. But is higher education defined and fixed by its providers as a given to be promoted and sold or is it a service to society (including industry and commerce) which must be responsive and therefore is to be designed and delivered by service provider organisations? Pye (1991) has discussed higher education as perceived by students, suggesting a number of reasons why they might attend a course. These include job training, a qualification, personal growth, entertainment, escape from unemployment and pressure of expectations of parents and peer groups. This suggests that there is no single product/service and associated benefits to be 'sold'.

The traditional view of education is that the institution provides a service to the student as a consumer and that courses must be designed to satisfy their needs. However, if government (as funders), society and industry (as beneficiaries) are seen as the ultimate customers, then education is a value-adding process and the student is the end product. The

35

institution must then concentrate on producing qualified employees-to-be. Thus, the educational institution is a manufacturing organisation and the manufacturing process itself should add value. These two types of customers have different perceptions of value (Conway and Yorke, 1991). This is a major problem for the education marketing manager. How can clear marketing objectives be set when the picture is complicated by the need to adopt a combination of service marketing and product marketing approaches? The issues involved in identifying customers in the public service sector has been examined elsewhere (Varey, 1993). Conway and Yorke have suggested that unless perceptual congruence can be achieved among employers, students and teachers (i.e. a common view of needs and satisfiers), then a successful marketing strategy is difficult to achieve.

Gronroos (1980) does not see a conflict between service and product marketing, although a large body of literature discussing major differences has grown up in the past two decades. Gronroos urges the understanding of a wider role for marketing than the selling of courses to students. This should encompass the buyer/seller interaction and requires senior management responsibility for marketing. The interactive marketing approach includes the permeation of the understanding and acceptance of the marketing concept to all layers of, and throughout, the organisation. Internal marketing (Robinson & Long, 1987) is a process for marketing the marketing concept within the organisation as satisfied employees will provide satisfying service to customers (Berry, 1984). A market-orientation does not guarantee a marketing-orientation, nor vice-versa.

The Prevailing Situation

Who are the marketers in higher education? The new marketers have often been seconded officers, often without specialist knowledge of marketing, often lacking experience of putting the tools and techniques to work effectively and usually without the influence, authority and resources needed really to impact on planning service provision.

How is the marketing philosophy and its associated tools and techniques applied in the higher education sector? There is much activity in the running of higher education institutions which may be identified with some aspect of marketing. Even where a marketing approach has not been consciously implemented, it is possible to offer marketing theory to explain institutions' responses and some prescriptions for managing the process of effective competition in student recruitment and funding. What is harder to discern is co-ordinated activity which could be described by the term 'marketing management' as being:

> the process of planning and executing the conception, pricing, promotion, and distribution of ideas, goods, and services to create exchanges that satisfy individual and organisational objectives' (American Marketing Association, 1985).

and as having:

> the task of influencing the level, timing, and composition of demand in a way that will help the organisation achieve its objectives' (Kotler, 1991, p.11).

It is still the case that marketing-related decisions are being made based on some basic assumptions about what is needed. It would seem that marketers in higher education lack detailed knowledge and understanding of their markets and customer groups. Market research is one of the first tools to be used but this is often in an ad-hoc manner which may not answer the real issues of strategic management.

Marketing is still widely equated with publicity, public relations and communications in general. Much of this has centred on the obvious need to recruit students to courses, and has more recently included image building and institutional branding as the binary divide has placed the 'new' universities (from the polytechnic sector) alongside the 'old ' universities, often with two or more institutions in close proximity and realising the need to differentiate themselves with clearer identities.

Taking the concept of the 'marketing mix' from consumer marketing, early education marketers have tried to create suitable mixes which typically have consisted of:

> a communications program, distribution channels, pricing and product policy, with reference to the three functions of non-profit marketing - resource attraction, resource allocation and persuasion   (Shapiro, quoted in Kinnell, 1987, p.156).

Kotler and Fox (1985) favoured an approach which could be related more specifically to the needs and context of the educational institution; product design (education programmes), pricing, distribution (availability and accessibility), communication and advertising.

A number of problems can be identified in the adoption of the marketing concept in higher education. Institutional objectives are usually set 'top down' (by non-marketers), there often are no separate actionable marketing objectives and both are often not quantified and hence performance is not measured against clear targets. Few 'managers' have the discretion to manage due to inflexible organisational structures which in the past have been more conducive to meeting the needs of the staff than of the students. There are no rewards for marketing success in meeting of ten vague objectives and marketing objectives, if any, do not align well with corporate objectives.

Many of those engaged in 'marketing' activities (often limited to advertising, publicity and print design) have no line authority and therefore have little influence in policy setting and decision-making. Many members of staff are still sceptical as, for them, marketing is synonymous with exploitation and is considered disreputable in an educational setting.

Finally, marketing may have been adopted in such a way and at a time when the real benefits are not clearly identifiable. This has produced demonstrated 'failure' of marketing as predicted by the sceptics. There is often little market research and marketing activity is limited to promotion. It is, therefore, not marketing in the sense of anticipating market needs and product/service development to meet them. For example, the development of a new course is seen as an academic rather than a managerial concern.

Ex-polytechnics, including Sheffield Hallam University, tend to have better-developed and centralised marketing functions than the longer-established universities. This stems from their vocational mission, close links with commerce and industry, and the need aggressively to approach student recruitment in the early years from establishment. The established universities have tended to emphasise fund-raising and student recruitment, with the former being the concern of academic staff and the latter being administered by the Registrar's office. Considerable sums are spent on recruitment advertising and print, and almost every former polytechnic and more than half of established universities have invested in a major visual identity change in the last five years (Sargent, 1993).

Kinnell (1987) observed that marketing is no longer novel in higher education, being recognised as one of a range of management tools by UK institutions but that there was a lack of overall marketing strategy or policy, a lack of co-ordination of efforts and activities, and a failure systematically to apply formal procedures. A discussion of the need for a systemic approach in higher education is available elsewhere (Varey, forthcoming). Although there is often a considerable body of work which can be termed 'marketing', it is usually work on course initiation (often carried out by academics rather than managers), student recruitment, income generation and so forth. Strategic assessment, in which a university gives 'corporate consideration to the questions of where it stands academically in relation to quality, spread and market performance, and where it wants to be in five years time' (quoted in Kinnell, 1987, p.149), is less-well practised as part of corporate management.

Marketing Joins Corporate Management at SHU

As part of a major programme of new developments, Sheffield Hallam University appointed a Director of Marketing and Corporate Affairs in late 1993, to join the marketing officers located in five of the twelve Schools. The new Director intends to develop centralised corporate marketing services and a network of 'local' School-based marketing officers who are empowered to run the necessary marketing activities for their own service/market portfolios. This clearly puts marketing on a strategic and tactical level at the corporate and sub-system layers of the organisation.

Co-ordination will be a major challenge in an organisation consisting of twelve Schools, essentially strategic business units, each with their own sub-culture and financial responsibility, each contributing to considerable diversity and serving their own target markets with particular approaches to meeting their needs. The Sheffield Hallam University 'product' is perhaps best understood as a combination of the place (location, facilities, building fabric, environment), the student learning experience (relationship with other students and staff, assessment, support services), the degree or other award and the successful learner. A major concern of the Marketing Director will be to develop a view of SHU as a service provider and promoter of education in a competitive marketplace, consisting of alternative service offerings from other service providers targeted at enabled consumers who can increasingly exercise their right to choice. Major emphasis will be given to understanding the need to transform the university into a customer-focused organisation and to manage various types of relationship with a range of different customers.

Foretelling the Future

Of course, no one can know what the future holds, and it would be foolish to deny the complexity of factors which may impact upon the decisions and actions of the huge 'industry' we call higher education. But it is essential to envision the way things could be, and to decide how we want them to be, before taking action. It would seem possible to anticipate the perhaps inevitably slow evolution of marketing in higher education in a special form, in which it moves away from being a support service to being a core management activity. The future research work should focus on problems of adaptation and then adoption, rather than to perpetuate the false pursuit of ideas which come from another era and a different set of circumstances. It is vitally important that marketing in higher education is evolved beyond the abuses and misuses cited here so that marketing management takes its rightful place in strategic and corporate decision-making.

Will marketing academics assert their positions as experts within their institutions and take an active part in advising and supporting developing practice? (Robinson & Long, 1987). Certainly, the 'management team' of universities who are presently almost exclusively academics or teachers, rather than professional managers, will have to be converted to an understanding and acceptance of the merits of a market-oriented approach. If they are not, marketing will remain a peripheral and under-exploited service function.

Institutions of higher education are going to have to find meaningful answers to the question 'what business are we in?'. This will lead, I predict, to differentiation by specialisation as funding will not be available to do a good job across all markets and market segments. At the same time, the removal of the 'binary divide' will further erode distinctions between institutions. However, it is important that differentiation decisions are made in terms that are meaningful to students and other 'customers'. Just why would students and their influencers favour any particular institution when considering the growing choice in higher education study?

Marketing will have to become strategic marketing management rather than tactical and piecemeal PR and advertising efforts, and marketing managers in educational institutions will have to develop and implement more integrated and proactive plans and programmes to take account of both customer and institution needs. Marketers will have to ensure an efficient flow of information both ways between the institution and its market. This adaptation to changing market conditions, including more discriminating individuals and companies, will require an approach which can effectively determine the needs of each market segment to be served, ensuring that courses of study and student support services (academic and welfare) meet students' needs, budgeting, and implementation and evaluation of the marketing programme.

Universities will need both a market orientation which focuses attention on identifiable customer groups and their specific needs, and a marketing orientation which places each member of the organisation with a clear role within a legitimate marketing process and organisation. Continuous marketing effectiveness review will have to become part of the organisation's and managers' performance review responsibilities. The role of marketing will develop as government continues to put pressure on efficiency and effectiveness by funding on a reward-for-quality in research and reward-for-numbers in teaching basis. Quality in terms of satisfied customers will increasingly influence decision-making about resource allocation as moves toward higher levels of participation in higher education drives a growth market in higher education services provision. There should be plenty of jobs for good marketers in the coming few years!

Bibliography

Adonis, A. (1992) 'Survey of Management Education and Training: Adapting to Hard Times', *Financial Times* (9 April).

Ames, C. (1970) 'Trappings Versus Substance in Industrial Marketing', *Harvard Business Review* (July-Aug) pp.93-103.

Berry, L. (1984) 'The Employee as Customer', in Lovelock, C. (ed) *Services Marketing* (Prentice-Hall).

Conway, A. and Yorke, D. (1991) 'Can the Marketing Concept Be Applied to the Polytechnic and College Sector of Higher Education?', *International Journal of Public Sector Management,* 4(2) pp.23-35.

Gronroos, C. (1980) 'Designing a Long Range Marketing Strategy for Services', *Long Range Planning,* (13 April).

Hall, N. (1992) 'University Challenge', *Marketing Week* (7 February) pp.26-29.

Keegan, W., Moriarty, S. & Duncan, T. (1992) *Marketing* (Prentice-Hall).

King, S. (1985) 'Has Marketing Failed Or Was It Never Really Tried?', *Journal of Marketing Management, 1*(1) pp.1-19.

Kinnell, M. (1987) 'International Marketing in UK Higher Education: Some Issues in Relation to Marketing Educational Programmes to Overseas Students', *Proceedings of the Annual Marketing Education Group Conference*, pp.143-166.

Kotler, P. (1991) *Marketing Management: Analysis, Planning, Implementation, and Control* (7th Ed) (Prentice-Hall).

Kotler, P. & Fox, K. (1985) *Strategic Marketing for Educational Institutions* (Prentice-Hall).

Pye, J. (1991) *Second Chances: Adults Returning to Education* (Oxford University Press).

Robinson, A. & Long, G. (1987) 'Marketing in Non-Advanced Further Education - A Cause for Concern?', *Proceedings of the Annual Marketing Education Conference* (Warwick University) pp.203-218.

Sargent, V. (1993) 'Back to School', *Marketing Business* (March) pp.18-21.

Saunders, J. & Lancaster, G. (1980) 'The Student Selection Process: A Model', *Higher Education Review, 13*(1).

Smith, G.(1987) 'The Application of Marketing to the Non-Profit Making Sector', *Proceedings of the Annual Marketing Education Group Conference* (Warwick University) pp.515-534.

Varey, R. (1993) 'Locating Customers in the Public Sector', *Proceedings of the Waves of Change: Strategic Management in the Public Services Conference* (Sheffield Business School) (April) pp.569-590.

Varey, R. (forthcoming) 'Systemic Perspective on Higher Education', in Knight, P. (ed) *Staff Development and Institutional Change in Higher Education* (SEDA).

Wills, G., Cheese, J., Kennedy, S. & Rushton, A. (1983) *Introducing Marketing (Revised Ed) (Pan Business Books)*.

MANAGING A GROWING BUSINESS - OR SHARING A COLLEGIAL EXPERIENCE? EXPERIENCES FROM HIGHER EDUCATION

Ranald Macdonald, Sheffield Hallam University

Introduction

Higher Education has gone through many changes in recent years as a result of external pressures and internal responses. These changes have been variously seen as opportunities by some and threats by others.

After outlining these changes, the paper examines contrasting responses, ranging from a managerial perspective to the collegial approach. Some of the responses which relate specifically to the University of Derby will be examined from the author's perspective as a former divisional manager within the Business School there. As such responses to change are still very current, many of the likely effects and conclusions can only be surmised. They might also be perceived differently from the perspective of different institutions or at different levels within those institutions. However, this article makes use of a framework which might be adopted elsewhere, perhaps providing the basis for a more analytical comparative study. The Report of the National Commission on Education, *Learning to Succeed*, provides a timely examination of the education system in the UK, with a wide range of useful suggestions for managing change, not least within the Higher Education sector.

The Nature of Change Within Higher Education

In recent years Higher Education institutions have faced a significantly changed political and financial climate. For all concerned this has resulted in a sense of uncertainty and instability and there has been a variety of responses from institutional managers, for whom the demands of change have been unprecedented (Brown and Sommerland, 1992). To highlight one example, since the granting of corporate status in 1988, former Polytechnics and Colleges of Higher Education have had to make the transition from merely administering to actively managing their resources. This has stretched professional academics and has resulted in the more widespread recruitment of professionals in the areas of finance, personnel and marketing.

The abolition of the binary divide in 1992 has resulted in both new and old universities having to re-focus their core activities. This is particularly marked in the distinctions previously made between research and teaching institutions and between academic and vocational courses. These stark stereotypes can no longer be held so dear.

Concern at the comparatively low participation rate in the UK led to the government persuading universities to expand numbers significantly whilst achieving significant efficiency gains. Worries about the cost of financing the expansion in student numbers have been exacerbated by the debate over the measurement and achievement of quality and its link to funding. It would be true to say that the Quality Assessment activities of the Higher Education Funding Council for England (HEFCE) have not met with universal support. Innovations in learning and teaching to cope with increased student numbers and higher SSRs have come very much to the fore, though many of these require significant investment in learning resources such as libraries and computers and staff time to develop appropriate packages and undergo staff development.

Changes to funding arrangements have put additional strain on institutions as unit costs have been pushed down. In 1992-3, unit costs in the old universities were 83 per cent of what they were in 1987-8 and in the former polytechnics they were 81 per cent (figures from the *Report of the National Commission on Education*, 1993). In addition, significant funding (which may affect the overall financial vialbility of some institutions) is now on a contract basis and this, and other sources, are linked to performance, as in respect of the recent research assessment exercise.

Reductions in student fees and grants announced in the last two budgets will also hit universities and students adversely and increase the degree of uncertainty about funding in the future - except perhaps that it is unlikely to rise! Increased centralisation through the control of HEFCE over the allocation of funds is likely to hit the fastest-growing institutions most significantly. Whereas reductions in resources per student had previously been met by increases in student numbers to cushion the effect on total funding, institutions now face real cuts in centrally-provided funds, with tough penalties being introduced for institutions which over-recruit.

The initial response to the demands from government to increase participation rates was met by a general widening of access to higher education, much of it in collaboration with colleges of further education. The introduction of foundation years and more kite-marked access courses has resulted in a far less homogeneous student population, though there is still a significant imbalance in terms of social background. The needs of a more mature intake have been addressed through more flexible modular schemes and credit accumulation and transfer schemes (CATS), though these have still not fully met the needs of the growing number of part-time students as much of the provision is still largely day-time based.

Responses to Change

Brown and Sommerland contrast the various responses to change as ranging from the corporatist approach of appointing a Chief Executive who is empowered to run the institution 'like a business', and where decision-making and resource allocation is increasingly centralised, to, at the other extreme, a cautious response and even outright opposition where a high degree of autonomy is maintained at departmental and individual levels. Somewhere between these two extremes are institutions that develop managerial structures which can respond appropriately to change. The *Report of the National Commission on Education* (1993) notes that:

> a new atmosphere of competition and managerialism has been introduced into a culture which has traditionally put more emphasis on co-operation between colleagues.

Bennett *et al* (1992) summarise the approaches as Model A, where managers exercise a control function through segmentation of the work of the organisation within a rational world, and Model B, with an emphasis on shared commitment, empowerment of the work-force and delegation. They contend that, whilst Model A grew out of scientific management, as modified by Mayo and others, Model B developed partly from Mintzberg's notion of management in a non-rational setting. A further distinction might be between that of managing change and coping with chaos!

	Model A	Model B
Relationship between manager and managed	Control	Empowerment
View of organizational activity	Segmentation	Holism
View of world	Totally rational: one best way	Limited rationality: multiple and perhaps competing rationalities

Table 1:
Two Models of Management

Source: Bennett *et al* (1992) p.8

Model B is seen as being closer to the emerging orthodoxy of educational management, particularly within schools, namely collegialism.

To quote from Bennett *et al* (1992) p.10:

> Collegiality is seen as a means of creating unity by involving staff in the policy-making and decision-making process. Its simple principle is that by owning the decision one is more likely to put it into practice and support it, since agreement creates a unity between the individual and collective self-interest. Its language is the language of holism, consensus, co-operation and interdependence.

The role of the headteacher is seen as crucial in providing leadership and vision as to the values of the institution and where a culture of co-operation and the value of the individual is instilled.

However, some writers (for example, Hargreaves in Bennett *et al*) contrast 'real' with 'contrived' collegiality where, in the latter, "collegiality becomes a contrivance through which the leader can bring about what he or she wants".

The contrast can be summarised as follows:

Collaborative Culture	Contrived Collegiality
Spontaneous	Administratively regulated
Voluntary	Compulsory
Development oriented	Implementation oriented
Pervasive across time and space	Fixed in time and space
Unpredictable	Predictable - leading to inflexibility and inefficiency

Table 2:
Collaborative Culture or Contrived Collegiality?

Source: A. Hargreaves in Bennett *et al* pp.85-86

Whether collaborative or contrived, successful collegiality requires a cultural change in the way many staff work. They have to become far more interdependent and work as a team. It may be that it is only achievable when certain key or senior staff are replaced by those who are more open and comfortable in a changed working relationship.

The University of Derby - A Line Manager's Perspective

Derbyshire College of Higher (as it was at the time) entered the 1990s facing a number of changes which were seen as opportunities by many of the staff new to the institution and as threats by a number who had been there for some time. The granting of corporate status allowed for a period of rapid development of diploma, degree and postgraduate programmes which had previously not been permitted because of regional agreements. Whilst BTEC programmes had been offered, the College was now able jointly to validate courses with the Council for National Academic Awards (CNAA). When the author joined the Business School in the college in September 1990 the first cohort of 60 undergraduate students were about to be admitted unto the BA(Hons) Business Studies. By September 1993, within the Business School there were well over 1,000 students on the BA(Hons) Business Studies, BA(Hons) Business Administration, BA(Hons) Accounting, LLB(Hons) Law and the BA/BSc(Hons) Modular Degree Scheme. Similar increases were seen across the whole institution, together with significantly increased numbers on BTEC and postgraduate programmes.

Autumn 1991 saw the College being granted the powers to accredit its own degrees, this being an important stage in moving towards Polytechnic status. However, soon after this, the announcement was made that no more Polytechnics would be created because the abolition of the binary divide meant that all institutions could apply to proceed directly to University status. The initial despondency at Derby was replaced by the determination to be granted research degree awarding powers, this being the main criteria necessary for the designation of new universities. Intense hard work by many staff during the Spring and Summer of 1992, led not least by the Assistant Director (Academic Planning), saw a close decision to grant these powers, though with conditions.

In September 1992, Derbyshire College of Higher Education became, at the time, the only College to be granted Privy Council permission to call itself a University, and the University of Derby was born.

These developments were led dynamically from the top, though a significant number of staff were involved at all stages, resulting in a fairly widespread sense of owned achievement. Many new staff had joined the institution during this period, with more than 50% of the staff at the start of the 1993 academic year having being there for less than 3 years. There had also been a significant number of departures through early retirement at all levels, including the Directorate.

The achievement of University status, together with large-scale course development, with the concomitant planned increases in student numbers would have been enough to manage in themselves. However, there was a need for significant investment in buildings and student accommodation - a situation not helped by the burning down of a major building on the first day of the Spring 1991 term. Significant appointments were made to the Directorate which, whilst strengthening the financial, resource and personnel management of the institution, were seen by some as further removing academic staff from decision-making. There was a feeling that the educational interests of students, and those who taught them, were taking second place to the balance sheet and the management of a rapidly growing business.

The next shock to the system came in changes to funding arrangements as the Government faced up to an ever-mounting Public Sector Borrowing Requirement. In the academic year 1993/94, Band 1 fees (classroom based subjects such as Humanities and Business Studies) were reduced from £1850 to £1300, at a time when student numbers were rising rapidly. The Autumn 1993 Budget announced a further 45% reduction, with the balance to be distributed by HEFCE. Derbyshire Business School responded in 1992 by a massive increase in full-time student numbers, particularly on BTEC programmes and with the coming on stream of various undergraduate courses. In the BTEC Division in particular, Staff-Student Ratios had deteriorated to over 40:1 and in other parts of the Business School it was over 30:1. Staff were slightly bemused to hear of complaints about SSR's of 15:1 or 20:1 elsewhere in the University!

With internal restructuring of the Business School into 4 so-called 'product' divisions, the author found himself as Business Manager of 23 full-time academic staff, together with an increasing number of part-timers, responsible for 3 major degree programmes which, though not yet fully on stream, cater for around 800 students. Many of the staff were new to teaching and were faced with heavy teaching loads and other responsibilities such as the supervision of final year projects and placement students. Working in teams, staff shared experiences in developing strategies for dealing with large numbers with limited resources. Over the period 1990 - 1993, many new course developments and associated initiatives emanated from staff and were taken through to validation by groups acting very much in the collegiate approach. This highly dynamic momentum has largely come to an end with instructions from senior management to consolidate the existing provision, if not retrench.

Further uncertainties were caused by the decision to set up a working party to consider the academic structure of the University. This was one of a number of working parties on a range of topics, including the Structure of the Academic Year, the University Mission Statement, Teaching and Learning, and a Collegiate University. Many in the Business School saw the primary intention of the Academic Structure group being to break up the School as it now accounted for around a third of the students within the University. The final decision (if such it is) was, and remains, controversial but involved moving from a University structure of five faculties to one of nine schools, with the Derbyshire Business School being divided into a Management School (comprising the BTEC and Post Graduate

Divisions) and a School of Business (comprising the Undergraduate and Accountancy Divisions). Consultation was fairly widespread, though the final decision seems to have been met with resignation, if not disinterest. The more cynical believe that the decision had already been made as to how to restructure and that, though they did not use the term explicitly, they were merely engaged in 'contrived collegiality'.

To those at the chalk/whiteboard face in Higher Education the location of real power in an institution is sometimes difficult to locate. Increasingly, senior managers, though appearing to act semi-autonomously, are answerable to the Vice-Chancellor/Chief Executive, perhaps through a Pro Vice-Chancellor. The Vice-Chancellor in turn is answerable to the University Governors and a number of sub-committees, comprised of representatives/appointees from the University together with a majority of external appointees from industry and commerce. The academic welfare of the University is managed through Academic Board and its Academic Standards or Quality Sub-Committee (or equivalent). Senior management may be called to account to these bodies where their activities impinge on academic matters such as library or computer services, rather than the pure financing of these services. In addition, each Faculty/School has its own Board which has a certain degree of autonomy, though they are again answerable to Academic Board. Whilst staff are represented on all these bodies, there remains a sense of being distant from the real decision-making and poor communications can make the distance seem even greater.

Some Tentative Conclusions

In the sense of managing growth, the last few years have seen staff in Higher Education, particularly in the new universities, being given their heads to develop new courses and programmes of study. Whilst more managerialist structures were being put in place, much of the new development was collaborative in nature and team working encouraged the development of innovative approaches to learning. However, there was a feeling among some staff that elements of this collegiality were rather contrived and too narrowly focussed on achieving specific ends, such as accredited status or the power to award research degrees, rather than on involving all staff in the management of change over a longer time horizon. Admittedly, many of the externally imposed changes were unforeseen, but poor communication and over-hierarchical structures have not helped senior managers disseminate information and take staff along with their decisions.

Most staff in higher education see themselves as professionals though, as again noted by the National Commission on Education, whilst non-manual earnings have risen by 53 per cent in the UK since 1979, academics' pay has risen by only 9 per cent in the same period. It is little wonder that many staff do not feel valued by society when they feel themselves to be doing more for less and getting little recognition for it from government. The lack of organisational slack has meant a growing tension between 'a growing business' and the statement in most institutions' Mission Statements (however it is worded) of 'putting students first'. There is equally a sense amongst many staff of senior managers becoming distanced from the realities of dealing with large numbers, maintaining quality and holding on to educational values. As noted by Bennett *et al:*

> educational management is about facilitating teaching and learning, and managers who forget this basic fact, or who act in ways which interfere with teaching and learning, should not be deemed competent.

Whilst many managers do realise the primacy of our purpose, poor communication and attempts at contrived rather than real collegiality have served to increase cynicism in those who would prefer to be positive and make a contribution to managing the change.

There may be those in Higher Education who would take issue with this, perhaps rather jaundiced view, but the mere fact that it is perhaps more widespread than realised by institutional managers should be cause for concern. Whilst this article contains the very personal perceptions of one individual, there is perhaps scope for testing them out across and within institutions to see whether there is real or contrived collegiality at work or merely a sense of growing managerialism, with staff feeling alienated from decision-making and the consequent outcomes. The main issues to be resolved are how to maintain staff motivation and morale in the face of reduced funding, the provision of appropriate managerial and professional development and the creation of organisational 'space' to give more equally distributed opportunities for research and other activities. There is very genuine and heartfelt concern amongst many of a serious detrioration in the quality of Higher Education which may not be addressed by the rather narrow and idiosyncratic approach of HEFCE visits.

References

Bennett, N. *et al* (eds) (1992) *Managing Change in Education* (The Open University).

Brown, H. & Sommerland, E. (1992) 'Staff Development in Higher Education - Towards the Learning Organisation?', *Higher Education Quarterly, 46* (2).

National Commission on Education (1993) *Learning to Succeed: Report of the National Commission on Education* (Heinemann).

Mintzberg, H. (1990) 'The Manager's Job: Folklore and Fact', *Harvard Business Review* (March-April).

REVIEWING SERVICE QUALITY IN THE PUBLIC SECTOR

Sonny Nwankwo and Bill Richardson, Sheffield Business School

Introduction

The role of service quality in public sector organisations has continued to attract critical reviews by both researchers and practitioners (Hudson, 1990; Wagenheim and Reurink, 1991; Burns, 1992; Morley, 1993). A popular view is that strategic quality service management is no longer the exclusive preserve of the private sector. Comprehensive quality customer service is now seen as being equally important to both public and private sector organisations. Until recently, quality issues were left out of any rigorous reviews of customer services provided by the public sector organisations. Ironically, while studies in this area have tended to concentrate on the private sector marketplace (Lewis, 1990; Narasimham and Sen, 1992), consumer problems have long been acknowledged as a significant issue in the public sector (Young, 1977).

Within the sector, anecdotal evidence abounds to suggest that public service employees are less concerned than their private sector counterparts. Burns (1992), for example, in relation to service encounters, reports that:

> Anyone who in the morning shops at Marks and Spencer, and in the afternoon queues up outside their local housing office is going to be very much aware of the differences in quality of service.

Nonetheless, the situation is no longer as gloomy as hitherto perceived. There is an increasing awareness amongst providers of public services that a lackadaisical attitude to quality of customer service is no longer adequate. Most of them now acknowledge the need to position service users as the centre-point of strategic focus (Nwankwo, 1992).

It is clearly the case that, with the growing attraction and application of market-based performance measures in the UK public sector, providers of public services are increasingly demonstrating an interest in service quality, how it is constituted and in how it should be operationalised and monitored. The government, with the launch of the Citizen's Charter, seems to have initiated a bold attempt to map out the field of public sector consumerism (*The Citizen's Charter*, 1991). This is bolstered by the Next Steps Initiatives (NSI) which have stimulated greater enthusiasm and commitment to improving service quality (*Next Steps Agencies Review*, 1992)

Defining Customer Service Quality

Customer service quality is not a straight-forward phenomenon to define, and yet a clear definition is a pre-requisite to the design, implementation and maintenance of an effective customer service improvement programme. Problems of definition arise to a great extent from three main sources (Nwankwo, 1993):

(i) *The offering*: There may be problems in evaluating what is offered. Quality attributes of tangible products may differ in generic terms from those of intangible products (services). The distinctions between products (tangibles) and services (intangibles) are not as simple as is very often assumed (Lewis, 1989).

(ii) The customer: Identifying and defining user segments may present some difficulties in terms of evaluating service processes and outcomes and this, in turn, complicates the perception of quality. For example, different customers will expect, want and/or need different things from essentially similar offerings (Hooley, 1993).

(iii) *Organisational boundaries*: The public sector marketplace consists of organisational types (public enterprises, on the one hand, and other sorts of organisations which are not enterprises on the other (Nwankwo and Curwen, 1993). These organisations differ in terms of their purposes, functions and characteristics. The underlying differences have in the past had an effect on the quality of service perception.

In spite of these problems, a common ground can be established with which to begin to explore and define customer service quality. Frequently, customer service quality is associated with customer care, marketing orientation, total quality management and so forth. These concepts have their basic roots in marketing and support a case for a marketing-based definition (Hooley, 1993). Viewed from this perspective, service quality is at the heart of an approach which focuses on a clear understanding of one's target customers with a view to creating superior value for them, compared to competitive offers, on a continuous basis. Hooley (1993) opines that:

Quality is concerned with supplying superior benefits in the opinion of the customer. Thus the pursuit of quality is the pursuit of greater customer benefit.

Wagenheim and Reurink (1991) define customer service quality as:

An organisational perspective and process that focuses on meeting customer expectations by doing the right things right the first time. It is based on an understanding that the organisation will attain its goals effectively and efficiently through satisfying its customers.

The tacit acknowledgment in the above definitions is that enduring, long-term organisational interests are best served by strategic moves which position the customer as the central focus of activities.

Problems Associated with a 'Lip Service' Approach to Customer Service Quality

A major problem confronting public sector organisations seeking to create an effective customer service programme is deciding how to structure an appropriate response strategy. Very often, such organisations concentrate their attention on the management of extrinsic factors by emphasizing peripheral service attributes such as physical facilities and 'smile' training at the expense of intrinsic organisational factors such as creating the value system which will enable employees to become more responsive, caring, courteous and knowledgeable and thus able to express trust and confidence. This, in turn, creates another set of difficulties, viz:

(i) difficulty in assessing performance objectively, given the more ambiguous goals of public sector organisations. This, in turn, creates ambiguity in the strategic posturing of many such organisations.

(ii) difficulty in gaining the support, and a change in attitudes and behaviour, of employees who interact with customers at service encounters.

(iii) difficulty in managing a cultural transition from 'the way we always do things' to 'the way we need to do things to be successful' (Piercy and Morgan, 1990).

(iv) difficulty in creating a visionary and sustainable quality customer service management strategy.

Lack of an effective internal organisational arrangement accounts to a great extent for the difficulties (Morley, 1993) which many public sector organisations encounter while striving towards a sustainable quality of service effectiveness. 'Charity', as is often said, 'begins at home'. Without the needed 'homework', service users will continue to be exposed to sub-optimal service delivery.

What is needed to achieve an effective customer service function is a complementarity of an externally-oriented strategic service vision, such as dealing with the 'customer delight' package, with an inner-directed vision, such as internal organisational arrangements for achieving the 'customer delight' goal (Heskett, 1987).

A Value Based Approach to Customer Service Effectiveness

The literature is replete with a variety of approaches to customer service effectiveness (Schneider, 1986; Wagenheim and Reurink, 1991; Berry, Conant and Parasuraman, 1991; Bitner, Booms and Tetreault, 1990). A major weakness in some of the approaches, within the context of the public sector, is that they appear to be overly prescriptive and very often concentrate on the process of planning rather than the resolution of actual strategic problems and the redesign of organisation features (Berkowitz and Flexner, 1978; Tompkins, 1987; Bryson, 1988).

The framework offered in this paper follows the increasingly popular method of using private sector management concepts to reform the general approach to management in the public sector (Morley, 1993). The framework is a diagnostic tool which can be helpful, not only in analyzing and evaluating organisational perspectives but also in identifying existing inadequacies and developing thought toward the organisational changes which might be necessary to improve management response to the challenges of the service revolution now sweeping across the public sector. It builds on the recognition that quality customer service is value-driven rather than technique-driven or based on 'charm school ethics' (Brown, 1989). This consideration is important because many public sector organisations provide 'social/political goods' (Lane, 1983) and are not subject to the discipline of the competitive marketplace. Users accordingly cannot 'exit' - although they may have recourse to the political mechanism - to signal a need for improved service quality (Hirschman, 1970). Quality effectiveness is to be attained and sustained through values and slogans. Values are reflected in the systems and behaviour which permeate the organisation, become its culture and drive it forward (Ginsburg and Miller, 1991).

A well-observed characteristic of public sector organisations (albeit a changing perception) is that unless provoked or stigmatised by negative publicity to act otherwise, they tend to deal with today's problems in the same way that worked yesterday, even though the context giving rise to the new problems may be different. Thus, creating an appropriate quality service involves far more than good intentions and 'lip service' structural changes. It involves an effective internal organisation. This is the basis of strategic service quality management and constitutes the foundation upon which success can stand.

It is dangerous to assume that quality customer service programmes are working effectively simply because short-term goals are being achieved. Service performance can quickly slide into mediocrity unless the basic attributes are rooted in a philosophy that recognises the delicate balance of internal organisational dynamics such as competence and motivation of staff, shared values, leadership, authority relations and decision processes. These express and create patterns of behaviour, create an awareness of where the organisation 'is coming from', what it strives to achieve, its purpose, norms and values and makes clear the role of organisational members before, during and after service encounters.

A Framework for Measuring and Achieving Quality Customer Service

The value-based approach advocated in this paper is consistent with current exhortations in the literature such as the dichotomous 'new management' model for the Civil Service which outlines the migration path from a bureaucratic to a progressive management model (Morley, 1993). Our model implicitly acknowledges that, in general, quality perspectives among providers of public services are, at the present stage, on a low profile path. The challenge, therefore, is to seek ways to engineer a turnaround to a high profile path. To effect this, four steps are necessary; (1) ideation (2) design (3) delivery and (4) maintenance. These steps form the basis for the development of our customer service evaluation framework.

Step 1: *Ideation*: This is about idealising or conceptualising value-focused behavioral patterns which can help chart the course the organisation wants to embark upon. It involves creating a philosophical awareness of a desirable state: Who are we? Whose interests do we serve? Where are we coming from? Where are we now? Where do we want to be? Why must we strive to get there? How and why should everyone be involved? For some organisations which already know 'who they are', it may be more important to focus on questions such as: Do we have the best qualified employees for the job? Are our recruitment strategies effective? An open-minded evaluation of these organisational aspects is likely to a loosening of the structural rigidities inherent in public sector (and other well-established, 'steady state') organisations. Since such a value-focused approach to change requires a fundamental questioning of deep-rooted beliefs together with the internalisation of more appropriate value systems, it should help to resolve the identity crisis which is characteristic of organisations in transition.

The issue of the organisation's identity, being the answer to the question 'who are we?', is critically important. At its heart lies the question of customer *definition*. Putting customers at the heart of the answer 'who are we?' is, according to Maddux (1991), the first rule of effective management in a competitive environment. Thus, does the organisation visualise itself through its target users' eyes or from the perspective of its service operation? Does it view itself as a service delivery mechanism or as a customer satisfying organism? *Definition* on this basis provides a yardstick to facilitate the location of the organisation's position on a service effectiveness continuum. This continuum can be modelled in a bi-polar way. Thus, the continuum can be constructed to facilitate assessment of the extent to which the organisation uses an implicit definition of its customers which is based on (i) customer specific factors or (ii) organisation/service specific factors.

(i) *A customer specific definition requires that the organisation has:*
- clear ideas about customers and their needs.
- customer characteristics underpinning the design of service attributes.
- customer service goals which articulate and communicate both the customers' and the organisation's aspirations.
- feedback systems which enable the organisation to reach its customers and vice versa.
- an effective customer education and information system.
- genuine concern for marketplace pluralism. Customers should not be considered as a monolithic group. There is a need to recognise the heterogeneity of the marketplace, that is, the diversity among users of public services in terms of their categories and needs.

(ii) An organisational, introverted definition of customers will be evidenced by a know-it-all stance about the needs of its customers. The presumption, in this instance, is that the organisation knows what customers want and how best to satisfy them. Customers are seen to be unsure about their needs and sometimes irrational in the expression of, and in the means to gratify, those needs. The role of the organisation, as a consequence, involves directing user behaviour along a desired path. This perspective cannot augur well for effective customer service because it assumes that customers are zombies. Basic features of an organisation which operate from this perfective include:
- a lack of a customer-driven mission.
- a lack of an effective customer-satisfaction-measuring information system.
- a lack of, or minimal customer input into, decision mechanisms.
- a lack of customer involvement in the setting of service objectives and standards.
- a lack of customer-oriented value-driven behaviour. Rather, organisational behaviour is activity-driven and ignores behavioral antecedents - service orientation is not directed at 'user motivation'.

Step 2: *Design:* Having clarified its existing definition of 'customer' and its preferred future definitions, the 'design' step seeks to answer the questions: How can we get to where we want to be? What actions are necessary? Who should do what? What level of support should be provided (in terms of training, motivation, etc)? This step involves planning how the entire organisation's members might be sensitized to view higher levels of customer service performance as an organisational imperative.

Very many public organisations are inadequately oriented to detect or predict underlying customer concerns. Frequently, core customer problems lie outside management's purview until a shock event occurs to highlight the inadequacy of existing approaches and, consequently, to expose the organisation's failure. The extent to which the organisation is able to scan and interpret environmental signals is summed up in the issue of *sensitivity*. This is central to the design of an effective, customer-focused service programme. A two-state schema can be applied to categorise levels of sensitivity in the same way as a two-state schema was applied to the issue of customer definition; (i) pro-active and (ii) reactive sensitivity.

(i) *Pro-active sensitivity:* This arises from a genuine desire to integrate customers' interests into the decision mechanism of the organisation. Ways in which an organisation can demonstrate such a level of consciousness to its customers will include:

- emphasizing customer and employee expectations and devising actionable programmes for meeting the expectations of each category of stakeholder. Employee welfare is important because a dissatisfied or a disgruntled employee is unlikely to be in the best position to deliver a quality customer service programme.
- articulating customer problems through a planned and co-ordinated approach instead of a 'fire fighting' approach.
- developing customer policy based on perceptive research into customer needs and perceptions.
- adopting an anticipative and preventative stance in formulating consumer policies.
- viewing all customers as marketing opportunities.

(ii) *Reactive sensitivity:* This perspective underpins a more mechanical approach to customer service management. It addresses the symptomatic factors rather than the underlying issues. Reactive sensitivity is characterised by:

- passive, often confused or misguided attention to customers.
- defensive attitudes in responding to customer enquiries and complaints.
- Coerced management attention, that is, management usually only acts for the customer when forced to act under pressure.
- management being guided by a 'band wagon effect', that is, a predilection to copy what other organisations are doing.

Step 3: *Delivery:* This is a critical aspect of the customer service experience because it is at the core of service encounters, that is, the organisation/customer interface. Delivery, in a broad sense is all about *implementation*.

It is easy to have a well-defined customer service strategy in place or have it eloquently articulated on paper. It is more difficult to translate the ideals into action. Policy statements represent 'stated strategy' but by themselves are not sufficient evidence of an 'enacted' customer perspective. The conclusive evidence about customer service levels achieved emanates from what people do inside the organisation. Here, the role of leadership is crucial in fostering a quality service culture (Webster, 1988; Goldsmith and Clutterbuck, 1984).

Delivering and implementation can be considered from two broad perspectives; (i) orientation to action (ii) statement of intent/passiveness.

(i) *Action orientation:* This entails designing and putting together actionable schedules of activities. Two principal issues form the basis for organisational action: implementation responsibilities and implementation tasks.

Implementation responsibilities deal with control systems (leadership being a very prominent feature) which reinforce customer responsive structures and strategies. Here, pertinent questions to ask and answer are: Who is responsible for doing what? What is the degree of motivation amongst employees to strive for better performance in their interface with customers? What is the nature of the customer care training provided, and of the degree of delegation of authority (decentralisation of decision-making and discretion allowed to operating staff) and communication within the organisation? These are important determinants of employee conduct and form the context of customer service strategy implementation. In this sphere, quality of leadership makes a great deal of difference to ultimate success or failure. The leader may be regarded as 'the customer strategist' - the pivot who must give clear signals and establish customer service values and beliefs. The leader holds the primary command and control responsibility - providing guidance and ensuring that the whole organisation is striving towards a common purpose.

Implementation tasks relate to organisational systems and activities for packaging, delivering and monitoring customer service strategies and, ultimately, facilitating a shift towards an integrated quality customer service management perspective. Here, one would be looking to evaluate the organisation in terms of: What tasks are emphasised? Is the structure adequate for the effective performance of those tasks? How is customer service performance monitored?

A high-profile approach requires that quality customer service management must take its place at the heart of the organisation's strategy process, not at the periphery.

(ii) *A statement of intent orientation* represents a do-nothing or delayed action strategy. It is characterised by weak leadership, ineffective organisational arrangements and poor management. Strategic choices neither reflect conscious efforts nor systematic approaches. In such cases, management becomes atavistic in searching for solutions to strategic challenges such as quality customer service. It might espouse a customer orientation but it does little or nothing to ensure a quality customer interaction.

Step 4: *Maintenance*: Many public sector organisations have well-developed planning processes, but the extent to which customer service goals are included, implemented and monitored is inadequate. Important questions to ask in evaluating an organisation's customer service maintenance function are: Are we doing well in continuing to satisfy customers? Are we truly understanding our customers? What do customers think of the services we offer? Are we listening to what customers are saying about our organisation? What mechanisms are available to obtain and process customer information? Are there gaps between what we aspire to achieve and what we actually achieve? Regular reference to these questions will monitor the organisation's changing customer service situation and its goals and objectives and related performance; how goals are expressed, interpreted, enforced and the degree of commitment for them within the organisation.

One of the easiest traps top management may fall into is to take for granted the disposition of employees on quality issues. This is the classic 'inside out' perspective. Having defined and articulated a vision statement of quality customer service, there is thus a need to check to see if employees' ideas concur, and are consistent with the requisite values, and if not, why not?

The need to provide maintenance measures for customer service programmes must be seen not just in symbolic terms but in the light of what they seek to achieve. Maintenance measures, if they are functional, will stimulate a more focused and integrated organisational effort, and provide a benchmark for determining whether customer service strategies are working as intended. Maintenance measures can be carried out through (i) formal or (ii) informal techniques.

(i) *Formal techniques:* Use customer-based quality performance measures to gauge true perceptions as well as subterranean factors which impel customer behaviour.

One major problem with formal measurement techniques is that, very often, efforts are directed at measuring satisfaction with core offerings, with the emphasis of measurement on surrogate variables. It is clear that the issue of surrogate variables, on a stand-alone basis, is inadequate. The focus on surrogate variables neglects other important factors such as the antecedents of behaviour. However, formal techniques do enable management to set criteria which warn of deviations from targets.

(ii) *Informal techniques*: Informal measurement takes place in two ways. The first is where there are no set standards - rules of thumb are applied. The second is where standards exist but are neither clearly articulated nor show objectively, and are thus difficult to measure. In this sense, informality refers to the lack of care and pro-activity involved in the design and implementation of these techniques.

The four-step approach to evaluating the present pertinence of customer interaction approaches and ways in which existing approaches might be improved can be summarised as follows:

Step 1: Ideation ⟶ Definition ⟶ Define your customer focus.

Step 2: Design ⟶ Sensitivity ⟶ Create and promote service mentality
as an organisational imperative.

Step 3: Delivery ⟶ Implementation ⟶ Pay attention to service delivery.
Effective delivery should address key
issues, such as tasks and responsibilities
and employees' skills.

Step 4: Maintenance ⟶ Measurement ⟶ Overall effectiveness will depend
on sustainability. Devise mechanisms
which warn of possible lapses.

An organisation's customer service performance (high or low-profile) will depend on how it **defines** its customers; the level of *sensitivity* it shows in creating a 'service mentality'; the *implementation* mechanism it chooses to deliver its customer service programmes; and the *measurement* technique it utilizes to maintain its strategic thrust. These determinant factors are likely to exhibit a consistent pattern of relationship such that a customer-centred definition, for example, will characteristically relate to pro-active sensitivity, action-based implementation processes and formal measurement standards. The dichotomous nature of the relationship is presented in Figure 1.

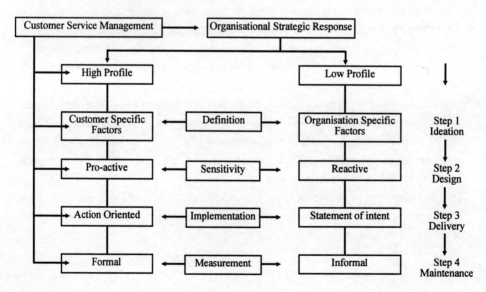

Implicitly, it can be deduced that each organisation's customer service profile will vary according to variations in management beliefs and behaviour. Management behaviour creates and, in turn, is reinforced by internal organisational characteristics. Consequently, a change in organisational behaviour in pursuit of quality customer service goals requires, first and foremost, a customer oriented attitude on the part of the organisation's top leaders.

The Customer Service Quality Framework Contextualised in the Case of British Telecom

In order to be more helpful to readers who are interested in operationalising our customer service quality framework, this section examines some of the attitudes, systems and behaviours attributed to British Telecom (BT), a former public enterprise which is recognised as having managed successful change towards a customer-responsive state. Presented below are illustrations of BT's organisational characteristics categorised under 'definition', 'sensitivity', 'implementation' and 'measurement' criteria. The illustrations indicate an organisation system which has moved from left to right on each of our customer service quality continuum, over the past five years.

Definition: 'Subscribers' became 'Customers'

When the erstwhile UK national telecommunications carrier (British Telecom or BT for short) was privatised in 1984, it quickly became obvious to the management that the organisation needed to adopt a new value system as an anchor for the 'quality revolution' that was to unfold. At that time, it was widely acknowledged that the company had almost a cultural vacuum, with customers out of sight and out of mind.

The company did not simply need to shift from a public to private culture, but more importantly from a monopolistic to a competitive culture. The main challenge rested on turning an introverted organisation into one looking outward towards the customer. Quality of customer service became an imperative.

Actively driven from the top, the move towards greater consumer responsiveness started with a reconceptualisation of organisational values based on the imperatives of putting customers first. Telephone users, for example, became 'customers' and were no longer referred to as subscribers or 'subs', for short. Through a wide array of channels used for staff briefing, the company started to create the awareness that its service orientation is to build a business culture aimed at 'meeting customer requirements first time, every time'. This philosophy was encapsulated in the company's early promotional campaign theme: **'It's you we answer to'**.

A more purposeful user-profile strategy was adopted (for example, delineating private, business, local and international user categories) and reflected in the reshaping of the organisation. The new customer-driven philosophy was a radical move away from the earlier engineer-dominated culture.

(Adapted from Richardson, Nwankwo and Curwen, 1993).

Designing in Sensitivity:

In 1987 when Mr Iain Vallance succeeded Sir George Jefferson as the CEO, the organisation started a programme of massive restructuring aimed at simplifying management structures, changing attitudes and, very importantly, moving closer to customers. To be able to provide a more responsive, flexible and efficient service to customers, BT created new divisions to focus on the needs of various customers segments respectively, and better management of overall network services. Quality customer service was not simply regarded as the centre-point of the organisation's philosophy but bolstered through specific initiatives such as Total Quality Management (TQM), Project Sovereign and 'Involving Everyone'.

The thrust of these initiatives was to propel the company towards service-mindedness, better customer service effectiveness and improved organisational efficiency - keeping customers happy and maintaining growth and profitability. Project Sovereign, for example, is wide ranging, geared in part towards improving the skills and overall competence of organisational members (management retraining absorbed £260mn in 1992 alone). It also led to a tighter coupling of organisational arrangements - review of job descriptions, personnel selection criteria, 'de-layering' and lay-offs (about 24,000 between March 1992 and April 1993).

To underpin the company's approach to quality customer service, it launched the *BT Commitment* - a complete set of service standards, backed by an improved Customer Service Guarantee scheme. The BT Commitment represents its own *customers' charter* -a bundle of quality service commitments which is vigorously promoted by the CEO and clearly permeating through the entire hierarchy of the organisation.

The CEO is reported to carry a copy of the 'BT Commitment' in his wallet wherever he goes.

(Adapted from Richardson, Nwankwo and Curwen, 1993).

Delivery: Implementing Quality Service at BT

The vision:

'There is far more pleasure in giving good service than in taking brickbat'. (Vallance, BT's CEO)

'We will not compromise our pursuit of continued improvement in service to our customers. The need for us to build customer loyalty is more important than ever as we face increasing competition in all parts of our business'.(Vallance -BT Annual Report,1992)

The practice:

'We do a lot of market research ... Customers are telling you what they think of you ...We have corporate communications unit which run consumer panels whereby managers in local and district areas meet consumers on monthly basis or something like that... They get together to talk about issues, not specific complaints ... BT is one of the first, if not the first to introduce something like that ... We actually take away a great number of issues that come up from those panels and try to feed them back into the policy making process.(Source; Director,BT - personal interview)

The result:

'More than 99% of faults are cleared in two days'

'More than 96% of public pay-phones are working at any one time'

'More than 98% of calls get through to the directory assistance first time, with 92% of those calls answered within 15 seconds'

'Timed appointments have become part of standard service for BT customers'

(Source; BT Reports - various)

ues to make remarkable progress in not only maintaining its
seeking ways to improve them. For example, through its
ems - one of the biggest computerised information system in
ate wider scope for 'getting in touch' with customers. This is
one way of monitoring and evaluating service perceptions.

Also, the Customer Service Guarantee imposes penalties on the company if it fails
to maintain stated standards of service. There are now grounds for compensating
customers who suffer poor services, with the organisation accepting liability for
delayed fault repairs and delayed provision of new exchange lines. The CEO sees
this as "a strong, external, self-imposed hair-shirt, to make sure that give good
quality of service".

A system of target-setting and target improvement is now well-established and many
aspects of customer performance are continuously monitored. Middle managers are
supported in their attempts to answer questions of 'where are we now'?', 'where do
we want to be?' and 'how do we get there?' in the context of BT's organisation
culture and the need for it to change and develop (Richardson, 1992; Daniels, 1993).

Conclusion

Most public sector organisations are facing enormous challenges in their approaches to
customer service management. The reason, in part, is due to their limited experience of
being governed by customer and market-based values rather than those of public policy
makers - hence their initial faltering steps. Moreover, customers are getting more
sophisticated in the demands they direct at organisations, the ways they express their needs,
the choices they make and their reaction to service quality.

Adopting a strategic customer service perspective offers a new opportunity for public
sector organisations, given the complexity of changes that are occurring in their
environments. To succeed, a sustained customer service focus is a *sine qua non*. It is not
possible to achieve an integrated and high-quality customer service simply by marshalling
policies which extol the virtues of service to customers, unless there is a sufficient prior
organisational support. The framework provided in this paper constitutes a foundation upon
which a planned approach and an effective customer service management can be based.

References

Brown, A. (1989) *Customer Care Management.* (Oxford: Heinemann).

Burns, T. (1992) 'Researching Customer Service in the Public Sector', *Journal of Marketing Research Society, 34* (1) pp.53-61.

Berkowitz, E. & Flexner, W. (1978) 'The Marketing Audit: A Tool for Health Service Organisations', *Health Care Management Review, 3* (Fall) pp.24-29.

Berry, L., Conant, J. & Parasuraman, A. (1991) 'A Framework for Conducting a Services Marketing Audit',*Journal of the Academy of Marketing Science, 19* (3) pp.255-268.

Bitner, M., Booms, B. & Tetreault, M. (1990) 'The Service Encounter: Diagnosing Favourable and Unfavourable Incidents', *Journal of Marketing, 54* (January) pp.71-84.

Bryson, J. (1988) *Planning For Public And Non-Profit Organisations* (Jossey Bass).

Daniels, J. (1993) 'Involving Everyone In Change at BT: How to Do It', in B. Richardson (ed), *Managing in Enterprise Contexts*, (Sheffield: Pavic Publications).

Ginsburg, L. & Miller, N. (1991) 'Value-driven Management', *Management Decisions, 29* (4).

Goldsmith, W. & Clutterbuck, D. (1984) *The Winning Streak* (London: Weidenfeld & Nicolson).

Heskett, J. (1987) 'Lessons in the Service Sector', *Harvard Business Review, 65*, pp.118-126.

Hirschman, A. (1970) *Exit, Voice and Loyalty* (Cambridge, Mass.: Harvard University Press).

Hooley, G. (1993) 'Market-Led Quality Management', *Journal of Marketing Management, 9* (3) pp.315-335

Hudson, B. (1990) 'Free Speech, Not Lip Service', *The Health Service Journal* (June).

Lane, S. (1983) 'The Rationale for Government Intervention in Seller-Consumer Relationships', *Public Studies Review, 2* (3).

Lewis, B. (1989) 'Customer Care in Service Organisations', *Marketing Intelligence and Planning, 7* (5/6) pp.19-22.

Lewis, B. (1990) 'Service Quality: An Investigation of Customer Care in Major UK Organisations', *International Journal of Service Industry Management, 1* (2) pp.33-44.

Maddux, G. (1991) 'Managerial Responsibility: The Re-emergence of the Corporate Conscience', *Management Decisions, 29* (5) pp.12-15.

Narasimham, C.& Sen, S. (1992) 'Measuring Quality Perceptions', *Marketing Letters, 3_* (2) pp.147-156.

Next Steps Agencies Review ,1992 (London: HMSO)

Nwankwo, S. (1992) 'Viewpoints from the Consumer Marketplace', Mimeo, Sheffield Business School.

Nwankwo, S. (1993) 'Internal Marketing: A Guide to Customer Service Effectiveness in the Public Sector'. Sheffield Business School, *Occasional Paper No.13.*

Nwankwo, S. and Curwen, P. (1993) 'Towards A Reconceptualisation of the National Enterprise'. Sheffield Business School, *Occasional Paper No.10.*

Piercy, N. & Morgan, N. (1991) 'Internal Marketing: The Missing Half of the Marketing Programme', *Long Range Planning, 24* (2) pp.82-93.

Richardson, B. (1992) 'Crossed Wires at British Telecom', in B. Richardson *et al, Case Studies in Business Planning* (London: Pitman).

Richardson, B., Nwankwo, S. & Curwen, P. (1993) 'Regulating Consumer Responsiveness in Public-to-Private Organisations in the UK'. Paper presented at the Second International Conference of *The International Institute of Administrative Sciences*, Toluca, Mexico, 27-30 July.

The Citizen's Charter (1991) CM 1599 (London: HMSO)

Tompkins, C. (1987) *Achieving Economy, Efficiency and Effectiveness in the Public Sector* (London: Kogan Page).

Wagenheim, G. & Reurink, J. (1991) 'Customer Service in Public Administration', *Public Administration Review, 51* (3) pp.263-269.

Webster, F. (1988) 'Rediscovering the Marketing Concept', *Business Horizons, 31* (May/June), pp.29-39.

Young, D. (1977) 'Consumer Problems in the Public Sector: A Framework for Research', *Journal of Consumer Policy, 1, pp.205-226.*

MAKING THE MOST OF DEVOLUTION

Professor Kevan Scholes
Director, Sheffield Business School

The late 1980's and early 1990's in many large organisations have been characterised by an almost missionary zeal to **devolve**. This is true of both public and private sector organisations and is a trend discernible in many countries. This article reflects on some of the reasons for this rising importance of devolution, the *range of choices* open to organisations wishing to increase the extent of devolution and, most importantly, some guidelines on how to benefit from devolution. There are many dangers in blindly taking on any new management approach - and devolution is no exception.

What is Devolution?

Until the mid 1980's devolution had been a word largely confined to the political arena and was concerned with the desirability - or otherwise - of sharing power between central and regional or local governments. In the corporate context devolution is concerned with a handing down of power and accountability for decisions to managers outside the central *strategic apex* of the organisation. This may mean to managers of departments, divisions or subsidiaries.

However, this definition is somewhat inadequate since it fails to describe the complexity and range of choices available in the process of handing down this power of decision making. For example, does this mean *all* decisions - or just operational decisions? Does it mean w*ithout reference to, or approval of, the central management?* These are critical questions to answer for those managers planning to increase devolution in their organisations.

Why Devolution?

It is probably no accident that this recent interest in the importance of devolution has coincided with a sustained period of market and financial pressure for most large organisations. Many public services too have seen their budgets significantly curtailed whilst large private sector companies have felt the bite of the market brought about by an extended recession. This has triggered senior managers to take action to address a number of issues they were, perhaps, avoiding:

- Top managers becoming out of touch with the "sharp-end" action in the markets and operations of the business. In fast moving markets, or during periods of significant change in the public services, there has been a feeling that more authority is needed *close to the action* in order to improve corporate performance.

- Some would say that it has largely been a reaction to the previous era of over-centralisation. Indeed a key theme in this paper is that the issue of devolution should be discussed as a *continuum* from highly centralised to highly devolved and not as a black and white choice.

- In the public services - and many large private sector organisations too - there was a belief that the performance of the organisation - in terms of competitive advantage or the creation of value-for-money services was significantly below the potential capability of the organisation. The inference being that over-centralisation had resulted in organisations losing their way and becoming too concerned with internal matters at the expense of serving the customer or client.

The Role of the Centre

In large organisations most of the managerial activity which occurs between the centre of the organisation and its parts - departments, divisions or subsidiaries - has tended to be concerned with targeting and controlling the activities of those managing the parts. If organisations are to benefit from increased devolution then these activities of assessing the performance and value added by each part of the organisation remain important. However, a critical question which also needs to be answered is what value the centre of the organisation adds to the activities of these separate parts. So asking the radical question "do we need a centre at all?" can be a valuable discipline in understanding the role of the centre of the organisation and the centre/parts relationships. There are many different ways in which the centre can add value:

- **Scale Advantages** - for example in purchasing or access to investment funds. Joint marketing or distribution between business units may also reduce costs. Most large organisations will attempt to gain some benefits in this way.

- **Corporate Image** - the credentials of separate operating companies or divisions can be enhanced by the corporate reputation of the parent. So an increasingly diverse international company such as Pilkingtons or the new separate businesses of the Post Office would expect to gain advantage in this way.
- **Providing Investment** - particularly during the early days of new ventures. The benefits from investment should not be limited to financial investment. Investment in creative thinking in the organisation could be facilitated by the centre through providing a wider forum or *peer group* through which individuals improve their knowledge and skills. This is particularly important in knowledge based organisations in both the private and public sectors. The lack of this creative investment is one reason why small consultancy companies often run out of steam.
- **Mitigating Risk** - is a very important function of the centre and can occur in two main ways:
  - by managing *the balance* of the organisation's activities and the portfolio of activities. The centre can provide a more secure environment for up and coming businesses or services than they would experience if they stood alone. This is an important way in which *specialisation* becomes possible without an unacceptable level of risk. So the establishment of satellite television in the UK - through B Sky B - was crucially supported by being part of a multi-national communications company - The News Corporation.
  - by *smoothing-out* short term fluctuations which an independent unit may not be able to ride. This could range from the management of bad debts or sickness leave costs through to the problems created by currency fluctuations. Businesses operating in commodity markets are particularly susceptible to such risks. For example, in minerals mining the exploration and mine development period may extend over several years during which time the world market price for the product will have fluctuated considerably. Companies operating as single site/single product units would be highly vulnerable to these uncontrollable risks. A larger parent company can mitigate this risk.
- **Access to opportunities** - either in the market or in resource supply. The parent organisation may have contacts and networks which are advantageous to the division or subsidiary. Many public sector service departments obtain funding which their private sector "competitors" cannot access. These opportunities could be lost if the separate service departments were either privatised or so devolved that they become out of touch with the centre of their organisation.
- **Facilitating and co-ordinating collaborative ventures** - either between different parts of the organisation and/or with external agencies. This is the benefit which the centre of a health authority, or a university should provide to its separate departments -

collaborative efforts often produce unique and valuable services. This is one competitive edge which the New Universities have had over their traditional counterparts. The federal structures of the older universities have often made collaborative ventures and "cross-department" programmes more difficult to pursue.

- **Providing specialist services** - needed by the separate parts of the organisation which they cannot provide themselves on a cost efficient basis. Many financial services such as payroll, billing and credit control are often best provided this way. However, other traditionally central services may be more sensibly devolved. In fact, in most organisations there could be a case for these central services to be optional - since larger departments or divisions may choose to undertake the activity themselves whereas small units may value central assistance - recruitment might be an example.

Clearly the importance of each of these factors will vary in any situation. It will be seen below that the critical issue is deciding in which ways the centre is able to add value and ensuring that decisions concerning the devolved structures are consistent with this role.

The Role of the Parts

The organisation and its clients are unlikely to gain advantage from devolution unless there is a strategic view on how the *modus operandi* of departments and divisions should change to turn the potential benefits into real benefits. Again the guidelines are simple:

- There will be a need to recognise, and encourage, *diversity* of operation and performance criteria between the different parts of the organisation. This is a crucial change the importance of which many public service organisations are now realising. It requires managers to have a much clearer view on the *positioning* of their division or department. For example, recent changes in the Health Service should allow health professionals to accept that where speed and geographical proximity are important - as Emergency and Accident Units - this will require a multiplicity of providers within a region as against say, Cardiology, where a few national - or even international - *centres of excellence* could be allowed to emerge and attract additional funding and/or resources. So, divisional and departmental managers need to think hard, and honestly, about the positioning of their own unit and which services should be provided in house and which are better contacted from other providers.

- Understanding and assessing the performance of a particular unit in terms of the *value for money* of its services is an essential part of understanding positioning. Public service managers have been too involved with traditional line-by-line budgets and spent insufficient time thinking about *cost structure* and value-for-money from a strategic viewpoint. For example, the mix of professional staff and support staff may be sensibly adjusted to provide a better value-for-money service to clients and a division of responsibilities which better suit each set of staff. This requires a *strategic* restructuring of the budget, which devolution should allow. The early experience of managing devolved budgets has been disappointing in this respect. The operational benefits of devolved budgets have been pursued - less paperwork and speedier decisions, but strategic re-appraisal of the cost structure has been more limited.

Dividing Responsibilities

It has already been mentioned that the key to benefiting from devolution lies in a proper definition of the role of the centre of the organisation and its various parts. This is essentially concerned with how responsibilities for decision making are divided between the centre and the divisions or departments. Goold and Campbell (1) provide three valuable stereotypes of different ways of dividing these responsibilities. These are summarised in figure 1 and illustrated in figures 2, 3 and 4.

- **Strategic Planning** (figure 2) - is the most centralised of the three approaches. Here the centre of the organisation operates as a *masterplanner* and prescribes detailed roles for divisions and departments which are seen as agencies which deliver part of the organisation's plan. Their role is confined to the operational delivery of the plan. In the extreme form of strategic planning the centre is expected to add value in **all** the ways outlined above. The centre orchestrates, co-ordinates and controls all of the activities of the departments/divisions resulting in the extensive use of the management devices shown in figure 2. This is the classic bureaucracy familiar to many public sector managers. However, this is not a public sector issue *per se*. Indeed, multi-national fast food chains, such as McDonalds, would arguably come closest to this stereotype. It is the problems experienced with this approach which have encouraged many organisations to devolve further. In particular, the relationship between the centre and divisions/departments tend to become entirely tactical and characterised by a "special pleadings" mentality in the divisions/departments.
- **Financial Control** (figure 3) - is the most extreme form of devolved structure - short of complete dissolution of the organisation. The centre behaves like a *shareholder* or *banker* for divisions. There is little concern for the product/market strategy of divisions - even to the extent that they can compete openly with each other. They might even have authority to raise funds from outside the company.

    Here the role of the centre is confined to allocating capital (against bids), setting financial targets and appraising performance. The centre, therefore, is only attempting to add value in a few of the ways listed earlier - in particular through its corporate image (particularly in money markets) and mitigating the risk of individual divisions through the management of a **portfolio** of activities.

This extreme is rarely found - even in the private sector. Some public sector managers appear to hold this as their "ideal" as to what devolution means - but in reality such extreme devolution is likely to remain unacceptable within the public sector for reasons of political accountability.

- **Strategic Control** (figure 4) - which lies between these two extremes necessarily defines the way in which most organisations operate. In a sense it is not a single stereotype since it bridges all of the space between strategic planning and financial control. So, figure 4 provides the *checklist* against which an organisation can establish its own particular brand of strategic control.

Here the centre operates as a *strategic shaper* and this defines the **minimum core** role of the centre as follows:

- Defining and shaping the *overall* strategy of the organisation - particularly through the allocation of resources.
- Deciding the balance of activities and the *role* of each division/department.
- Defining and controlling organisational *policies* (on employment, market coverage etc).
- Assessing the *performance* of the separate divisions/departments.

However, the centre does not fulfil these roles through an imposed masterplan. Rather it is built through the process of agreeing business plans produced by divisions - but within central guidelines. So, referring to the earlier discussion the centre would expect to add value through links and collaborations between divisions and departments - for example through internal suppliers or collaborative product developments. Gaining advantage through *synergy* would often be an important objective in organisations. Central Services may be optional rather than imposed. A key decision is which services should be provided on which basis.

An example should serve to outline the key differences between these three approaches. Consider a company like Laura Ashley - an international clothing company traditionally providing the majority of its merchandise through its own manufacturing division, and having expanded to some 500 outlets internationally by 1991. Faced with difficult trading conditions in the USA market (with almost 200 outlets) how should the company respond? A strategic planning approach would consider the impact on the whole company of (say) new product lines and attempt to work through an optimum strategy. By way of contrast financial control would give the American division complete freedom to solve this difficult market problem itself - providing it met financial targets. This could include diversification or sourcing from non-Laura Ashley factories.

Strategic control would probably disallow diversification - on the grounds that it fell outside the company's preferred scope of activity. It would probably lay "ground rules" about third-party sourcing of goods by the American division. For example, they may be allowed to do so after they had offered the contract internally and demonstrated the significant advantage which third-party supply would bring (in cost or quality or speed of delivery). They may also have central policies regarding supply - for example not wishing to source from particular "slave labour" economies.

The Internal Market

It should be clear from the above that one of the important changes which increased devolution brings within organisations is a gradual move away from relationships which are *compulsory* to more opportunities for managers of departments/divisions to exercise choice. This could apply to sourcing of supplies and services and/or to choosing clients and customers. So, it becomes an important management task to regulate and manage within this *internal market* as well as the external markets at both the supply and customer ends of the organisation. Many managers see this as a welcome shift in the approach to internal relationships. *Compulsion* - for example having to source all your IT or catering or financial services internally has often led to poor performance by internal "supply" departments and a feeling of resentment by internal "buyer" departments. Where internal markets have been operating for some time this relationship should shift to one of *mutual* benefit. A *good* internal supplier is probably the best arrangement for most buyers of internal services.

...and making it work

There is now a considerable amount of experience in many organisations of the operation of internal markets and some simple guidelines can be drawn from these experiences:

- The most important issue is for people to remember that an internal market is not the same as an external market. A key difference is that an internal market will always be subject to some degree of short term - or even long term *constraint*. The extent of these constraints clearly depends on the degree of devolution. Organisations operating close to the stereotype of *financial control* may limit these constraints to issues of internal availability of capital - and closely approach the external market situation. However, for many organisations *strategic control* will require policies, rules and guidelines which constrain the internal market. The Laura Ashley example above, illustrated a commonly taken position where the internal supplier must be given first option, but the possibility of third-party supply (or sales) is not excluded.

  A pharmaceutical manufacturer which owned its own supplier of a strategically crucial ingredient naturally disallowed any third-party sales from that company. However in that case, as in many others, an important management decision concerned internal *transfer pricing* of the ingredient in circumstances where the market was being constrained (by disallowing external sales). This is an example of how *strategic control* as a management approach would attempt to regulate the internal market to best achieve the overall corporate purposes and minimise the risk of suboptimisation - ie one division doing well at the expense of another.

At a practical level, there are two types of behaviour which can be triggered off by creating internal markets and which are to be discouraged. First, is the escalation in *bargaining* between units which eventually diverts important management time from the real task ahead. Second, is the creation of a new bureaucracy monitoring all of the *internal transfers* of resources between units. Indeed, it is essential that devolution does not fall into disrepute through trying to devolve too many detailed and trivial items down the line. For example, in a service organisation budgetary responsibility could be passed down the line for all of the costs related to delivery of each service. However, two important costs - secretarial time and photocopying may be provided centrally within the organisation and not separately for each service. It may not make sense to create a new bureaucracy to measure, record, and allocate each item to separate services - so these items need to remain under central control. Good management philosophies need to be tempered by level headed interpretations of how to manage in practical situations.

Letting go

One major problem of making devolution work is that the centre can't let go. This may not be because top managers are against devolution, nor that they fail to understand the wider implications of the concept as discussed in this article. It is because the whole *culture* of the organisation is a bureaucratic culture. So changing the structures, systems and even the power axes will not shift the behaviour and attitudes of the vast majority of staff who simply carry on doing things in the same old way. This is not to suggest that people are necessarily resistant to change, it is just that management have forgotten that for those people who implement the organisation's strategy, little, if anything has been done to educate, develop and encourage them to take on change. Above all it is a reminder that an organisation's culture is enshrined in the *work routines*. If these are not changed nothing will shift. So in reality, change is frustrated by the *inertia* of old approaches rather than through organised resistance to change as is often suggested.

Changes in outlook and behaviour

One of the most important issues for managers of divisions/departments is coming to terms with the reality of *being* a devolved manager. Most can see the positive benefits of more self-determination, but have forgotten the responsibilities which this implies. In particular that managers cannot keep running back to the centre to bail them out or provide special funding for new ideas. This is often a painful realisation for managers who have developed skills in bargaining for discretionary resources. They need to learn more about *self-sufficiency* and setting *priorities*. A related issue is that no longer is there someone else to blame for one's own shortcomings, which forces managers to reassess their relationships with their subordinates. It is no longer a plausible management style with subordinates to be "one of the troops" fighting the real enemy (mean-minded central managers).

One type of behaviour in centralised bureaucracies which is hard to change in a move to devolution is the desire to prescribe and measure everything that moves. Senior managers may have encouraged managers of divisions/departments to decide how to deploy their resources and the difficult choices and priorities which that brings.

However, there will inevitably be pressure for "more rules of the game" as to how much resource they *should* be deploying on various services and activities. There is a key distinction between the centre producing a *rule book*, which is very much against the spirit of devolution, whilst accepting that managers do need some guidelines on key aspects of their operations. Strategic control would try to find a "half way house" by providing an *enabling framework* where there is a high level of openness in the organisation as to what priorities and choices are being made together with an expectation that managers of devolved units have a key responsibility to shape corporate thinking on these issues rather than simply awaiting instructions.

This can be an essential part of ensuring that an *implementation* gap does not emerge between the aspirations of the organisation as a whole and the sum total of the strategies of the separate divisions or departments. The public sector has traditionally used its democratic forums and committees to bridge this gap, but these are now being successfully supplemented by more involvement in a direct advisory capacity (to senior executives) from middle managers within the organisation.

Finally

Improvements in the strategic performance of organisations will not be brought about by any single change or management device - such as increasing devolution. Successful change requires a whole series of related adjustments to be made to the organisation's operations - including new work routines, management systems and most importantly, the motivation of people inside and around the organisation to accept change and make new strategies work. For example, it is vital to the success of devolved management that those managing divisions or departments are provided with good quality *management information*. This has proved to be a very difficult transition for most public services whose financial information systems have traditionally been concerned with external reporting and not internal facilitation. Also the skills of business *planning* need to be developed in divisional managers who have been used simply to receiving line-by-line budgets.

Within this wider position the reconsideration of responsibilities - the subject of this article - may play a vital part. Devolution needs to be viewed in this wider context and figure 5 provides a checklist which managers can use to assess the extent of devolution in their own organisation and whether it could be changed to good advantage.

References

1. M Goold and A Campbell, *Strategies and Styles*, Basil Blackwell, 1987
2. G Johnson and K Scholes, *Exploring Corporate Strategy*, Prentice Hall, 3rd Edition, 1993

	Key Features	Advantages	Dangers	Examples
STRATEGIC PLANNING	• 'Masterplanner' • Top-down • Highly prescribed • Detailed controls	Co-ordination	Centre out of touch Divisions tactical	BOC Cadbury Lex STC Public sector pre-1990's
FINANCIAL CONTROL	• 'Shareholder/banker' • Financial targets • Control of investment • Bottom-up	Responsiveness	Lose direction Centre does not add value	BTR Hanson plc Tarmac
STRATEGIC CONTROL	• 'Strategic shaper' • 'Stategic and financial targets' • Bottom-up • Less detailed controls	Centre/divisions complementary Ability to co-ordinate Motivation	Too much bargaining Culture change needed New bureaucracies	ICI Courtaulds Public sector post-1990

Figure 10.8
Centre-division relationships

Figure 1

From G Johnson and K Scholes *Exploring Corporate Strategy,* Prentice Hall, 3rd Ed.

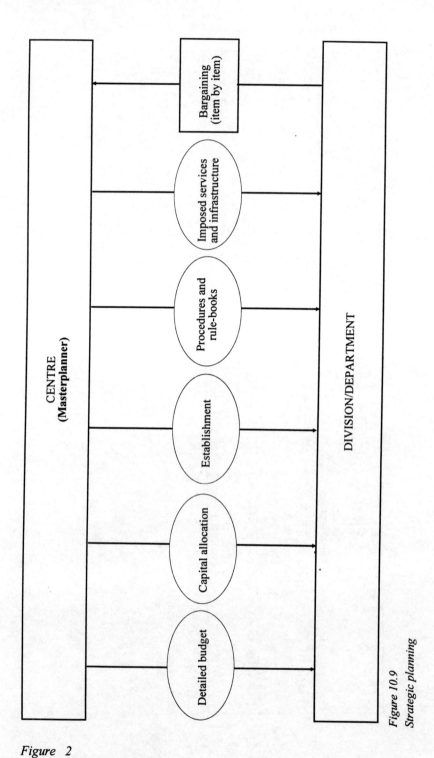

Figure 10.9
Strategic planning

Figure 2

From G Johnson and K Scholes *Exploring Corporate Strategy,* Prentice Hall, 3rd Ed.

78

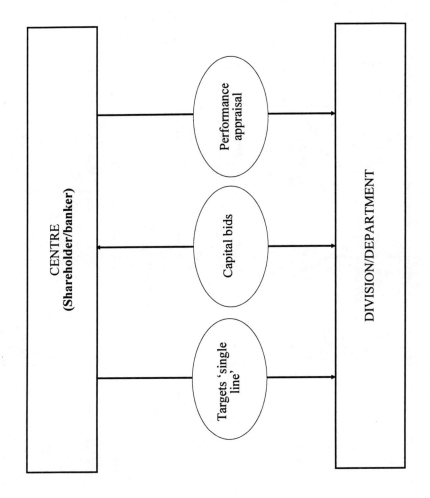

Figure 19.10
Financial control

Figure 3

From G Johnson and K Scholes *Exploring Corporate Strategy,* Prentice Hall, 3rd Ed.

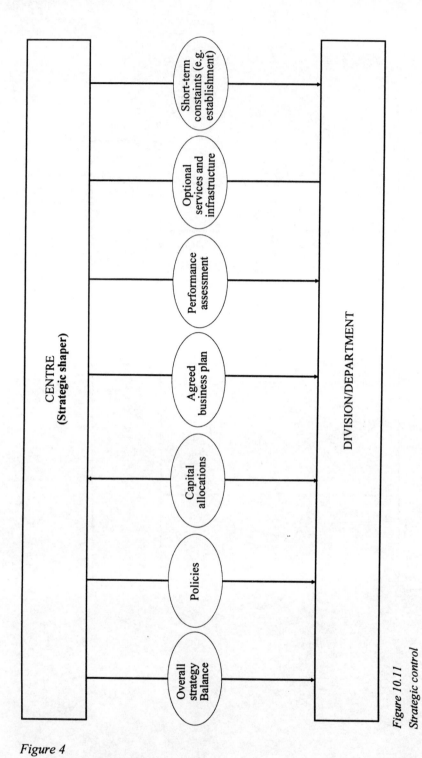

Figure 4

From G Johnson and K Scholes *Exploring Corporate Strategy,* Prentice Hall, 3rd Ed.

		Yes/No	Performance assessed by (eg):	Yes/No

1. Role of the Centre	Does the Centre add value in the following ways:
	
	- Scale advantage?
	- Corporate image?
	- Investment?
	- Mitigating risk?
	  a) Portfolio management
	  b) Smoothing fluctuations
	- Accessing opportunities?
	- Facilitating collaborative ventures?
	- Providing specialist services?
			- Reduced unit costs
			- Price premium, additional funding
			- New ventures supported
			
			- Balanced portfolio
			- Smoothing devices
			- High level networks
			- Cross-unit products/services
			- Lower cost or better quality	

2. Role of Divisions/departments	Which philosophy is being pursued: - Strategic planning? - Financial control? - Strategic control?		Is this *modus operandi consistent* with this? - Budgeting/business planning - Central policy framework - Procedures/Rules - Capital Allocations - Central Services - Performance assessment	
3. Assisting the move to more devolution	Is attention being paid to: - Regulating the Internal Market? - Controlling bargaining? - Limiting cross-charging? - Involvement in central policy making? - Devolving business plans as well as budgets? - Changing management systems? - Providing management information?			

Figure 5

WHAT BUSINESS ARE WE IN? OR ARE WE IN BUSINESS?

Peter Lawless, Sheffield Business School

Introduction

In a recent edition of *The Observer*, Andrew Campbell, director of the Ashridge Strategic Management Centre, wrote that -

> A better understanding of legitimate business purpose could ...help allay the deep suspicion of 'big business' common to employees and society at large - a suspicion which leaves companies well down on the list when graduates and school leavers come to choose their careers (24 October 1993)

It is my contention in this paper that there is something more profound than a "deep suspicion of 'big business' " underlying such issues and that in fact there is an underlying mythology about business which not only influences recruitment but actually impedes the development of certain types of organization.

Based on my involvement with a growing co-operative and related research, what I intend to present here is a general consideration of how popular interpretations of the images and language of business can be a limiting factor in the creation of organizations which seek to break away from the accepted modes of business practice in order to find ways of working which give expression to the deeply-held ideas of the organization's members.

There are many examples of businesses which have prospered because of a guiding ideal. For example, we are familiar with Rowntree and Cadbury, the Quaker industrialists, the Rochdale Pioneers who instigated what became the CWS and many others. Indeed, the rise of capitalism itself has been associated with the growth of Protestantism. No doubt, for every one that succeeded there were many which fell by the wayside, but I mention these because for some, especially the Quakers, social, ethical and spiritual considerations were not a later addition to their business practices but an essential founding principle, and I feel that currently we are also seeing the creation of organizations for which similar considerations are of primary importance. However, the importance of these considerations can be seen as both a spur to action and a hindrance.

The Problem of Determining and Articulating Strategic Objectives

In their analysis of the failure of radical projects Landry *et al* (1985, p.32) recognised that:

> The problem - of how to clarify objectives, create a strategy to carry them out and find means to make them happen, is one that few radical organizations recognise explicitly - most muddle through. The lack of strategic clarity can only be a recipe for disaster, as the history of failure in this sector over the last few years plainly demonstrates.

Obviously, the issue in relation to setting objectives is crucial to the long-term success of an organization, but before this must come an even more basic step, that of the organization deciding 'What business are we in?'. However, for certain types of organization a more fundamental question must be 'Are we in business?'. If this latter question is unresolved, then to attempt to come to terms with the issue of 'What business are we in?' and to create strategy is difficult, if not impossible. In addition, if the question of 'What business are we in?' is unanswered, then other issues cannot be addressed. As an illustration of the significance of this question we need only to look to a modified version of Weisbord's Six-Box Development Model as shown in Figure 1.

On the face of it, 'Are we in business?' should be an easy question to answer, so what makes it such a difficult question to answer for some types of organization? As a starting point, we could consider a definition such as the following from Cole (1993, p.89):

> A Business organization ... exists to provide goods or services at a profit. Making a profit may not necessarily be the sole aim of a business, but it is certainly what distinguishes it from a non-business organization.

It would be easy to consider that the difficulty in answering lies in the apparent central role of profit in this definition, but my contention is that it is a problem which has deeper roots than the problematic issue of profit and rather lies in the organization's culture.

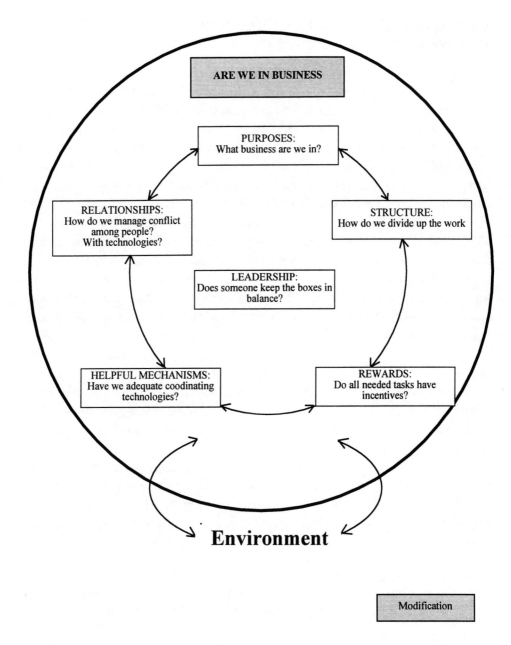

Figure 1
Weisbord's Six-box Development Model

Source: Burke (1987)

Cultural Influences On The Issue of 'Are We In Business?'

Much attention has been given to the role of metaphor, myth and legend in the creation and maintenance of organizational culture and its role as a powerful facilitator of change (Krefting and Frost, 1983; Marshak, 1993; Morgan, 1986; Pondy, 1983) but it appears to me that a great deal of this work considers the creation and maintenance of organizational culture in established companies. The role of the founder and leader in the origin of the culture has been acknowledged (Deal and Kennedy, 1988; Peters and Waterman, 1982; Schein, 1985 and 1991a) but how is culture developed from Day One in an organization that has no leaders but only a collection of founders, i.e. a workers' co-operative?

Whilst the internal aspects of culture, 'the way we do business round here' aspects, are often mentioned, there are also crucial external dimensions to culture. Externally, culture provides the organization with a way of looking at the world and interpreting it but, assuming that interpretation plays a fundamental role in the subsequent enactment of the organization's environment (Weick, 1977), what is the basis of the organization's initial interpretation and assessment of its environment? Obviously each member of the organization brings to it his or her own experience of existence, values, and meanings - effectively, his or her own paradigm, which is important if we consider paradigms to be not only ways of interpreting the world but of responding to the world (Lincoln and Gubba, 1985). Even though, within the group, there are some shared experiences, their only common ground is what at this point I will loosely call the mythology(ies) of the society(ies) to which they belong. Included in these mythologies are those related to the world of business and how it pursues its objectives.

If Schein's (1985 and 1991b) model of the three levels of culture is considered as shown in Figure 2, it can be seen that the hidden roots of culture lie at the level of basic assumptions about the nature of time, space, human interaction and so forth. It is only from awareness and understanding of these roots that culture can be understood and, if possible, managed and it is in regard to this that Weick's concept of enactment can be understood, since it:

> stresses the proactive role that we unconsciously play in creating our world. Although we often see ourselves as living in a reality with objective characteristics, life demands much more of us than this. It requires that we take an active role in bringing our realities into being through various interpretive schemes, even though these realities may then have a habit of imposing themselves on us as 'the way things are'. (Morgan, 1986, p.130)

However, where in the founding situation do the founders get these assumptions from, particularly their assumptions about the world of business? This comes partly from their

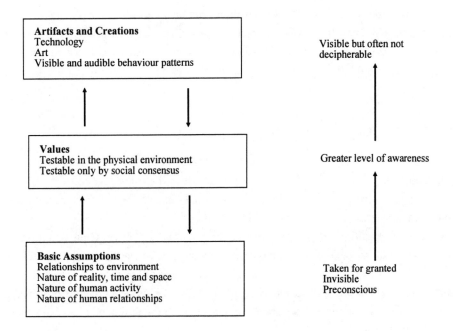

Figure 2
Levels of Culture and Their Interaction

Source: Schein (1985) p.14

experience and observation of it; partly from their political and social analysis of events in the world of business; partly from the image of business that is promoted not only by the media but also through the media by some of its exponents who wish to be seen as power players - high rollers who manifest this in their displays of fast cars, flash suits, high profiles and low morals.

Additionally, many ideas surrounding business, even in regard to small business, come as a consequence of what Mintzberg (1989) calls the alliance of the economist and the engineer, one given to the optimisation of profit and the other to the optimisation of the machine. This constitutes an alliance which presents the world with the still popularly-held image of the grinding heartless machine that has little regard for either its employees or other stakeholders other than the owner/stakeholders. Along with this image come commensurate issues relating to power and authority. If this analysis is to be considered outmoded in the light of the new ways of considering and designing organizations, we need only look at how efficiency and cost effectiveness are well-publicised aspects of the way that businesses are run, especially newly-privatised businesses or those being prepared for privatisation. Indeed, these are the organizations that the majority of the population have to do business with, and these aspects appear to take precedence over other areas which would present the organization in a more humane light, for example one reflecting the possible social desirability of the maintenance of employment, not profit, at a time of recession.

Issues Of Power, Authority and Conflict

Looking at Weisbord's model, it is also possible to see other areas of conflict within the organization. In fact, an area of crucial significance is that of leadership. Whilst the Weisbord model equates leadership to keeping the boxes in balance, it is often perceived in terms of power and authority when related to business.

An obvious manifestation of this linkage of power and authority comes with issues relating to the management of internal business meetings, particularly in respect of taking the chair of such meetings. When all are involved on a basis of equals in these meetings, it is difficult to accept any permanent role, particularly one associated with power and authority. Often the chair is elected for a single meeting or the notion of a revolving chair is introduced, but whilst this may give a semblance of democracy what is significantly lacking is continuity of action and purpose as the meeting effectively has to re-constitute itself on each and every occasion it meets until such a time as quasi-permanent roles evolve over time. Such roles often evolve by default as the more willing take up roles which other members of the group are reluctant to undertake, and as a result certain members may find themselves making a disproportionate contribution to the running of the organization.

Similarly, the resolution of organizational conflict is beset with difficulties, especially those conflicts which in other organizations would be regarded as matters of discipline. Here again the issue of power and authority arises, especially when it comes to dealing with the behaviour of individuals whose actions are disruptive or potentially damaging to the development of the organization. Such behaviour is inevitable when any group comes together and tries to form its own norms, and must be seen as an essential, though distressing, part of group formation as any basic organizational behaviour text will indicate. The issue is, however, how the individual is brought into line in a manner which is conductive to the ethos of the organization and acceptable to the other members.

A Demonology Of Business

It is undoubtedly the case that amongst the founders there may be many other issues relating to personal/political/sexual agendas, but underlying their transactions is not so much a mythology related to business but a demonology which presents the organization's founders

88

with a problem when they come together to create a co-operative business. Indeed, the very use of the word co-operative in this context seems at odds with what they are trying to create, since what is co-operative about business as it commonly perceived?

Fear Of Business And The Need To Confront It

If organizations are considered to be constructions which help their members to come to terms with anxieties that would be difficult to deal with individually (Morgan, 1986), how can such a mythology of business serve to do anything but enhance that collective anxiety to such an extent that an 'underlying pathology ... (of) ... unresolved fear' (Critchley and Casey, 1989, p.7) is created? As a consequence of this, the organization can become 'stuck' as that fear distorts its world view and affects its subsequent interpretations and actions.

Hirsch and Andrews (1983) have written about the use of language at times of organizational takeover, seeing it (p.150) as an:

> indicator of normative confusion, and functions to distance both participants and observers from the stress and fast pace involved in an organisational sequence amply spiced with drama, pain (for many), and uncertainty over legitimacy and final outcomes.

and a parallel is to be found in the way language is used, and interpreted, at times of organizational foundation in the context of a perceived hostile environment. Fears are projected onto the environment as the organization's members try to come to terms with that environment and their relationships to it. Indeed, at such times the imagery and metaphors used can provide the key to the deep structure of the organization and the individuals involved (Krefting and Frost, 1985). Having recognised these factors, however, the issue is to consider what can be done to help the organization overcome its problems and handle the issues that such a mythology of business creates. Bradford and Harvey (1972) and Harvey and Albertson (1971a and 1971b) suggested that organizations need to deal with dysfunctional myths and fantasies by a process of reality testing since the underlying attitudes and behaviours they reflect are seldom tested. This, however, is a long process and presupposes that the organization has more than a brief history, but if the organization's founders have an active part to play in the creation of its culture and history, then it is inevitable that they have an active involvement in the creation, enactment and maintenance of the organization's reality. The issue accordingly becomes one of getting the members to accept their part in that process.

Landy *et al* (1985) write that an understanding of the capitalist market place is essential for the survival of radical organizations. This may be doing little more that stating the obvious, as well as pre-dating the opening comments of Andrew Campbell, but in gaining that understanding there is no need to take it to mean that an organization has to take upon itself the values of that world - a taking on of values which, I feel, is the source of certain of the organization's anxieties. The organization has to come to realise that, rather than accept these, a process of internal re-definition can occur. Roles and related matters can be defined within the context of the organization as it is, and not within terms of the world of business as it appears to be. In effect, a process of de-mythologising can occur.

The organization may feel that it can do little about the external environment, but what it can do is come to realise that it can engage itself in a process of de-mythologising the world of business in respect of its internal processes. For example, as a consequence of the de-mythologising of their roles in meetings, members should come to see that such roles only possess that power and authority which other members of the organization allow them. In turn, this will have an effect upon their interpretation of the external environment and have a consequent effect upon their enactment.

Over time, it is hoped that such a process will allow a positive resolution of the question 'Are we in business?' as the organization members develop an understanding of what business means for them. Similarly, over time a change will occur within the basic assumptions upon which the organization's culture is based as these unconscious roots are confronted and evaluated and changed as the organization develops.

In situations like this it would be too easy to place the blame for misunderstanding the nature of business on those who misunderstand, but what is it about the world of business that gives such a mythology a seeming validity? Part of the answer may lie in more widespread discussion, and application, of notions of ethical business, but until this takes place what can be done to prevent the hidden costs to organizations and the economy if talent and skills are lost because large numbers of people are put off being in business simply because of the myths surrounding it?

References

Bradford, L. and Harvey, J. (1972) 'Dealing With Dysfunctional Organization Myths', in Burke and Hamstein (eds) *Social Technology of Organization Development* (NTL Learning Resources Comp Inc).

Burke, W. (1987) *Organizational Development: A Normative View* (Addison-Wesley).

Campbell, A. (1993) 'A Question of Purpose', *The Observer* (24 October).

Cole, G. (1993) *Management Theory and Practice* (DP Publications Ltd).

Deal, T. and Kennedy, A. (1988) *Corporate Cultures* (Penguin).

Harvey, J and Alberson, D. (!971a) 'Neurotic Organizations: Symptoms, Causes and Treatment, Part 2',. *Personnel Journal* (September).

Harvey, J and Albertson, D. (1971b) 'Neurotic Organizations: Symptoms, Causes and Treatment, Part 2', *Personnel Journal* (October).

Hirsch, P. and Andrews, J. (1983) 'Ambushes, Shoutouts and Knights of the Round Table; The Language of Corporate Takeovers', in Pondy, Frost and Morgan (eds). *Organizational Symbolism* (JAI Press).

Krefting, L. and Frost, P. (1985) 'Untangling Webs, Surfing Waves and Wildcatting: A Multiple-Metaphor Perspective on Managing Organizational Change', in Frost, Moore, Louis, Lundeberg and Martin (eds) *Organization Culture* (Sage).

Landry, C., Morley, D., Southwood, P. and Wright, P. (1985) *What a Way to Run a Railroad - an analysis of radical failure* (Comedia).

Lincoln, Y. and Guba, E. (1985) *Naturalistic Inquiry* (Sage).

Marshak, R. (1993) 'Managing the Metaphors of Change', *Organizational Dynamics* (Winter).

Mintzberg, H. (1989) 'The Case for Corporate Social Responsibility' in Iannore (ed) *Contemporary Moral Controversies in Business* (Oxford University Press).

Morgan, G. (1986) *Images of Organization* (Sage).

Peters, R. and Waterman, Jr R. (1982) I*n Search of Excellence* (Harper and Row).

Pondy, L. (1983) 'The Role of Metaphors and Myths in Organization and in the Facilitation of Change', in Pondy, Frost and Morgan (eds) *Organizational Symbolism* (JAI Press)

Schein, E. (1985) *Organizational Culture and Leadership* (Jossey-Bass).

Schein, E. (1991a) 'The Role of the Founder in the Creation of Organizational Culture', in Frost, Moore, Louis, Lundberg and Martin (eds) *Reframing Organizational Culture* (Sage).

Schein, E. (1991b) 'What is Culture' in Frost, Moore, Louis, Lundberg and Martin (eds) *Reframing Organizational Culture* (Sage).

Weick, K. (1977) 'Enactment Processes in Organizations', in Staw and Salancik (eds) *New Directions in Organizational Behaviour* (St Clair Press).

PARADIGM SHIFTS IN A LOCAL AUTHORITY SETTING: NEW ROLES FOR THE CORPORATE PLANNING FUNCTION

Andy Stephens and Bill Peel

Introduction

This paper is concerned with the impact of 'paradigms' on the strategic development of organisations and, in particular, on the strategic development of a Metropolitan Borough Council (MBC). The paper begins by discussing the concept of the paradigm and the reasons why new paradigms are necessary in turbulent business conditions before organisational change to meet the demands of new environmental situations can be effectively made. It then provides some brief contextual material to describe one organisational context which has changed radically over the past few years and which has required a matching fundamental shift of paradigm. The nature of the old, and the required new, paradigms are then juxtaposed and a discussion on the work of the Authority's corporate planning personnel as agents of paradigm change is undertaken.

The Nature and Importance of Organisational Paradigms

According to Gerry Johnson (1988):

> The [organisational] paradigm is the set of beliefs and assumptions, held relatively common through the organization, taken for granted, and discernible in the stories and explanations of the managers, which plays a central role in the interpretation of environmental stimuli and configuration of organizationally relevant strategic responses.

Thus, for our purposes, 'paradigms' are those deep-rooted beliefs about how the organisation should operate in adapting to its environmental situation. They relate to the

93

basic views which people in the organisation hold about their world and their organisation's role in it. These hard-to-change beliefs are clearly visible in the structures, systems, strategies and behaviours of the organisation. Thus, deep-rooted paradigms which are part of a world view which sees the organisation as undertaking appropriate behaviours from a dominant position in a safe world, tend to hold fast even when the world around the organisation has changed to become threatening and hostile. An appropriate analogy might be that of the the change of environment which would take place should a boat drift from the calm waters of Lake Erie over the edge of the Niagara Falls and into the more foggy, noisy, chaotic and fast-flowing conditions below. Such a change in environment demands a changed view of reality - one which acknowledges that safety and serenity have been superseded by dynamism and danger. Only after the boat's crew and its pasengers have accepted this new reality will they begin to behave in ways more appropriate to the new reality. Such a change in environment has occurred in the case of what we will call Teflon MBC and such a change of paradigm needs also to take place.

Context of the Case and the Traditional Paradigm

Teflon MBC is a unitary authority delivering the full range of local authority services. These include education, social services, leisure provision, housing, development planning, economic regeneration, statutory functions such as building control, health and trading standards and supporting professional disciplines such as engineering, architecture, legal and financial services.

The Authority employs over 11,000 people serving a population of 222,000 with 66 elected Members. The political environment has been stable for many decades and the Authority is Labour controlled with a large majority having always been the norm.

In 1991/92 the authority's gross expenditure was £233mn, of which £17mn was raisd through the Community Charge. In 1993/94 the estimated gross expenditure will be £250mn of which £20mn will be raised through the Council Tax.

The traditional employers in the borough were coal-mining and heavy engineering. However, 20,000 jobs have gone from the coal sector in the last ten years. The last working colliery closed recently.

Traditionally there has been a strong sense of community, and an expectation that heavy engineering work for men will continue to be the major source of employment, with the Council providing or helping to generate much of this work as well as providing standard local authority services.

Not surprisingly, given the many decades that Teflon MBC has functioned in its traditional way, a strong paradigm has taken root. We have identified what we consider to be key elements of the organisation's dominant paradigm as follows:

- We care for our community from a very paternalistic standpoint.
- We are the 'natural' and 'rightful' providers of services for the community around here.
- We are the most effective providers of what we do and new providers would not do the job as well as we do.
- Our primary responsibility is to the people of our community.
- Our position is unchallenged and unassailable.
- We manage our resources prudently but the key financial issue is how to share out our funds more than how to raise them.
- We aim and expect to improve:
    the welfare of our community
    the positions and prospects of our staff.
- We take account of our wider economic, political and social environment but, ultimately, we are separate from and can control it.
- Hierarchical structures and committee systems are the most effective ways of conducting local government 'business'.

Over the past few years, central government-led changes have altered the nature of our situation. For example, the coal industry has been decimated following changes in the structure of the energy industry and the related British Coal pit closure programme. The organisation is being required to adopt competitive tendering policies with the implication that our internal department suppliers of services might no longer maintain the right to supply these services. New agencies such as the Training and Enterprise Councils have been set up and have become the conduit for central government investment monies which were formerly under our control. Our tax-raising capability has also been constrained following central governmental legislative intervention. These specific changes have combined with other legislative changes, economic recession and Europeanisation to create a much more turbulent and less amenable environment within which Teflon MBC must operate. Before fundamental operational changes will be made, however, people must 'take on board' the new reality and the implications that it holds for new policies and practices. The new paradigm from which environmental-matching organisational changes might be made is at odds with the old one. The following tenets seem to be more suitable for the new conditions in which we operate:

- We are not the natural providers of services to our community - we do not have an automatic right to do this job.
- Parental care is no longer an appropriate concept - the 'retailer' concept of 'value for money' and 'customer care' is a more appropriate concept.
- The community is not our major customer (although it might be our major end-user) - rather, central government and other important financial resource providers are major customers.

- An economic basis for action is a more fitting basis than is a social one.
- We can no longer control or ignore our environment - it is imposing strategic change on us and our very survival is threatened.
- Competition is now the name of the game - and cost reduction is the dominant competitive strategy.
- The key financial issue is how to get more resources - a basic shortage of resources is the fundamental problem for us and this simply intensifies the problem of how to share what we have around our departments.
- Instead of standing aloof, and separate, from elements of our environment (for example, the local Training and Enterprise Council), we need to collaborate with them.
- People inside the organisation and the community we serve can no longer expect us to 'grow' their qualities of life - some things will inevitably get worse.
- We need to devolve the power to make big strategic decisions about types and levels of services and about employment numbers and conditions to our managers (who are likely to need awareness and skills training). Structures need to support and develop 'bare bones', low-cost, flexible, innovative and best-value activities.

The Paradigm Gap

Clearly, for elected Members, Authority personnel and people in the community, big changes have occurred which need to be recognised and internalised. The reality gap between the forces of the 'new order' and long-established, cherished beliefs is enormous. Closing this paradigm gap will involve changes for leaders, managers, rank and file personnel and the people of the community. This gap is modelled in Figure 1.

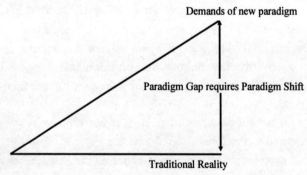

Figure 1
The Paradigm Gap

96

The Corporate Planning Function and the Paradigm Shift Problem

Where do today's Corporate Planners stand on this issue of paradigm change? Should they perform the role of traditional paradigm protectors or new paradigm propellors? Clearly, people need to be moved to the new paradigm and, equally clearly, the Corporate Planning function is one which aims to articulate a more appropriate view of reality and to help move people towards an acceptance of it. However, this process of change is a difficult and painful one for the Corporate Planner and those affected alike. Ideally, the Corporate Planner as change agent should stimulate change in a protective way. He or she should seek to enable people to become aware of the differences between their views of reality and that which is demanded by the situation prevailing. A process of reconciliation to facilitate an embracing of the new paradigm is required. A catalogue of models and concepts can be helpful in these tasks. For example, the 'No Longer-Not Yet' model illustrated in Figure 2 can help people to recognise that they are always in a 'zone of transition' - that situations are always shifting and that paradigms might themslves be in a phase of transition.

The 'No Longer-Not Yet' model is useful in helping people to structure their understanding about the relationships between the past, the present and the future, the consequences of passive or active behaviour and to generate a point of reference against which change can be measured.

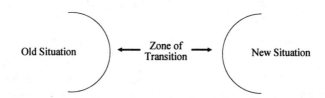

Figure 2
The 'No Longer - Not Yet' Model

In order to explore the proces of paradigm change more deeply, the zone of transition can be developed into the 'transition curve' shown in Figure 3. This model identifies the feelings and behaviours associated with the process of coming to terms with a significant new reality and is one well known to psychologists and those concerned with crisis management.

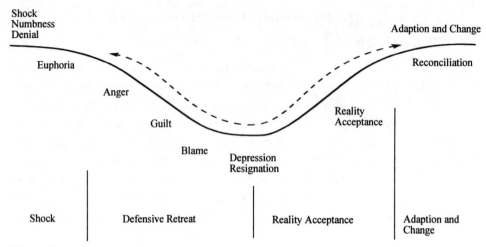

Figure 3
The Transition Curve

By expressing the model in terms of everyday language, in the way indicated in Figure 4, people are able to identify with their own responses to pressure for paradigm change and this can help them come to terms with the need for further personal change. Typically, in responding to a traumatic change such as the death of a loved one, people initially adopt shock and denial responses. Although the new situation confronting Teflon MBC is not of such traumatic proportions, it is one of a fundamental nature and managers exhibit many of the feelings and behaviours shown in Figure 4. The feelings of shock, denial and anger are forerunners of the acceptance of a new managerial reality and moves towards adopting new, more appropriate behaviours. However, this process of realisation and change is a complex one which does not run in the strict sequence suggested by the transition curve model. It involves regression as well as progress. Although regression tends to reduce with the passage of time, it rarely disappears completely.

Behaviour/Feelings	Characteristic Language
Shock, numbness, denial	I don't believe it!
Euphoria	Thank goodness, I know where I stand.
Anger	I hate them
Guilt	Why me? What did I do?
Blame	They're all idiots. Bloody management!
Depression/Resignation	What's the point? Why bother?
Reality acceptance	Well it has happened.
Reconciliation	What shall I do now?
Adaptation and change	Let's get on with it.

Figure 4

It is important to understand that people are often least-well equipped to deal with change when they are first confronted with it. When they are on the left-hand side of the transition curve their feelings are strongly engaged and their thinking is at its least-clear stage. The extent to which individuals or groups come to terms with new situations, and the speed with which they do this, depend upon such things as the extent to which the changes taking place have been pre-planned and the people involved in the planning, the extent to which they have been clearly informed about what is happening or might happen and how deeply they hold the beliefs which the changes challenge.

Helping Managers to Make the Change

At Teflon, when assisting people to 'face up to the new reality,' we pay heed to the ancient Chinese Proverb:

> Tell me and I will forget.
> Show me and I will remember.
> Involve me and I will understand.

We aim to achieve a highly involved style of working for participants in the change programme, both at individual and group levels. Here, the 'No Longer - Not Yet' model referred to earlier can underpin a process which facilitates an 'involved' confrontation of the environment in which managers operate. This involves helping a group of managers through the following steps:

(a) The group is asked to describe to each other how the environment used to be. This enables the group to establish a yardstick against which to measure the change which has taken place both at individual and group levels. It also enables individuals to perceive that members of the group are not all experiencing the same change.

(b) The second step is to identify the changes that have taken place already, the changes taking place in the present and what those changes mean for the group.

(c) The third step involves an assessment of where the current trends are leading and what dominant management styles and characteristics will be required.

(d) The transition curve model is introduced after step two or three, depending on whichever is considered to be the most appropriate point for the group. Its function is to help explain the process in which the group is involved so that this knowledge can be brought to bear on decisions about how to manage the next steps.

(e) The next step is to determine strategies for change. At this point, the group has a shared picture of past, present and future. Hopefully, they have a shared understanding of a new paradigm. They are thus in a position to address the issue of what the changes and the new reality mean for them; which issues and concerns need to be dealt with; what is likely to happen if they do nothing; what needs to be done to move things usefully forward; what might get in the way of progress; and how they will know whether new behaviours are succeeding.

Conclusion

In this paper we have discussed what form the traditional, dominant paradigm at Teflon MBC took, why it needed to be altered and what form it needs to take in the future. The role of the Authority's Corporate Planning function has also been alluded to in its capacity as a facilitator of paradigm shift. Personnel from the function lead participative workshops which are designed to help personnel, working together, to understand how the environment has changed, to confront their own world-views, to share different views of reality as well as a new combined understanding of it and to set in process necessary changes in behaviour.

At Teflon we still use traditional corporate planning tools such as SWOT (strengths, weaknesses, opportunities and threats) analysis, STEP (social, technological, economic and political) analysis and the PDSA (plan, do, study, act) cycle, but these more standard techniques are used in conjunction with change management techniques such as the 'No Longer - Not Yet' model and the transition curve. Cognitively rational and planned approaches to strategic development need to be undertaken in conjunction with approaches designed to address emotions and to change attitudes. Without attitude change based on the acceptance of a new environment-fitting paradigm, planned strategies will be 'wide of the mark' and lacking in commitment to their implementations.

References

Johnson, G. (1988) 'Rethinking Incrementalism', *Strategic Management Journal, 9* (1) pp. 73-91.

Meyers, G. C. with Holusha, J. (1987) *When It Hits the Fan:* Managing the Nine Crises of Business (Unwin Hyman).

MANAGING PROFESSIONALS IN THE NEW LOCAL GOVERNMENT ENVIRONMENT: A POTENTIAL SURVIVAL KIT FOR THE LOCAL AUTHORITY PROFESSIONAL

Roger Hawkins, Sheffield Business School

Introduction

This paper is presented on the basis of the author's experience:

(i) as the organiser/marketer/presenter of a small number of courses designed specifically for local authority managers facing change.

(ii) as a teacher of local authority staff on higher education courses.

(iii) as a local authority manager.

The last was over ten years ago. However, it appears that everything is different yet nothing has changed. Everything is different because of potential or previous changes in the environment due either to the central government prescribed Compulsory Competitive Tendering, to the result of local initiatives to create competition or simply as a natural consequence of organisations developing to meet the perceived needs of their 'customers' - in inverted commas because many of those providing the services are by no means sure precisely who the actual customers are. Hence the currency of the term 'end user'.

Everything is the same because, at least in the minds of many professionals, the Members still hold the key to any attempts to introduce new ideas or major change, a point made by several of those responding to my questionnaire and vocally at the actual courses. The 'all pervasive' nature of Members' influence was the main topic of debate at times when professionals considered their chances of surviving in the new world. The perceived 'fact' that Members 'would not allow officers the freedom of operation' that will, in their view, be necessary to make an effective challenge and 'win the first one, because if you don't you won't be around to try for the second one' (as one DSO manager accustomed to a competitive environment put it) appears to be an adequate reason for some not to get started. It is felt that the threat of competition has not altered the Members' perception of their role and 'privileges'. While in many instances they appear to officers actually to welcome change, Members are said to decline to make concessions in terms of their current power to make all the decisions and request/require officers to provide services that could not be supported in a contract situation unless the cost was agreed within the contract.

Objectives

The objective of this paper is to highlight the issues and difficulties faced by public sector professionals (most of whom are managers), in coming to terms with the need to compete to survive in the new environment. This environment includes, among other changes, compulsory competitive tendering (CTT) and the internally and professionally perceived need to be competitive (demonstrably efficient), and a growing awareness that there is a need for new skills and techniques to be learned to enable this to happen. In writing the paper, I have consciously sought to synthesise three things: information obtained by questionnaire and informal discussion; theory related to the management and marketing of professional services and professional service organisations; and positive, clear options for consideration by professionals who have contributed to this work.

McNulty *et al* (1992), writing about the NHS, make a number of points of considerable relevance to the local government professionals' situation. Their paper relates to a study of the changes that took place in Industrial Research & Development Laboratories following privatisation, particularly looking at the effect of the need to be 'market orientated', and goes on to assess the similarities to the situation that currently prevails in the NHS. It is my view that the situation reviewed is equally relevant to the present situation of many of the professionals in local government, although the nature of political control makes for an even more complicated management environment for those professionals involved in attempting to secure their futures.

McNulty *et al* make a number of interesting points regarding the process undergone by the research professionals in the laboratories. In particular, they outline the way in which the scientists initially resisted any attempt to manage their work along lines that were more immediately marketable. Eventually, forced by the need to secure finance for their research, they reconsidered the position and moved strongly towards the needs of the market. Following this move, and realising the implications of the swing of the pendulum on the 'stock of developable ideas' on which they would have to depend for future saleable products, they adjusted the balance back towards pure research until what was thought to be the correct mix of activities was reached. In other words, too much emphasis on pure research ignored the needs of the market, too little was the equivalent of eating the seed potatoes. I believe that local government professionals will have to undergo a similar process, and that they could, in fact, learn from this experience. They will have to come to a series of decisions about a number of aspects of their work which can utilise some of the classic models and concepts that are taught to final year Business Studies students, MBA's and others.

The local authority professional is also, as part of this process of reorientation, going to have to rethink (dare I say re-engineer?) her/his mindset and administrative/business processes, regarding cultural norms. For example, there are a large number of local authority values that are taken for granted and which are unlikely to be sustainable in a competitive environment. These are related in several aspects to the previous reference to Members and their requirements. Currently, for example, a Member expects, and is expected, to make requests for action, information and so forth and see the request acted upon more or less immediately, depending upon circumstances. This approach is unlikely to fit into a contract situation in which specified types of activity at specified frequencies at specified prices have been agreed to be provided for a specified period. Other factors 'taken for granted' by officers include, for example:

(i)   the recruitment of qualified professionals at a predetermined range of salary levels.

(ii)   availability of administrative support.

(iii) availability of technical, legal, financial and health advice, on demand, at no cost.

(iv)   unlimited access to information at no cost.

(v)   the assumption that 'qualified' staff are required to carry out the full range of services, and that qualification automatically brings the appropriate salary, as on the career grade structures.

(vi)   time consuming decision-making processes.

(vii) the lack of need to constantly monitor expenditure, *in detail*.

I believe that these assumptions all need to be challenged *before* the arithmetic for the calculation of the tender figure that is designed to 'win that vital first one' is attempted. The professional service group that goes out to win the first one, among other things, will need to be:

(viii) flexible, adaptable and innovative.

(ix)   economical in the use of highly-paid staff.

(x)   led by people who become and stay involved.

(xi)   capable of developing new, market-orientated attitudes to the needs of customers.

(xii) cost conscious. A cost accountant, or regular access to accounting services could be 'a must'. Access to and familiarity with, at least the basics of PC and spreadsheet use is essential.

(xiii) multi-skilled, by which I mean that professionals are going to have to be prepared to carry out tasks that they have previously regarded as the province of technicians, clerical, secretarial or administrative staff.

(xiv)utilise structures that are relatively so 'flat' that by current standards they are like pancakes.

(xv) prepared to work in low-cost accommodation.

(xvi)able to get its sums right or it will not be in a position to try for contract number two. Unless these issues are addressed in a positive and serious fashion I do not believe that existing professional departments will be able successfully to defend their positions.

Finally, at this stage, there is the issue of identification of what will make the professional service offered by the new professional service groups unique and desirable to the customer. In terms of marketing, it is the unique selling proposition that we are discussing. I have listened to several officers asking themselves and each other 'what is it that will make us attractive to the council once we lose our current knowledge/experience base?' In some cases it is very difficult to visualise what could be offered that will differentiate the group from the competition. Currently, and for some time past, particularly in the private sector, architects' services for example have been purchased purely on price. Is one architect the same as another architect or a housing manager the same as any other when offering/selling services on the basis of a specification? What makes this or that architect different, and/or what do they offer such to suggest that one should employ them? It should be remembered that the specification, if properly drawn up, will allow little or no flexibility in terms of delivery to the end user, let alone the Member, whose influence may be substantially reduced or even eliminated as a result of the tendering process. It is this very flexibility of service and advice that differentiates the current local authority professional from those in private practice. Of course, the cost of this service in terms of time that is consumed is real enough, but it is not obviously apparent in the form of an invoice.

Sources of Information

The information presented for discussion and debate above was collected from a self-selecting sample of senior local authority managers who attended one of a number of courses that were run in late 1993. The courses were specifically designed and marketed for this group of professionals, two being run in Bolton and one being run in-house for a District Council in Lincolnshire. The group is not, therefore, claimed to be statistically representative in terms of either sample, profession or status, to name but a few of the different cohorts that could legitimately be surveyed. It simply represents the views of a proportion of those who, for whatever reason, decided to attend a course in business planning or marketing for local authority managers. Some 'control' may be assumed by comparison between the 'miscellaneous attenders' who came to Bolton from all over the north of England and Wales for one-day courses and the fifteen managers of the Lincolnshire authority who, in theory at least, brought to their two-day purpose-designed course some common values and a shared environment. The sample was self-selecting because only those who felt so inclined returned the course evaluation questionnaires and/or the local authority professional questionnaire which was handed out at the end of each course. As was expected, not all of the participants returned both questionnaires. Unfortunately, the local authority did not carry out its own course evaluation so I am dependant upon the few forms that were returned to me. The promoter of the Bolton seminars carries out a simple course evaluation, but this does not provide information on anything but the quality of the course delivery, content or accommodation.

Professionals in the New Local Authority Environment?

Professionals represent a major group in local authority departments, as indeed they do in large areas of the public sector such as the NHS. Indeed, some departments are staffed almost exclusively by professionals who operate with a relatively small administrative support staff. Their management is something that has been ignored, at least in terms of their education, until comparatively recently. At the time of local government reorganisation in 1974 there was a brief flurry of activity following the Bains Report which preceded the event itself. Numerous articles appeared in technical journals with titles such as 'The Role of the Valuer-Manager'. Only in recent years have the professional bodies begun to include any form of management training in their syllabi, and some do not do so even now. The best example is my own profession of town planning, others being architecture and, until this year, the certified accountants.

While referring to the management training of professionals it is also relevant to point out on the basis of my own experience and the observations of others, that whereas professionals often talk of a need for management, or complain of a lack of it, they do not generally respond to it. In fact they positively dislike it and are very good at subverting it, usually introducing factors such as professional judgement, professional accountability and professional competence/freedom to justify their need to make their own decisions. What they will and do respond to is leadership, although they see that as management. The leadership style of the head of a professional service organisation is accordingly of paramount importance if he or she is to motivate colleagues and take them in any given direction. Regarding the point about professionals not liking 'being managed', neither do they take easily to management. The reluctance to 'give up the drawing board' as evidenced by the presence of a board in the office of many a city architect or planning officer is physical proof of this. Witness the comment, by a civil engineer, that he is now a general manager, not a professional. In their minds many professionals would find that step a difficult if not impossible one , and will always describe themselves as an architect or a housing manager.

Three Categories of Public Sector Professionals

The professions and individual professionals discussed above can be grouped broadly into three categories, namely exclusively public sector, substantially public sector (usually by choice) and 'mixed' (those who have served in both public and private sectors). I am talking here about those working in local government unless it is specifically mentioned to the contrary.

Many of the 'local authority professions' practise only in either local or central government (including the NHS), or at least this is the case for the vast majority of their members. Town planners are one example, environmental health officers, housing managers and Cipfa members (Institute of Public Finance Accountants) are others. These professionals have never, until recently, had to contemplate any form of competition for their work. They are, therefore, in many ways quite unique.

Some of the local authority professions naturally provide services outside local government, for example architecture, accountancy and engineering, and one would expect that these professionals would be more than equal to the task of organising for a competitive environment. However, many of these individuals have in practice never worked outside the public sector, having made successful careers totally within local or central government. They are, therefore, feeling every bit as vulnerable as their colleagues in the exclusively public sector professions.

The third group is not only accustomed to competition but appears to welcome it, albeit not liking the current rules which place major restrictions on the areas and terms on which they can compete. This group includes architects, builders, civil engineers, personnel managers and surveyors, many of whom have worked in the private sector for a major part of their professional lives and some of whom by training are very entrepreneurial.

The above are the 'organisational professionals'. There is a fourth group comprising those operating in private practice. In the case of architects, surveyors and some others this is where the majority actually do work, but management in such organisations is not the topic of this paper, nor is the issue of defining a profession or a professional. The term professions/professionals used here is as commonly understood by those engaged in local government activities; an architect is a professional, being a local government officer is an occupation.

The problems of managing such people in the new environment - people who on initial consideration may appear to be easy to manage as they are highly trained and well educated - are therefore substantial, particularly when considering the other aspects of professionals, for example the need to exercise judgement, to take independent action and to operate on the basis of predetermined responses to standard situations. These problems are relatively well documented as in the professional configuration (Mintzberg, 1984) and the work of

Raelin (1991) and others. Moreover, the structures within which the local authority professionals work are by their very nature not designed to facilitate the type of entrepreneurial activity which will become necessary for the current groupings to plan and provide services on a competitive basis, let alone survive and prosper. Indeed, the converse is the case since innovation is positively discouraged in many cases. The barriers are numerous, for example:

(i) bureaucratic decision-making systems.

(ii) the current and traditional perceived need for political control.

(iii) the 'mind set' of the career local authority professional.

(iv) lack of knowledge, experience and skill in competing.

(v) lack of systems to facilitate competition such as information on costs. This has been a major problem in the NHS, but should be more manageable for local authority managers as they have far better and more comprehensive accounting and budgetary systems and procedures.

The Sample Population

Attendance was made up of a wide variety of local authority managers. Professions represented included accountants (finance officers), architects, builders, building control officers, committee administrators, civil engineers, environmental health officers, forestry officers, housing managers, landscape architects, personnel managers, research officers, trading services managers, chartered secretaries, social workers, chartered surveyors and town planners.

Their status, and those of the individuals returning questionnaires, ranged from Chief Officers to Principal Officers (middle managers), although due to the wide variety of titles and their use across the country too much emphasis should not be placed upon actual status, with the exception of Chief Officers who are clearly in a unique position.

Reasons for Attending

The reason why most participants attended was to learn about the process of business planning and marketing. Many, particularly the town planners, had been 'handed the task (by the Chief Planner) of preparing the department's business plan, due for completion in six months, and been told to get on with it', as one worried planner put it. Other reasons for attending included:

(i) 'Did a DMS a few years ago and wanted to find out if there is anything new. I did get something that I had not learned before'. *(Chief Trading Services Officer)*

(ii) 'To find out whether there is any value in this for us'. *(Personnel Manager)*

(iii) 'To prepare for CCT and enable the in-house team to compete and win'. *(Lincolnshire authority personnel officer at the commencement of the discussions about the course)*

(iv) 'We realise that we are going to have to sell ourselves as a service, the competition is increasingly from outside the local authority'. *(Social Services)*

The reasons quoted above give some idea of the pressures felt by professionals in local authorities at the present time. As a consequence of the extension of the Local Government Planning and Land Act 1980, housing departments are expected to submit their tenders for management of the local authority stock commencing in 1996, and other professions are likely to be subject to a similar process within the next two to three years. In particular, Corporate Administration and Personnel, Legal Services, Financial Services, Construction Related Services and Information Technology are brought within the scope of CCT by the extension. This follows the introduction of CCT for blue collar services by this Act during the 1980s, and the list of services currently subject to competition is long. Ranging from catering to sports and leisure management, ten separately identifiable activities are regularly the subject of competitive tendering, or will become so once the initial period of the first tenders expires. Observation of the results of this process has raised the awareness of those in the white collar departments who have until now felt safe from the rigours of having to 'obtain work' as compared to 'secure a job'.

The PSO Professionals' Opinions and Comments

The following is a resumé of the issues covered in the questionnaire, and of the responses[1]. The questionnaire was designed to ascertain the views of respondents on some major professional-related issues and the advent of CCT. The questions were designed to discover information and check the consistency of attitudes. For example, questions regarding where respondents thought they would be working in two years time related to those on possible changes to structure, those on training undertaken to those on anticipated training needs, those on career prospects of professionals to the perceived adequacy of their professional training for a competitive environment and those on work/income generation to perceptions about future responsibility for survival of their organisation, responsibility for financial control and understanding of the implications of competition for their service.

Not surprisingly, there were some contradictory and potentially damaging opinions. For example, most of those responding thought that they realised the implications of CCT for

---

1   A full analysis of the responses and a copy of the questionnaire can be obtained from the author on request to Sheffield Business School

their organisation, but that their superiors did not! Given this, there appeared to be an element of over-optimism in that almost all respondents anticipated working for the same authority two years hence. The exceptions were those whose authority is likely to be merged with others. Organisation structures were universally expected to become flatter. Opinions on career prospects were divided; two-thirds felt that there would be opportunities, one-third that things would get worse. The latter thought that elected members would retain power over decision making with the result that staff would not get an adequate opportunity to compete.

The most worrying responses concerned responsibility for obtaining work and survival of the organisation. Several respondents thought that it would be the responsibility of the Chief Officer to ensure that adequate work was obtained, surely a serious misunderstanding of the nature of a competitive environment. For example, an architect, writing many years ago offering advice to those in similar professions, offered this advice to budding town planning consultants: 'The job of the senior partners in a professional practice is two-fold. The first is to get work to keep the staff gainfully occupied, the second is to ensure that you get paid. The latter is usually more difficult than the former'. Perhaps this is one lesson that the fourth group I defined can offer the new entrepreneurial PSO managers. Finally, a message for the professional bodies. Not one of the respondents thought that his professional training had equipped him for a competitive environment.

Overall it can be seen that there is a lack of consensus among those responding regarding the impact of a competitive environment, and that there are some potentially serious misunderstandings about the way in which entrepreneurial PSOs will need to operate.

What Can Be Done to Prepare for the New World?

I have previously referred to the issue of unique selling propositions for Professional Service Organisations. One of the difficulties for professionals is that, in general, the standard of the service offered is taken for granted by the customer. So far as the public is concerned, an architect is an architect, one solicitor is the same as another. Only in the professional world is it realised that some professionals specialise, and that inevitably some are more effective than others. This was graphically illustrated to me in discussion with a business manager for a large hospital when he stated that 'the public take the quality of health care for granted, it is the ease of getting parked that dictates which of our hospitals they prefer to visit'.

Given that level of faith in their abilities, how can professionals identify and/or create a USP that will enable them to differentiate the service that they offer? Van Dierdonck (1992) offers the view that only by relying upon interpersonal skills and personnel related factors can the service organisation differentiate itself from other similar organisations. He goes on to argue, on the basis of his own model, that they need to move along a scale towards three physical and process components, namely physical infrastructure, material components and processes and procedures, in order to prevent the almost immediate imitation of any advantageous differentiation gained. He advances the view that only by developing these 'physical systems' can the service standards be replicated, thereby allowing growth of the service organisation. This probably seems highly academic to the local government professional wondering how to prepare for the struggle to survive in the new world. However, if we look at the basic principles put forward by Van Dierdonck, the development and maintenance of high standards of personnel practice in terms of customer relations is something at which the local authority professional is adept, at least in one specific area. Delivering a professional standard of work while 'keeping the members happy' is a skill that substantial numbers of local government officers have developed and constantly practice. Those that do not do so tend to leave the scene or survive by their outstanding professional abilities and other qualities.

Possibilities using this approach could include:

(i) Ensuring that premises are easily accessible; that customers feel comfortable, welcome and important. Children's toys, free coffee in the reception area and making life easier for the family caller is the kind of approach that could be used.

(ii) Use of appropriate IT or other equipment to give an exemplary service such as three-dimensional representations of buildings, colour copies, personalised stationary, conference or on-line inquiry facilities including use of fax/copier machines, that allow instant response to enquiries by elected members or the public.

(iii) Integrated information and decision making networks that cut out time-consuming processes; clear explanatory leaflets; information gathering sessions, that save customers making their own way through professional's service delivery systems.

A second way to differentiate the professional organisation, as already suggested, is by price. This already happens, despite the theoretical existence of recommended fee scales. Normally price would relate to quality, and the usual model of 'High Price, High Quality: Low Price, Low Quality' could be applied. As we have already defined the professional standards as a 'taken for granted', this leaves us with a problem. No professional service organisation will wish, or possibly be able due to their professional body's Code of Professional Conduct, to offer less than a full professional standard of service. To use a phrase often utilised in promoting services, a 'Professional Standard' is seen as 'the best'. The issue of positioning a PSO in the market place is accordingly not an easy one to resolve. The use of systems to create time/money saving potential for the organisation and customers is important.

One answer to the problem of positioning might be to relate price to the standards offered in terms of personal care, speed and range of options in terms of supplements. These might include the use of premises, technical facilities and negotiating skills. The range would clearly vary according to the actual professional service offered.

This brings us to another option for differentiation, namely related professional skills. Most PSO's operate in one service or professional area of expertise. Only large private practices offer, for example in the contracting industry, a full range of services such as architecture, planning, quantity surveying, building surveying and civil, mechanical, electrical and structural engineering. In the normal course of events one of the professions acts as the coordinator of the others, in this case normally the architect. However, this is not always the case, and in the case of house purchase for example, an activity which most of us have undertaken, the individual purchaser is left to grapple with the coordination of all the various activities which need to be carried out. As many of us are given to comment after a move, 'It is amazing how many people that we employ to carry out a service for us who do not see the need to talk to each other, but prefer to leave it to us!'

You have only to try to use the homemaker service of one of the national building societies to realise just how much really needs to be done to offer the type of totally integrated service that the local authority member takes absolutely for granted. What I am suggesting is that the ability to offer a networked service could give groups of apparently unrelated PSOs a competitive advantage, and position them as 'standard price/extra service' organisations. There is an obvious comparison here with the role of project leader, or the activity of project management. Indeed, major building contractors perform, for a price, such a role in coordinating multi-million pound schemes such as Broadgate, London. The potential for local-authority-orientated PSOs to work together to offer 'a fully coordinated and integrated service' to local authorities seems to me to be a way of building upon the existing linkages that they already have, in themselves a USP.

We have here a number of bases for planned action by local authority professionals which would enable them to identify and utilise their existing distinctive skills (core competencies) and knowledge to build a distinctive offering. There will be complications, and no doubt the limitations of the legislation will require careful thought in order to avoid accusations of prejudice in allocating work. However, if the individual local authorities can decide in clear terms what they require from their future contractors, for that is what the PSOs will become, and specify accordingly, there seems to me to be no reason why they cannot both protect their service standards *and* enable their staff to have an opportunity to continue to provide them at an appropriate cost and quality.

In relation to the issue of positioning therefore, *the potential exists to position either an individual PSO operating as one of a group, (depending on the particular service and tender), or a group of linked and potentially fully integrated PSOs (for the benefit of*

111

particular customers) as offering the highest standards of *specific and related services at competitive cost.* This, I believe, would be extremely difficult for competitors to emulate, at least at the time when the current home team is fighting to 'win that vital first one'. Subsequent development of advantage through more efficient and effective linkages is beyond the scope of this paper, although I am certain that it exists. Application of many of the 'usual academic or private sector techniques' is eminently possible in the present local authority framework and will be even more so in the new world of competition.

Conclusion

Briefly, the problems of the local government manager as she/he enters 1994 and, over the next two years, the new world of a competitive environment, can be summarised as follows:

(i) the need to keep existing services operating to the required standards while planning for a different professional and operating environment.

(ii) the need to evaluate the new environment and assess how to approach it.

(iii) the need to learn new skills and techniques for that new environment, and practice their application.

(iv) the need to realise the need for, and to identify, those skills.

(v) the need to decide upon, and as necessary lobby for the freedom to use, new and existing skills to build new organisations. These should retain the best of the old yet develop new flexible, innovative attitudes to help secure survival, and if desired, growth.

(vi) the need to find the time to implement (v) above.

(vii) the need to learn to manage change, developing staff and the organisation to enable it to relate to a rapidly changing and developing environment.

The following approaches are put forward for consideration and development:

(i) First, but by no means most obviously, each embryo professional service organisation should carry out an audit of skills already available within its orbit, placing an emphasis upon seeking to identify those which it takes for granted, but which are not, or are unlikely to be possessed by new entrants to the field at the time of that vital 'first one'. These are the initial source of competitive advantage which, assuming success, will need to be sustained and developed. The results of this audit will form a part of the matters which follow.

(ii) Assuming the standard of service offered by professionals and professional service organisations is a 'taken for granted', unique selling propositions could be developed on the basis of *standards of personal service and customer care offered.* In practice, the application would vary between professions but, put simply, could range from a basic service to the full service (all our facilities are at your disposal, call us day or night for home based service and advice). This latter is not as odd as it may seem. For example, elected members are accustomed to telephoning their officers and arranging meetings outside normal office hours.

A third option would be differentiation by price alone. This is the option that many potential PSOs will feel compelled to adopt, particularly if little or no planning is undertaken. Here again, however, the actual level of service offered will need to be carefully understood by both parties, and the link to levels of personal service may be unavoidable. The necessity for clear definition of service levels will be crucial, as there is potential for considerable misunderstanding between parties, particularly at the early stages, as there is the risk that both sides will make a number of assumptions based upon the previous 'taken for granted' levels of service. The quality of specification will be important here, and the existing providers are in a position to influence the process and ensure that the requirements are adequately identified and set out.

A related activity that could be undertaken in parallel or sequentially with the above, and integrated into the option which follows, is for each individual service to consider the physical and process components of the service that is offered. The aim would be to identify all the individual elements, placing particular emphasis upon those which a competitor would find difficult, expensive or impossible to replicate. This could, for example, involve unique linkages between professionals and/or PSOs. It would also be appropriate to seek to identify new elements. By involving staff in the exercise, the aim would be to commence the introduction of new, competitive thinking into the culture and to strengthen the armoury of unique aspects of the service that would be offered. In the case of networked service groups there would be numerous opportunities for links that competitors would find difficult to copy. These linkages, which could be related to the value system of the potential customer(s) as discussed by Michael Porter (1985), would be the basis of a strong competitive position.

The development of networked or 'multi-professional group' service organisations able to offer fully integrated services, if taken to the limit, could virtually remove the need for the local authority to operate its own coordination function. This could result in a 'minimal' local authority, which might appeal to some, but that is not the intention behind the concept. The intention is to provide a basis to enable small groups of professionals to develop value-added services, and by so doing to be competitive with the larger practices which might be interested in obtaining local authority contracts. There is an apparent opportunity for small groups of professionals to gain strength in this way, in particular if they use the techniques outlined above.

The use of the vital aspect of local knowledge should be part of the audit discussed above, but is so much a 'taken for granted' that it is likely to be overlooked. Housing Associations and large local authorities (small ones already knew) discovered the value of local knowledge a long time ago. The ability to talk to local members about a problem involving their wards, and understanding the full significance of how they see the issues, is something that an incoming organisation would find extremely difficult to copy. Its only practical strategy would be to 'win the first one' in order to recruit the necessary expertise. This is not necessarily going to be available, depending upon opportunities elsewhere and the age profile of local staff. This is an asset that many serving professionals will not identify as saleable.

I am conscious that the ideas and suggestions set down here are not progressed much beyond the formative stage, although they may appear more developed to those in practice who presently have all their time cut out to continue the provision of services to their members and customers. Accordingly, it is my intention to continue to develop them, together with any new ones that emerge.

References

McNulty T., Whipp R., Whittington, R. & Kitchener, M. (1992) *Managing Change in Professional Service Contexts*, presented at the Employment Research Unit 1992 Conference 'The Challenge of Change: The Theory and Practice of Organisational Transformation', Cardiff Business School, University of Cardiff.

Mintzberg, H. (1984) *The Structuring of Organisations* (Englewood Cliffs NJ: Prentice-Hall International).

Porter, M.E. (1985) *Competitive Advantage: Creating and Sustaining Superior Performance* (New York: Free Press).

Raelin, J.A. (1991) *The Clash of Cultures; Managers Managing Professionals* (Boston: The Harvard Business School Press).

Van Dierdonck, R. (1992) 'Success Strategies in a Service Economy', *European Management Journal, 10 (3)* pp. 365-73.

ATTEMPTING TO IMPLEMENT CHANGE THROUGH NEW TECHNOLOGY: AN ANALYSIS WITHIN THE LOCAL GOVERNMENT CONTEXT

Eamonn Sweeney, School of Accountancy, Law and Management, University of Huddersfield,

Introduction

The paper is based on a study of three local authority organisations in the North of England. The aims of the research, were:

(1) To identify the nature and extent of perceived environmental changes within the local government business environment.

(2) To identify the importance of information technology within the context of these changes.

(3) To present findings of a survey of management and non-management perception of change specifically in relation to the role, purpose and validity of information technology.

(4) To identify a number of key factors which may facilitate the use of information technology as a vehicle for organisational change.

Method

Between 1988 and 1991 an attitudinal survey was conducted among staff in four local authorities of different sizes. 240 questionnaires were distributed and 187 were returned, a response rate of 78%. Of the returned questionnaires 85 were from managers and 102 from non-managers. Although salary scale and the number of staff supervised were identified as being important variables in relation to the definition of management/non-management, an earlier study (1) helped to identify the acceptable working definition of management as being "someone who has supervisory line management responsibility for staff, and who is accountable for their actions". Information was also categorised along the dimensions of functional occupation, length of service, academic qualifications, gender, ethnicity and disability, although these findings are not referred to within this paper.

The questionnaire addressed fifty aspects of perception of actual and proposed organisational change, with the major section addressing the issue of the use of information technology within the local government context. Given the potentially volatile nature of the inquiry respondents were guaranteed anonymity. A number of follow-up qualitative interviews were conducted between 1991 and 1992 with managers and non-managers in order to clarify further and explore the concept of 'usefulness of information technology' within the local government setting. These results are incorporated within this paper.

The Changing Local Government Business Environment

The significance of local government as an employer cannot be overemphasised. Apart from having responsibility for the provision and monitoring of a diverse range of key services to the population of England and Wales, including for example housing, education and social services, local government also employs approximately two million people and is accountable for the management of nearly 12 per cent of the gross national product. However, the many decades of management stagnation and "creeping centralisation" (2) came to an abrupt end in the early 1980's with a number of major reviews of the service provision offered by local authorities, and indeed many other public sector organisations. The traditional image of local authority service provision was declared defunct by the Audit Commission (3) and an era of major change was introduced. Regardless of ones political views and the perceived merits or otherwise of existing and proposed changes, there can be little argument about the extent to which local government has been, and will continue to be affected (4).

The nature and extent of change in Britain's local authorities over the past 14 years has been both dramatic and extensive, making synthesis difficult. The market serviced by local authorities is becoming more complex. Economic, technological, social and environmental changes have been unprecedented (5). The local-central government relationship has altered significantly, and a wide array of legislative changes have redrawn the boundaries of local government financing, service responsibilities and customer expectations (6,7). Local government had to survive within a business environment driven by a central government crusade whose underpinning 'market driven' political ideology has incorporated principles of efficiency in service delivery, effectiveness in the impact of the service upon the end user, economic value for money and a changing emphasis on the proactive role management should play in relation to these changes.

Local authorities have had to confront reductions in central government grants, continued and often increased demand for services, increasing costs and new powers in relation to crime prevention, environmental care and community care. Each of these areas has been complicated by the political flux of both national and local politics, and by the additional controls introduced by the Citizen's Charter. Customer empowerment, the single market, the debate over whether local authorities should assume an 'enabling role' rather than direct service provision and the recent directive from central government that local authorities must expose a wider range of their services to market forces (8), serve to highlight further the major imposed changes confronting local government.

Until the late 1980s, the response of many local authorities to these changes was one of attempting to increase revenue incrementally whilst simultaneously imposing a variety of expenditure cutting measures (9, 10). In so doing, they failed to question the fundamental inadequacies of the structural features of the existing service delivery pattern, attempting instead to deliver 'historic' service packages within the imposed constraint of reduced resources. In the 1990s, local authorities are now having to address a number of essential questions concerning their future roles, particularly when one considers the unequivocal constraint of capped budgets and the declining proportion of expenditure over which a local authority has discretionary control. They are having to address issues relating to management skill, strategic management, management development, the appropriateness of existing organisational culture and the importance of the human resources and information technology to the success or otherwise of the change process.

The changes indicated above should not, however, be viewed only as a threat to local government, for just as the Chinese understand the word 'crisis' to mean dangerous opportunity, a number of exciting opportunities are also opening up for local government. Customer empowerment, demands for increased service quality, delegation, increased accountability, and competition in the form of compulsory competitive tendering need not be regarded as constraining measures. Rather, they should be seen as opportunities for promoting economic development, of identifying and refining the services which the organisation is efficient, effective and economic at providing, and competing as an equal with certain commercial enterprises. New markets are opening up domestically and within Europe, and offer many opportunities for the proactive organisation. The historic conflict between political ideology and professional values need not escalate. The local government business environment has altered and will continue to do so. A powerful axiom is that local government must become and remain proactive in the way in which it perceives and reacts to the future (11).

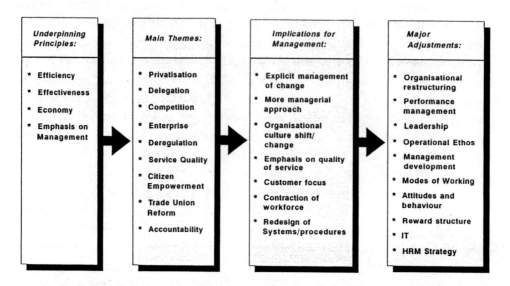

Underpinning Principles:	Main Themes:	Implications for Management:	Major Adjustments:
* Efficiency * Effectiveness * Economy * Emphasis on Management	* Privatisation * Delegation * Competition * Enterprise * Deregulation * Service Quality * Citizen Empowerment * Trade Union Reform * Accountability	* Explicit management of change * More managerial approach * Organisational culture shift/change * Emphasis on quality of service * Customer focus * Contraction of workforce * Redesign of Systems/procedures	* Organisational restructuring * Performance management * Leadership * Operational Ethos * Management development * Modes of Working * Attitudes and behaviour * Reward structure * IT * HRM Strategy

Figure 1
The Changing Face of Local Government: 1979-93

Perceived Environmental Changes

Having identified the actual changes impacting upon local government and the implications for the future of the service, it is appropriate to examine briefly the environmental changes as perceived by the respondents in the study. Pertinent results from the qualitative element of the analysis are illustrated in Table 1, and are intended to be an indicative illustration of a number of the key areas of perceived environmental change in local government as it was in the 1970/80s (perceived old system) and in the 1990s (perceived new system). No attempt has been made to differentiate the views of management and non-management, and only the views of those respondents who had experience of the two systems of local government were included. One can see clearly that the management of change is perceived as a critical operational component, and that the changes impacting upon local government are seen to encompass a diverse range of dimensions over which the organisation has different degrees of discretion and control.

Aspect	Percieved Old System	Percieved New System
Change Catalyst	Internal/External	Primarily external
Nature of Change	Incremental/Reactive	Incremental/Radical/Reactive/Proactive
Business Objectives	Social/Non-profit-making	Social/Business/Profit-making
Organisational Tasks	Functional Service delivery	Business development/Functional service delivery
Financial Base	Secure/Marginal	Insecure/Reduction in real terms growth
Structure	Centralised and bureaucratic	Decentralised/Less bureaucratic
Role of Management	Organisational perpetuation	Strategic change/survival
Role of Customer	Recipient of service/s	Empowered, increasingly assertive
Decision Making	Rules and regulations	Greater personal initiative
Responsibility	Senior/Middle management	Increasingly delegated downwards
Accountability	Senior/Middle management	Increasingly delegated downwards
Power	Seniority/time/experience/nepotism	Experience/Qualification/Nepotism/Information/Change/control
Managerial Promotion	Internal	External recruitment at senior levels
Union Power	Strong/Diminishing	Weakening

Table 1
Perceived Environmental Changes between 1979 and 1993

Information Technology and Change

Ohmae (12) believes that the main beneficiary, if not the driving force for the introduction of information technology, is the customer, and that the key trend in any business environment is the increasing power of the customer. This means that the key objective for organisations is to create added value for customers. He understands the term strategy to mean "*the creating and sustaining of value for the customer better than any competitor*". This is especially pertinent given the changing nature of the local government business environment. However, the increasing importance of companies staying close to their customers has also been recognised by a number of other writers, for example, Peters and Waterman (13) found that one of the basic principles of their "*excellent*" companies was staying close to the customer combined with what they referred to as "*sticking to the knitting*" to ensure that they had a keen sense of the market.

119

The business environment is, however, much more complicated that this simple observation would suggest, and when identifying the significance of IT in relation to change, one should be conscious of the complicated social relationships which exist within every organisation. IT is inextricably linked to each of these key elements.

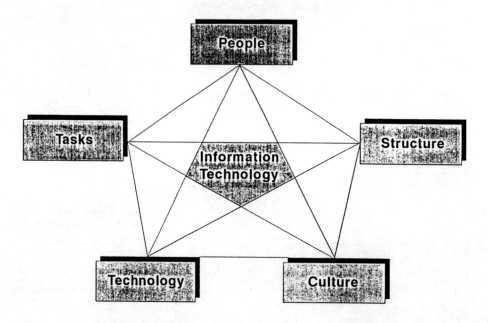

Figure 2
The Organisation as a Social System

If the business environment as a whole is changing rapidly then Information Technology (IT) is changing even faster and is assuming an ever-increasing importance in determining the way business is conducted. The key trends according to Yates et al (14) are:
- The compression of time and space
- The expansion and transformation of stored knowledge, and
- The increasing flexibility of IT applications.

These changes are helping to create knowledge rather than data and increasing the power of the technology available.

It is argued that IT is being used to facilitate new ways of working as organisations change to more flexible forms, such as networks which embrace customers, suppliers and partners (15). Brown et al (16) believe that knowledge-based corporations employing knowledge workers will create *"a human/technology partnership"* which will be at the core of every organisation's future success and survival. As a result, it is suggested that IT has

120

a unique characteristic which means that it has the power to alter an industry's competitiveness and the nature of inter-firm rivalry within an industry (17). This vision of IT presents a picture of, in effect, a new industrial revolution using IT as the key enabler for creating a knowledge-based society which appears to fit the contention of both Handy (18) and Drucker (19), namely, that we are entering an age of discontinuity.

Reality, however, appears to be very different. The evidence available suggests that, with a few well known exceptions IT has failed to live up to its promise. Coulson-Thomas (15) quotes an OECD report which concluded that the returns on investment from IT were, and still are, problematic. It is also suggested that the service sector has been automated but productivity (20) has fallen because workers have been added faster than productivity has increased. It appears that many organisations have made the wrong choice when investing in IT in that they have chosen to automate their existing process rather than to use IT to look at their formal and informal processes, the tasks required and the activities performed afresh. Zuboff (21) also makes it clear that technology is not neutral in its effect on an organisation and that it is important to use it in a way that adds value to what the organisation does. This illustrates the need to take a holistic view of the organisation, its values and structure and if necessary change them to get 'value' from IT by exploiting opportunities and increasing productivity. This implies that the promise offered by IT both now and in the past, albeit sometimes exaggerated, has not been completely false and that the failure has been at the strategic level in both strategy formulation and implementation.

Traditionally, Information Systems and IT have tended to be regarded as support activities concerned with the efficient utilisation of their resources to provide the level of information support required by management to carry out their chosen strategy. Writers such as Earl (22) have taken the generally accepted differentiation between the various levels of strategy which are; corporate, business (SBU) and functional and have suggested that the various elements of management strategies for IT should be aligned accordingly in support. Venkatraman (23) suggests that the traditional support role for IT needs to be changed to reflect the more central strategic role IT can now play. He argues that there is now a body of literature which gives examples of organisations which have used IT in a central strategic role to gain a competitive advantage, albeit sometimes short-lived. As a result, he believes that IT can play a critical rather than a supporting role in both strategy formulation and implementation at all levels of strategy. Such an approach gives IT a much more dynamic role and will perhaps enable it in the future to live up to its promise.

The Implications of IT for Organisations

It is argued that organisational competitive advantage can be created and maintained through the appropriate use of IT (24). Indeed, in a recent survey by Kearney (25) it was shown that the primary reason given by many local government departments for increasing IT investment was to give the organisation greater competitive advantage. Hence, one of the most important questions for senior management to ask is not "should we be using IT?", but rather, "can we use it to reduce costs?; change the power balance with customers and/or suppliers?; make it unattractive for customers to shift to other suppliers?; create barriers against competitors?; improve the quality of service to customers?; or improve or differentiate services?" McFarlan (26) suggests that when assessing the ultimate impact of information system technology in relation to competitive advantage, an organisation must ask five fundamental questions:

(i)   Can information system technology build barriers to entry?
(ii) Can information system technology build in switching costs?
(iii) Can the technology change the basis of competition?
(iv) Can information system technology change the balance of power in supplier relationships?
(v)   Can information system technology generate new products or services?

He argues that if an organisation can answer yes to one or more of these questions, then information technology represents a strategic resource that requires the immediate attention of senior management. As such, it is inappropriate for managers to detach themselves from the decision-making in relation to IT investment (27).

Drucker (19) states that rapid, knowledge-based change will require organisations to build the organised abandonment of everything and the creation of the new into their very structures. To do this they need to build the management of change into the organisation which will in turn change what is required from the workforce, altering the power and authority relationships within organisations. Workers will be empowered participants working in teams taking an innovative approach to their work thereby allowing them to act as intrapreneurs. Handy also believes that the boundaries of jobs will become permeable, with no clear job descriptions as workers become more flexible.

One solution could be to create a learning organisation which according to Amited (28) is a "coherent approach to maximising human potential in the service of organisational effectiveness". It is the capacity of people to learn individually, and therefore organisationally, which can provide companies with a huge asset. It appears to be possible to create such an organisation, as Leonard-Barton's (29) research shows.

The Implications of IT for Managers

Kanter (30) suggests that, as part of their need to increase their responsiveness, the power and authority structure within organisations will change because she suggests knowledge workers should not be controlled or supervised in the traditional way. The reason for this is that creativity and innovation do not derive from order. This will particularly affect the role of first line managers and supervisors. She suggests that managers and professionals will work in a world of vague assignments, overlapping territories and uncertain authority, resources and mandates. They will work through teams rather than unilaterally. This links in with Handy who says that people will be project heads and co-ordinators rather than traditional managers. The term 'manager' will no longer be a definition of status but a skill which can be taught. He mentions three broad areas where new skills are required; analysing, human and conceptual.

The question arises, however, of how different the skills required by managers are from the ones they need now. Surely 'managers' already have, or should have, the skills mentioned by Handy and already work in the confused environment suggested by Kanter to a greater or lesser extent depending on the organisation. It appears that it is the 'how' of managing, and, the emphasis on which skills will be the most important which has changed. Coulson-Thomas suggests that, among others, leadership, facilitating, counselling, mentoring, trust, responsiveness, learning and listening will be important attributes of managers.

It is interesting to note that Kanter steps back from the complete demise of traditional management in that she makes it clear that the delegation of power and authority, as part of the empowerment process, means the delegation of responsibility not abdication. The parameters are set and controlled by management in accordance with organisational goals. She also accepts that in some circumstances unilateral action is best. Leadership is seen as an increasingly important part of a manager's task, although Kanter, among others, believes that it can come from anywhere and anyone within the organisation. Harvey-Jones (31) regards leadership and vision as a crucial role of the Chief Executive and Handy also links leadership to vision, believing it is important anywhere that networks or alliances are important.

Unfortunately, it is not possible to come to any firm conclusions concerning what will happen to the role of managers, or their career prospects. Dopson et al (32) concluded that there was an urgent need for more research in this area. They found that they could only make broad generalisations because the pattern of what was happening to managers varied so much and depended on the organisational context. They did, however, state that, overall, middle management were undertaking more general jobs with greater responsibilities; were performing a wider range of tasks with increasing spans of control; were responsible for a wider mix of staff and were being held more accountable for their work, in part because IT made their performance more visible.

The Implications of IT for Local Government

At a time of increasing competition within the local government business environment, information technology and information system management must add value to the process of management. Otherwise is little point in making a major capital investment. Information technology and the dynamic business environment should combine to create dynamic change catalysts (33)

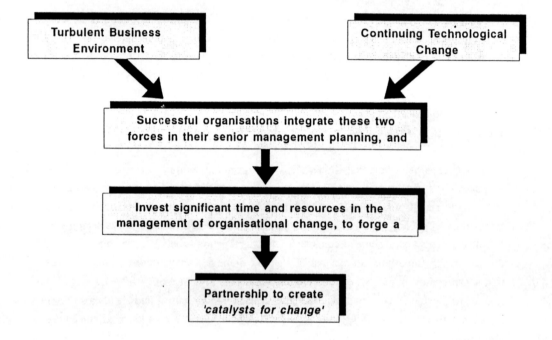

Figure 3
Creating a Technological Partnership

Clearly, the importance of IT within the local government context is recognised. Spending on IT by local authorities exceeded £1 billion in 1991/1992 (34). However, the scale of investment is small compared to the impact of IT upon the local government business environment, the changing nature of which dictates that the creation, management and distribution of information will increasingly depend upon IT to meet departmental and corporate information requirements. It is interesting to note that the value of IT is not frequently expressed on the annual balance sheet (35), although there are examples of IT systems failure causing havoc in relation to service delivery (36). It is also noted that resource constraints due to public expenditure cuts will further limit investment in IT. However, a desire to share funds equitably may dilute the investment required.

A major dissimilarity has been identified between the efficiency and effectiveness of the IT adoption processes used by the private sector and the public sector. It is suggested that, unlike the private sector, public sector organisations (37):

(i) have an inclination to move into unproven technologies.

(ii) have decision-making which is non-interactive, i.e. there is no customer feedback.

(iii) have no bottom line decision-making, i.e. new resources can be used to conceal mistakes.

(iv) have separate policy-making and administration.

(v) must be responsive to political masters.

(vi) have a short time scale.

(vii) tend to prefer large-scale projects.

A number of additional pertinent observations can be made. The very nature of many of the services provided by local government, for example social services to the vulnerable members of the community, dictates that risks cannot be taken with the introduction of new technology. This is particularly important when one considers that it is not uncommon for the introduction of new technology within an organisation to be fraught with problems (38). One is conscious of the capacity of machines and humans to contribute to a systems failure. Local government experience and history of IT usage is not necessarily a pleasant one (39), and one must therefore question organisational readiness for change.

The strategic maturity of the organisation is also in question (40), which is particularly important when one considers that it is necessary to take a more strategic approach to the study of information technology, rather than viewing it narrowly and as a cost-cutting tool (41). Information overload is also a characteristic of local government administration (42,43). *"All human beings know more than they can say"* (44), therefore codification of that knowledge leads to a considerable wastage of information, often of a valuable nature. The combination of information systems and information technology often creates management problems, in that it may become increasingly difficult for managers to identify and prioritise appropriate data. In the words of Tarrant (45), *"the machine spews out endless scrolls of information that the manager does not need and cannot use. He would be best advised to throw it away. But that is not in human nature."* IT will create more information and make the job of managing more challenging. However, success requires total commitment from senior management in that *"even the favourable combination of leadership and computing resources will fail unless a distinction can be made between key management information and the burden of routine information collection"* (46)

Change and Organizational Culture

The critical stages of the change process are easily delineated and are illustrated in Figure 4. However, successful management of the introduction of information technology change requires the manager to move beyond this simplistic analysis. It is essential to understand the impact its exploitation can have upon the ultimate efficiency and effectiveness of the overall process. The author contends that the personnel employed by an organisation are the key strategic resource which will ultimately determine the success or failure at each stage of the change process, particularly in relation to IT related changes.

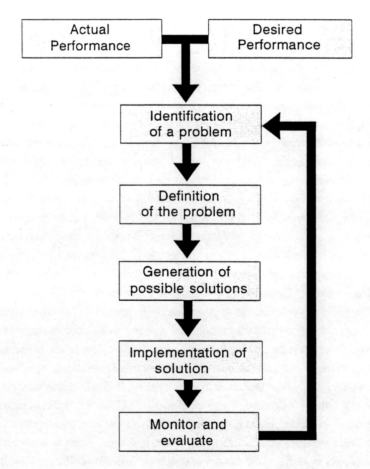

Figure 4
Critical Stages in the Change Process

Consequently, it is argued that it is not the environmental forces, organisational capabilities or information technology alone that identify, create and implement competitive change, rather it is the people within the organisation who use these resources who are responsible for the creation of competitive advantage. This is a particularly important observation when one considers the dominant influence organisational culture can have upon the behaviour and attitudes of employees within the organisation. A number of researchers suggest that management is essentially a cultural process (47), and that it is the culture and values of an organisation that are crucial for matching the organisation's resources to its environment, and ultimately for determining its level of commercial success. Of course, using the metaphor of culture to understand organisations has its limitations as well as strengths (48), but the author contends that it can provide invaluable insights into the management of change. Indeed, recent work by Kotter and Heskett (49) concludes that only cultures that can help organisations to adapt to environmental change, by paying attention to the needs of stockholders, customers and employees, are likely to be associated with superior financial performance in the long term. Indeed, Flannery and Williams (50) argued within the health care context that it is possible to create healthy management cultures in turbulent environments, a view which receives support from a number of other sources (51).

One of the most pertinent definitions of organisational culture is that of Schein (52), who defines culture as "the deeper level of basic assumptions and beliefs that are shared by members of the organisation, that operate unconsciously, and that define in a 'taken for granted' fashion and organisation's view of itself and its environment." In relation to the change process, organisational culture is therefore reflected in the way in which people set personal and professional objectives, perform tasks and administer resources to achieve them. Culture effects the way in which people consciously and subconsciously think, make decisions and ultimately the way in which they perceive, feel and act towards opportunities and threats presented by the introduction of IT.

Accepting the critical role played by people in all organisations, Johnson and Scholes (10) put forward the concept of a 'cultural recipe', in which culture is seen as a composite of a number of variables, including the type of leadership, prevailing stories and myths, accepted rituals and symbols, the type of power structure, the form of organisational structure, the decision-making process, functional policies and information systems. They argue that the strength and intensity of each of these cultural variables may vary from person to person, and from group to group within an organisation, but that the dominant organisational culture will prevail as a common theme. They also argue that the behaviour of an individual or group at each of the critical stages of the change process serves to preserve and legitimise the existing culture of the organisation, and that when people make decisions they are constrained by the cultural ethos.

The author stresses the importance of this observation. Each stage in the overall change process is a critical component. Influenced by the dominant organisational culture, an individual or group responsible for the monitoring of the environment may or may not even identify the existence of a problem. Assuming a problem is identified, their definition of that obstacle may or may not be in tune with commercial reality. The generation, and selection of potential solutions might also be constrained or enhanced by the nature of the organisational culture, and the eventual implementation of the desired 'solution' will ultimately be dependent upon the cooperation of people at different levels within the organisation for its success.

The impact of organisational culture upon management and non-management will clearly affect their perception of what is happening in the internal and external environments, and their ultimate reaction. How they perceive and respond to internal and external IT-related change, whether it is voluntary or imposed, will as a consequence be determined by the prevailing cultural recipe to which they conform. In order to achieve successful management of the change process, it is important to gain an insight into the different perceptions which particular groups within an organisation have of the culture of the organisation.

Incremental change is more easily assimilated into the prevailing culture. However, the radical change demanded of many organisations in the 1990s may result in a conflict of personal and professional interests and hence active resistance to the proposed change. By differentiating between the perception different groups have of the organisational culture, it may be possible to facilitate the change process. Analysing the potential causes of resistance to change is a valid part of the change process in that, if one can identify the key elements of opposition to the planned change, one can start to establish a framework for overcoming the resistance.

An earlier study within the public sector (53) identified that management and non-management had significantly different perceptions of the same change process, depending primarily upon their position in the organisational hierarchy. Whilst conforming to the overall culture of the organisation, the different groups were simultaneously influenced by different subcultures or cultural recipes, and their response to the change was significantly different, varying between commitment to the proposed change to sabotage of attempts to introduce the proposed change. This general picture of substantial differences in perceptions between managerial and non-managerial employees in the public sector is reinforced when the results of a more detailed survey of managers (n=85) and non-managers (n=102) in several local authorities are considered. The main areas of agreement between managers and non-managers are identified in Table 2, below.

128

| (1) IT will make all employees personally more responsible and accountable for their work |
| (2) IT will result in the process and content of work becoming more challenging to the individual |
| (3) The quantity of work will increase |
| (4) IT will induce greater levels of personal work stress |
| (5) Feelings of personal insecurity will increase |
| (6) Additional training will be a prerequisite to coping with the new technology |
| (7) The potential of unemployment will increase |
| (8) Historic IT related changes create an atmosphere of mistrust of senior management |

Table 2

Agreement Between Managers and Non-managers on the Impact of IT

As can be seen from Table 3, there are many significantly different perceptions of the likely impact of the changes between the two categories of employees. Different assessments of the outcomes of proposed changes are not unusual and have to be taken into account in the management of most change programmes. Improved communication and appropriate programmes of training and support can often help in this respect. However, the findings suggest that the situation in the local authority needs a more fundamental re-assessment when one takes into account perceptions of the current process of managing the introduction of new technology.

Aspect of Change	Perception of Impact
Agreement with change	Agreement is high among managers
Autonomy	Management believe they have more job related freedom
Benefits	Management see tangible and non-tangible benefits Non-management see no personal benefits
Customer Relations	Management perceive a positive reaction to IT induced changes Non-management see IT failing to empower the customer
Decision-making	Management see IT creating an improvement in this area Non-management only perceive senior management benefiting
Dehumanising Impact	Non-management see IT change as being impersonal
Involvement in Change	Management perceive a high level of involvement Non-management perceive a high level of personal isolation
Productivity	Management percieve an improvement in this area Non-management see no real change in this area
Quality	Management perceive an increase in the quality of service Non-management perceive a degradation of the service

Table 3

Differences in Perception of the Impact of IT By Managers and Non-Managers

The literature on the management of change makes it clear that there are no simple prescriptions in this area, but a few basic factors associated with successful change usually emerge (54). These typically include trust, shared vision, effective leadership, ownership and so on (55). Unfortunately, none of these are perceived to be present by both managerial and non-managerial employees in the study. In particular, the findings indicate that many employees, regardless of their level, have little or no trust for their peers, immediate manager and the senior management team. This climate will almost certainly undermine any attempts to 'manage' IT change unless it is addressed as a matter of urgency. It is aggravated by the fact that neither managers nor other employees have faith in the ability of senior management to ensure that the right changes take place at the right time. The lack of trust is not the only stumbling block in the way of the change process. Although most managers perceive that there is open communication, respect for the views of others, participation and shared vision, very few non-managerial employees share these views.

Worker Perception and Co-operation with IT Change

It is apparent that both management and non-management are the primary resource in relation to each of the critical stages of the IT change process whether they are involved in problem identification, option analysis or at the point of change implementation. Given that workers conform to specific organisational cultures and, by definition, organisation sub-cultures, individual and sub-culture perception of the benefits of change is a critical element in relation to worker co-operation in the overall change process. A perception of gain is likely to result in a high level of co-operation, whereas a perception of loss may result a low level of co-operation, or indeed, in negative co-operation.

From the qualitative interviews with respondents, a range of individual worker and group responses which were predominantly determined by individual worker perception of personal and group benefits to be derived from successful implementation of the IT related change was identified. Using the above framework, an analysis was undertaken in relation to:

(1) The perceived *personal* benefits of change, and the corresponding level of worker co-operation.

(2) The perceived *group* (sub-culture) benefits of change, and the corresponding level of group co-operation.

Given the focus of this paper, the author addressed the specific issue of the level of management and non-management co-operation with the change process depending on their perception of the benefits to be derived, six useful reactions to the proposed change were identified, each of which assumed an active analysis and response on the part of the individual concerned. Using these reaction categories, the perception and anticipated level of co-operation with the change process by each group from the two population samples was modelled, and the tentative position of management and non-management from each of the population samples was superimposed on this illustration. Given the qualitative nature of this particular data, the author felt that it was inappropriate to validate statistically and position the size and shape of each group. The model is therefore indicative. One should note, however, that in a follow-up pilot study of managers (n=12) and non-managers (n=15) between 1991 and 1992, there was consensus regarding the group position using the above model framework.

Even with the above limitations, the model does provide a useful overview of the fundamental differences between management [1] and non-management [2] within local government, and certainly indicates the need for the senior managers within the organisation to ensure that resources are invested in altering the 'perception of personal benefits' this group has towards the proposed IT-related change if the proposed change is to be implemented successfully. The issue is not, however, a simple one, and will draw upon many 'human resource management' issues, for example work motivation theory, information processing, leadership, group dynamics, decision making and so on. The importance of each discipline will depend upon a number of factors, for example the importance of the individual/group to the overall process of change.

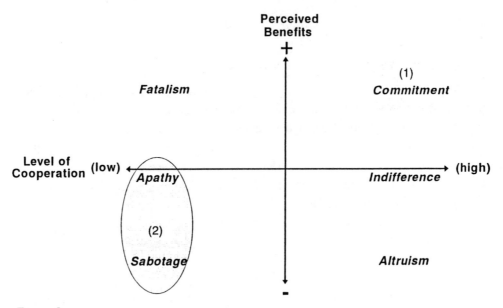

Figure 5
Worker Perception of and Cooperation with IT Change

Consensus existed between management and non-management regarding the reasons for adopting new technology. The research findings are summarised in Table 4.

Financial/Economic	Service Delivery	Introduction to Strategy
To increase profitability	To improve the management of the information	Softly-softly approach
To improve efficiency	To keep up with new technology	Float idea of new technology
To increase productivity	To speed up information processing	Select/train key staff
To improve budgetary control	To improve control	Presentation by management
To compete effectively	To better integrate information	
To reduce overall costs	To improve quality of service	
To reduce staff costs	To improve flexibility	
To respond to skill shortage	To facilitate service innovation	
	To increase staff skill	

Table 4

Additional feelings towards IT-related change were identified during the follow-up interviews. In the main, the findings were of a critical nature and are set out below under two separate categories.

Signs of Poor IT Design/Implementation

(i)   Failure to evaluate the new technology prior to implementation.

(ii) No consultation before the purchase of new technology.

(iii) No communication or right of feedback between the design and implementation stages.

(iv) Poor technical support in relation to recurrent systems faults.

(v)   Apparent poor understanding of the technology by the "experts".

(vi) Similar equipment being used by different departments/sections with different results.

(vii) No allowance for the discretion of skills/profession of specific personnel.

(viii)The introduction of new technology resulted in unforeseen problems developing in other parts of the organisation.

(ix) Lack of a long-term perspective in relation to the use of the new technology developments.

(xi) The organisation loses competitive advantage because the opposition has better technology, or uses the same technology in a more imaginative way.

(xii) New organisational/systems inefficiencies develop because of the system design/use of the technology.

Signs of Poor HRM/IT Integration

(i)   IT is regarded as purely a technical matter and left to the "experts".

(ii)   The new technology in use is clearly inappropriate for its intended use.

(iii)   The equipment is either not used or is used inappropriately.

(iv)   Staff are unable or unwilling to use the new technology.

(v)   An implicit belief exists that it is impossible to learn about the new technology.

(vi)   Poor conceptual understanding of what is possible.

(vii)   Lack of knowledge about the types of application suited/not suited to the new technology.

(viii) Personnel (particularly managers) spending a disproportionate amount of time on low level work feeding the information demands of the system

(ix)   Continuing simultaneously to operate old manual systems following the introduction of the new technology.

(x)   A failure to exploit new opportunities created by the introduction of new technology

(xi)   Lack of cooperation with/sabotage of the new technology by individual personnel.

(xii)   Failure/unwillingness of one department/section to communicate its experiences of the new technology with other departments, especially in relation to greater task effectiveness and customer service.

(xiii) The new technology is underutilised because nobody cares.

(xiv)   Conflict arises out of system unreliability.

Conclusions

The preceding analysis suggests fundamental problems for the effective implementation of IT change in local authorities. The difficulties facing local authority managers cannot, however, be taken as reasons for not addressing the problems of different perceptions about the effects of change and the process of managing change highlighted in this research.

There seem to be two key areas which require more careful attention. These are respectively the level of co-operation of workers in relation to the IT change process and perceptions of the benefits of these changes. If these are ignored, then it is highly likely that the difficulties experienced regarding implementation will intensify. They will simply be implemented in an ad hoc way which will not be in the interests of any of the parties involved. All service organisations are now beginning to face the challenges of obtaining productivity and quality increases without corresponding increases in resources. In many ways, they are following the path manufacturing industries have already gone down with varying degrees of success. Managers in the public services have a responsibility to ensure that the cultural changes to support these developments are brought about.

If desired IT change is going to be achieved in an efficient and effective manner then senior management within local authorities need to address a number of critical issues, each of which is significant in relation to each of the stages in the change-making process. In short, improved management of the IT change process requires:

(1) Acceptance of the inevitability of change, and the importance of IT in relation to this change. Managers need to adopt a proactive approach by developing a conviction that the new 'privatised' model can work within the public sector. There may be no second chance (56).

(2) Resource implications, including job losses need to be identified as quickly as possible.

(3) Active 'risk free' vertical and horizontal communication should be encouraged as a prerequisite to successful change management. Such a process would facilitate management understanding of non-management perception of the proposed change.

(4) Ownership of the change process has to be accepted at all levels. If workers oppose or sabotage the proposed change then it may never take place in the intended form. It is arrogant of management to assume that only they have a monopoly on information and how it should be disseminated, and to assume that they are the innovators in relation to idea generation.

(5) Time is a finite resource. It is essential that priority is given to developing a more speedy resolution in relation to structural and job changes.

(6) Clarity of direction appropriate to local circumstances which will enable a better performance orientation to be achieved.

(7) Perhaps the most useful suggestions regarding how to tackle IT implementation within the dynamic resource constrained local government business environment are contained in Table 5, below.

• Define the information technology requiements
• Define the objectives of the project
• Identify the structural implications
• Commit staff resources to the project
• Evaluate all information technology proposals
• Allow appropriate resources for the planning and implementation
• Test the system
• Train staff
• Implement the project
• Conduct a post-implementation review

Table 5

Framework for the Monitoring, Control and Implementation of IT Acquisitions

References

(1) Sweeney, E. & Smith, D. (1993) 'The Significance of Worker Perception in Relation to the Change Process: A Comparison of Two Service Sector Organisations', Paper presented to the conference *The Waves of Change: Strategic Issues in Public Services.* 5 & 6 April.

(2) Isaac-Henry, K. & Painter, C. (1991) 'The Changing Face of Local Government: The Reforming Impetus Continues', *Local Government Policy Making, 18* (4) pp. 29-34.

(3) Audit Commission (1988) *The Competitive Council.* Management Papers. No 1, March. HMSO.

(4) Thompson, P. (1992), 'Public Sector Management in a Period of Radical Change: 1979-1992'. *Public Money and Management, 12* (3) pp. 33-42.

(5) Isaac-Henry, K. & Painter, C. (1991) 'The Management Challenge in Local Government: Emerging Themes and Trends', *Local Government Studies, 7* (3) pp. 69-90.

(6) Clark M. (1993) 'Changing Prospects for Local Government', *Local Government Policy Making, 20,* (2) pp. 3-8.

(7) Leach, S. (1993) 'Local Government Reorganisation in England', *Local Government Policy Making, 19* (4) pp. 30-35.

(8) Stewart, J. (1991) 'Considerations on Strategic Management in Local Government', *Local Government Policy Making, 17* (4).

(9) Ibrahim, M. and Proctor, R. (1992) 'Budgetary Decision Making Under Fiscal Stress', *Local Government Policy Making, 19* (3) pp. 51-59.

(10) Johnson, G. and Scholes, K. (1993) *Exploring Corporate Strategy* (London: Prentice Hall).

(11) Carr, D. & Littleman, I. (1991) *Excellence in Government: Total Quality Management in the 1990's* (London: Coopers and Lybrand).

(12) Ohmae, K. (1990) *The Borderless World.* (London: Collins).

(13) Peters, T. & Waterman, R. (1982) *In Search of Excellence* (London: Harper and Row).

(14) Yates, J, & Benjamin, R. (1991) 'The Past as a Window on the Future', in Scott Morton, M. (ed) *The Corporation of the 1990s* (Oxford: Oxford University Press).

(15) Coulson-Thomas, C. (1992) *Transforming the Company* (London: Kogan Page).

(16) Brown, J. & Watts, J. (1992) 'Enterprise Engineering: Building 21st Century Organisations'. *Journal of Strategic Information Systems, 1* (5).

(17) Rotenberg, J. & Saloner, G. (1991) 'Interfirm Competition and Collaboration', in Scott Morton, M. (ed) *op. cit.*

(18) Handy, C. (1989) *The Age of Unreason* (London: Arrow Books).

(19) Drucker, P. (1993) *Managing the Future.* (London: Butterworth-Heinemann).

(20) Thurrow, L. (1991) 'Forward', in Scott Morton, M. (ed) *op. cit.*

(21) Zuboff, S. (1988) *In The Age of the Smart Machine* (London: Heinemann).

(22) Earl, M. (1989) *Management Strategies for Information Technology* (London: Prentice Hall).

(23) Venkatraman, N. (1991) 'IT Induced Business Reconfiguration'. in Scott Morton, M. (ed) *op. cit.*

(24) Porter, M., (1985) *Competitive Advantage: Creating and Sustaining Superior Performance.* (London: Macmillan).

(25) Kearney, A. (1990) *Breaking the Barriers: IT Effectiveness in Great Britain and Ireland.* (London: Chartered Institute of Management Accountants).

(26) McFarlan, F. (1984) 'Information Technology Changes the Way You Compete', *Harvard Business Review, 62* (3) pp. 98-103.

(27) Knight, K., Algie, J., Dale, A. & Fonda, N. (1986) *Management of Technology* (Middlesex: The Brunel Institute of Organisational and Social Studies).

(28) Amited, C. (1993) 'Becoming a Learning Organisation', *Training and Development* (March).

(29) Leonard-Barton, D. (1992) 'The Factory as a Learning Laboratory', *Sloan Management Review,* (Fall).

(30) Moss-Kanter, R. (1983) *The Change Masters.* (London: George Allen & Unwin).

(31) Harvey-Jones, J. (1989) *The Changing Climate for European Business.* Proceedings of the Third Amdahl Executive Institute Conference. 7 July. London.

(32) Dopson, S. & Stewart, R. (1990) 'What is Happening to Middle Management?', *British Journal of Management, 1.*

(33) AMDAHL (1989) *Innovation Through IT: Managing Change.* Proceedings of the Third Amdahl Executive Institute Conference.

(34) Hurford, C. (1991) 'Acquiring IT Successfully'. *Public Money and Management, 11* (3) pp. 11-16.

(35) Thompson, P. (1992) 'Public Sector Management in a Period of Radical Change: 1979-1992'. *Public Money and Management, 12* (3) pp. 33-42.

(36) Angel, I & Smithson, S. (1989) *Technology: A Crisis of Confidence. LSE Department of Information Technology. Working Paper No. 20.* (London: London School of Economics).

(37) Margetts, H. & Willcocks, L. (1993) 'Information Technology in Public Services: Disaster Faster?', *Public Money and Management, 13* (2) pp. 49-56.

(38) Hughes, J & Bayes, J. (1991) 'Managing IT - the Introduction and Adoption of New Systems', *Public Money and Management, 11* (3) pp. 31-36.

136

(39) Morris, T. (1989) 'Information Technology: Servant or Master?', *Public Money and Management, 9* (2) pp. 35-40.

(40) Stewart, J. (1991) 'Considerations of Strategic Management in Local Government', *Local Government Policy Making, 17* (4) pp. 62-64.

(41) Willsocks, L. & Mark, A. (1989) 'IT Systems Implementation: Research Findings from the Public Sector', *Journal of Information Technology, 4* (2).

(42) Willsocks, L. & Margetts, H. (1991) 'Informatization in UK Public Services: from Implementation through Strategy Management'. Paper at the EGFPA Conference *Informatization in the Public Services*. The Hague, The Netherlands.

(43) Brussard, B. (1988) 'Information Resource Management in the Public Sector', *Information and Management, 15* (2).

(44) Argyris, C. (1980) 'Some Inner Contradictions in Management Information Systems', in, Lucas, C. & Land, F. (eds), *The Information Systems Environment. (*Amsterdam: North Holland Publishing Company). p. 16

(45) Tarrant, J. (1976) *Drucker: The Man Who Invented the Corporate Society* (Boston: Cahner Books). p 87.

(46) Hughes, J. & Bayes, J. (1991) *op cit.* p. 36.

(47) Handy, C. (1986) *Understanding Organisations* (Handsworth: Penguin Books).

(48) See, for example, Morgan, G. (1986) *Images of Organisation* (London: Sage).

(49) Kotter, J. & Heskett, J. (1992) *Corporate Culture and Performance* (New York: Free Press).

(50) Flannery, T. & Williams, J. (1990) 'The Shape of Things to Come - Management Culture and Process', *Healthcare Forum, 33* (4) pp. 52-57.

(51) Hopfl, H. Smith, S. & Spencer, S. (1992) 'Values and Valuations: The Conflict Between Culture Change and Jobs', *Personnel Review, 21* (1) pp. 24 - 37.

(52) Schein, E. (1989) 'Corporate Culture is the Real Key to Creativity', *Business Month* (May) pp. 73 - 75.

(53) Sweeney, E. (1989) *The Attitude of Management and Non-Management to the Introduction of Information Technology* (An unpublished MBA Thesis).

(54) Drennan, D. (1992) *Transforming Company Culture: Getting Your Company From Where You Are Now To Where You Want To Be* (London: McGraw-Hill).

(55) Hofstede, G. (1991) *Cultures and Organizations: Software of the Mind* (London: McGraw-Hill).

(57) Stewart, J. & Stoker, G. (eds) (1989) *The Future of Local Government* (London: Macmillan).

137

MANAGING IN ADVERSITY: OR THE TALE OF A DIRECT LABOUR ORGANISATION MANAGER

Graham P. Bratley, Wakefield MDC

Introduction

This paper describes some of the critical ingredients which constitute the context in which management has to be undertaken in a Direct Labour Organisation (DLO) Department of a Local Authority. It provides information on the DLO in question - one operating from within the City of Wakefield Metropolitan District Council. It introduces and discusses, from a Chief Officer's perspective, some of the managerial challenges currently being faced because of externally imposed environmental change on the one hand and an internal resistance to change on the other.

The Organisation and Its Markets

Wakefield Metropolitan District Council (Wakefield MDC) is the parent organisation of the Department which is the focus of this paper. Wakefield MDC provides traditional local authority type services over a comparatively large (compared to neighbouring Authorities) geographical area. Its constituent townships include the old City of Wakefield, Ossett, Horbury and the 'Five Towns Region' which encompasses Castleford, Pontefract, Featherstone and Normanton. The Authority has a total budget of around £240m and a population of approximately 400,000.

The Building Services Department of the Authority has a turnover in excess of £42m per year and operates through its four divisions - Construction, Highways, Maintenance and Engineering. Its markets are diverse and are internal to Wakefield MDC as well as external, comprising other Local Authorities, Health Authorities and Housing Associations. The internal market services the Housing, Education, Social Services and Municipal Services Departments of Wakefield MDC. The major external markets are related to the

Department's PVC-U window manufacture and its new construction, build for sale homes, function.

The Department is represented through its Chief Officer on the Authority Management Team which consists of eleven Chief Officers and the Chief Executive who deal with the general management of Wakefield MDC including budgetary controls, setting of standards and setting of service level agreements.

The Department's Competitive Position and Market Conditions

The Building Services Department wins 95 per cent of its work in open competition in the general construction industry - an industry which is in its worse recession since the 1930s. Turnover has fallen from £3,300m in the peak year of 1990 to a current level of less than £1,850m - a reduction of some 40 per cent in three years. This reduction in volume within the market has caused contract tender rates to be forced ever downwards, and many contractors are currently tendering at prices below the projected costs of the completed work. As a result, 20 of the top 30 contractors are currently losing money. For example, AMEC have reported losses of £30m, Trafalgar House has recently published results showing losses of over £300m and last year Tarmac lost over £300m. There is little evidence that this situation will recover quickly over the next few years.

With over 500,000 construction employees out of work, this has enabled many major contractors to reduce labour pay-rates to sub-contractors to below nationally agreed rates. This adversely affects our competitive position. As Local Authority employers we are tied to national agreements, which incorporate rates of pay and conditions of employment that are much more favourable than those being worked to within the private sector.

Recently agreed conditions within the Local Authority sector will certainly cause us problems over the next six months. These include the harmonisation of sick pay whereby pay is harmonised to incorporate bonus payments over any period of sick-leave, and the introduction of a 37 hour working week. The effect of this harmonisation of sick pay has already caused difficulties. Following its introduction, sickness within the organisation rose by around 4 per cent. However, this increased level of sick leave has been arrested and reversed following the introduction of an attendance bonus scheme and attendance rates are now back to the levels which existed prior to the harmonisation of sick pay. The new bonus scheme seems likely to require renegotiation as this will create a competitive disadvantage.

In addition to this, the Building Services Department is not able to sustain operating losses in the way that many of our competing contractors can. In the private sector, strategic development can allow for losses and debts to be incurred over the short term (say two years) and for debts to be written off by the corporate centre to enable successful 'come-backs' in, say, years three and four. In contrast, Local Authority DLOs must, under Department of the Environment rules, make a rate of return of 5 per cent on capital employed in any one year (this rate might be increased to 6 per cent next year).

Any private contractors producing profit rates of 5 per cent or 6 per cent on capital employed in current market conditions would undoubtedly be considered to be top industry performers. As stated above, much of the industry is in a loss-making situation. Nevertheless, DLOs are expected by Central Government to maintain this positive return on capital employed. It is not, perhaps, surprising that some Local Authority operations were closed down by the District Auditor last year, having been served non-compliance orders. Authorities affected in this way included Sheffield which lost £1.9m on maintenance works and Newham London Borough Council with losses of £1.8m on new construction work.

The hostile conditions which prevail in the construction industry have also created problems over our sub-contractor position. Many large and medium sized contractors have gone into liquidation in the last two years and many of our local sub-contractors have followed them into demise as part of a knock-on effect. When our own sub-contractors and suppliers get into difficulties then our ability to perform our current contracts is likely to be undermined by the disruption to works which is involved. One topical example is that of the reletting of contracts at higher rates because the original supplier (of timber) went into liquidation with a a school roof only half-completed.

The internal market within Wakefield will also be affected over the next three years by the need to reduce budget spending year on year by £30m. This has been brought about by a reduction in Central Government support to Wakefield MDC. Although the reduction this year was not as large as anticipated, we will still have to achieve a reduction of between £7m and £8m in this year's budget.

Political Threats

During the lifetime of the current Government, major pieces of legislation have been introduced which have directly affected the Building Services Department. For example, the 1980 Local Government Planning and Land Act introduced a compulsory competitive tendering system for all building works projects in Local Authorities and reduced the DLO market by restricting new construction contracts available from other Local Authorities to those of maintenance and fabrication only.

Two examples of the effect of this legislation are :

(a) A market which we have recently sought to develop our position in, that of new build for Housing Associations within the Wakefield boundary, was taken outside our jurisdiction by the District Auditor. Within 2 hours of our winning the tender for one such contract, the District Auditor challenged the legal position on which we had tendered for the work and our tender had to be withdrawn.

(b) The District Auditor is also looking at cross-boundary tendering in general, and particularly at our PVC-U window fabrication operation. A High Court challenge may be imminent. If this action proves to be successful then it is unlikely that our Metroglaze Factory will remain viable producing windows exclusively for an internal, Authority, market.

Further legislation is currently being proposed under the umbrella of the Citizen's Charter and this will call for compulsory competitive tendering in the context of contracts for the services of housing managers, architects, surveyors, solicitors and accountants. Our major customers are the Authority's Housing Department and Education Department. Both will be affected by the new legislation. Our housing service may well be restructured into thirteen units, with each controlling a large community estate and each being independent with its own local management. The housing contractual arrangement, from my Department's viewpoint, might then change from the present situation of one contract covering the whole of Wakefield, and involving a value of over £16m, to one involving thirteen smaller contracts. This would change the competition structure of the market for my Maintenance Division from a situation where it is a market suitable for large contractors, able to provide service covering all building trades over a large geographical area, to a situation attractive to small contractors offering local services. Further, it is likely that these smaller companies will operate with much lower overheads than the Building Services Department, and this may well confer a competitive advantage which outweighs any economies of scale that we may be able to muster. It is also possible that the District Auditor will insist on contracts being split even further into trade packages with the effect of producing up to 48 small contracts.

Recent legislation not directly focused on DLOs has, nevertheless, had consequences for our market-place and our ability to compete successfully within it. One example of this is the legislation aiming to stimulate locally-managed schools. Another is the latest 'twist in the tail' - the infamous clause zero which has been inserted at the beginning of the new Education Bill and which may well lead to the destruction of Local Education Authorities throughout Britain. Even more recently the Government has announced that funds will be available for parents and pressure groups to start new schools in competition with Local Authority schools. Once the Local Authority's role in Education has been diminished, with more schools being centrally funded, it is then but a small additional step to make centrally-funded schools and the local Technical Colleges a closed market to the DLOs.

This has already occurred with our Health Authority market-place where we often obtained, in competitive circumstances, heating, electrical and painting jobs in hospitals within the local health area. Recent developments in the Health Sector have meant that many hospitals have been removed from the control of Health Authorities and have become self-financing trusts. These newly constituted hospitals are deemed to be outside our scope of work and, therefore, this has again restricted our market place.

European Union Legislation

EU legislation requires that all large works contracts are advertised in the Community Journal and it is possible, as has happened in respect of, for example, cleaning and refuse collection, that French companies will be attracted into Britain in order to take over our major maintenance schemes. Worse still, countries such as Portugal which customarily provide very low rates of pay will also be attracted. Recently, I have even read a report that describes how a Polish company was hoping to be able to tender for the rebuilding of the Royal Palace at Windsor.

One of the major threats which comes from our EU membership is due to the fact that we British are extremely observant of the law and work within it. The Local Authority sector is, perhaps, particularly law abiding. Many of the EU Regulations which affect us such as the Cosh Regulations, Manual Handling rules and the latest 'Six Pack of Safety Regulations' require strict observance by all Local Authority employers. Many of our competitors may not, however, be as diligent in fulfilling the legislation, and this will undermine our competitive position to the extent that they can do the job more cheaply, easily or quickly.

It is within this climate that the Department must attempt to formulate a competitive strategy. I feel sure that Michael Porter of the Harvard Business School would advise a strategy of market withdrawal in the face of such a gloomy picture. However, DLOs are not just about making profit and the Building Services Department of Wakefield MDC, for example, is an organisation which aims to provide a quality service at a minimum cost and to maintain rates of return greater than those laid down by the legislation whilst supporting local employment. It is evident that internal changes are required in any organisation facing such externally imposed market changes and aspiring to achieve the objectives described above.

The Existing Organisation Culture

This author was recruited to the Building Services Department as its Construction Manager about 4 years ago. This career change followed a period of work with a dynamic, fast growing private sector company where I had been employed as Contracts Director. The change of job and organisation created a big 'culture shock'. I walked into an organisation that, despite having made changes which had been driven by the Competitive Tendering

Regulations introduced in 1980, still had its roots firmly fixed in a typical Local Government hierarchial structure and culture. These characteristics of the Department were strongly reinforced by bureaucratic control systems and an Information Technology (IT) based management information system and management hierarchy that was difficult to manage, and which provided little support for any worthwhile decision modelling. The nature of the central control system was such that the system often interfered with, rather than helped, the smooth operation of the front line services.

Thus, there was a major mismatch of cultures and management systems between the organisation which I had left and the one into which I had been recruited. My new organisation had long established working practices based on a tradition of operating in a stable environment. In terms of change receptivity, many of its staff suffered from the 'we've seen it all before' syndrome. In other words, it exhibited some of the classic symptoms of the large and ageing organisation described by Henry Mintzberg in his article on structures of organisations.

In contrast, the organisation from which I had come had been young, organic and fast-growing. It had not been restricted by long established bureaucratic systems. Its culture and ways of working seemed more suitable to the task in hand for the Building Services Department than did the actual approach adopted by the Department.

There were two choices available to me in terms of how I should approach my new job. The first was one which my new colleagues recommended I should adopt. This required me to change my managerial style and approach to management. The other choice required that I attempt to change the culture of my new organisation (which was itself grounded in a wider, bigger organisation culture based on rigid Departments with hierarchial structures and often led by professionals and staff motivated more by protecting their own departments or sections than providing a service either to other departments or the general public).

I chose the second option and am pleased to say that changes are being effected within Wakefield and in relation to some of its senior officers and that these changes are helping the organisation to achieve a revolution in service delivery and working practices.

However, these changes are not easily made in an organisation which has developed in a particular way and in a particular type of environment for many years. Often I have been required to demonstrate personally how things might be done more effectively and with greater resolve.

A typical example of how the traditional approach to doing things worked against better departmental performance can be drawn from the occasion when, at one of my general staff meetings, a Site Agent reported that he was unable to obtain reinforcement for the foundation work on a College extension. The site buyer, for his part, said that he could not obtain the additional steel needed immediately to keep the job going because he was awaiting three tenders to comply with Standing Orders and one of them was late in arriving.

144

He was also busy with producing data for the annual tender, and he was not aware, anyway, that the steel was urgently needed. When the agent was asked why had he not 'chased' the delivery of the steelwork through the buying department, he replied, "No, that's not my job, its a Project Planner's job". The Project Planner's view, however, was that he had demonstrated clearly on the works programme provided to the buyer that the materials should be delivered on time. Thus, he had fulfilled the description of his job. Meanwhile, the steel fixer was on site with no steel, delayed and feeling very frustrated.

I used my own initiative, without breaking Standing Orders and had the steel delivered within two days by special order. The point being made was that 'it could be done', the problem was that 'nobody wanted to do it'. The prevailing attitude was part of the 'blame' culture. If you do nothing, you cannot get it wrong, and in Local Government nobody is allowed to fail so everybody keeps his head down - nobody takes responsibility for getting things done. This blame culture stands in the way of the ability to learn. This non-acceptance of failure is a major problem in Local Government.

The performance of the Construction Division had to be improved and quickly. I set about trying to improve the structure of the organisation. One structural problem involved the Site Agents who were supported by Project Planners and Quantity Surveyors based at Head Office. The general feeling of these Site Agents was that they were isolated and were given insufficient help in the day-to-day management of the contracts - whether in relation to labour inputs, planning or help from surveyors on claims and unanticipated delays. The structure which existed at that time is shown in appendix A.

To overcome this problem we restructured so that Contract Management, Quantity Surveying and Contract Planning were combined to form one Department. This has allowed greater flexibility in the delivery of services and the implementation of a multi-skilling approach to staff development. Small groups of personnel now work together to service a number of site agents. This, in turn, has allowed a reduction in staff cost related overheads. One Planner has been redeployed to a Site Manager's job and a Surveyor has been transferred to Contract Management. Appendix B illustrates the new structure which was put in place.

Strategic Management of the Organisation

The general belief of many of the personnel when I arrived was that they (their organisation and their present jobs) would survive without making major changes to the way things were done. The belief was that they had survived since 1974 and that they always would. The philosophy which underpinned strategic development was likewise related to the way the organisation had always operated. The key development was that of winning the three year maintenance contract at the highest possible price and thereafter hoping that enough capital projects would be available to keep the major Construction Division alive. The Highways Division attracted approximately 70 per cent of its work in a competition-free context and so it was considered that there was no need for modern management techniques such as strategic planning. Budgets were set at six monthly intervals to meet the expected demands of Wakefield's Client Departments.

Market positioning, market focus and an environmental analysis of the total market were not raised as issues for long-term planning exercises.

The Early Moves to Strategic Planning

Because of the support for the maintenance of the status quo, the organisation had little or no strategic view. This has started to change with the creation of a strategic plan for survival which has led to the generation of some new market opportunities. For example, we are now involved in build for sale projects and sell houses to the public both at the luxury end and at the starter-home end of the market. These strategic developments were undertaken to provide a continuous flow of work to our operatives on those occasions when major projects were not being undertaken by the Department. The plan has also helped the Department to have more control over its workload. It has also helped in the achievement of a reduction of our base labour force through the planned development to take out peaks and troughs through the employment of temporary staff, an idea which is used by many Japanese companies who have a core workforce and bring in additional temporary staff as and when required.

Strategic planning for the whole organisation is in its infancy, but recently attempts have been made to implement a strategic planning process on a six monthly basis. Medium and long-term strategy for the Department is tied to the major strategic plan for the Wakefield Metropolitan District as a whole. The strategic plan contains proposals for the reduction of overheads whilst maintaining front-line services at existing levels despite the budget reductions. A strategic decision has been made to form a new organisation which is to provide direct services for building, cleaning, highways, health and leisure under one leadership. A diagram containing this new Department appears as Appendix C.

I have personally been involved in the planning of this new Department. The initial challenge will be to bring about major structural changes and similar changes in existing management systems in order to 'free up' the individual managers of the Business Units within the new Department. The Business Units will be managed as independent units with management systems capable of giving accurate and timely financial information. These Unit Managers will be responsible for the preparation and updating of their own business/strategic plans and agreeing these with their Head of Department. They will then be allowed to compete in their own particular market place without petty restrictions.

146

I expect to face similar challenges in leading this change as I faced when I brought about the initial change within the Construction Division.

Leading the Change and the Problems Involved

Gaining acceptance to the changes proposed was achieved without great difficulty. Construction Department people agreed to change their roles and working practices and to be re-skilled. Office accommodation was identified. The change was accepted as being required, possible and acceptable.

I next turned my attention to the parties who might be affected - central Personnel, unions, other managers and people from the other Divisions. These were not receptive to any ideas of change. Every possible objection was raised. The following are examples of blocking statements used against me on many occasions during the last four years :

(1) It is not as simple as that.
(2) You cannot change what they do - there may be effects we cannot calculate.
(3) It is not the Wakefield way.
(4) The Chairman won't allow it - we now have a new Chairman!
(5) The Auditor won't allow it.
(6) It is against Standing Orders.
(7) It is not policy.
(8) The union will resist it.

All of the above, or a combination, were used as a means of preventing change in working practices. I have continually run up against the no-change culture. The unions and the Personnel Manager ran to the politicians to report that I was changing staff conditions without consultation. As a result, I met with the Chairman of the Public Works Committee and explained my position. He saw the logic of better front-line services at lower cost. Unions were unable to defend their objections when all the staff involved were seen to be in agreement with the moves. The main resistance, however, came from other managers who saw this as a decentralising radical change and not the Wakefield way.

However, the changes were made and have now been completed for some time. The Planning Section no longer exists. My next move will be to look at other independent Sections and form these into cells. The Incentives Section cell structure in Construction should be absorbed within other Departments before the end of this financial year.

Leading the Change to a New Department

Much time needs to be consumed in breaking down resistance to change. Leading change is also a dangerous occupation, as was recognised by Machiavelli in his advice to Lorenzo de Medici in 1514:

> It should be borne in mind there is nothing more difficult to arrange, more doubtful of success and more dangerous to carry through than initiating changes in a state's constitution. The innovator makes enemies of all those who prospered under the old order and only lukewarm support is forthcoming from those who prosper under the new.

As evidence in support of Machiavelli's assertion, I can refer to the fact that Departmental staff recently organised a vote, on the question: "Do you believe the following members of the Management Team are acting in the best interests of the Department and its staff?" I received a 13 per cent 'Yes' vote. Machiavelli's statement appears to have been validated. The change management drive must continue to continue.

Appendix A

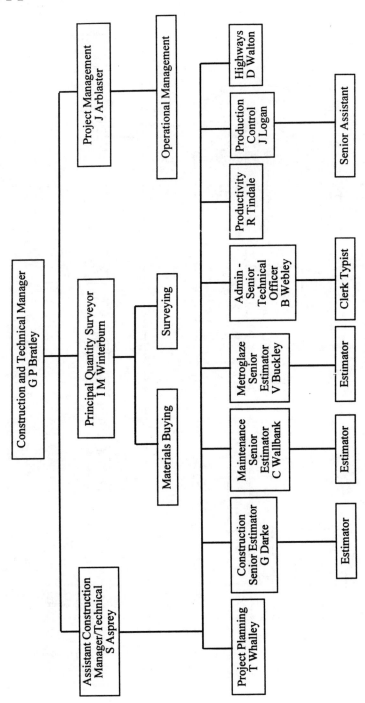

Appendix B

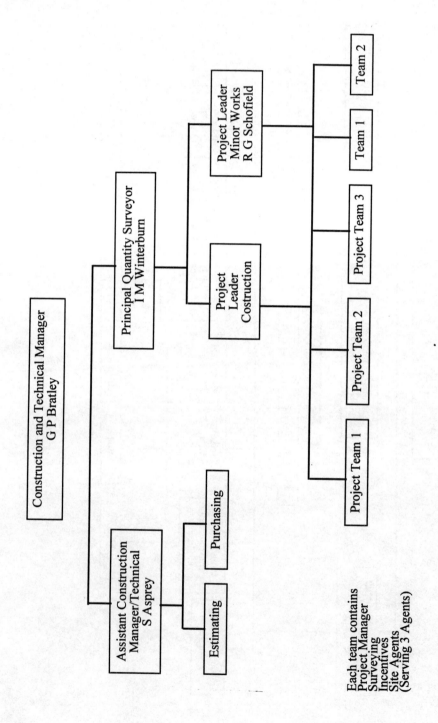

Construction and Technical Manager
G P Bratley

Principal Quantity Surveyor
I M Winterburn

Assistant Construction Manager/Technical
S Asprey

Estimating

Purchasing

Project Leader
Costruction

Project Leader
Minor Works
R G Schofield

Project Team 1

Project Team 2

Project Team 3

Team 1

Team 2

Each team contains
Project Manager
Surveying
Incentives
Site Agents
(Serving 3 Agents)

Appendix C

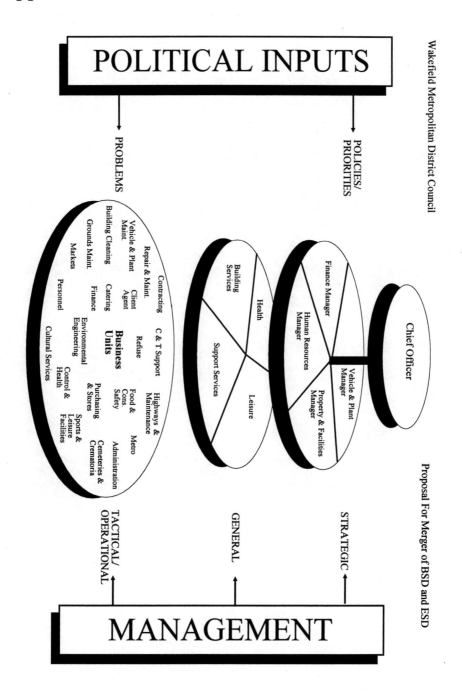

Proposal For Merger of BSD and ESD

151

MANAGING ENTERPRISING LOCAL AUTHORITIES: APPROACHES TO THE EUROPEANISATION OF UK LOCAL GOVERNMENT

Joyce Liddle, Sunderland Business School and Steve Martin, Aston Business School

The 'Europeanisation' of British Local Authorities

In recent years a growing number of UK local authorities have attempted to assess and respond to the impacts of European integration. The 'Europeanisation of local government' is a somewhat vague (even clumsy) short-hand which has been increasingly used to encompass a range of local authority activities relating to 'European issues'. It is, however, indeterminate both in terms of geography and local government functions. Thus, some researchers have employed the term to refer to the overall process whereby authorities have become more outward looking and 'international' in orientation. Some researchers include within Europeanisation, central and eastern European countries and, even, former Soviet Republics. Others refer to Europeanisation as a process which involves contact with other states in western Europe and a third group have interpreted it as being primarily related to issues involving the European Union.

The second major ambiguity in the phrase 'Europeanisation' concerns the activities which it encompasses. The phrase has been used to refer to a wide range of different functions, but on the whole four basic categories of 'European response' can be identified (John, 1994).

Sub-national government throughout the European Union (EU) has been required to respond to an increasing volume of primary and secondary legislation and directives from the European Commission covering areas such as public procurement, trading standards, environmental protection and health and safety standards. Much of this has been of direct concern to local authorities as employers and as the providers of services; in other cases they have been the monitoring, enforcing or licensing agencies (LGIB, 1991).

Even the least active or 'Euro-minimal authorities' have therefore had to deal with EU legislation and with information about its implications. Among less-active authorities, the response to directives has typically been at a departmental level although some have nominated a central point (often just one officer) from which Euro-information is disseminated within the authority. Individual departments will also often act as brokers of Euro-information for other local agencies. Many UK authorities have become increasingly aware of the implications for their areas of the completion of the Single European Market through, for example, one-off 'Europe weeks' and on-going training programmes. In many cases this issue provided the first area of interest in Europe among elected members, and even the least 'Euro-active' authorities have tended to pass information about the Single Market to local businesses. County councils and metropolitan boroughs, in particular, have often been involved in comprehensive analyses of the needs of local employers and assisted them in identifying and taking advantage of the new opportunities offered post-1992 (Audit Commission, 1992).

The second level of 'Europeanisation' involves attempts to gain EU financial assistance - 'financially driven' (or 'grant getting') authorities have seen European financial assistance as a way of compensating for the erosion of UK domestic regional policy assistance (Martin and Pearce, 1992). This is particularly evident in the North East which has been perceived as "one of those Unfortunate Regions : a boom area of the coal age with an enormous legacy of obsolete social capital, a slower rate of economic growth, an accompanying higher rate of unemployment, a poorer standard of health and social services and a not unrelated outward migration of population" (Cullingworth, 1970). Their initial involvement in attempts to 'Europeanise' often stemmed from a desire to maximise the amount received, particularly from the structural Funds (Keating, 1992). Many parts of the UK have been eligible for structural Funds assistance as Objective 1, 2 or 5b areas, and even the ineligible have been in receipt of European Social Fund aid and, in some cases, have also received finance from the wide range of Community Initiatives (including programmes such as HORIZON, NOW, CONVERE etc). In addition, over the last eighteen months, many authorities that have not previously qualified for assistance have intensively lobbied both central government and the Commission in an attempt to persuade them to designate their areas for Objective 2 or 5b status. In most cases, such activities have been led by Economic Development Departments or specialist European Teams, often based in Treasurers or the Chief Executive's Department.

Some authorities have moved beyond a desire to maximise financial receipts and have sought to find ways of influencing the Commission policy-making processes. Most have been pleasantly surprised by the welcome which they received in Brussels and the enthusiasm with which the Commission's officials have pursued its declared aim of establishing a dialogue with sub-national government. In pursuit of influence on, and

154

advance intelligence about, Commission policy-making, a growing number have opened Brussels offices (either jointly or on their own) and employed full-time European staff both in Belgium and the UK. As the number of authorities involved in such lobbying grew during the 1980s, however, the Commission's officials found it increasingly impractical to attempt to liaise with individual authorities. As a result, authorities have tended in recent years to join one or more of the plethora of local authority networks which have sprung up between sub-national governments across the European Union and, increasingly, the rest of Europe. Coupled with the Maastricht Treaty's recognition of a role for sub-national government in the Union's policy making, these developments have helped to reinforce a move among UK authorities away from an initial pre-occupation with funding to a broader appreciation of the value of playing a fuller part in the Union's affairs and of 'putting something back into Europe'.

Networking of this kind can also be related to financial considerations. Domestic inter-authority alliances have been prompted by the Commission which now specifies the existence of meaningful sub-regional and regional partnership as a pre-condition for receipt of structural funds (Martin and Pearce, 1993). Trans-national networking has also often been prompted by a desire to tap initiatives which require authorities to have partners in other member states. Authorities which have joined multilateral networks such as the Euro-cities, RETI or Atlantic Arc associations have normally been concerned with influencing broader policy making.

A small number of UK authorities have gone a stage further in 'Europeanisation' by becoming advisers to the Commission on implementation issues. This group also tend to have an authority-wide awareness of European issues and to have developed corporate strategies which address the European dimensions of all their departments' activities.

On-going Research

The PhD research is focused on the changing power relations between local national and transnational governance, with particular emphasis on the North East of England. By assessing the implications of Europeanisation on local authorities and other collaborative public and private sector agencies, it is anticipated that a map can be drawn of the relationships currently being built up in this Region of the UK.

Taking as a theoretical starting point the 'differentiated policy' developed by Rhodes (1988) and the provocative notion of a 'centreless society' formulated by Luhmann (1982), it is hoped to survey the existing networks of sub-central government in the North East and to explore the collaborative arrangements already in place or currently being established in response to the opportunities and threats of European integration. By deliberately rejecting the traditional Centralist perspective on the study of British policy (with its concentration on Westminster and Whitehall), Rhodes and Luhmann stake a claim for the importance of sub-central government in bringing about policy change and in some instances of "developing and implementing policies unbeknown or unwelcome to the Centre". Clearly "local authorities are located in networks of organisations both public and private and the gestation and implementation of policy cannot be explained by the actions of any one organisation" (Rhodes, 1988).

Research into the work of local authorities has in the past been very parochial and isolationist in nature, primarily because they have been regarded as distinct entities with their own particular problems to solve and specific issues to resolve. Researchers have traditionally restricted their unit of analysis to the confines of the local authority and its surrounding locality or they have regarded the local authority as a sub-unit of the wider political systems and concentrated on central/local relationships.

If one accepts the fact that policies at the local level cannot be explained by the actions of one organisation then not only is it appropriate to analyse the inter-agency relationships at the local/regional/central and transnational levels of government but it may also be interesting to use the concept of Europeanisation to test the theory of "lesson drawing in public policy across space and time" (Rose, 1993).

Rose's theory bridges the time and space dimension and explains how policymakers with familiar problems can aid their decision making by comparative analysis of other agencies' approaches and then transfer the lessons learned and apply them to their own policy problems. By observing the way other governing units respond to common problems, it can be possible to avoid the faults of governance and thus improve policy decisions. Europeanisation of local governance seems a likely policy area for the application of Rose's theoretical model as it has already become apparent that, throughout the UK, responses to Europeanisation in one Region may well benefit another Region. In the case of the North East of England, this model may be a useful way of explaining the transfer of ideas between agencies, so the PhD research will focus on Europeanisation of the Region. In the process it will also seek to identify how different agencies may, or may not learn from each other in this policy domain.

Closely related to this is an ESRC two-year study of the Europeanisation of Local Governance and responses in Local Economic Development. This involves in-depth case studies of approximately 40 UK Local Authorities in order to examine how closer integration might affect the activities and functions of sub-national government in the UK followed by a wider postal survey of all other local authorities.

In order to gather the necessary information on the overall response to Europeanisation, the case studies involve two members of the four-person research team visiting each of the 40 designated local authorities (this includes those identified as *actively* European and *less actively* European) for a period of 3 to 4 days. During this time other agencies in the locality

156

that have an interest in, and an effect upon, Economic Development are also being visited Follow up visits, as necessary, are being made.Meetings in each case study authority are being conducted with Chief Executives, Leaders of the Council and other leading members who sit on relevant European committees, Chief European Officers and their staff, European Officers in other service departments and key personnel in other local and regional agencies. Eight such case studies have so far been completed.

Emerging Findings

Both studies are, therefore, at an early stage. However, a number of interesting findings have already emerged.

The PhD research has revealed a high degree of awareness of Europeanisation and a relatively high level of inter-authority and inter-agency collaboration at both sub-regional and regional levels. The region is considered by many to provide a good working model of partnership in action and key actors in the North East believe that it 'has done well out of Europe' because it has been able to present a united front to the Commission. A number of interviewees have highlighted the quality of the relationships between local authority officer and officers from central government's offices as having been particularly important.

A range of significant structural changes in some of the important organisations and agencies in the Region seem to be providing a better interface with 'Europe'. These include:-

(i)   The new unified regional offices of central government departments.

(ii)   The merger of three existing Chambers of Commerce (Tynedale, Teeside and Tyne and Wear) to become The North East Chamber of Commerce with the HQ in Durham City. It is claimed that this change is in line with the position adopted at the Eurochambres Conference where discussion centred on the recognition of a Europe des Regions.

(iii)   Local Authorities and other private and public agencies are collaborating very closely at the European level. This close relationship has led to the establishment of the Northern Assembly of Local Authorities, with a Brussels Office financed and supported by a plethora of central government agencies, quasi government agencies, local and regional bodies and the private sector.

(iv)   At the level of regional political parties there is a well-established non-partisan Campaign for a Northern Assembly supported by the Labour Party, the Liberal Democrats, and the trade unions.

The ESRC funded research has highlighted some of the key factors which promote or constrain Europeanisation within UK authorities. These are the focus of the remainder of this paper. We firstly examine those aspects of the internal management of 'European' activities which seem to have been pivotal in ensuring the success of individual authorities before considering some of the more general external factors which may play an important part in constraining the capacity of UK sub-national government as a whole to play a full role in 'Europe' in the future.

Critical Internal Success Factors for 'Europeanisation'

(i) Almost all of the local authorities described as 'actively European' have a history of applying for EU structural Funds as a way of alleviating perceived economic decline in their areas. Many established their European Teams or European Officers with the primary aim of securing finance from the EU to aid economic development.

(ii) All successful local authorities have found some way of financing and developing their European function. In some cases this is through commitment from their own authority, in other cases it is by means of European finance, and there are also instances where finance is raised by a combination of inter agency (public and private) finance.

(iii) Having moved on from obtaining structural Funds, there is clear evidence to suggest that business development activities are now at the core of European activities, for example provision of seminars on the SEM, legal advice on the effects of EU Directives, and increasingly local authorities are accessing EU Funds to develop cross-national business networks.

(iv) Most of the Chief European Officers interviewed could be described as risk-taking, dynamic, innovative and entrepreneurial. There seems to be a cadre or breed of charismatic and visionary European Officers who drive the European effort.

(v) There is a network of the Officers (mentioned in point iv) who maintain informal links with their counterparts in other authorities throughout the UK. Indeed, one interesting point to emerge from the findings is the fact that there has been a very clear pattern of mobility between authorities over the last few years. This gives some credence to Rose's 'Lesson Drawing in Public Policy Theory' as it seems to suggest that many of these Officers have gained much experience in 'Europeanising' one local authority before they move on with a range of expertise to 'Europeanise' another one.

(vi) There is not, as yet, a clear picture emerging on how important belonging to a specific professional body might be in disseminating European ideas.

(vii) In the very actively European local authorities there is clear evidence of Senior Officer backing for involvement in any new initiatives (especially CEO backing). There appears to be a corporate recognition of the importance of Europe and a willingness to let the European Officers 'get on with the job'.

(viii) Successful local authorities also seem to be characterised by strong commitment from the Leader of the Council and Chairs of the relevant European Committee or sub-committee.

(ix) A large degree of trust and informality between the European teams, the CEO and the leading members seems to be essential because there is a reliance on, and deference to, the expertise of the European Officers.

(x) Nearly all European Units have been set up by a strong European Officer over the last 10 years (mainly to access structural Funds). Over the last 5 years or so, with the necessary political backing, these Officers have surrounded themselves with a group of like-minded individuals possessing a new skills mix encompassing languages, legal, business development and research skills. Many European Units have grown from a one or two man band to larger teams of up to 15 people.

(xi) In terms of committee structures, most local authorities have some form of European committee, but in the main they are sub-committees of other main committees, for example Economic Development, Transport or Environment. In some cases, the Town Twinning aspect of international sub-committees has been subsumed under the European committees as members and officers recognise the need to move from 'handshaking' to a more strategic approach.

(xii) Actively European local authorities can be seen to have 'their act together' at many different levels:
  (a) with other local authorities in the UK
  (b) with other local authorities in their locality and region
  (c) with their sub regional partners from the public and private sector
  (d) with the European Commission
  (e) with national government at the regional level

(xiii) In terms of information flow throughout the authority, best practice seems to be very strong dissemination from a European team throughout all other service departments of the authority. There is also evidence to suggest that in very active authorities there is a strong relationship and clear information flow with businesses in the area, with external agencies like the EU, central departments and other regional and local partners.

There are many examples of extremely good relationships between local, regional, national and transnational partners.

Finally, two distinct models of Departmental structure seem to be emerging:

Model A: Service Department Led Approach to Europe

This is characterised by a European Unit instigated or formed in one of the service departments (quite often in Economic Development). This unit is usually given strong backing by other Chief Officers and Members and effectively services the other local authority departments. In some cases the establishment of a nominated European Officer in each service department then leads to an amalgamation or merging of the European function to service the whole authority.

Model B: Corporate Approach to Europe

In this model the European function is located from its inception in the Chief Executive's department. It is regarded as a central function because of the locality and each service department then uses the expertise available in this central service area. There may be designated European Officers in each service department who meet as a working group with the Senior European Officer from the central department as the Chairperson but this is mainly for the dissemination of information. The decisions on European strategic direction rest with the European Department.

External Constraints On Europeanisation

In spite of the considerable progress made by many authorities in responding to Europeanisation, there are a number of important external influences which may limit the ability of British local authorities to play a fuller role in the future development of Europe, even if they have in place all of the critical success factors which have been identified above. Three seem likely to be of particular importance.

The Structure of Local Government

Britain continues to be out of step with most of its EU partners in not having a constitutional regional tier of sub-national government. The increasing emphasis placed by the Commission upon the need for a regional response to its policies adds an international dimension to the domestic debate about the structure of local government. There is growing concern the existing English and Welsh counties and Scottish 'regions' are too small to present an effective 'voice' in Europe, and that a move towards smaller unitary authorities will make it even harder for sub-national government to establish effective working relationships with EU institutions and policy makers (ACC, 1992; Martin and Pearce, 1994).

The present British government's 'principled and political opposition to regionalism' (Moore, 1992), represents perhaps the greatest impediment to the further Europeanisation of UK sub-national government. There is no sign of a willingness in Whitehall to extend

160

the principle of subsidiary beyond its own relationship with the Community, a stance which was backed up by the Edinburgh Summit declaration at the end of 1992. Central government continues to guard jealously its role as 'gatekeeper' to the Union, and whilst in some areas such as the North East there are good relationships between local authorities and regional offices, the new 'unified' regional offices of the DTI, DOE, DE and DTp from April 1994 are seen by some as enhancing of the dominant position of central government administration (Morphet, 1992).

Resource Limitations

Many local authorities in the UK have received significant amounts of EU financial assistance. However, these resources remain thinly spread. Despite reforms, the Common Agricultural Policy continues to dominate the Community budget to the detriment of the UK. Germany unification led to resources being spread more thinly and the rejection of increases in the structural Funds envisaged in the original 'Delors package' has meant that, though enlarged, the ERDF and ESF for 1994 to 1999 will not be as large as some UK regions had hoped. In addition, the benefits of obtaining EU funds may in practice be limited because of the lack of additionality which has, until now, been attached to ERDF receipts, and the inability of UK authorities to raise the matching funding which is required in order to 'draw down' EU assistance.

The Lack of a 'Participative Tradition'

A further widespread constraint upon UK local authorities is that it has proved difficult to persuade local economic and social elites to become fully involved in 'European issues', particularly where tangible benefits are not immediately apparent. The fragmentation of traditional local authority functions, and the Commission's insistence on the greater involvement of 'social partners', has meant that local authorities will have to work increasingly with other regional actors. However, the participative tradition which exists in some member states seems to be largely absent in many UK regions. In particular, local Chambers of Commerce lack the statutory basis and funds of their German and French counterparts and, despite the growth of private-public partnerships, many businesses remain wary of collaboration with local government. The lack of a strong corporate tradition in the UK at either national or sub-national levels has been emphasised by the withdrawal of state aid for businesses, which in conjunction with the transfer of public services to newly formed quangos, unaccountable to elected local government and which, elsewhere, might have formed part of a regional tier of government, implies that Britain may be unable to participate fully in a 'Europe of the Regions' should this eventually emerge within the Union.

Nevertheless, there are some positive signs, and a growing number of local authorities report involvement in 'European issues'. In the longer term, these trends must be seen in the context of the much wider debate both at EU and national level, regarding subsidarity, upon which the outcome of attempts to shift power away from national towards sub-central government will ultimately depend.

Note: This paper is based in part on some of the preliminary findings of a two year study of the Europeanisation of local governance which the authors are undertaking with two colleagues at Aston Business School - Tanya Crook and Graham Pearce. They acknowledge the ESRC's financial support for this work.

References

Association of County Councils (1992) *The New Europe: Implications for UK Local Government, London.*

Audit Commission (1992) *A Rough Guide to Europe* (HMSO: London).

Commission of the European Communities (1990) *XXIIIrd Annual Report on the* Activities of the European Commission 1989 (Office for Official Publications of the European Communities, Luxembourg.

Cullingworth, J.B. (1970) *Town and Country Planning in England and Wales* (Allen and Unwin) p.297.

John, P. (1994) *The Europeanisation of British Local Government: New Opportunities and Management Strategies* (Joseph Rowntree Foundation, York).

Keating, M. (1992) 'Regional Autonomy in the Changing State Order: a Framework of Analysis', *Regional Politics and Policy, 2* (3) pp.45-61.

Local Government International Bureau (1991) *Responding to the Challenge of EC Law,* Paper Number 9 (London: LGIB).

Luhmann, N. (1982) *The Differentiation of Society* (NY: Columbia University Press) pp.353-5.

Martin, S.J. and Pearce, G.R. (1992a) 'The Internationalisation of Economic Development Strategies', *Regional Studies, 26* (5).

Martin, S.J. and Pearce, G.R. (1992b) 'European Regional Development Strategies and the Europeanisation of Sub-national Government', *Regional Studies, 27* (6).

Martin, S.J. and Pearce, G.R. (1994) 'Implications of Local Government Review for Local Authority European Functions', *Local Government Policy Making* (Forthcoming).

Moore, C. (1992) 'Regional Government in the UK: Proposals and Prospects', *Regional Politics and Policy, 2* (4).

Morphet, J. (1992) 'Mandarins Lay Strategy to Seize the Regional Ground', *Planning 989.*

Rhodes, R. (1988) *Beyond Westminster and Whitehall* (Unwin Hyman).

Rose, R. (1993) *Lesson Drawing in Public Policy* (Chatham House Publishers) pp.77-117.

162

INTRODUCING BUSINESS PLANNING TO FACILITATE FIREFIGHTING

Darrell Davies, West Yorkshire Fire & Civil Defence Authority

Introduction

This paper aims to pass on some of the issues raised, procedures adopted and lessons learned during a local authority fire service's first tentative steps on the road to a Business Planning culture within the West Yorkshire Fire and Civil Defence Authority.

I shall begin by recalling the first question I asked myself, when presented with the task of initiating my Authority's first formal business planning process, namely..."Is it possible, in the setting of a local authority fire service, to produce a Business Plan in the purest sense of the term?" I did not know it at that time, but Ray Puffit, Senior Lecturer at the Institute of Local Government Studies at the University of Birmingham, had already asked himself a similar question and the answer he arrived at was "no". He said that he believed that the private sector Business Plan/Business Planning Process was designed primarily to address the following issues (Puffit, 1993):

> What price is the entrepreneur prepared to pay for the factors of production, such as labour, equipment and premises, and exactly how is the entrepreneur going to mix these factors of production together in order to yield a surplus (profit) between the factors of production and the market price that the customer is prepared to pay?

There is, at present, no interest being shown by any entrepreneur to compete with my brigade, but then who would ever have predicted that any entrepreneur would come forward and capture a corner of the HM Prison market? The fact remains that, at this time, fire service managers have only a limited influence on the price of their fire service. This price is fixed by the elected members of the West Yorkshire Fire and Civil Defence Authority - the Fire Authority. They decide the price based on political and moral grounds. It is the role of the fire service managers to advise the Chief Fire Officer/Chief Executive, who in turn advises the Fire Authority on all matters to do with the delivery of the services, but it is always the Fire Authority who make the final decision on price.

If we are correct in our belief that it is impossible, in the setting of a local authority fire service, to produce a Business Plan in the purest sense of the term, can it also be true that Business Planning in an alternative sense of the term is possible? The answer to this question is an emphatic "yes!". It is possible to identify, adapt, and integrate many Business Planning principles in order to produce a document which will further assist the elected members in critical decision making about the future survival of the Fire Authority as the sole provider of the fire service needs of the West Yorkshire community.

Service, rather than business, is a key word for strategic planners in organisations similar to mine because it focuses on the raison d'être of the organisation. In the case of the Fire Authority this is derived principally from the legal directions on the provision of fire services outlined in the Fire Services Act 1947, section 1(i) which states:

It shall be the duty of every fire authority to make provision for firefighting purposes and in particular every fire authority shall secure:

- the services for their area of such a fire brigade and such equipment as may be necessary to meet *efficiently* all normal requirements.
- the *efficient* training of the fire brigade.
- *efficient* arrangements for dealing with calls for assistance...and for summoning members of the fire brigade.
- *efficient* arrangements for obtaining... information required for firefighting purposes.
- *efficient* arrangements for ensuring that reasonable steps are taken to prevent or mitigate damage to property resulting from measures taken in dealing with fires.
- *efficient* arrangements for giving, when requested, advice in respect of buildings and other property... as to fire prevention, restriction of the spread of fires, and the means of escape from fires.

It can be seen that the section 1(i) of the Act makes numerous references to *efficiency*, but in the 1990's we would be more inclined to focus on the three key aspects of high-quality service, namely, efficiency, effectiveness and economy.

What then do we mean by *Service Planning?* Service Planning means the Fire Authority's coordinated short/long-term planning of its entire resources and activities in order to achieve a desired future. Service Planning is concerned with helping to decide on the action to take *now* in order to ensure the effectiveness of the organisation as a whole. Service Planning for the Fire Authority is concerned with what, where, how and why.

The Service Plan is the document, crystallised from the process of Service Planning, setting out in detail, at a particular point in time, the resources, management strategies and action programmes necessary to provide the best possible fire service to the public of West Yorkshire. The framework of the Business Plan can be separated into four distinct stages, and it can be readily adapted into a framework suitable for a Service Plan (Richardson and Jennings, 1988):

- Stage I - where we've been and where we are now.
- Stage II - where we are now and where we want to be.
- Stage III - where we want to be and how we intend to get there.
- Stage IV - how we intend to get there - in full detail.

Thus, the process of business planning is aimed at ensuring that an organisation anticipates and adapts safely and successfully to its future environments. However, before we got carried away with evangelical zeal for Service Planning we had to address the question of cost. Service Planning is not cheap - it demands a substantial investment of thought, time, money and effort. It represents a significant financial expenditure at a time of shrinking budgets. It also represents the beginning of a move to a new organisational culture. Add on to this the awareness that Service Planning will not guarantee success, and the prudent newcomer is induced to consider a pilot scheme as the first step in the transformation of organisation culture.

Although Service Planning will not guarantee success, the lack of it is likely to increase the chances of lost opportunities and, in the worst scenario, may lead to the destruction of the Fire Authority as we know it. The intention is that Service Planning in my Authority will help to develop managers to make the right decisions **now** about the future of the Authority. It is the planning process itself which will develop each manager's understanding and knowledge of service planning. The more skilled managers become at Service Planning, the more likely it is that it will become a familiar and valuable tool to aid them in their tasks.

The Technical Services' Service Planning Model

We decided to construct a Service Planning Model, and we agreed that the people likely to benefit most from the pilot scheme would be those in the Technical Services Department. This is accordingly where the first process is being implemented. If this first project proves to be successful in this Department, then we intend to develop Service Planning across the whole of the Fire Authority. The Technical Services Department has responsibility for the functions of Technical Services, Transport, Communications, Information Technology, Property Management, Supplies, Research and Development and Brigade Safety.

Top of the list of candidates for the introduction of a Sevice Planning process within Technical Services was Transport. The Local Government Act 1988 provides that a wide range of local authority services should be open to competitive tendering at regular intervals. The Act states, amongst other things, that the maintenance of fire service vehicles is to be subjected to market testing in preparation for Compulsory Competitive Tendering (CCT). Clearly, the Fire Authority wishes to ensure that its Transport Section continues to provide it with its transport needs. CCT represents a substantial threat to the Fire Authority Transport Section. Hence, producing a winning Service Plan has never been more important to the survival of the Transport Section, and this also goes for the whole Technical Section.

The Technical Services' Service Plan.

The three fundamental approaches to the system of Business Planning are, 'top down', 'bottom up' and a combination of 'top down' and 'bottom-up'" planning (this mixed approach being referred to as the 'team approach'). The Service Planning approach most appropriate for Technical Services is the team approach because this enables the Head of Department and all of the Department's managers and decision makers to contribute to and become part of the whole planning process. The team needs to consist of the *contributors* (any person who can contribute to the success of the Service Planning process), the *evaluators* (a combination of self-evaluation done prior to submitting the contribution, and final evaluation done by the senior managers) and the *constructors* (the people who design the format of the document in readiness for publication).

As someone charged with the job of making Service Planning work, I knew that the Head of Technical Services was a believer in Service Planning but I was less sure about the individual section managers' attitudes to the Service Planning process and its implementation in their parts of the organisation. Accordingly, I decided to meet face-to-face with managers and found that reactions to the concept of Business Planning covered the whole range of possible reactions. As one might expect, they were all extremely busy people and prone to falling into the trap of allowing the urgent to take priority over the important. Their reactions to the idea of Service Planning varied from the wildly enthusiastic ("about time too, when can we start!") to indifference ("interesting, but what about these more important problems - when am I to get some computer training") to the mildly interested ("interesting, but we don't need it do we?" and, "you don't mean us do you?") to the extremely hostile ("I've been in charge of this Section for twenty years and I've heard all this management rubbish before, you can tell the Deputy Chief to ..."). Of course, if the Technical Services managers have difficulty in understanding or accepting the concepts of Service Planning for the Fire Authority then there is little chance that it will create improvements for our customers - and as is becoming increasingly clear, we operate in an era where the customer needs to be treated as 'King'.

Implementation of the Service Planning Process

The Service Planning sequence we chose was:
- the provision of introductory meetings and a help-line.

166

- the setting up of planning teams (consisting of "our" people and "my people" - I solicited help from academic experts from the Institute of Local Government Studies at the University of Birmingham, and from Sheffield Business School, Sheffield Hallam University and I read some books in the field of Corporate/Strategic Planning such as Johnson and Scholes (1988), Steiner (1976) and Argenti (1974)).
- the setting up of planning timetables and deadlines.
- the setting up of workshops to design and carry out 'performance analysis', a process involving the setting up of performance objectives, standards and criteria for the forthcoming Service Planning period, and the designing of the service statement, and primary and secondary objectives for the Department.
- the production of a co-ordinated action programme.
- the setting up of planning, monitoring, review and revision systems.

The Service Plan we are constructing in the above way is intended to be simple. The plan, ultimately, should possess the following features:
- it must be understood by all management.
- it must lead to conclusions and objectives.
- it must be moderately accurate having avoided the temptation of wasting time and effort on pedantic accuracy.
- it must state fairly and objectively strengths and weaknesses; strengths must be strengthened and weaknesses must be eliminated.
- it must prepare managers for action.
- it must provide all managers (and interested parties) with a fuller knowledge of Technical Services and its potential.
- it must provide the means for managers to convert the plan into action
- it must be the expression of the commitment of managers to convert the plan into action.
- it must be capable of being monitored.

The Service Planning Checklist

After a series of introductory meetings, each Section manager was given access to their own copy of the *Service Planning Guide*. The document had been amended earlier in order to avoid it appearing too much to be 'instructions from above' as compared to our desire that it should act as a valuable aid to managers and Fire Authority decision makers when used as a systematic and sequential Service Planning aid to be worked through topic by topic, or dipped into from time to time for explanations and clarification of one or more aspect of the Service Planning concepts.

The most important part of the guide was the Service Planning Checklist. This focuses on the practical aspects of the collection and analysis of Service Planning data/information (see Appendix A). A practical approach to the important task of setting section objectives is facilitated by the checklist's passage on 'Service Aims' and on the associated testing of objectives generated against criteria adapted from the Ashridge Test (Campbell and Yeung, 1990 and see Appendix B). Fire Authority managers are being encouraged to establish section (or Department) objectives and to use this test after they have re-examined the Fire Authority Service Aim.

The Fire Authority Service Aim is as follows:

> This Authority will provide a fire and rescue service that is of the highest possible quality within the resources available...our aim is to protect the life and property of all people by expert and comprehensive fire safety measures and by dealing with every call for assistance promptly and with the appropriate response of well equipped, committed and professional personnel...

> The Service Aim implies that the Fire Authority provides the public with services which aim to rescue persons from fire and other emergencies, to protect people, property and the environment, and to provide fire safety expertise.

The Fire Authority Service Aim should be the starting point from which all managers and decision makers should begin their section's Service Aim analysis and deliberations. The Service Planning Guide offers practical help on how to evaluate and test the quality of the Technical Service Section's Service Planning Aim.

The Service Objectives flow naturally from the Service Aim, and in order to assist managers in the creation of their performance objectives we have provided them with the test suggested by Ray Puffit (op. cit.). Puffit proposes that three test questions should be applied to proposed service objectives to clarify whether they rank as primary objectives, secondary objectives, or are not even objectives at all. These questions are as follows:

- *Question 1* - Under what circumstances would the Section or Department *NOT EVEN TRY* to achieve the proposed service objective?

The expected answer must be *NONE* - this is because if the proposed service objective were truly a primary objective, then it must be part of the fundamental purpose of the Authority and as such, regardless of the circumstances prevailing on the Authority, it would at least TRY to achieve the objective.

If the proposed objective fails to give the expected answer the clear implication is that the proposed objective is not a Primary Objective. Even when the answer is *NONE* on this question, it is vital that the next part of the test is carried out before it is possible to accurately determine whether it is a Secondary Objective or not even an objective at all.

- *Question 2* - Why must the Fire Station, Section or Department achieve the proposed objective?

The expected answer must be..." in order to survive as an Authority or withstand fundamental criticism". If the answer obtained was significantly different to the expected answer, then again it would suggest that it is not Primary Objective. However it is still necessary to complete the final question before it is possible to determine accurately whether the objective being scrutinised is a Secondary Objective or not an objective at all.

- *Question 3* - If the Fire Station, Section or Department failed to achieve the proposed objective, would the Authority also fail as an Fire Authority or be threatened or prejudiced in the discharge of its function?

The expected answer must be *YES*. If any other answer is given, then this again tends to suggest that the proposed objective is not a Primary Objective.

The pattern of answers that emerges from this line of questioning establishes the status of the objective under review.

The Pattern of Answers

- If there is agreement with all three of the above questions this signifies that the objective is a Primary Objective.
- If there is agreement with the expected answer to Question 1, but disagreement with the expected answers to Question 2 and Question 3, then it is not a Primary or a Secondary Objective.
- If there is agreement with the expected answers to Question 2, but disagreement with the expected answers to Question 1 and Question 3, this signifies that the proposed objective is likely to be a Secondary Objective.
- If there is disagreement with all three of the above questions this signifies that the objective is neither a Primary Objective nor a Secondary Objective.

Service Planning and the Service Plan - Conclusions

Business Planning for the Fire Service came to prominence in the early 1990's and some Brigades are already working on and through their fourth 'Business Plan'. The Technical Services pilot scheme described in this paper is our first attempt at Service Planning. The majority of first-time Service Plans require reshaping and pruning to fit the available or projected resources. A Service plan without doubts or apprehension first time round should be viewed with suspicion. My guess is that it will take us between 3-5 years really to become proficient at Business Planning Techniques. Service Plans do not necessarily need to be complex but they must be tailored for the individual needs of a complex organisation such as my Authority so that the probability of achieving the agreed objectives can be assessed against the effects of both internal and external constraints.

It is now the norm for local authority fire services to be affected by change and, as a result, it is the responsibility of management in them to attempt to anticipate the changes coming and to be prepared for them. In times of stress and a confused social and economic climate the Authority with the most disciplined approach will be best able to weather the economic storm. Service Planning, and the Service Plan, equips each Fire Authority decision maker with the means to become more disciplined in management activities.

Finally, let me return to the reason for Service Planning in the West Yorkshire Fire & Civil Defence Authority - it starts and finishes with the Fire Authority Service Aim:

> This Authority will provide a fire and rescue service that is of the highest possible quality within the resources available...our aim is to protect the life and property of all people by expert and comprehensive fire safety measures and by dealing with every call for assistance promptly and with the appropriate response of well equipped, committed and professional personnel...

This aim is timeless, in that it can never be achieved; rather it is something which the West Yorkshire Fire & Civil Defence Authority is continually striving to attain. Professor Peter Drucker (1990) said..."to make service institutions and service staff perform does not require genius... it requires first, clear objectives and goals. It also requires organised abandonment of the obsolete".

It is a matter of..."turning ploughs into swords"...it is time to re-examine some of our more agricultural methods of planning for the future and fashion them into precision instruments to strike at the heart of the difficulties facing the Fire Authority. Service Planning is central to my Brigade's survival strategy. More than ever before we need to Service Plan as a matter of survival.

Service Planning is facilitating firefighting - our aim is to ensure that the only firefighting that is taking place is in response to 999 calls - there is no place for firefighting at the fire station or in the office or in the Board Room.

References

Argenti, J. (1974) *Systematic Corporate Planning* (Nelson Publishing).

Campbell & Yeung. (1990) *Do You Need a Mission Statement?* (Economist Publications).

Drucker, P. F. (1990) *Managing the Non-Profit Organisation* (Heinemann).

Puffit, R. (1993) *Business Planning and Marketing* (Longmans).

Richardson, B. & Jennings, P. L. (1988) *Both Sides of the Business Plan* (Sheffield Business School).

Scholes, K. & Klemm, M. (1987) *An Introduction to Business Planning* (Macmillan Education).

Steiner, G. (1976) *Strategic Planning* (Macmillan Publishing).

Appendix A

Service Planning - Performance Management - Performance Analysis

Part A - Your Service Planning Team (continue on a separate sheet if necessary)

Fire Station/Department/ Section	
The Service Planning Team	
Contact Manager/Officer	
Telephone Extension	

Part B - Your Service Planning Timetable (continue on a separate sheet if necessary)

State the timetable set for the production of the Service Plan - comment on any timetable changes would you suggest for the next Service Planning period:

Part C - The description of Section, (continue on a separate sheet if necessary)

Provide a brief word picture of the Fire Station, Section or Department:

Part D - The Service Aim and associated objectives (continue on a separate sheet if necessary)

State the Fire Station, Section/Department Service Aim, including associated objectives - refer to the Fire Authority Service Aim first:

Part E - The "Resources Analysis" (continue on a separate sheet if necessary)

> Financial Resources (eg the budget allocations, expenditure and income statements including salaries etc - also comment on the effect these resources have in assisting toward the achievement of the performance targets and the service statement rather than simply listing the resources available):

> Physical Resources (eg buildings/rooms, machinery, fixtures and fittings,stocks - comment on the suitability of these items in assisting toward the achievement of the performance targets and the service aim rather than simply listing them):

> Human Resources (eg the management structure - including any temporary or permanent changes - numbers and names of personnel, knowledge, experience and qualifications held by your personnel - comment on their capacity and capability to enable each of them (and the team as a whole) to assist in the achievement of the service aim:

> Systems Resources (eg briefly describe any systems, either formal or informal, for managing the resources available to you in order to ensure that performance targets and the service aim are achieved. Comment on the effect these physical resources have in assisting toward the achievement of the performance targets and the service statement rather than simply listing the systems resources available:

> Intangible Resources (eg comment on the morale, aspirations and commitment of your personnel. Comment on the effect these resources have in assisting toward the achievement of the performance targets and the service aim rather than simply listing the intangible resources available:

173

Part F - Your Section's SWOT Analysis (continue on a separate sheet if necessary)

> List strengths, weaknesses, opportunities or threats affecting your performance and targets:

Part G -Past Performance (continue on a separate sheet if necessary)

> List the major tasks and performance levels achieved in the past - 3 years to 5 years is desirable, but if that is impractical comment on the previous year - comment on the completions, partial completions and those which were cancelled (if any):

Part H -Future Performance Performance/Targets (continue on a separate sheet if necessary)

> List, in order of priority, the performance standards and targets you intend to achieve during the next Service Planning period - consider 1 year, 3 year, and 5 year Service Planning periods if possible, but if that is impractical focus on an annual Service Planning period - make comments on any foreseeable critical factors which will substantially affect these performance standards and targets and the achievement of the Service Aim:

174

Appendix B

Service Planning - Do You Have a Good Service Aim?

*Answer each question O = No, 1 = To some degree, 2 = Yes			
Purpose Does the statement adequately describe the ultimate rationale of the Section ? Does the statement describe the Section's responsibility to each Section within the Authority and the Fire Authority as a whole?			
Strategy Does the statement adequately define the activities designed to ensure that the Section always gives of its best? Does the statement make reference to CCT and/or associated potential competitors?			
Values Does the statement identify values that link it with the Fire Authority's purpose and act as beliefs that employees can feel proud of? Do the values complement and reinforce the Fire Authority's Service Planning strategy?			
Behaviour standards Does the statement describe important behaviour standards that serve as "beacons" of the strategy and the values? Are the behaviour standards described in a way that enables individual staff to judge whether they have behaved correctly or not?			
Character Does the statement give a portrait of the Section depicting its culture and it's cultural relationship with the Fire Authority? Is the whole statement easy to read and understand?			
Total score			
Maximum score is 20; good score 15; poor score less than 10			

CULTURE CHANGE THROUGH TRAINING IN A HEALTH SERVICE CONTEXT

Graeme Currie, Derbyshire Business School

Background

The teambuilding training was carried out against a background of change in the health service. This was initiated by two government White Papers; *Working for Patients*[1] and *Care in the Community*[2]. The former emphasised the business management of health service provision. The latter promoted community care rather than ward-based care for the mentally ill and geriatrics.

The second White Paper, in particular, necessitated the co-operation of professionals from different disciplines and different agencies, for example housing and social services as well as health authorities, in order to meet organisational objectives. Health professionals would now be required to participate in, and in some cases to lead, effective and efficient multi-disciplinary teams. Hence, a culture change was required to support the business emphasis and greater teamworking.

Training Intervention

The training intervention took place within athe Family and Preventative Services Unit of a District Health Authority. This unit could be regarded as the community arm of the health authority. It was responsible for ten community health centres and the neighbourhood teams which worked out of these centres. The unit also covered the area of geriatrics, providing ward-based and community care.

The training programme itself consisted of five modules, each lasting one day, which covered those skills areas deemed to be essential to the effective working of teams. These areas were leadership, motivation, problem-solving and decision-making, group dynamics and handling conflict, and had been identified by a senior management group in conjunction with the training department. The training came under the broad heading of 'Organisation

177

and Management Development'. This indicated that on the surface at least there was senior management commitment to the training. It was also a recognition that the training needed to be integrated with cultural change.

Rationale for Training

It was felt strongly by senior management that the clinicians who were given responsibility for leading teams often lacked the knowledge and skills to do so. Their professional training had equipped them with clinical rather than managerial skills. There was recognition that training needed to be supported by organisation development initiatives such as quality circles and task forces in order to facilitate cultural change necessary for different modes of teamworking and for a more business-like emphasis.

Selection of Participants

The programme was aimed at first line and middle managers. As there was a re-organisation taking place, individuals who were potential as well as actual team leaders were nominated. In all, 30 potential or actual team leaders participated in the programme. Participants included district nurses, health visitors, neighbourhood health team managers, occupational therapists, physiotherapists and ward nurses.

Modes of Delivery

Courses were classroom based, and a variety of techniques were used. Individual self-assessment questionnaires, groupwork with feedback, roleplaying, videos, lecturettes and action plans were complemented by icebreakers and rejuvenators in order to create the right environment for relaxation and participation.

Working Theme

As a working theme for analysis, Mintzbergs' work on configurations was examined. A district health authority is an example of a professional bureaucracy, as identified by Mintzberg. For those readers who are unfamiliar with Mintzbergs' work in this area, there follows a summary of the characteristics of a professional bureaucracy:
- Standards originate largely outside its own structure and its operators join with their colleagues from other professional bureaucracies in self-governing associations.

- Professional bureaucracies cannot rely extensively on the formalisation of professional work, or on systems to plan and control it. The professionals' close relationship with their clients means freedom from having to respond to managerial orders.
- Thus, managerial attempts to influence professionals radically are unlikely to be successful, and this includes management development interventions.

Reference must also be made to other configurations identified by Mintzberg. Of particular interest are those of the machine bureaucracy and adhocracy. Briefly, a machine bureaucracy is a structure that rates high in complexity, formalisation and centralisation whereas an adhocracy is a structure characterised as low in complexity, formalisation and centralisation.

As a result of the business management emphasis, structures and processes were being converted into machine bureaucracies. Such conversion resulted in temporary forms within some parts of the organisation which were reflective of adhocracy. Thus, there was a combination of configurations within the same organisation comprising professional bureaucracy, machine bureaucracy and adhocracy. The concepts of a combination of configurations, and of conversion from one to another, are useful for understanding where management development is likely to meet with success.

We must also refer to Mintzbergs' later work which emphasised that forces for efficiency and innovation were becoming more evident than the force for proficiency in the professional bureaucracy. The idea of forces pulling in different directions emphasises that the organisational environment is dynamic rather than static. It would suggest that business management can influence the responses of clinicians to management development by integrating other changes alongside management development.

Using Mintzbergs' ideas, we can seek to identify the structural variables in terms of differing configurations and forces which influence the success of management development initiatives.

Evaluation of Training[3]

At the end of each training module, an action plan was drawn up regarding intended actions. These formed the basis of the action plan which was drawn up at the end of the programme. Six months following the end of the programme, the action plans were followed up through the medium of a self-report form for participants, which focussed on the end of programme action plan. By this means, the transfer of learning between classroom and workplace could be evaluated.

Quantitative evaluation complemented the approach outlined above. A questionnaire based on Woodcocks'[4] teambuilding blocks was completed prior to the commencement of the programme and again six months following the end of the programme. Statistical analysis (Wilcoxson test)[5] was carried out to assess the degree of change. In conjunction with these approaches, observation was carried out on a day-to-day basis.

The evaluation strategy outlined represented a practical, even opportunistic, response to a situation which was political. By political we mean, firstly, the precedence given by participants to clinical duties over managerial duties in a professional bureaucracy, including management development. The divide between attitudes towards clinical and non-clinical aspects of the job must be recognised in the design of the evaluation. Secondly, we mean the role that the district training function undertakes following government reforms. In this case, the role was one of internal consultant and change agent.

The implication of the political situation was that the evaluation strategy should minimise time spent by participants and their managers in order not to compromise clinical requirements. This had an impact upon the methods and techniques utilised for evaluation. Action plans followed by structured self-reports, and questionnaires with statistical analysis were used and represented methodological triangulation. This maximised data collected without causing resentment by participants and their managers in respect of the time taken to respond.

There were problems associated with this opportunistic evaluation strategy. There was the contamination of responses over a six-month period due to non-attibutable factors such as the heightening of awareness following training and suspicion regarding confidentiality of evaluation. The action gap may have been lengthier than allowed for, and unanticipated outcomes may have been missed. The training intervention was also rendered less effective as a whole. Such problems cannot be denied, and there may be other potential evaluation strategies, such as post-course projects or diaries with line manager involvement which the trainer would wish to explore. However, the research emphasises that political considerations represent a constraint upon rigorous evaluation strategies.

Results of the Programme

Examining questionnaire responses as a whole, it can be concluded that there was a significant improvement in team behaviour as desired by the organisation. Success was also evident in respect of a number of specific issues; for example there was an improvement in the participation of team members following the problem-solving and decision-making module. Given traditional professional autonomy, this represented a radical behaviour change. However, some district nurses felt a participative philosophy was not appropriate. This was the result of traditional barriers between district nurses and auxilliary nurses.

Most respondents felt able to evaluate their own roles and the roles of others within the team, and to act accordingly. In a number of cases, Belbins'[6] inventory had been used as a basis for evaluating team roles.

Where team leaders were in charge of a single professional group, such as superintendent physiotherapists and chief speech therapists, this facilitated training success. Team meetings were regular, highly participative and concensus decision-making was encouraged. Views were sought by the team leader outside meetings, and decision-making power delegated downwards where appropriate. All this indicated structures, and more importantly culture, which did not reflect the typical professional bureaucracy[7].

The post of neighbourhood health team manager provided an example of a new position in the organisation. It co-ordinated the work of professionals from different disciplines, as the organisation moved towards a machine bureaucracy. Their responses reflected the difficulty of such co-ordinating roles in bringing together professionals from different disciplines.

If action plan responses are examined, those intended actions which occurred frequently were clear objectives and agreed goals, regular review, improving inter-group relations and sound working and decision-making procedures. Intended actions which rarely appeared were being more open with each other, more support and trust, individual development of team members and appropriate leadership. This was also reflected in the incidence of actual actions. Hence, the participants on the teambuilding programme were more comfortable with notions whereby their teamwork was proceduralised rather than vague notions of openess and confrontation or support and trust. The autonomy of their professional team members was also recognised. Team leaders did not wish to take responsibility for leadership or individual development.

If individual responses are examined, there are a number of critical respondents who were illustrative of the processes and outcomes of the programme. Taking a typical example of a team leader of a single discipline, dietetics, progress had been made in a number of areas. Communication channels had been changed, information sharing improved, and an internal performance review set up. The organisation of the team encouraged transfer of the philosophy put across in the teambuilding programmes. Its members were spread across a number of units within West Birmingham, and they came together as a single discipline team which was innovative and highly participative.

The action plan which was the fullest and most successfully implemented was that in the physiotherapy area of geriatrics. The approach the respondent took in formulating her action plan was one encouraged by the teambuilding programme. It involved the participation of all team members, and was reflective of the culture in this area. By way of contrast, the neighbourhood health team managers had taken the view that structural change was necessary to meet objectives identified by the team. This was indicative of a machine bureaucracy approach to the problem.

A team leader within a neighbourhood health team formed a multi-disciplinary task force in order to improve communication. Thus we can conclude that team leaders participating in the programme made the transfer of learning from the classroom to the workplace. F.P.S.U. was more progressive to the extent that it had moved towards meeting objectives outlined in the White Papers, and was more orientated towards community care. It had moved away from the archetype professional bureaucracy structures and culture. The teambuilding programme was successful because the unit reflected the culture of a machine bureaucracy, and even an adhocracy in parts.

The multi-disciplinary nature of the teams, and the fact that they were neighbourhood-based, encouraged behaviour which was not previously brought out during professional training and socialisation. Structure and culture impacted upon the success of the programme, as we might expect. Specifically, multi-disciplinary teams moving towards a machine bureaucracy were less likely to resist actions as a result of the teambuilding programme. Some single-discipline teams were also seen successfully to implement the desired behaviour changes because of the democratic way in which they operated.

Problems Associated with the Teambuilding Programme

Although the teambuilding programme was successful judged on questionnaire and action plan responses, observation identified a number of problems. For example, the organisational climate on return to the workplace did not support transfer of learning. This may have been due to the managers in the area, but more often stemmed from team members. For example, district nurses and auxilliary nurses were not accustomed to participative decision-making.

Transfer of learning was also hindered by the control over their actions that participants have back at work. In a highly-proceduralised environment such as a geriatric ward, only incremental change was possible. Operational aspects of the job were often assigned a priority over self-development. Many participants carried very heavy caseloads as a result of financial constraints in the health service. This was also related to the fact that a clinician is judged by what goes wrong so far as health care of a client is concerned.

Some professionals were isolated by the nature of their jobs, such as health visitors. They were more likely to resist behaviour consistent with a multi-disciplinary team situation. There was a lack of commitment from some participants on the programme. Some were not clear why they were attending, particularly those who were potential rather than actual team leaders. In some cases unsuitable participants had been nominated. The geriatrics area had taken the view that this was not an integrated programme and sent different participants on different modules. They sent those who were less valuable on the ward, or who needed a break from the job. Often such nominees were older, stuck in their ways and at the lower end of the organisation. This represented a traditional response from a ward-based area in a professional bureaucracy towards management development initiatives.

182

This was reinforced by a few of the participants who brought in an attitude of 'us and them'. They saw the trainer as representing management, and on a number of occasions used the training session to voice their grievances about the increasing business emphasis of the health service.

Finally, variables associated with the participants learning style caused some problems. The learning style[8] of participants tended to be passive, reflecting previous professional training and socialisation. Some participants found reflection upon previous experiences difficult to carry out. They found groupwork and discussion threatening.

Conclusion

Radical behaviour change was dependent upon a number of contingent factors. In some cases, structural change towards machine bureaucracy or adhocracy initiated by the organisation facilitated behaviour change. In other cases, conditions which supported behaviour change were almost accidental in their occurrence. What is meant by this is that they were not encouraged by any explicit organisational strategy. For instance, it was often down to the individual participant in the teambuilding programme, and his or her personal management style.

The most radical behaviour change took place in single-discipline teams which had existed for a long time prior to any ideas of teambuilding. In general, behaviour changes were not of a radical nature, but were of a type which fitted in with existing culture. This existing culture was one of working in a formal proceduralised environment. Any change beyond this was unlikely, and further inhibited by lack of commitment from participants on the programme.

Comparision With Other Units

To reinforce the lessons drawn from the training intervention in the Family and Preventative Services Unit, it is worth examining the success of training interventions in other units; that is, the General Acute and Maternity Services Unit (G.A.M.S.), and the Single Specialty Acute Unit (S.S.A.U.). Within G.A.M.S., problem-solving and decision-making training had relatively limited response in terms of behaviour change. The scientific/rational approach put forward should have fitted in with the professional bureaucracy. However, the participative nature of the problem-solving model was contrary to existing professional ways of working which discriminated on the basis of expertise. In addition, formalised procedures and organisational hierarchy in the unit constituted a barrier to transfer of learning. More general interpersonal skills such as communication, assertiveness and presentation skills were more readily adopted by participants and transferred back to the workplace. Such behaviour changes were less dependent on structural and cultural factors.

Within S.S.A.U., team briefing was introduced in order to improve communication in the unit. Communication was perceived as relatively effective prior to team briefing where structure was moving towards machine bureaucracy. This was particularly true where a businesslike culture was increasingly evident in place of the professional culture. Audiology services was a prime example of this. Improvements in these areas were greater following the introduction of team briefing.

Those areas whose structure and culture reflected the archetypal professional bureaucracy perceived communication to be initially poor. In addition, they were resistant to the impact of team briefing. Examples of such areas were the specialist eye and skin hospitals. Within S.S.A.U., senior management were attempting to effect changes in the structures and cultures in the unit. They were moving away from the professional bureaucracy towards machine bureaucracy. They had been successful in non-clinical areas, such as transport and catering, but made little impact upon specialist hospitals. The impact of team briefing mirrored this.

To summarise, structural and cultural factors influence the types of management development interventions that are successful. G.A.M.S. approximated to the archetypal professional bureaucracy. Thus, radical training interventions such as participative decision-making will not be transferred back to the workplace. Within S.S.A.U., favourable responses were a result of the configuration of the work area. For example, the transport department was akin to a machine bureaucracy rather than a professional bureaucracy. Unfavourable responses were the result of an autonomous, isolated and professional environment. Examples of such an environment were the specialist eye and skin hospitals.

References

1. Government White Paper (1988) *Working with Patients* (London: HMSO).
2. Griffiths, R. (1988) *Community Care - Agenda for Reform* (London: HMSO).
3. Easterby-Smith, M. (1980) *Evaluation of Management Education, Training and Development* (Gower).
4. Woodcock, M. (1980) *Team Development Manual* (Gower).
5. Greene, J. and D'Oliveira (1990) *Learning to Use Statistics in Psychology* (Open University).
6. Belbin, R. M. (1981) *Management Teams, Why They Succeed Or Fail* (Heinemann).
7. Mintzberg, H. (1989) *Mintzberg on Management* (Free Press).
8. Honey, P. and Mumford, A. (1986) *Manual of Learning Styles* (Honey).
9. French, W. L. and Bell, C. H. (1990) *Organisation Development - Behavioural Science Interventions for Organisational Improvement* (Prentice Hall).

STRATEGIC DECISION-MAKING: ISLE OF MAN

Jacqui Yates, Sheffield Business School

Introduction

The neo-classical economic view of strategic decision-making sees decision-makers choosing strategic developments for their organisations which optimise the organisation's performance. In this theoretical perspective complete knowledge, precise computational ability and an over-riding desire to profit-maximise work together to achieve rational decisions.

In contrast, many management theorists of the *contingency* school see the present activities, structures and processes of organisations as having been shaped by the effects, in combination, of a range of 'strategic pull' (1) or situational contingency (2, 3, 4) factors. 'Rationality', for such theorists, is less to do with the making of economic optimising choices and more to do with the state of informed decision-making which the strategists achieve. The need, from this perspective, is one of generating and making sense of the important decisional variables so that 'best fitting' choices over strategic developments can be made. From the contingency perspective, the choosing of strategic developments is often a very messy and ambiguous process which involves making sense of, and decisions about, a range of interactive social and political as well as economic variables.

Factors which these contingency theorists have raised as being important influences behind the present strategic situation of a particular body include:

- the history, tradition and age of the organisation.
- its dominant culture.
- the values of its people and the society in which it operates.
- the people who are influential in the organisation's decision-making processes.
- its product and market operations.
- the nature of the environment in which the organisation operates.

185

These factors also influence the future developments that an organisation will pursue.

This paper provides a discussion of the strategic development of the Isle of Man community as it moves through a decade in which environmental changes seem likely to affect this development and so increase the need for governmental strategists to take it into account in the context of other situational variables. In this way, in accord with the assumptions of the strategic planning movement, strategists might expect to reach better decisions on how the community should develop.

In providing this discussion, the paper will utilise the framework created by the above 'situational variables' and will indicate the multi-variable and difficult processes that can characterise strategic decision-making in governmental contexts. The major strategic issue upon which this paper focuses is that of the nature of the relationship between the Isle of Man and the European Union (ex-Community).

The Isle of Man: Strategic Situation Variables

History, Tradition and Age

The Island's Celtic and Viking history established political behaviour and institutions which are still in existence today. The Island's parliament, Tynwald, is of Viking origin and is certainly one of the oldest in the world. From the thirteenth century the Island became a pawn in a game of war between Scotland and England, with control passing back and forward between the two nations. Sovereignty passed to the English Crown at the beginning of the fifteenth century and for nearly four centuries the Island was governed under an hereditary Lordship.

In the eighteenth century the Island's offshore independence made it a major centre for the smuggling trade, causing a considerable loss of revenue to the English Treasury. As a result in 1765, the British Government bought the Island for £70,000. With this Act of Revestment began a period of subjugation to the British Crown, and it was not until the mid-1800s that the Island regained a measure of control over its internal finances. Since that time political power has gradually devolved from London to the Island, and an old colonial-style administration has given way to a relatively modern democratic government. Its long history of independence combines with strong Royalist traditions to produce a set of institutions with ancient and modern facets. The Tynwald has an upper house, the Legislative Council, elected largely from the membership of the lower House of Keys which is itself elected by popular suffrage on a modified system of proportional representation. The two houses of Tynwald sitting separately and together legislate for the Island and scrutinise the activities of the Council of Ministers led by a Chief Minister.

The Island is a Crown Dependency of the UK with its own legislative processes, subject to the requirement that it seeks the Royal Assent for legislation. It frequently apes UK legislation but is not required to do so. The UK government has ultimate responsibility for the 'good government' of the Island, and liaison with the sovereign power is through the Home Office. It has complete freedom over all taxation decisions except that of VAT which is levied at the same rate as in the UK. There is, therefore, no customs barrier between the IOM and the UK. Thus the Isle of Man has a special, free-market based relationship with its major market and supplier, the UK which is, in turn, a full member of the EU.

The IOM is not a member of the EU, nor is it an associate member. Its relationship with the Union is defined by Protocol 3 to the UK's Act of Accession 1972. The IOM is accordingly treated as part of the EU customs territory and, as a result, there are no tariff or quota barriers on the trade in goods between the IOM and EU member states, and the IOM applies EU tariffs on non-EU goods entering the Island. Further, the EU rules on trade in agricultural and fisheries products and goods processed from them are applicable to the IOM, and the UK and the IOM are treated as a single member state for the purpose of applying those rules. EU competition rules apply directly to the IOM only in respect of agricultural products.

There is nothing in the Protocol about trade in services. In all other respects the Island is treated as a third country and is therefore able to draw considerable advantages from being in the Union. However, as it is not a full member it makes no contribution to, and receives no benefit from, EU funds.

The Island is in a peripheral position both geographically and in relation to its ability to take part in major economic and political decision-making processes in Europe. The costs of peripherality are many, for example in relation to transportation, high energy prices, the absence of both domestic markets and an industrial hinterland and the lack of a qualified labour force. With the possibility of enlargement to include Austria and Hungary and the programme of assistance to former Eastern-bloc countries, the geographical centre of gravity of the Community is moving away from the Atlantic Western region. In a geographical sense, the IOM is likely to become more remote from the heartland of the EU - an off-shore island off an off-shore island.

Dominant Culture and Values of Society

The majority of Manx people are proud of their independence and have espoused their right to be different on numerous social issues from homosexuality to breath-testing for alcohol. Separate currency (at sterling value), different stamps and a distinctive culture and heritage all give testimony to the Island's desire to run its own affairs. The recent growth in the finance sector has brought a new sense of economic security to the Island though there are still those who remain sceptical about its durability and its capacity to provide the variety of forms of employment needed to meet the needs of the population. Culturally, the link with the UK is an accepted given and only a small but vociferous minority would advocate complete independence. Nevertheless, the Manx people and their governors exhibit an introverted and parochial attitude which is leading to a failure to recognise the importance of the EU as a political and economic threat and opportunity. There is a lack of awareness in government circles of the implications of EU legislation as it applies to a vast array of government services, exports and environmental matters. For example, one former Tynwald member illustrated this as follows:

> We've got this ship steaming along and no-one is steering at all...There should be a proper process of scrutiny of European legislation that charts the course for the Isle of Man. It should be going to a Committee which is capable of making a consistent series of decisions. If that ability to legislate for ourselves has any meaning then it is at that level that it works. If you're a rubber stamp, OK, but don't talk about independence -it's a pretence. (6)

Influential Decision-makers

The Tynwald is made up almost entirely of non-party independent members, many of whose politics is right-of-centre and who are concerned to maintain the Island's obviously successful independence. The government's Policy Report clearly states that its policy on constitutional development is:

> to promote and continue the evolution of the constitutional relationship between the Isle of Man and the United Kingdom towards more complete self-government and to ensure appropriate recognition of the Island's interests internationally.(7)

Most influential decision-makers on the Island accept this level of independence as given, and there is little enthusiasm to change what to date has been a successful arrangement. Where opposition occurs, it is primarily extra-parliamentary, particularly through the Celtic League and Mec Vannin, nationalist groupings within the Island. One particularly vocal opponent is the President of the Transport and General Workers Union, Bernard Moffat, who also heads civil liberties and nationalist pressure groups. His forthright views have frequently forced pro-establishment figures to re-state their viewpoints if not to re-evaluate them.

Nevertheless, Chief Minister Miles Walker and his Council of Ministers adhere to the view clearly expressed in the Policy Report and even the Alternative Policy Group makes little attempt to challenge the fundamentals of the relationship with the EU.

The considerable recent development and probable future growth of the Financial Services sector results in its representatives having an important influence on the policy-making process. The continuing diversification within the financial sector represents strength for the Island's economy although the government recognises the need for other forms of employment and for diversity in general. Companies operating in this field welcome the government's policy of not overburdening the sector with excessive bureaucracy and controls, and prefer the freedom from regulation. Nevertheless, one of the strengths of a tax haven is that it is well-regulated and thus safe for investment, and this is clearly understood by the sector.

The EU is a newer and most influential decision-maker for the Island. The EU recognises the costs of peripherality, ranging from transportation of imports and exports, high energy prices, absence of both a domestic market and an industrial hinterland to the lack of qualified labour force. The appreciation of these disadvantages of peripherality lead to direct aid in the case of the Mediterranean Projects in particular, but also in Ireland.

The particular problems of small island communities are also recognised with a Union programme of measures for the French Overseas Territories (POSEIDOM), another for Madeira and the Azores (POSEIMA) and a third for the Canary Islands (POSEICAN). Whilst the special problems of remoteness, small size and island situation are significant, in the case of these programmes there is also a recognition that there is a generally poorer level of prosperity and economic development which warrants special protective measures. In the case of the French, Dutch and British Overseas Territories, European Development Fund monies and assistance under the Lomé Convention have also been provided. The Commission's action has generally been that of protector and developer of island communities mirroring their regional development programmes generally.

In the case of the Isle of Man, its special constitutional relationship and relative prosperity have so far meant that no special assistance has been given apart from the economic advantages derived from Protocol 3 itself. The Manx government may subsidise agriculture to a level equal to the assistance that a UK farmer can receive from the national government and the EU combined. It may also subsidise manufacturers to whatever level it chooses. But the fact remains that it may not seek financial assistance from the EU for agriculture and industry. An application has recently been made for assistance with the development of a reed bed sewage treatment project on the grounds that it could prove beneficial in other parts of the EU, but this is unusual.

Whilst access to financial assistance is impossible, the Island nevertheless benefits from the free movement of manufactured and agricultural goods. The constraints on the Island arising from the Protocol 3 arrangements are the absence of free trade in services between the Island and the Union at a time when financial services form an increasingly significant part of the Island's economy, and the restrictions on Manxmen (as defined in the Protocol) preventing them from benefiting from the Community provisions relating to the free movement of persons.

The IOM is not a sovereign state and does not have the right to negotiate membership of the EU for itself. Even were it to do so, there would be disadvantages in having to make a financial contribution and having no choice but to implement the legislation jointly agreed by the member states both past and future. Membership would represent an enormous loss of decision-making sovereignty and a substantial move to the Left politically, both of which would be unacceptable to the Island community and would mean an end to fiscal independence and hence the attractions of the tax haven.

The EU has not been over-enthusiastic in dealing with applications from small states (witness the Mediterranean islands of Malta and Cyprus whose applications have been indefinitely deferred for further investigation). There is nothing to suggest that it would be any more welcoming to the IOM. The UK's position, however, is straightforward; it respects the Island's wish to choose its own constitutional status. If the IOM wishes to become completely independent or to change its present relationship, the UK government would be unlikely to prevent it. It tolerates a tax haven on its doorstep because of the advantages this brings to the British business community.

Product-Market Operations and Strategies

The traditional industries of the Island, namely farming, fishing and tourism have been in relative decline over the second half of the century. Nevertheless, they provide considerable employment and have political, social and strategic importance. The UK and increasingly the rest of the EU provide the major market for agricultural and fish products.

The manufacturing sector is the main provider of full-time employment in the Island and is second only to finance in terms of growth and contribution to the economy. Industrial concerns, ranging from small cottage industries to large factories, provide jobs for around 4,000 men and women. They export their products to the UK, continental Europe and beyond. Because of additional transport costs many successful companies concentrate on achieving a high value for their Manx-based processes.

The finance sector now contributes 35 per cent of total income and, in view of the anticipated further growth in demand for financial services and the growing reputation and status of the Isle of Man as an offshore centre, appears likely to be the area of greatest growth in the future. The rich and varied nature of the sector, including banking, insurance, asset management and trusts provides a modicum of security. In recent years the Manx Shipping Register has grown in size and importance, offering yet another facet to the service sector of the Island's economy.

The reasons for the growth in this sector are its geographic proximity to the UK, ease of establishment, good communications, capacity for growth and political stability. The affinity of the Isle of Man's culture and business practices, culture, language and law are further attractions as are the government's flexible approach, an absence of unnecessary bureaucracy and relatively low compliance costs.

For these new sectors the EU represents a major source of potential growth. The IOM government has not, however, taken an entirely coherent approach to the application of EU legislation and the awareness in government circles of the serious implications of the EU as a political and economic opportunity or threat has been too low.

A detailed report by the consultants Peat Marwick McLintock on the impact of the introduction of the Single Internal Market was produced in 1989 (8), and the Manx Government has taken on board its recommendations to monitor developments of relevance to the EU, inform relevant organisations and respond to opportunities thus identified.

Pursuant to these ideas, the government has continued its involvement with the Conference of the Peripheral and Maritime Regions of the EU (CPMR) where (particularly through the Islands Commission), the Island benefits from an exchange of ideas and experience and can lobby the Commission through the CPMR executive. As all foreign affairs are dealt with by the UK Home Office on the Island's behalf, any alternative channels of communication with the EU institutions are important, even when the IOM perspective is only one amongst many. Often fact-finding trips and inter-parliamentary conferences and meetings are a means of building contacts without risking being accused of circumventing official procedures.

With a view to building further links and raising awareness and understanding of the Union within the Island, a Euro-Club of government, business and other interests has been created which welcomes speakers as illustrious as Lord Cockburn who has close links with the Island. The Island also profits from its membership of the Irish Seas Study Group, effectively using the Republic of Ireland's EU membership as a way of presenting an alternative opinion on pollution of the Irish Sea and nuclear waste disposal at Sellafield.

Despite these initiatives awareness of the power and importance of the EU in government circles is limited and a parochial attitude prevails. Some mechanism designed to respond coherently to proposals for change at an early stage would at least prepare the Island community for changes rather than coming as a surprise.

Environmental Change

Many environmental changes effect the Island's economic and constitutional position. In concentrating here on the EU as an aspect of the environment, the cultural, political and economic antecedents to the Island's strategic choices are revealed. As noted above, in a geographical sense the IOM is likely to become more remote from the heartland of the EU. Nevertheless, an enlargement of the Union also represents an opportunity for further growth provided that the major actors in the process can recognise the potential and adapt to the changes in their environment that this represents.

Assessing the Strategic Options

The Peat Marwick McLintock consultants' terms of reference stated that Protocol 3 should continue to provide the basis for the Island's relationship with the European Union and that all recommendations should be on that basis. This was assumed on the grounds that Protocol 3 had been generally beneficial and that any change would require ratification by all member states.

However, the Island cannot afford to ignore the question of this relationship. Whilst the birth of the finance industry and its recent expansion into new sectors has brought prosperity, low unemployment and the development of service industries, there is no room for complacency. The challenge is to ensure that the Island preserves the quality of life and its natural beauty whilst promoting economic development in order to retain its young people and enable them to enjoy a comparable standard of living to the inhabitants of the EU. In order to progress as intended the Island must have something different to offer. (9) Places on the periphery do not generally do well unless they have a unique advantage; something which makes them different from the surrounding area and this really comes down to the fiscal difference. Tourism can no longer provide that advantage and agriculture is no longer a source of potential new business to boost development. The manufacturing sector is most successful with a very limited range of high value-added products which overcome the transport disbenefits of peripherality. Hence, finance is the only sector which can overcome the disbenefits of peripherality and attract business to boost employment and wealth. The growth of the sector is testament to the fact that fiscal policies are appropriate and that there is potential for further growth.

A suitable relationship with the UK and the EU is essential for that development but not a prerequisite to it. The essential first step is to make decisions and projections on the likely nature of the developing economy. The Island must decide where its future lies and adjust its policies accordingly. In essence, there are three policy options regarding the Island's relationship with the EU:

(i)   as currently, but possibly tinker with aspects of the current relationship.

(ii)   withdraw completely from the EU by abrogating the Customs and Excise Agreement.

(iii) become a full member of the EU.

Strategic planners advocate a very wide trawl of options, and the above three might be operationalised in many different ways or decision-makers could choose to do totally unconnected things. If we concentrate on the third option, becoming a full member, we can illustrate many of the arguments that strategic decision-makers must contemplate. We can set up a simple 'for' and 'against' score card for that option.

The disadvantages of becoming a full member of the EU are that:

(i) it would destroy a relationship which has served the Island well until now, giving it access for industrial and agricultural goods to the UK and EU market-place without tariff barriers.

(ii) the Island would have to begin making contributions to the EU budget.

(iii) the Island would lose its much valued autonomy in decision-making and a part of its precious identity and distinctiveness.

(iv) the free movement of labour provisions would apply to the Island so that it could no longer operate the work permit system which is currently intended to protect the interests of Manx workers.

(v) the Island's essential differences would be eroded thus damaging its best claim to economic success on the periphery.

The advantages of becoming a full member are that:

(i) the Island would have access to EU markets in all sectors and most importantly open up financial markets.

(ii) the Island would have some (small) influence on decision-making processes and a presence at the heart of European affairs.

However, this option is unrealistic in the extreme. At the moment the IOM is not a sovereign state and does not have the capacity to negotiate membership for itself. That would require a complete change in the legal and constitutional status of the Island.

There is also the possibility that the EU would not consider the application. Should it accept one small island community as a full member then there is a host of others who would be clamouring for the same status such as Cyprus, Malta and Gibraltar. In the latter case, this could provoke confrontation with Spain. In the former case, attempts to secure this status may be accompanied by violence. Were island communities to be treated this way, other small ethnically diverse communities might also see fit to press their claim, particularly the Basques, Bretons and Catalans. The application by Malta (whilst the subject of some dissension internally given its strategic position between the Arab and European worlds) has not been ruled out by the Commission on grounds of small size. Developments there are of some significance for the IOM.

Realistically, option 1 - maintaining the present relationship and enhancing the 'political process', monitoring and influencing machineries - offers the best alternative. Constant tinkering with the system, whilst suffering the disadvantages of an incremental approach, would preserve some vital advantages.

Conclusion

This Paper has not been about reaching a decision on behalf of the IOM government. Rather, it has been more about providing a governmental contextualisation of a strategic decision-making situation and the use of management theory to articulate and make sense of problems facing governmental strategists.

Like most strategic thinking, the Island's decisions concerning its relationship with the UK and with the EU must be made in the context of many variables, some of which contradict one another. These are also dynamic, and whilst the decision to maintain the existing constitutional relationship for the time being seems most apposite, as changes occur strategic thinking must also move on.

References

(1) Mintzberg, H. (1979) *The Structuring of Organizations* (Prentice Hall).

(2) Handy, C. (1993) *Understanding Organizations* (Ed.4) (Penguin).

(3) Johnson, G. and Scholes, K. *Exploring Corporate Strategy: Text and Cases* (Ed.3) (Prentice Hall).

(4) Mintzberg, H. (1981) 'Organizational Design: Fashion or Fit', *Harvard Business Review* (Jan/Feb) pp.103-116.

(5) Isle of Man Government Policy Report (1993) Appendix 7.

(6) Dr. J. Orme, former Member of the House of Keys, in personal interview with the author.

(7) Isle of Man Government Policy Report (1993) p.1.

(8) *The Economic Implications of 1992: A Report to the Isle of Man Government*. Prepared by Peat Marwick McLintock and Salford University Business Services Ltd. June 1988.

(9) Webster, J. (1990) 'The Ecological Sustainability of Economic Growth in the Isle of Man', in Beller, W., d'Ayala, P. and Hein, P. (Eds) *Sustainable Development and Environmental Management of Small Islands*. (Parthenon: UNESCO).

THE GARIBALDI SCHOOL: THE UK's 'EAST MIDLANDS COMPANY OF THE YEAR' - A CASE STUDY IN ENTREPRENEURSHIP

Inger Boyett, School of Management and Finance, University of Nottingham and Don Finlay, Coventry Business School, Coventry University

Introduction

There are approximately 25,000 state primary and secondary schools in England and Wales employing 350,000 qualified full-time teachers, teaching 6.5 million pupils aged between 5 and 18 years of age. In 1988, the Government's Education Reform Act decisively affected the management of schools by devolving financial responsibility and accountability to schools and creating a degree of competition in the education market between schools. The creation of a 'quasi market' introduced the conditions intended to encourage the development of entrepreneurial activity within schools, in the belief that the discipline of the market would result in greater school effectiveness and efficiency. However, entrepreneurial alertness and action is not widespread in UK state education where there remains a deep and inherent suspicion of business terms and practices. Nevertheless, a few schools have used their new-found freedoms to act in a businesslike manner and to radically improve the effectiveness of their pupils' education. The Garibaldi School in Mansfield, Nottinghamshire recently won 'The East Midlands Company of the Year' award. The school's management and educational practices became the subject of an award-winning detailed case study (1) and the salient features are summarised in this paper. The school believes that its management practices offer a blueprint for other schools throughout the country.

The Development of the 'Quasi-Market'

The 1979 general election victory of a radical Conservative government has had a profound impact upon the structure and management of all public sector organisations. Inherently

195

profitable state industries which produced tangible 'private' goods were privatised, but for those public sector services whose product characteristics or welfare implications did not lend themselves to full-blown privatisation an alternative route was sought by the government. The generic strategy adopted centred around the creation of 'internal markets' with budgetary devolution to agents at the business unit level being accompanied by contracts, substituting the traditional hierarchical structure of policy implementation. The 'quasi-market', perhaps best illustrated in education and health, is characterised with the state remaining primarily the funding source but with each public sector service unit buying its resource inputs from a variety of competing suppliers and selling its services direct to the final consumer (education) or through an agency on behalf of the final customer (health). The UK public sector context is now characterised by a competitive contract system with incentives (and losses) to reward opportunistic behaviour. This lends weight to Druker's (2) comment that:

> Public sector institutions will have to learn to be innovators, to manage themselves entrepreneurially. To achieve this, public service institutions will have to learn to look upon social, technological, economic and demographic shifts as opportunities in a period of rapid change in all these areas.

The UK Education Context

All European countries spend a considerable proportion of their GDP on the provision of pre-primary, primary, secondary, further and higher education. Table 1(3) contrasts certain education statistics between selected European countries and their respective expenditure (excluding higher education).

	Public Ependiture on Education	Pupils per 1000 Population	Teachers per 1000 Population
UK	4.01	168	11.2
France	4.36	220	12.9
Germany	3.3	171	8.7
Belgium	3.89	193	18.8
Italy	4.21	180	16.6
Ireland	4.71	256	11.5

Table 1
Education and Europe

Along with other European countries, the UK has over the last decade experienced a major economic recession, but unlike its major European partners, the government remained firmly wedded to the belief in the primacy of the market as a mechanism for allocating resources.

196

Consequently, it wished to extend this concept into the 'non-market' domain of the public sector. This dominant political philosophy, allied to the economics of financing education expenditure, itself a very high opportunity cost, led government policy-shapers to re-examine the prevailing efficiency and effectiveness of the 25,000 state schools in England and Wales.

The 1988 Education Reform Act marked a watershed in UK education policy. It was characterised by a number of elements. Financial management and accountability was devolved from the regional or local authority to the individual school itself; individual schools were entitled to 'opt-out' of local authority control if a parental majority in a school ballot was obtained; control over the curriculum and subject content became centralised in the standardised form of the national curriculum and competition was developed in the education market with the introduction of formula funding and the publication of exam results in the form of school league tables.

The practical consequences of the 1988 Act were two-fold. Firstly, schools now compete with each other for students in the local education market since the schools' main income is financed according to its level of student numbers - the greater the student numbers the greater the income received. Secondly, students and parents have access to information enabling them to contrast respective schools' performances before making their school choice. Never before have education suppliers and education consumers been more visible, thereby underlying the government belief that the discipline of a competitive education market would force under-achieving or inefficient schools to improve their performance or else forego resources to those schools which education consumers value more highly.

Whilst neo-classical economic theory predicts that competitive markets, in contrast to imperfect markets, generate resource efficiency gains and higher welfare for individuals and society, little if any role is attached to the entrepreneur whose judgemental decisions about the co-ordination of scarce resources (4) is paramount. This serious omission of the entrepreneur from standard economic theory has been likened by Baumol (5) to Shakespeare's 'Hamlet' without the central character, the 'Prince of Denmark'. In other words, it gives an incomplete picture of the market and its processes if decision-making is confined to the unexplored 'black box'.

If the entrepreneur is central to decision-making in private markets with profits as the incentive and reward for risk-taking, then equally, the public sector entrepreneur is vital to understand the nature and processes of the burgeoning 'quasi-markets' within the broad public sector. However, the introduction of markets alone will not guarantee greater efficiency or effectiveness regarding resource allocation. The key independent factor is the existence of the entrepreneur (6). What is irrevocable is that 'quasi-markets' have introduced elements of varying uncertainty into a formally-regulated public sector environment (7). Uncertainty provides a rich source of opportunities for entrepreneurs irrespective of private or public sector contexts. Whether public sector 'quasi-markets' will be effective in line with prescriptive government philosophy will be determined by the supply of individuals who are sufficiently perceptive of market opportunities and who also possess the confidence to act upon them. Indeed, the speed at which a market adjusts to market imbalances will be a test of its overall efficiency. Slow-responding markets are likely to indicate a shortage of public sector entrepreneurs unable to recognize disequilibrium, a clear sign of unsatisfied opportunities which capable individuals could exploit. Conversely, where markets respond quickly to change, it is a likely indication of the existence of successful entrepreneurship (8).

Using a Case Study

Detailed case studies are well-established pedagogical tools for effective teaching and learning strategies. Furthermore, in relation to research, the case study is recognised as an acceptable research methodology. Using a case study to teach management students of any type, practitioners, undergraduates or postgraduates, the desired outcome is that the exercise should extend students' learning and their understanding of management processes. The case-study approach adds to the learning experience by simulating management activity, elucidating key management functions, developing an understanding of decision-making, integrating management theories and evaluating the effectiveness of processses and outcomes as well as examining future strategic choices. The better the case study, the higher the likelihood of meeting these multiple objectives.

However, the subject matter of a management case study and the quality of the associated material is more prone to good fortune. The original idea behind the Garibaldi School Case Study was formed after reading an article printed in a local newspaper about a comprehensive school which had won a regional business prize, 'The East Midlands Company of the Year 1992'. The school seemed likely to make an interesting case study for a number of reasons. Firstly, it was extremely unusual for a school to enter a business competition, let alone win it outright, and in so doing the school had beaten several well-known companies. Secondly, the school itself had suffered from a very poor local reputation only a few years earlier, yet not only had it managed to improve significantly its educational performance but it was now winning business prizes with the result that other schools and companies were requesting advice on how to raise finance and market their schools. Thirdly, the case might provide hard, concrete data to aid the construction of 'public sector entrepreneurship theory' and, in particular, that of the educational entrepreneur in the post-1977 education reform period.

The Garibaldi School Case Study

Essentially, the Garibaldi School Case Study documents how one public sector organisation managed to transform itself over a three-year period (1990-93). It highlights the role of the senior management team and in particular one entrepreneurial individual, Bob Salisbury, the headmaster. The case is a story of how an organization managed to innovate successfully by changing its culture and by developing sufficient organisational flexibility to allow it to implement those new ideas seen as opportunities within its immediate environment. In short, the Garibaldi School Case Study is a classic example of entrepreneurship in action.

To illustrate how the case can be taught, it will be placed in the context of an MBA programme. Normally, the MBA is delivered through a series of discrete modules, for example strategy, marketing, financial management and entrepreneurship used on a variety of modules, but its main domain is entrepreneurship where the focus would be on innovation and the entrepreneurial change process. After all, high levels of innovation and entrepreneurship do not guarantee organisational effectiveness!

Assuming that the students have read the case study and become familiar with the industry's characteristics and the personalities involved (allied perhaps to the use of a professionally-produced 15 minutes video which accompanies the case study, teaching notes and audio tape (9), the starting point for class discussion may be to ask students how one could measure organisational effectiveness. It is almost inevitable that students will respond with the three traditional business yardsticks of:

- whether the organization's goals are being met,
- how effective are the processes used to meet these goals
- and of ultimate importance, whether the organisation has survived and will survive in the future.

The first is often easiest to answer provided the information has been clearly developed within the case study itself. Likewise the third, but the second may require more teasing out. Ideally, students themselves might develop a framework against which the generation of their ideas can be tested. Alternatively, it may be provided by the lecturer. Figure 1 illustrates such a framework.

Figure 1

After goal identification, the processes used to meet these objectives would constitute the next student discussion. Four key management processes can be pinpointed - a process of cultural change and development of new values and priorities is required, as is revenue generation to lessen the school's financial constraints, marketing to change the school's image and finally the development of a decision-making process which encourages entrepreneurial endeavour. Each of these can be examined in greater depth against the backcloth that the common theme of these key identified processes is human action (that is, people). The business of the school is people-orientated, the systems are driven by people and entrepreneurial activity consists of individuals recognising opportunities and acting or encouraging others to act upon them. People can work as individuals or in teams, but their effectiveness is often linked to style of management leadership and its chosen system of organisational communication. Thus the effectiveness of each sector must be reviewed in relation both to outcome and also the involvement of people within the overall system.

The first process is entitled culture. It may be introduced with reference to the well-known cultural web (see Figure 2). Students need to be able to recognize the overall importance of culture and its impact on change management outcomes. Moreover, they should be able to identify from the case study the problems of low morale, reluctance to try new teaching methods in case they do not work, unapproachable and hidden management and the pervasive power of ones place in the hierarchy.

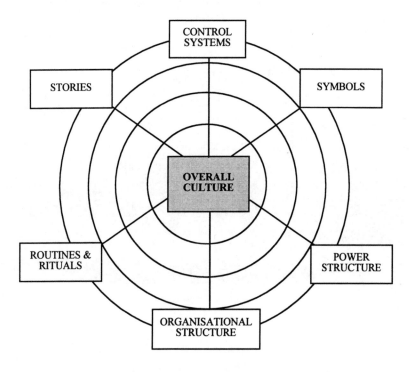

Figure 2

Indeed, using each of these strands of the web allows one to contrast the old with the new culture at the Garibaldi School. For example, when considering organisational structure, students will have perceived that the school has moved from a traditional hierarchical structure to a much flatter organisational structure. The process adopted was to replace posts with scale points, with new posts on the basic teaching salary as vacancies arose. The interwoven web can be highlighted by noting the power and leadership styles. Bob Salisbury's leadership may be described as a soft management style. Certainly, he is not the overpowering charismatic leader so often portrayed in respect of the entrepreneurial figurehead. Symbols, too, are often used to cement and encourage cultural change. Frequent use was made of stories and analogies. The 'bobbing corks' symbolism is probably the most important (see Figure 3).

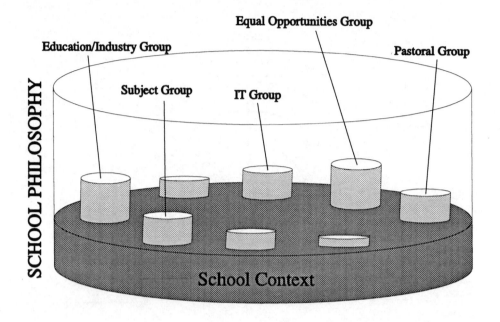

Figure3
Bobbing Corks - The Entrepreneurial Organisational Archetype

Time and time again during the research, interviewees referred to the 'bobbing corks' to describe the opportunities available to individual teachers to explain the dominant driving force at work at the Garibaldi School. The corks depict the Garibaldi staff in the river of education who are guided by the strong school ethos or current towards the outcome of an efficient and effective education experience for the school's students. This river is bounded by high banks symbolising the basic philosophy of the school, which constrain any extreme or high-risk action. At any time one of the corks may bob higher in the water to start an education initiative to be displaced subsequently by another cork after the first innovation is completed. This imagery illustrates that innovatory activity may be initiated by an member of the staff team at any point in time.

As the strands and references to the cultural web are developed, students should be able to identify a series of positive outcomes. These are depicted in Table 2.

202

Removal of inertia and resistance to change:
"It was almost like people wouldn't think of having a cup of tea without coming to ask first..."
Raising of staff morale:
"...it's the recognition of what you are trying to do that's important."
Raising of staff motivation:
"The vandalism bill for 1992 was £0, three years before it peaked at £42k!"
Idea generation has become the norm:
"If you try something and it doesn't quite work you're not hauled over the coals any more..."
Increase in student motivation:
"I come to school because it's fun, not because I have to!"

Table 2

Cultural Outcomes

The second process identified is marketing. The traditional marketing perspective can be reviewed with its emphasis upon the '4 P's' (price, product, promotion and place) and the associated marketing mix. However, the Garibaldi School Case Study allows a critique of the dominant marketing paradigm. Two further 'P's', people and parameters might also be included in order to allow the marketing mix a greater relevance for the public sector and education in particular. Schools are populated by individuals with excellent communication skills. Marketing is communicating product information to potential consumers with the intention of increasing sales on a repeat basis if the product's portrayed image is supported by reality. Teachers are natural marketeers, in fact arguably superior, given their closeness to the end customer, where teaching and learning strategies are often customised for the greatest effectiveness.

All schools contain numerous human resources with a potential competitive marketing edge if grasped by the senior management team. However, public services operate for the 'public good' and thus operate within a more clearly defined social and ethical context significantly different from the private sector. Frequently in education, it is remarked that teachers did not enter the teaching profession stimulated by the profit motive, but instead by the desire to work with, and for, people rather than inanimate objects.

It must be recognised that there are perhaps, greater limits to school marketing than the forms of marketing adopted by, for example, a financial services company. Ethical, people-orientated marketing can still be extremely effective. Table 3 summarises a few of the positive outcomes of the Garibaldi School's marketing.

External image of school:
Increasingly favourable reports in the local press and increasing numbers of adult learners.
Increase in Sixth Form numbers:
In 1990 there were 8 students, by 1993 115 students
Increase in Education/Industry links:
Alton Towers, British Thornton, Trent Copyfax, Mansfield Brewery, Training & Enterprise Council, Mansfield 2010 Assoc.,etc.
Increase in pupil numbers:
Year 1 pupil numbers have increased from 112 to 176.
Increased involvement of parents:
Average parent attendance at meetings three years ago was 30, today it is 300.

Table 3

Marketing Outcomes

The third main process identified was the financial process of income generation. This case study contains numerous examples of beneficial outcomes which have been dependent upon the extra generation of resources. Undoubtedly, the most significant was an innovative link, firstly with the American Adventure theme park and later with Alton Towers. Not only was Garibaldi the first school in the country to do so (others are now beginning to follow suit) but it also generates £10,000 to £15,000 profit annually for school funds. This enables the school to make the most of its opportunities. Other examples are depicted in Table 4.

Finance for educational improvements:
Alton Towers profit of £10k allows loan of French teachers to Junior Schools, £50,000 marketing prize will help towards the refurbishment of the Sports Barn.
Improvements in the environment:
Conference Room, Sports Barn, Reception Area, Carpets, Curtains, general decorative level, etc.
Additional technology:
French Street, Language Laboratory, Technology Rooms, computers, etc.
Enabling gain from future opportunities:
Euro-centre, Leisure Centre, etc.

Table 4

Resource Outcomes

The fourth and final process for student discussion is entitled the decision-making process. The case study indicates that the school has not been constrained by past management models but has instead developed their own which is displayed in Figure 4.

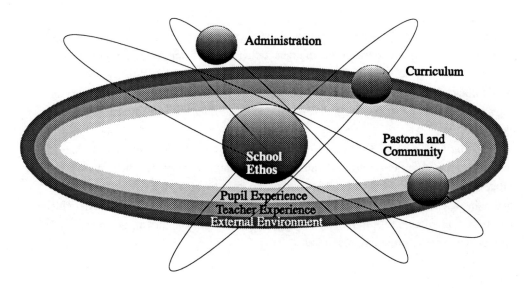

Figure 4
The Entrepreneurial Strategic Management System at Garibaldi

This 'Entrepreneurial Strategic Management System' is based on the principle that the best decisions are made when there is maximum involvement by all the stakeholders in the school, with full access to the best information available. At the core is the school ethos epitomised by the concept of the 'bobbing corks'. Around this are three rings of influence - the external environment, the teacher experience and the pupil/student experience. The 'planets' generalize the three key management decision-making areas - decisions involving what is to be taught in the school, how the pastoral and community educational issues will be managed and how the school's operations should be administered. The model's functioning can be illustrated with reference to a proposal of an innovative activity originating from the core. The idea is propelled into the orbits of the three planetary management areas in order to assess the respective impact of the innovation. Whilst it is driven along its respective orbits, the idea also passes through the three rings of influence allowing pupils, teachers and the external community to also assess the innovative activity. As the idea moves back towards the central core, all of this simultaneously-gathered information is assessed and a decision made by the senior management team.

Conclusion

Government-inspired reforms in education over the past decade have resulted in several key managerial issues coming to the forefront. Head Teachers face problems of coping with, and responding to massive change in a sufficiently pro-active manner; utilising a shrinking resource base to satisfy growing demands for ever-increasing quality in the services provided and attempting to transform an organization culture from one of punishment into one that genuinely tolerates mistakes encourages innovation and risk-taking. Finally, dismantling an historically hierarchical organizational structure and rebuilding it on flatter lines with accompanying flexibility and responsiveness to changes in customers' needs and demands.

The Garibaldi School Case Study indicates that successful innovation and change management require the careful co-ordination of each individual part of the management process, thereby engendering a cultural change as a lever to more effective and innovative marketing and income generating decisions and overall, entrepreneurial management. This co-ordination places a premium on the existence and development of educational entrepreneurs both now and in the future.

References

1. Boyett, I. & Finlay, D. (1993) 'The UK's East Midlands Company of the Year 1992 - A State Financed Secondary School?', *European Foundation for Management Development Winning Case Study in Entrepreneurship and the IBM Excellence in Management Award, Brussels.*
2. Drucker, P. (1985) *Innovation and Entrpreneurship* (London: Pan Books).
3 OECD in Figures (1991 Edition) (Paris: OECD).
4. Casson, M. (1982) *The Entrepreneur - An Economic Theory* (Oxford: Martin Robertson).
5. Baumol, W. (1968) 'Entrepreneurship in Economic Theory', *American Economic Review, 58,* pp. 72-83.
6. Boyett, I. & Finlay, D. (1993a) 'The Emergence of the Educational Entrepreneur', *Long Range Planning, 26* (3), pp. 114-22.
7. Boyett, I. & Finlay, D. (1993b) 'Awakening Entrepreneurship in UK Schools', *Working Paper, School of Management and Finance, University of Nottingham.*
8. Kirzner, I. (1973) *Competition and Entrepreneurship* (University of Chicago Press).
9. Available from the School of Management and Finance, Portland Building, University of Nottingham, NG7 2RD. Tel: (0602) 515486.

GOING FOR NEW GROWTH IN A CHRISTIAN SETTING

David Harper, Sheffield Business School.

Introduction

I have attempted in this paper to examine the main requirements for achieving growth in an organisation which is non-profit making, dependent primarily on voluntary workers and offers spiritual life as its raison d'être, namely a Christian church. This comes mainly from my own experience of being the overall leader of a new church formed seven years ago and from some studying and observations of other growing churches. These principles for growth are equally applicable in a secular organisation although their application will most likely differ in some key respects. First, however, I will look at the market characteristics facing any local church.

Market Characteristics

A market analysis for the Christian church looks something like this: If the product is spiritual life in Jesus Christ and the marketing organisation is the church then this industry is in serious decline. Measured in terms of total UK church members, there has been a decline of 1.5m members over the last 20 years (from 8.0m to 6.5m) a fall from 18.5 per cent to 14.0 per cent of the population that are church members (see Figure 1).

This includes an element of nominalism such that attendance is less than 10 per cent on any Sunday. An analysis of attendance by age groups gives little encouragement since the lowest percentage attendance is among young adults, that is 15-19 and 20-28 (Figure 2). In Derbyshire where I am based, 6.6 per cent of the population are church members though attendance rates are high amongst young adults.

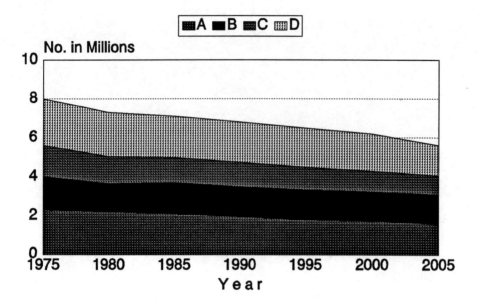

No. in Millions

A = Roman Catholic **B** = Presbyterian **C** = Free Churches & Orthodox **D** = Anglican

Figure 1
UK Church Members by Denomination 1975-2005

Source: The UK Christian Handbook

If a profit-making organisation lost customers at the rate the church has lost members then there would be a thorough review of products and organisation, heads would roll and new strategies would be implemented. Clearly, customers have lost faith in the product and the church, questioning its relevance and credibility. The church, like any other organisation, should face up to its own responsibility for this decline and not blame external circumstances. Our view is that the product is as good as ever and the church itself is in need of recovery of faith, reality and vitality in the message that it offers.

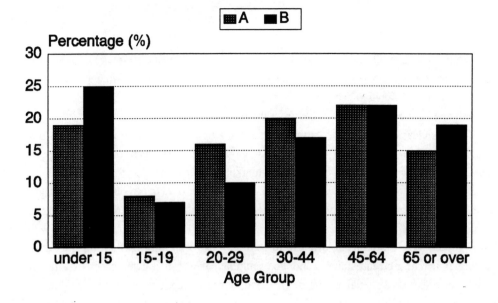

A = English Population   B = English Church Attenders

Figure 2

English Church Attendance Compared to Population by Age-Group 1989

Source: The UK Christian Handbook, 1994/5.

World sales of the product, new life in Christ, are booming and experiencing unprecedented levels with total world sales at 1.7 billion (32 per cent of the world population). Fastest world growth of over 8 per cent per annum is with the experience -centred version of this product (charismatic), whilst the more cerebral evangelical variant is growing at 5.4 per cent per annum. These represent the two fastest-growing major religious groups in the world. Latest market indicators suggest that by the end of the decade two-thirds of Christians will not live in the West (a reversal from two-thirds Westerners in 1960) and there will be more Christians on earth than in heaven. African, Latin and South American and Far Eastern markets are experiencing the greatest growth, for example 1,500 a day in China alone. If the non-west markets are riding the wave then the western markets are going against the tide. There are, however, some cases of growth within the UK and evidence of a change in the spiritual climate in the face of disillusionment with materialism and secularism and their consequences. There has been some very significant growth amongst the so-called new churches (formerly known as house churches) and also amongst particular local churches within traditional denominations, some of which have passed the 1,000 member mark. The new churches currently have 140,000 members, having been embryonic only 20 years ago. This growth is partly transfers and partly new additions (new believers), and attendance generally exceeds membership by up to 25 per cent. In our situation in rural Derbyshire, we have grown from an initial gathering of 15 adults and children to 120 adults and children and averaged growth of 35 per cent per annum. Our goal is to continue this growth and to plant out new churches from the increased base.

There is clear market segmentation in church membership. In a rural setting this has traditionally been church or chapel (conformist or nonconformist), each reaching a different market. The new churches represent a new market segment which after initial switching from other sub-markets are now experiencing net Christian growth. In our case, our target market is younger adults (<45 years of age) and their children (in total, 62 per cent of the local population).

We seek to be culturally relevant to this group presenting the Christian message in a setting which is non-threatening and non-religious, whilst being uncompromising on Christian essentials. A major obstacle is negative preconceptions or misunderstandings about 'Christianity' or 'Church' which we seek to help people overcome and to introduce them to a personal experience of God. Against that background I have identified 3 main requirements for growth that are evident in growing churches.

Principles for Growth

The three principles for growth I will briefly examine are vision, leadership and motivation. Churches are non-profit-making organisations and membership and participation is voluntary. Motivation is therefore potentially the most difficult area and the one where methods for motivating workers may differ from secular organisations, though I would contend that the principles for effective motivation remain the same in both types of organisation.

Vision

Vision is the grand design, the end result, the final picture. Detail may be lacking, how to get there unknown, but a visionary can see in his or her mind's eye a destination and goal. Such vision can inspire people because it gives purpose, purpose motivates and purposeful activity is the result.

Vision is relevant in a secular or spiritual context. Clearly, vision for a church needs to come from God and be God-given so that a church has a sense of purpose and destination and a clear mandate from God. He grows the church, but the people need the vision. Fresh vision has brought recovery out of decline many times in church history.

Secular equivalents are often called mission statements. Vision has to be shared and captured so that it is owned. This way a group of people can be motivated to work towards a common goal. Without vision there may be much activity but little sense of direction, with a maintenance mentality to the organisation.

The church I am involved in leading is in Derbyshire in the Peak District National Park. There are many villages and a few small towns with a total catchment population of 60,000 people. I would hope and expect most people in the church could tell you our vision which is summarised in a three-fold vision statement. This reads 'Our vision is to worship God, reach those who are seeking God and build Christian communities in each of the villages and towns of the Peak District area'.

In addition, we have found the need to define our values which are the foundations or distinctives upon which the church is being built. We have ten such values. For example, we value relationships highly and want to build the church on relationships and friendships whilst releasing people to work and serve in the church according to their gift or ability. The openness and trust resulting from relationships creates an environment in which authority and responsibility can be delegated and yet accountability maintained.

Leadership

Vision is a mark of leadership. There needs to be visionary leadership. J.P. Kolter of Harvard Business School in his book *The Leadership Factor* makes a clear distinction between leadership and management. Leadership has vision, communicates vision and is the ability to get people to follow. Such leaders can recruit and motivate people to work to the vision, by inspiring and directing. This is different from the management function which ensures an efficient and effective use of resources. Managers have an ability to organise and administer and are essential, but represent a different type of leadership. Both types of leadership are necessary and this is why team building is also an important part of leadership in order to harness these different skills and abilities. Team leadership is not one leader telling others what to do, nor is it a group representing and protecting individual interests (a committee), rather it is complementarily skilled people working together towards a common goal, releasing one another into their respective spheres of expertise. Such leadership, certainly in a church context, cannot be self-appointed but must be recognised and affirmed by those you seek to lead and indeed by more experienced objective outsiders, such as consultants or mentors.

The potential for the misuse or abuse of authority and power is an important issue and a possible source of fear. Consequently, some safeguards are needed. Accountability of the leader to others both within and outside the organisation is one safety factor, not only for people under a leader but for the leader himself. A determining factor in the use of authority and power is the motivation and attitudes of the leader. In particular, is a leader primarily motivated by personal gain or by the interests and needs of those he/she leads?

211

We adopt the principles that Jesus taught, that leaders are not to lord it over those under them and to seek to control and manipulate, but rather should develop a serving mentality and attitude. Such an approach values people and will release motivation. This is essentially a matter of values, but there is no inconsistency between clear leadership with authority and an attitude of serving others. The style of leadership adopted in an organisation can be defined in terms of how authority and power are executed. Four styles have been identified, namely dictatorial, authoritative, consultative and participative.

These styles vary, depending upon the degree to which others are involved in the decision-making process. There are times when different styles are appropriate. The style we have adopted is the consultative style.

Motivation

People are any organisation's most important resource, not only in their capacity to work and use their skills but also in their ability to be creative and to use their ideas in problem-solving and decision-making. Motivation of the people in an organisation increases productivity and gets the job done. Motivation is voluntary and releases the E factors: excitement, enthusiasm, energy and effort. Within a church context, there may be a number of negative forces to overcome before individuals see that involvement and participation in the work of the church is actually their job and not just that of the leader(s). There are a number of ways we have sought to motivate:

- Share vision
- Teach members to serve and minister to others
- Recruit personally
- Personal involvement on the job and off the job

The central value of building on relationships is important here because this values people and recognises their need for self-worth, security and significance. As relationships are built, so is trust and this creates a climate for risk-taking and 'having a go'. Failure can be used creatively and positively as a learning opportunity and achievement should be recognised. Leaders can delegate with appropriate responsibility and accountability, not only for the benefit of the individual but also to be more effective as a leader - doing what only he/she can do. Personal on-the-job involvement and training does motivate.

This co-operative style of relationships is used to motivate, to produce greater individual fulfilment and to maximise productivity from the resources available. Where such a style breaks down because of relationship problems then other styles will emerge such as the retaliation style, the domination style and the isolation style.

Relationship conflicts challenge a leader's own security and therefore an essential requirement for such an approach is learning to handle relationship tensions and conflicts.

This is a high order requirement in terms of time and commitment and the benefits of the co-operative style must be fully assured if the leader is to go through the challenge of addressing and resolving relationship tensions or breakdowns.

Conclusion

These principles have been learnt on the job and through observation of other church growth situations, and are generally accepted requirements for growth in organisations. The ability to apply these principles to a given situation and to develop and adopt them as an organisation grows is a test of leadership. The application of such principles will vary with the stage of development of a church and consequently there is a significant learning element as well as a need to be adaptable and flexible. In another five years it might be worthwhile repeating this study on a comparative basis in order to access what has developed or changed in my understanding and application of the three growth principles.

References

Rush, M. (1983) *Management: A Biblical Approach* (Victory Press).

Gibbs, E. (1986) *I Believe in Church Growth* (Hodder & Stoughton).

Brierley, P. (1994) *The UK Christian Handbook 1994-5* (Christian Research Association).

ECUMENICAL CENTRE PROJECT IN A NEW TOWN DEVELOPMENT: THE CASE OF SKELMERSDALE

Rev Rob Frost, Raynes Park Methodist Church.

Introduction

In this work the decline in the membership of people affiliated to the 'Christian' denominational churches is highlighted with especial attention being given to its accelerating level in recent years. This is in strong contrast to other types of church gatherings such as the 'House-Church' which is neither part of the established church movement in the UK nor stands on the broad church principles. In the last 20 years or so, the trend for church goers has been towards the 'House-Church' grouping-style which is less traditionalist in presentation and has a less rigid administrative structure. Organisational style can also influence the way in which church administration is conducted. Smaller and less structured management systems than those of the traditional committees and parish councils systems have been efficient in helping many to express their personal commitment to Christianity. Furthermore, as the 'House-Church' style tends to provide greater openness along with better mobility, smaller communities can find this more attractive than the traditional approach as a church model. The concept of church groupings along these lines emphasises the concept of taking the church affiliation to the people and their community. An ecumenical project, based on the principle of taking the 'church-to-the-people', is evaluated in this paper and provides a case example from the free church movement led by the Methodist denomination as an attempt to take into practical consideration some of the lessons learnt from the 'House-Church' model of church administration.

Mission in a Secular Society

The term 'secular society' is often used, but what is meant by it? How can we measure increasing secularisation? What kind of markers help to indicate the changing nature of society?

Accurate measurement of a 'phenomenon' such as the 'secular society' is impossible but there are at least five clear areas where there would seem to be a major sea-change in British society with special reference to community behaviour and church participation.

Decline in Membership

One possible way of measuring the growing secularisation of a society is by looking at the declining number of church members within the total population. It is clear that the decline in church membership over the last sixty years has not been a sudden phenomenon but that the trend stretches back deep into the nineteenth century.

Alan D. Gilbert (1981) traced some of the roots of Christianity in Britain up to the Victorian era:

> In their early days, for example, the Methodist and New Dissenting movements had been able to attract members from the labouring and artisan sections of the population in considerable numbers, but the Victorian working classes were virtually impervious to their existence. Such churches retain their relative position in the society only by relaxing membership standards to accommodate declining levels of commitment, and by improving methods of autogenous growth based on Sunday schools.

It is clear that the decline has been very steep. The Free Church membership figures in England during the late 1930s demonstrate a decline of about 1 per cent per annum, and this rate of decline roughly trebled from 1937 to 1947. The position stabilised in 1950, but decline began again at the end of the 1950s and accelerated during the 1960s and 1970s.

During this period there was a very significant change in the relationship between church membership and church attendance. Before 1914, it could generally be assumed that the numbers attending Free Church worship were two or three times as great as those formally in membership. However, since the First World War the Sunday attendance has generally been less than membership.

These figures also need to be set in the context of the continuing growth of the English population as a whole. Thus, the influence of the Free Churches was declining much more sharply than the church membership statistics alone were able to indicate.

Rupert David (1982) noted the psychological effect of this decline:

In the 1930's people began to feel that the problems of the 1920's were not merely transient, but had deeper causes; yet there remained an underlying optimism. In the 1940's despite, and partly because of the war, there were hopes for renewal and revival which were not entirely disappointed in the early 1950's. But by the later 1950's people began to feel that things would not improve, and in the 1960's and 1970's decline came to be accepted as normal; even to maintain membership figures was regarded as an achievement. There was therefore a slow but immense change in non-conformist psychology.

Recent church affiliation statistics and projections of future trends on the UK's Christian movement compiled by Marc Europe (1993) illustrate that the decline is very likely to continue. In the 1970s, for example, the Methodist Church lost 129,000 members, whereas in the 1980s it lost 46,000 and, if the forecast figures prove to be accurate, in the 1990s it will lose a further 25,000. Methodist Church attendance decreased by 11 per cent between 1979 and 1989. That means that there were 98 fewer adults going to Methodist churches each Sunday throughout the decade. Although the decline is bottoming out, it is still most disturbing. For the Methodist Church as a whole the estimated loss between 1970 and the year 2,000 is 30 per cent of membership, 34 per cent of church buildings and 31 per cent of church ministers.

Total figures for Protestant, Catholic and Orthodox church membership between the years of 1970 and 2000 indicate a loss of 30 per cent of total membership. Meanwhile, the population in the UK is expected to show a growth of 3.7 per cent between 1986 and 2001 (Brierly, 1994).

Relative to the total population, very few people in Britain attend church or are active members. About one adult in five goes once a month or more and about half do not go at all except for weddings and funerals (Marc Europe, 1993). Furthermore, British churchgoing in the Marc Europe's assessment reveals that only 10 per cent of the adult population attended church on 15 October 1989. One indicator of an increasingly secular society, therefore, is decline in number in both church membership and attendance.

Decline of Religious Education

Another important indicator of secularisation is the decline in the church's influence among young people. At one time, vast numbers of children received religious education (RE) in Sunday schools, and nearly all children were involved in worship and Bible study at day school.

The Spens report of 1938 advocated that "No boy or girl can be counted as properly educated unless he or she has been made aware of the fact of the existence of a religious interpretation of life". The 1944 Education Act provided that "religious instruction shall be given in every county school and in every voluntary school". In contrast, however,

217

although preserving religious education as part of the Basic Curriculum, the 1988 Act makes it clear that religious education is not a foundation or core subject. It does have related attainment targets set as do other core subjects.

The HMI report of 1985, on sixty two schools, found that eighteen of them had no RE in the fourth or fifth years apart from examination options, and that in two thirds of the remainder "ethical and social problems...were considered to the exclusion of other aspects of religion". The 1987 religious education statistics showed that 62 per cent of 15 year olds and 58 per cent of sixteen year olds were not given any religious education.

Reviewing the changes in school assemblies in his book *Schools Now*, Charles Martin (1988) concluded that "By the 1980's few secondary schools would be having a religious assembly for all pupils." Many interpreted 'worship' to mean 'celebration of worth', not necessarily religious worth but the values and achievements of the school and society. Primary schools have tended to maintain the traditional morning assembly, though the content of this meeting has tended to become less specifically Christian. Where there are pupils from other religious traditions, schools have tried to find some 'general' religious or community theme.

There have also been marked changes in the religious attitudes of secondary school pupils between 1974 and 1986. In 1974, 41 per cent felt that God was very real to them, whereas only 22 per cent could say this in 1986. In 1974, 36 per cent found it hard to believe in God, whereas the figure was 59 per cent by 1986. In 1974, 47 per cent believed that God listens to prayer, but by 1986 the figure had dropped to 29 per cent. This was taken to demonstrate "a consistent, widespread and large drift further away from the churches among secondary school pupils".

A. H. Halsey (1986) expresses concern about the current culture of adolescents:

> Their powerlessness is reflected in their collective amnesia, their unknowingness of the history of their conditions, and even more in their uncertainty as to the future. No wonder that fashionability, hedonism, and a desperate individualism serve as substitutes for a securely held morality.

It is disturbing to note that more than half of Britain's Methodist churches have no members or attenders under the age of 18. Perhaps the Young People's Working Group for the Nationwide Initiative in Evangelism were right when they observed that "the churches have not provided an atmosphere or a place which can receive the respect of young people and does not cause them to lose face with their peers".

Decline of 'Religious Assumptions'

Though it is difficult to demonstrate statistically, sociologists are noting changes in the underlying assumptions about life and faith among many British citizens. One important indicator of this is the change in rating figures for religious broadcasts. Broadcasted religious services that had audiences of 10 per cent of the adult population in 1940 were listened to by 3 per cent or less of adults by 1955. The popular 'People's Service' which still held 11 per cent of the population in 1964, had an audience of less than 5 per cent by 1970.

Religious television programmes have also lost much of their audiences. Between 1963 and 1970, the audiences for the televised morning service, the discussion programme 'Meeting Point' and 'Songs of Praise' had fallen by 60 per cent, 40 per cent and 30 per cent respectively. Today, about a third of the audience turn off immediately when a religious programme begins.

The European Value Systems study group reported in 1986 that as many as 85 per cent of British people claim affiliation to a church yet more than two thirds of the population do not believe in a personal God.

Richard Hoggart (1958), writing about working class life pre-1950 observed that "We're 'ere for a purpose' they say, or 'There must be some purpose or we wouldn't be 'ere'". That there is a purpose presupposes that there must be a God.

A. H. Halsey (1986) compared the underlying assumptions in working class families in the 1950s and 1980s as follows:

> I am struck by the integration of ordinary families in those days with the moral traditions of the old class and Christian society. That moral structure has ebbed away fast under the assault of the classless inequalities and the secular materialism of the post-war world.

Decline in Christian Monopoly of the Religious Scene

The loss of Christian influence in society has been further affected by the growth of ethnic minorities. According to the 1981 Census about 6 per cent of our population was born outside Britain, a total of nearly 3½ million people. Population growth among the ethnic minorities since that time now means that about 9 per cent of our population are first or second generation British residents.

These figures help to explain the growth of other faiths in British society. Buddhists are set to grow from 6,000 members in 1970 to 40,000 in the year 2000. Over a similar thirty-year timespan, Hinduism will grow from 50,000 to 220,000 members; Muslim membership from 250,000 to 1,500,000; Satanists from 1,500 to 20,000; and Sikhs from 75,000 to 275,000.

If by 'secular society' we are referring to a 'non-Christian' society then the growth of other religious groups is a significant factor. It is hard for many older people to understand that there are now more Muslims in the United Kingdom than Methodists. In total, the membership of non-Christian religions is set to rise almost five-fold from 538,321 in 1970 to a staggering 2,430,000 by the year 2000.

Decline in the 'Presence' of the Church in the Community

It is evident that presence must precede proclamation. If the church is not present it cannot possibly be relevant! Researchers believe that one of the major factors in membership decline has been the church's inability to respond to demographic change. It has not relocated to where the people are.

Robin Gill (1988) wrote:

> The Church of England continues to deploy a quite disproportionate number of its clergy in rural parishes...Today the village population is only a fifth of the size of its Victorian population and 90 percent of the British population as a whole is urban, not rural. Yet the Church of England still deploys half its stipendiary clergy in rural and small town situations.

The retreat of the churches from the Inner City is one illustration of declining 'presence'. In a comprehensive study of churches in Toxteth in 1974, Jim Hart showed that in Brunswick, the poorest part of the area, there were only 39 Protestant members in a population of 12,630. More than half of the 39 were elderly, single or widowed women.

In its disturbing analysis of the 'unchurched', Marc Europe (1993) has uncovered whole communities of people with little or no Christian presence or witness among them. Here are some examples:

- 1,100-1,500 people living in small private developments on the edge of Rossendale. Many teenagers and children. Adults employed in management, commerce and blue collar industrial work. No known Christians or witness.
- 20,000 Asians living in Blackburn, mainly coming from India and Bangladesh. Many young people, largely unemployed but some work in shops or small businesses. Only 30 per cent can read English. No known Christian witness.
- Young marrieds forming a quarter of the population around Thetford. They have various occupations and tend to live on new council estates. Non-manual class being under 1 per cent Christian. No known Christian witness.

Such communities are a far cry from the traditional English village, with its community culture firmly interconnected with the Church and Chapel.

In a masterly analysis of the social changes in industrial south-west Wales, a commission set up by the Blaendulais Ecumenical centre reported in 1969 that "A mobile living society confronts a comparatively immobile church". The hundreds of new churchless communities clearly indicate that the church is often not 'present', and its absence from the scene is in itself a contributing factor to the 'secular society'.

Membership Trends in the 'House-Church' Groups

Many religious analysts have asked questions about the reasons behind the declining number in the established churches and especially in relation to the Methodist Movement which was first initiated under the guidance of the brothers John and Charley Wesley. Some researchers even attempt to trace such a phenomenon in relation to the influence of the leaders of small groups - Class Leader - as they are recognised within the Methodist tradition. They also seek to discover whether the leadership system in terms of its authority over the membership has suffered a breakdown. Conclusions drawn so far indicate that the flame of spiritual revival which produced such amazing growth in the early years of the Methodist movement was no longer the inspiring guidance behind the Christian movement.

Robert Currie (1970), in his disquieting review of Methodist history and ecumenism described some of the changes in spirituality and church practice which occurred at the end of the nineteenth century:

> Gradually they extricated themselves from traditional doctrines and creeds. They began to construct a much looser, vaguer and more palatable Christianity ... Religion was a permanent Sunday School Anniversary, Christ the affable minister, the universe a tidy church hall full of happy faces. Traditional Christianity was dead.

Some would say that the newly formed 'House-Church' groups - based, to some extent, on the 'class leader' supervision - along with small independent evangelical and pentecostal groups are closer in spirituality to traditional Methodism than many of our High Street churches today. It is interesting to note, therefore, that these groups are experiencing dramatic patterns of growth. Figures up to 1979 show that Pentecostal churches are set to rise in membership by 34 per cent between 1970 and 2000, and the Independent and 'House-Churches' by an amazing 78 per cent. The latest figures, from the Marc Europe survey show that these trends are, if anything, accelerating. Between 1979 and 1989 the 'House-Churches' grew by an amazing 114 per cent. This trend is equally apparent in the United States, as mainline denominations lose millions of members to the evangelical groups. It is interesting to note what social observers say about these trends.

Richard Ostling (1989) wrote in Time Magazine in May 1989:

Explanations abound. No doubt cultural and demographic changes have eroded mainline churches. Constant organisation reshuffles have taken a toll. In addition far too many mainline churches are lacking in the marketing and communications savvy that the Evangelicals employ to win new members...A preoccupation with political and social issues at the expense of good old-fashioned faith has alienated many members. Not only are the traditional denominations failing to get their message across; they are increasingly unsure what that message is.

Another American, John Naisbitt (1990), writing in *Trend Reports* which monitors social trends in 6,000 US periodicals each month, also noted the decline of mainline churches and the growth of evangelical denominations and concluded:

As a society, we have been moving from the old to the new. And we are still in motion. Caught between eras we experience turbulence. A very important point is that the strictest and most demanding denominations, especially the Southern Baptists, are growing fastest - while the liberal churches continue to lose members. This should not be surprising. During turbulent times many people need structure - not ambiguity in their lives. They need something to hang onto, not something to debate. The demand for structure will increase - supplied not by the old established denominations - but by the great array of new native grown fundamentalist faiths.

The only established church to record encouraging patterns of growth in recent years is the Baptist Church. Baptists grew by 2 per cent from 1985-1989 after a decline in the previous six-year period. In their detailed assessment of Baptist Church growth in England, Paul Beasley-Murray and Alan Wilkinson (1980) echoed these American observers:

Growing churches seem to be those, predominantly, that are expecting great things from God and have that conviction underlying all their activity. Church growth is not simply doing the right things at the right time. It is also a matter of being a fellowship which believes that it is God's plan for his Church to grow and having the conviction that he wants it to happen in that particular church: it becomes a matter of faith.

Methodist Movement in the Early Days

Anglican Christianity in the eighteenth century was, in the main, little more than a spare religious ethic - sedate and timid. The appeal of many church leaders at this time was almost solely to the intellect, through works such as Conybeares' *Defence of Butler's Analogy*.

Deism was popular among the clergy, and for more than half a century a great debate over the Deity of Christ - the Trinitarian controversy - was waged within the church. John Tillotson (1630-94) and Thomas Tenison (1636-1715) both became Archbishops of Canterbury. They taught that reason by itself could provide all that was needed in the way of divine truth - and that its findings could be confirmed by the Holy Bible. During this period there was a declining emphasis on biblical doctrine and a greater reliance on the 'truths of natural religion'.

Large numbers of people of all social strata, believing Christianity to be false, dropped all pretence of religious observance. However, the majority, believing that the Church of England was a necessary support of the monarchy and a key factor in maintaining the peace of the realm, asserted that, despite its outworn dogmas, it ought to be retained.

The very culture of the established churches alienated the new industrial workers of the woollen, cotton and iron boom towns. This alienation was epitomised by the 'pew system', whereby the wealthy could purchase and even furnish their own areas of a church. Many of these pews were built with tall partitions, so that the affluent could worship in complete privacy. Sometimes they were curtained, sometimes filled with sofas and tables, some even provided with fireplaces. It was not uncommon for a servant to enter between the prayers and the sermon with sherry and light refreshments. The poor, meanwhile, were often put back into whatever part of the church was the coldest, darkest and most distant from sight and hearing. This traffic in pews excluded the poor, and symbolised the church's attitude toward them.

Wesleys' Preachers exercised a different style of leadership to that which many working class people had come to expect from the established church. In many communities the parson was dependent on the squire, a dependence which was often economic as well as being a social and cultural alliance. The role of the parson was generally to care for the rich and powerful more than the weak and oppressed. The result was that each bishop was left to do what he wanted in his own diocese. They typically spent two thirds of the year in London, not daring to miss voting time at the House of Lords if they wanted to rise to the higher echelons of church life. Confirmations, when they took place at all, were of vast numbers of people at once. Some bishops rarely visited their diocese. There was a surplus of clergy, and they were poorly paid. On average, at any time, over 1,000 parishes were simply left unattended.

Perhaps the established church's most evident weakness, however, was its inability to respond to the massive demographic shifts which resulted from the industrial revolution. The southern counties, except for Cornwall, Devon and Middlesex, continued to be a 'Methodist desert' well into the nineteenth century. It was in these southern areas that the most effective Anglican parishes of the 'closed' style existed in which the squire was still dominant, with all the sanctions available through which to enable social control:

> Where the national church required an Act of Parliament, a grant of money, an educated gentleman and a crop of lawyers, the Methodists required only a friendly barn and a zealous preacher - at least for the beginning.

The parish system was a legacy of medieval conditions and population. New parishes could not be created save by private Act of Parliament - a cumbersome procedure. Vested interests would look askance at change. In the new industrial areas, the church hardly touched the population at all.

In 1815 the Province of York still had only 2,000 parishes compared with 10,000 in the Province of Canterbury. In Manchester, there were still only 56 churches when the population was 515,581. In Liverpool, the total church accommodation amounted to about 21,000 seats for a population of 94,000; a little later, in Oldham, the figures were 1,700 seats for 18,000, in Stockport 2,000 for 33, 393, and in Walsall 700 for 9,389.

In the woollen towns the picture was much the same. In Bradford, between 1800 and 1840, only three Anglican churches were built as the population boomed from 13,264 to 66,715. It is little wonder, therefore, that in 1851 Bradford had the third highest proportion of Nonconformists in the urban areas of England.

Although the will to implement a 'satisfactory' structure for the church's role in the community seems to be widespread amongst christian denominations, most of the time, attempts to widen the church's presence in society are very unsuccessful. The early growth of the Methodist movement and the more recent mushrooming of the House-Church Movements provide church analysts with an important lesson. Much of the problem of declining church members is to do with the styles and structures characterised through the choice imposed by the traditional churches. To some extent, the denominational churches today are guilty of the same kind of inflexibility, so heavily rooted in the structural formations of the past, when it comes to responding to demographic change in the UK.

An Experience of One Innovatory Project

Against most of the background given above, church groups, especially under the Methodist denominational style, have undertaken projects aimed at addressing some of the issues associated with church attendance decline and innovative administrative style. As society is beginning to show signs of a deeper multi-cultural cliché, churches are nowdays also turning to inter-denominational structures. This is not dissimilar to small businesses grouping together to fight declining market share and, by becoming more integrated with each other, to attempt to ensure survival. Diverse branches of the Christian movement are, therefore, coming together to explore the benefits of 'ecumenical' association of faith-sharers. The upsurge of ecumenical community projects for church development based on the 'House-Church' has been very appealing to frustrated leaders who are trying continuously to find alternatives ways of increasing people's participation in church matters.

An ecumenical community project was put together recently under the leadership of the Methodist Church in Skelmersdale in England which was at the centre of this new town development. The plan drawn up for this undertaking embraced issues such as finance, the number of church groups, clergy input, household background, location, size as well as the most 'ideal' management style for a christian-church like project. On paper, at least, therefore, painstaking measures were taken to ensure a comprehensive approach to the project and its successful outcome. Certainly, it is not the intention of this paper to detail every one of the stages in this project's development. However, a detailed review of the Methodist church's approach to the church-planting and development of the project at Skelmersdale reveals the following problems with its overall project delivery:

- *Lack of planning:* In Skelmersdale, the denominations did not have a clear response to the New Town Plan, and this resulted in the allocation of an inappropriate site for the new church.

- *Lack of research:* The British Council of Churches received a detailed proposal from the New Town Ministers' Association for a research project into mission in new towns. Although this would only have cost the same as one medium sized church hall it was deemed to be too expensive. Promulgation of the Church's gospel in new towns has continued without any detailed research backing.

- *Inappropriate church models:* The 'Servant' model of church life adopted by the clergy in Skelmersdale did not lead to a strong congregation or financial base. Surveys of local residents and community leaders reveal a sense of inappropriateness about this model for the community in which it was placed.

- *Denominational bureaucracy:* It is clear from the weight of correspondence and archive material that there was a great deal of interference from the head offices of the different denominations in Skelmersdale.

- *Tensions:* There is a great volume of evidence to suggest that the existing church congregations resented the arrival of the incomers and the new church which resulted.

- *Social imbalance:* There was a social bias towards working class and blue collar workers in the new community at Skelmersdale...but the church membership did not reflect this.

- *Ecumenical tensions:* There is a great deal of evidence to suggest that much time was spent in attempting to keep the different denominational groups together rather than in tackling the priority of mission together.

- *Management model:* The model of ministry at the ecumenical centre in Skelmersdale was originally very professional and directive. Surveys of the congregation reveal resentment of this.

- *Buildings before people:* The design and structure of the new ecumenical centre in Skelmersdale was felt by many in the emerging community to be inappropriate as a church.

- *Financial dependency*: The grant aided funding which started up the new centre appears to have created a dependency culture, and to this day the centre still looks to the headquarters of the church for a great deal of financial support.

Conclusion

The current declining position on church attendees commonly affects the established and church traditional groups. Although there is wide evidence to corroborate this, too little is known about the causes and plausible solutions are not yet available. The trend downwards, experienced by major denominations, is very often associated with the changing social and economic nature of a secular society. Furthermore, churches, overall, seem to be equipped with leaders having limited managerial skill comparable to other areas of the economy and, especially the profit-making organisation sector. As most of the aims and objectives of the work carried out by ecumenical groups fail to be fully recognised by church goers, it seems that the downward trend is unstoppable, at least for the time being. Because bitter divisions exist amongst the mainstream denominations whose respective leaders and members have deep-rooted differences as to the most appropriate overall administrative style of churches, any attempt to bring leaders from different church background to work together have, so far, proved very wasteful. This paper provides one example of such a wasteful project - a management structure formed by church leaders of diverse commitment and believing principles resulted in failure in the case of Skelmesdale. Compared to the approaches used by the traditional Churches, the 'House-Church' movement has used a simplistic administrative technique on smaller scalle contexts and its attendees are still growing strongly. It is important to undertake further projects similar to Skelmersdale's so that lessons learned can be put to good effect in improving the success of these types of projects and in supporting and achieving the vision of a national church renewal. It is also recognised that both an inside assessment on objectives and performance of such projects, combined with principles based upon the business function of marketing as applied to the non-profit-making sector, would improve the managerial style and the strategic development of churches.

References

Beasley-Murray, P. and Wilkinson, A. (1980) *Turning the Tide* (Bible Society)

Brierly, P. (1994) *The U.K. Christian Handbook 1994-5* (London: Christian Research Association).

Currie, R. (1970) *Churches and Church-Goers: Patterns of Church Growth in the British Isles Since 1700*

Davis, R. (1982) *The Testing of the Churches 1932-82* (Epworth)

Gilbert, A. D. (1981) *Making of a Post-Christian Britain* (Longman)

Gill, R. (1988) *A Challenge to the Churches* (S.C.M. Press)

Halsey, A. H. (1986) *Change in British Society* (Opus)

Hoggart, R. (1958) *The Uses of Literacy* (Penguin)

Marc Europe (1993) 'Christian England', results of National Opinion Polls carried out in 1992.

Martin, C. (1988) *Schools Now* (Lion)

Naisbitt, J. (1990) *Megatrends 2,000* (Sedgwick and Jackson)

Ostling, R. (1989) *Time Magazine* (May edition)

MARKETING ON HALF A P

Simon Kelly and Harry Hellyer

Introduction

We will begin by explaining the meaning of the title of this article and by clarifying what this article is about. The article is not about managing marketing programmes on incredibly low budgets, as might be inferred by the title. Rather it is about the management of a Marketing Department in an enormous organisation, British Telecom (BT). The 'half a P' of the title refers to the extent of the control that the Marketing department in question holds over the '4Ps' (Product, Price, Place and Promotion) of the 'marketing mix' for those customers with whom the Department is concerned.

The article will be developed in the following way. First, we will give a brief overview of the changes which have taken place at BT over the past decade and in the telecommunications industry. Having conveyed a sense of the fundamental changes which have taken place and of the dynamic and uncertain nature of the present situation, we will move into a discussion of the role of the Marketing department and the difficulties it faces in seeking to influence the total marketing profile from a position of having direct control over only half the Promotion element of the 4Ps and none over Price, Product and Place. Finally, we examine the competencies which people in 'Marketing' require given the context in which they work. Given this we then examine the key competencies required for people working in Marketing. The central context to which this discussion relates is the Customer Marketing department in the Business Communications division of BT.

BT - a Brief History

In the early days of telecommunications, the telephone service in the UK was provided by the General Post Office (a government department) in competition with private sector companies. In 1896, the Post Office took over the private sector trunk service and in 1912 became the monopoly supplier of telephone services throughout the UK other than in a few municipalities, including Kingston-Upon-Hull where local service is still provided by the City Council.

In 1969, the Post Office ceased to be a government department and was established as a state public corporation. In 1981, the postal and telecommunications services of the Post Office became the responsibility of two separate corporations with British Telecommunications taking over the telecommunications side of the business. At the same time, the first steps were taken to liberalise the telecommunications market and to introduce new competition.

In November 1982, a Bill was introduced in Parliament to convert British Telecom into a public limited company (plc) and to enable the government to sell shares in the new company. In November 1984, the government offered 3,012 million ordinary shares for sale to the public whilst retaining the remaining 50% shareholding in its own ownership. British Telecom shares made their debut on the London stock exhange on 3 December 1984.

The last ten years, in particular, have been a time of dramatic change at BT, and in the UK telecommunications and IT markets and the more general environment in which BT operates. Shaped by the UK government's free market policies, the UK telecommunications market has become the most liberal telecoms market in the world. Since the formation of Mercury in the mid-1980s as BT's first network competitor, many new players have entered the market. Some of the more recent entrants include cable companies and Energis which was formed from the electricity industry. The Porter-based diagram shown below indicates the current competitive nature of the telecommunications industry in the UK.

General economic conditions have influenced the situation facing BT. The recessionary environment which prevailed throughout the late 1980s led many businesses to retreat to their core activities. Growth has been achieved increasingly through partnerships and the search for, and development into, new markets. Globalisation of market places is increasing. The rapidity of technological change has shortened product life cycles and an increase in choice of technology has created increasing complexity in the market place. In totality, the forces of politics, legislation, technology and economics have created an environment for BT which is much more dynamic, diverse and difficult and much more uncertain than that in which it traditionally operated.

Organisation Changes

In response to these environmental developments, BT has itself changed. Its operating structure has changed from one based on more than 60 telephone areas in the early 1980s to one based on 27 districts. This was followed by a radical change in organisation philosophy and structure which was reflected in the formation of functional directorates described below.

230

Five Forces Analysis

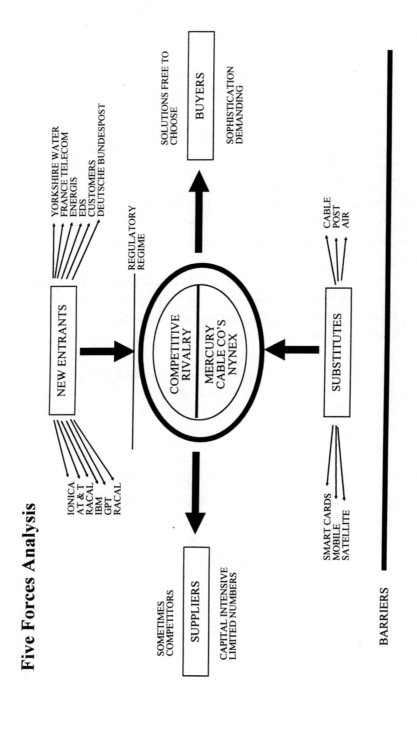

Figure 1

The three divisions which interface directly with customers are Business Communications and Personal Communications, for the core telecommunications activities, and Special Businesses for areas outside this. These divisions typically have their own Sales, Marketing and Service functions. They are also supported by central directorates including:

- Development and Procurement (D&P) which is responsible for researching and developing new technologies.
- Products and Services Management (PSM) who specify, develop and manage the portfolio of BT's products and services.
- Worldwide Networks (WN) who design, build and maintain the network platforms that deliver the products and services.
- Headquarters (HQ) which includes the support activities such as Personnel and Group Computing Services.

In an organisation with a turnover in excess of twelve billion pounds, some of the directorates have more people and resources than many corporations.

As well as planning and overseeing restructuring at BT, top management continually seek to improve the organisation's productivity. The competitive threats in the market place and the drive into global markets have created the need to reduce BT's cost base. This has led to a reduction in the workforce from around 250,000 in the mid-1980's to the current figure of around 170,000. This has taken place alongside the implementation of a number of change programmes including Customer Care, Total Quality Management (TQM) and ISO9000 registration.

Segmentation of the Marketing Function

So far as Business Communications is concerned, the market is addressed through its division into three segments and the allocation of responsibility to different units of the organisation: Global, UK Global and National Customers. 'Global Marketing' represents large mutinationals who have their main centres outside the UK. 'UK Global' comprises the top 350 corporate clients with national interests. 'National Customers' is responsible for the rest of the business community.

UK Global, and a unit of its Marketing function, Customer Marketing, are the focus of this article. UK Global is responsible for the top 350 UK corporate clients. Its marketing team is split into 4 key functions :

- Generic Marketing - whose job it is to develop, design and implement programmes across the whole of the UK Global customer base.
- Business Market Management - which is the key interface into the PSM function and responsible for Product Marketing.

232

- Planning and Infomation Unit.
- Customer Marketing - which is responsible for marketing to industry sectors. This department is the focus of this article and the functional home of the authors. Its fundamental role is to ensure that the needs of their customers are being met. How we attempt to do this will be discussed later.

Ownership of the 4Ps

The discussion to this point should have conveyed a sense of the size and complexity of BT and of the turbulent environment in which it operates. Market change and market challenges means that BT has to be better than ever at marketing. Organisational size and complexity mean, however, that the job of marketing is not so straightforward as that portrayed (or implicitly assumed) in many marketing text books and reports which put forward the view that although marketing is a job for everyone in the organisation, its base is in one 'tight' Marketing department which has clear responsibility for the design and operation of the marketing mix. As one example of this dominant and traditional view, Coopers and Lybrand claim that marketing, with its perceived role of 'identifying and meeting customer needs profitably' will best serve the organisation by genuinely managing the customer interface. They argue in *Marketing at the Crossroads* that successful organisations in the 1990s will be those whose marketing department will:

- Have within its remit all the processes that contribute to managing the customer and customer interface.
- Have clear and defined responsibility for these processes.
- Focus on activities that demonstrably add value.
- Be judged against these measures.

At BT the situation is not so simple, and many organisational functions and units play their part in arriving at choices on the marketing mixes which will eventually be operationalised in the market place. The Customer Marketing department, for example, operates from a position of little authority in relation to the various other departments involved in creating the customer interface whilst nevertheless having a great deal of responsibility for the success or otherwise of the marketing outcomes realised. To understand how Customer Marketing achieves its basic role of ensuring that its customers needs are met, readers need to understand the answers to "Who owns Marketing?" and "How much influence does Customer Marketing have?" Thus, the answer to the first question is: "Ownership is shared and negotiated", and the second answer is: "formally, only limited power, but potentially, through more informal and interpersonal mechanisms, a lot of power".

By way of explanation we will indicate which parts of the organisation have central responsibility for aspects of the marketing mix. Thus we have:

Price - which is controlled, ultimately, by PSM.

Product - which, in a service industry, needs to be regarded as all the component parts that are required to make the product or service purchased by the client work effectively. So far as the product is concerned, there are many influential stakeholders in the BT community:

- Research and Development, which decides which technologies to develop further.
- PSM, which, as we have already explained, specifies products and services and is responsible for launch and withdrawal (of products/services) decisions.
- Procurement, which makes the buying decisions that, in turn, affect the constitution and capability of the final product/service and also determinesto a large degree the service levels customers will be delivered. Who Procurement buy from, and what they buy, are critical decisions because BT does not manufacture its own products.
- Customer Service, which is the service arm of the Business Communication division and the policies they implement significantly affect what is perceived to be 'BT's product' in the eyes of customers. Everything from speed of installation and repair and knowledge of the equipment being fitted or maintained to the quality of customer interactions affects the final product offering.
- Sales. In an environment where the product portfolio runs into four figures the products and service mix offered to meet the customers' business needs is very complex. The quality of Account Management provided by Sales to clients is a crucial factor in influencing their views of the product offering.

Promotion/Packaging is another multi-influenced 'P'. For example:

- Customer Communications Unit has overall ownership of the BT image. This unit is responsible for commissioning advertising agencies, writing advertisement briefs and monitoring the effectiveness of communication campaigns.
- Customer Marketing, as already indicated, is the authors' work-home. It has responsibility only for some of the promotional input into the total marketing mix having direct budget and resource under its control for the undertaking of promotions into industry sectors. Its promotional budget is spent on activities such as industry events and newsletters. Customer Marketing is also the key player in decisions on how the portfolio of products and services is presented to a particular industry sector in order to ensure that our solutions are packaged in ways which clearly address industry needs.

Place is also determined by the interaction of a number of internal stakeholder groups including:

- Product and Service Management, which has ultimate responsibility for deciding where the equipment required to drive key products and services is to be deployed. This is a critical aspect of the marketing mix decision process as decisions made here affect the availability of services offered, particularly if they are network-based offerings.

- Sales, which decides on the number and the quality of sales people deployed. This obviously impacts on where, how and what gets delivered to the customer. Clearly, therefore, Sales has a big influence on client perceptions of the Account Managment Service they are being offered.
- Customer Service, the service arm of the Business Communications Division, which makes decisions about the quantity and ability of the people employed to install and maintain products and services. The decisions taken here will affect product/service provision and repair times and the customers' perceptions of the quality of service offered.
- Worldwide Networks, which is responsible for deployment of capital equipment in exchanges and in the ground. This impacts on the people deployment and management issues raised above and so has a big shaping influence on 'Place' (and the other Ps, for that matter).

Figure 2 indicates the multi-influence nature of the decisional processes which lead to the implementation of actual marketing mixes in our customer markets.

Ownership of the 4Ps

Price

Products &
Sevice Management

Promotion/Packaging

Brand Ownership:
Customer Communications
Customer Marketing

Product

Products & Sevices
Mangement
R & D
Group Procurement
Customer Service
Sales

Place

Products & Services
Management
Sales
Customer Service
Worldwide Networks

Figure 2

The Roles of Customer Marketing

The stated aim of Customer Marketing is to:

> drive change and innovation, influenced by people directly responsible for sales, service and marketing of BT's product portfolios by changing the focus of our business from concentrating on individual products and services, to providing solutions to satisfy customer needs.

This departmental aim needs to be considered in the context of its fit with the re-orientation of BT from a product-led organisation to a customer-focused and market-led one. Figure 3 indicates the nature of, and differences between, the old and the new BT philosophies.

PRODUCT LED INFORMATION FLOW

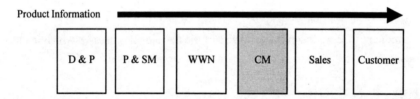

CLIENT FOCUSED MARKETING LED INFORMATION FLOW

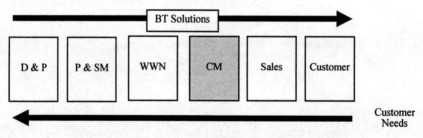

Figure 3

In the light of Customer Marketing's stated aim and the earlier discussion on 'ownership of the 4Ps', three clear conclusions can be drawn from the discussion in the above section:

- almost everyone in BT is involved in Marketing.
- to ensure success Customer Marketing must endeavour to embed the marketing philosophy throughout the company.
- Customer Marketing must extend its influence, in order to ensure that its customers' needs are met, beyond the level of influence inferred by its position and resource base in the formal scheme of things.

In terms of the first of these conclusions, it is worth making the point that as well as everyone being part of the marketing effort, the Customer Marketing department needs to adopt other functional perspectives (such as purchasing, production, personnel and fincance) and to interface with the departments which provide the specialist lead in these areas of organisational activity. Thus, Customer Marketing works with the Purchasing department with respect to the exchange of information regarding the markets that the two departments operate in, particularly when clients are also suppliers, and the planning of new products and the evaluation of trends affecting raw material supplies. It may work with the production department to discuss likely levels of product demand and production/marketing schedules, and it may work closely with production to help provide solutions to client problems. Customer Marketing also works with the R&D department, providing it with market research to ascertain client group needs and helping in the crucial function of new product development. Customer Marketing managers often also work with the Personnel department, both to provide criteria for selecting staff and for the provision of specific training across the organisation. Finally, marketing is a profit generating activity and so its staff need to be aware of costs, sales volumes and profits and should be able to work with the Finance department in order profitably to exploit corporate resources. In a client-focused company, the most important interface of all, for the Marketing department and the Company, remains that between itself and its customers.

This multi-faceted interface of marketing with other aspects of the corporation is illustrated in Figure 4.

Corporate Interface of Marketing

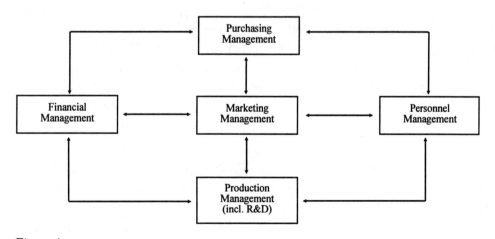

Figure 4

However, the model shown in Figure 4 provides an over-simplistic representation of the interlinked nature of Customer Marketing at BT. A more comprehensive (although still simplistic) view of the Customer Marketing/ corporate interface is provided in Figure 5. This acknowledges the interactions between the Customer Marketing department and the units referred to in the discussion about control of the 4Ps.

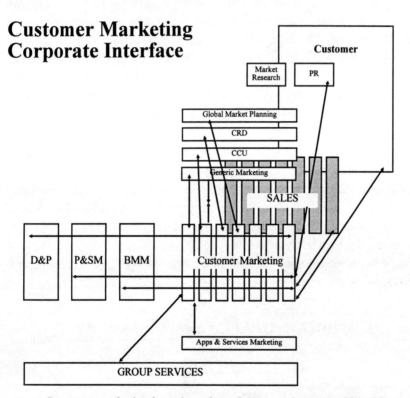

Customer Marketing Corporate Interface

- Customer marketing has a huge boundary spanning role within BT.
- IT covers the intersection of product lines and individual lines of business it helps integrate customer needs with products and applications to provide solutions

Figure 5

In terms of the second and third of the above-mentioned conclusions, the discussion in the previous section makes it clear that the policies and actions of a number of directorates significantly influence customer perception and ultimate success levels achieved in the market place. It also indicates that Customer Marketing has direct control only over some of the promotional aspects of the marketing mix. However, its job of ensuring that customers' needs are met requires it to be much more influential than its formal position and resource budget infers in shaping the ultimate 'Ps mix' which impacts in the market place. It has to influence 'the other three and a half Ps' despite the difficulties of this task, particularly given strong power bases for the Production and Sales departments (as is often the case with organisations producing high value capital goods with long life cycles). If this does not happen then potential dangers could become reality. For example:

- Research could become 'technology pushed', resulting in product and service development which does not satisfy customer demand and, consequentially, wasting investment resources and missing revenue generating opportunities.
- Products could be priced at levels which do not fit market requirements.
- Lack of industry knowledge could result in campaigns which aim to sell technological features rather than to market known customer/industry needs.
- Capital and people might be deployed without sufficient reference to market requirements leading to wasted cost, customer dissatisfaction and lost revenue.

The Technical and Political/Social Roles of Customer Marketing Staff

In ensuring that the organisation markets itself effectively, Customer Marketing staff need to be expert at functional (or technical) aspects of marketing and at 'politicking' and 'socialising' in order to influence other parts of the organisation. Skills associated with the first type of expertise are probably easier to understand, articulate and acquire than are those associated with the second type. Some important functional skill requirements are reflected in five areas of activity in which Customer Marketing plays key roles. These areas are:

(i) Understanding Customer Needs

Much has been said in the management literature about 'getting closer to the customer'. The Customer Marketing department needs to understand what this concept actually means in practice. A customer marketing specialist must deeply understand the customers and the industry he is working with and in. This understanding has to be sufficiently profound to enable BT to provide affordable solutions to the important communications problems of its key customers. These must meet real business needs and lead to satisfaction from the perspective of a business customer's end-user customer. In large multinational organisations, a knowledge of who the customers are and how an organisation can be segmented into different types of customer is also essential. In addition to this, a clear picture of what an industry's expects of BT, particularly with regard to service standards, has to be developed.

Understanding customer needs is thus only a means to an end - the delivery of customer satisfaction. The Customer Marketing department must therefore ensure that sound understanding is transferred across the relevant parts of BT. The trick, here, is to ensure that the link is made between the customer needs and the operational policies that need to be changed. This leads us to the next key activity area.

(ii) Driving the Planning Process

Understanding of customer needs must be used to drive the planning process in all parts of the business. If divisional plans are drawn up without regard for important, customer-related aspects of the market place and in isolated, non-integrated ways, all the dangers mentioned in the previous section will become operational reality. It is vital that industry market plans take into account what the rest of the organisation needs to deliver and are then used to drive planning activity in other areas. If this is not done then the only part of the Market Plan which can be guaranteed to be delivered is the promotional plan (or the Customer Marketing department's half of it).

(iii) Educating the BT Community

In every interaction with the rest of the business, Customer Marketing must seek to educate people about how industry needs affect the way they need to operate. It is not enough just to seek to impress others with a high level of industry knowledge. Positive, customer oriented changes are the fundamental objective of these communications and information exchanges involving the Department.

By showing customers that we are keen to learn what drives their businesses and to translate this knowledge into packaged solutions which meet their needs quickly and effectively, we will enhance our chances of maintaining organisational success. Further, our longer-term investments need to be clearly communicated as having been triggered by their expressed future needs.

(iv) Developing Solutions

At the end of the day, a Customer Marketing department is of little worth unless it develops solutions in response to customer needs and ensures that these are implemented. There is a clear link here between, on the one hand, the activity of developing solutions, and on the other hand that of driving the planning process. If ideas for new solutions are not sold effectively within the business, and incorporated into corporate and divisional business plans, they stand little or no chance of ever getting to market.

240

The above are merely five key activity areas for the Customer Marketing department and its staff, and do not provide an exhaustive list of the activities which need to be performed. Other important, traditional activities of competitive analysis, market research, market analysis and performance monitoring remain important.

The popular view of the mythical 'Marketing Man' is that of the eccentric wearing braces and tortoise shell glasses. The key physical attributes of 'Marketing Man' which relate to our Department's functional tasks include:

- Elephant sized ears - constantly listening for customer needs, for information on competitor activity and for opportunities to educate the business.
- Planet sized brain - full of innovative ideas to meet customer needs in a creative way from the enormous portfolio at his disposal - and to remember the key features of major product areas.
- Big smile - to help create a good impression with customers and to increase the chances of success when trying to sell ideas and propositions internally.
- Mans a spanner - prepared to turn his hand to anything to ensure that an identified need gets developed to the point where a new product of service comes to fruition
- Bush baby eyes - always on the look out for an opportunity.

These types of physical attributes are also required in other parts of large organisations where the percentage of total control over a business function that any one particular manager holds is often small to the point of insignificance. BT has acknowledged this by radically reshaping its appraisal process towards measuring performance in areas of key competencies and away from a straight linear measurement of objectives achieved. These personal competencies are particularly relevant to Customer Marketing and cover areas such as customer focus and commercial and business awareness. Standards have been set in each of these competencies in order to describe clearly what is regarded to be high performance.

Key functional roles and their associated skills need to be supported by interpersonal skills if they are to impact across the organisation characterised by a situation of shared power. Thus, people working in the Customer Marketing department need to be especially competent in political and social interactions. What is needed is a group of 'Marketing Man' types who possess the personal qualities associated with the ability to:

- Conduct an orchestra - this is a key ability and the one we will focus on in what follows.

This skill is a pre-requisite to the achievement of *internal* and *interactive* marketing thrusts - two key aspects of modern service marketing which extend the traditional '4Ps' approach to the marketing function (see Figure 6). In this new, enlarged model of the marketing function *external* marketing covers the work involved in designing and implementing the 4Ps whilst *internal* marketing refers to the efforts undertaken by the company in training and motivating its internal customers. *Interactive* marketing refers to the employees' skill in handling the customer interface - in its technical and functional quality dimensions.

Service Marketing Relationships

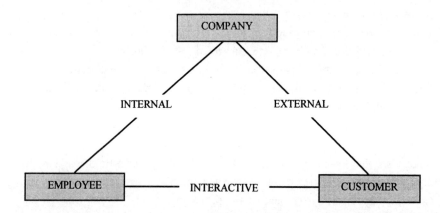

Customer marketing operates within an industrial marketing framework, as such it has direct influence on only one of the 4 P's - Promotion.

However it also wishes to operate in a service marketing environment, which includes the traditional 4P's + 2 marketing thrusts - these need to be managed effectively if BT is to succeed with its aims.

Figure 6

Given no direct management control over a large part of the budget and the people required to serve customer needs effectively, getting the relevant parts of the business to 'play in time' is perhaps the key job requirement of members of the Customer Marketing department. Associated competency areas in which people are being assessed at BT are those of leadership, motivation and people management.

The job of conducting an orchestra requires leadership skills for motivating teams of people to deliver high standards of customer-relevant performance in conditions where their 'pay and rations' are not directly under the control of the 'leader'. Thus a key requirement of personnel in the Marketing role is that they have the capability to a lead a 'virtual team'.

Leading a Virtual Team

All of the roles desribed earlier need to be combined and put into effective practice by the Customer Marketing team in order to avoid the dangers that can occur if there is insufficient marketing input into the organisation's strategic decisions. We have already said that isolated industry knowledge and expertise is worthless - it needs to be used to drive planning and educate the organisation.

Virtual business teams can be key enablers of success. The core members of such teams need to be the key customer-facing people from Customer Marketing, Sales and Customer Service. The aim of such teams should be to make the organisation become marketing-led and sales-driven. This aim can be said to have been realised when the rest of the business shares revenue and customer satisfaction goals. The core members of these teams bring together and integrate sector market plans and 'pull' the team key players from all those parts of the organisation who must collaborate in order to deliver successfully the key elements of the plan. Once this has been done, the key task is to track actual progress against the plan and to ensure that customer needs are being successfully satisfied. This leadership process is much more akin to orchestra conducting (involving the harnessing of expert contributions from groups of 'equals', as and when required, to achieve an effective overall outcome, in ways which acknowledge and give scope to each contributor's expertise and position) rather than to military leadership (wherein people are expected to work in blind adherance to the instruction of the hierarchical leader). Orchestra conducting is becoming a key requirment of managers in Customer Marketing and of managers in other parts of the organisation.

Conclusions

The traditional view of the Marketing department is one which sees the function being the ultimate responsibility of a department which has control over the elements of the marketing mix. This article has sought to cast light on the reality of marketing in a giant organisation - and specifically the organisation that is BT. This big organisation view of the Marketing department differs from the traditional model in that the ultimate forms in which combinations of price, place, promotion and product impact in the market place are the results of power-diffused decisional process wherein many personnel from different parts of the organisation play influential roles.

The job of the Customer Marketing department at BT is to make sure that customer needs are addressed in effective, customer satisfying and organisationally productive ways. Staff of the department, therefore, need high levels of skills in the functions associated with the achievement of a customer effective interaction and also need high levels of skills in 'conducting organisation stakeholders' from positions of only partial formal power and limited resource bases, in order to ensure that customer responsiveness gets embedded into the cultural fabric of the organisation, into its range of plans and, crucially, into its *customer interactions*. This is a boundary spanning role and is based on effective internal as well as external marketing.

Today's "Marketing Man" should most of all be an orchestra conductor who can lead a "Virtual Team", where the violin and cello players are not directly controlled by him/her. This involves facilitating the organisation towards a more task-centred culture where far more value is placed on expert contribution and team working.

Bibliography

Bender, H. (1989) 'Marketing Technologically Advanced Products', *European Management Journal*, 7(2).

Canton, I. (1988) 'How Manufacturers Can Move Into The Service Business', *Journal of Business Strategy* (July/August).

Jackson, R. and Cooper, P. (1988) 'Unique Aspects of Marketing Industrial Services', *Industrial Marketing Management, 17*.

Lysonski, S. (1985) 'A Boundary Theory Investigation of the Product Manager's Role', *Journal of Marketing, 49* (Winter).

McDermott, D. and Schweitzer, C. (1980) 'Product vs. Customer Focused Industrial Selling', *Industrial Marketing Management, 9*.

Ruekert, R., Walker, O. and Roering, K. (1985) 'The Organisation of Marketing Activities: A Contingency Theory of Structure and Performance', *Journal of Marketing, 49* (Winter).

Ruekert, R. and Orville, C. Jnr. (1987) 'Marketing's Interaction With Other Functional Units: A Conceptual Framework', *Journal of Marketing, 51* (January).

Saghafi, M., Gupta, A. and Sheth, N. (1990) 'R & D/Marketing Interfaces in the Telecommunications Industry', *Industrial Marketing Management, 19*.

Shostack, G. (1987) 'Service Positioning Through Structural Change', *Journal of Marketing, 51* (January).

JIM STEVENS AND HYDRO ENGINEERING

Bill Richardson, Sheffield Business School[1]

Introduction: Jim Stevens and the Pre-Hydro Engineering Days

Jim Stevens is enthusiastic about life and about his business. Conversation with Jim about his business seems inevitably to include many references to his approach to life and his self-stated need to "control my own destiny". As a young qualified engineer with a seemingly secure job with a British nationalised industry, his need to do something with his life, coupled with his belief in his ability to control his own destiny, led to a career move:

> I looked across the room one day at an older colleague. He was an engineer too. It was all he'd ever done and it was all he was ever likely to do. This was OK for many people in my area, lots of people from around here go to the same pub in an evening and sit in the same seat, year in, year out. I decided this type of life wasn't for me.

A career move into education, as a lecturer in a southern Polytechnic, followed.

> I was happy to spend some time in this post. The job was OK, I was learning all the time, although the pay was pretty hopeless. I asked one of my managers about promotion to the next level of the scale. He said that people usually get that type of move after around eleven years in the job. That wasn't for me and I decided to move on.

1   The author wishes to express his thanks for the assisstance proferred by Gregory Elliot, John Cullen and Michael Outterside in the preparation of this paper.

The next move for Jim was into his own business in industrial machinery. This didn't work out and he moved again, leaving the venture with some new insights that helped mould his views on business management.

> In particular, I learned a lesson about working in a partnership. For me, it didn't work out. Often, people who start to run their own business have this grand idea that being the director of a firm automatically implies success without any need to work extra hard. The reality of building up that organisation, however, meant eighteen hour days and being there whenever the situation demanded our presence. My partner didn't really want the long days and the weekend work.

A move to another continent followed as Jim pursued his machinery-related career, this time working on ships with an organisation based in Africa. After two years, Jim and family moved back to the UK, whereupon Jim met a local Yorkshire business man John Graham. Graham had a well-established business and was looking toward developing a new side to its activity, one which included a move into the hydraulic machinery industry. Jim was delighted to take a role with the Graham organisation, helping to lead this new venture. "I know hydraulics", he says, "it has been my life."

For John Graham, however, the move into hydraulics created more problems than he had envisaged. He became disenamoured with the project and decided to get out. Jim saw things differently:

> The hydraulics industry had a lot of potential and I had spent months getting the thing off the ground. The major problem with John was that he hadn't planned well enough and felt uncomfortable in an area he didn't really know. He wasn't really a 'hydraulics man'. I decided to keep the new venture going. I had three months to get a financial package together and to take over operations.

John Graham proved to be an important source of guidance:

> John was an astute businessman and I learned a lot from him. In particular, he taught me that the top manager's job is to take an overview and to act as the controller of what others do. Before working with John, I was very much a hands-on operator, I felt I had to do everything myself. Now I employ people to do things and I manage. I can still turn my hand to any job but, when you think about it, the manager sees more of the game than the player, doesn't he?

Given his varied and restless background, the question might be posed as to whether Jim is likely to become bored with Hydro-Engineering. Four years into the business, however, Jim is confident that the job of controlling and developing the company will continue to provide him with too many challenges and new venture opportunities for this to be the case.

246

Development of the Organisation

The newly-formed Hydro-Engineering was trading, as a partnership, in January 1989. Initial capital for the business was raised by Jim and his wife; this was added to via a range of hard and soft loans from banks and established Business Enterprise support agencies. Newly-acquired premises were small and barely adequate and little time was available for Jim to plan in a time-consuming, orderly fashion, the move from Graham's premises to the new site. He and his team of three former Graham employees had needed quickly to find a base from which to continue to grow the business and to keep its operations moving.

By autumn of 1991, it had become apparent that another move was necessary. Larger and more suitable premises would be needed if the business was to continue to grow. Such premises were located a short distance away and the pressure to move quickly - increased production was vital to satisfy potential orders - was once again apparent. Jim personally designed the layout of the new site and worked eighteen hour-plus days in an effort to ensure that everything was ready for the 'grand opening day', scheduled for March 1992. The day arrived and was a success. Jim was, as he put it, 'shattered'.

During the period when the focus of his attention had been on moving into the new premises in the short time available, Jim was aware that other sides of the business were being neglected.

> We were doing OK. A lot of our business just came through the post every morning. We do a lot of our work for British Coal - around 49 per cent of our turnover came from this and much of it was easily attracted. However, during those months when we were concentrating on the move, we weren't putting in as much effort as I would have liked into developing the sales side of the business. I was just waiting to get into the new premises and then we could start to push on that front again.

Once in the new premises, however, other organisational issues emerged and once again diverted the attention and effort away from the sales generation function:

> Our general manager and our foreman left in June/July 1992. It was a big blow to us and we needed to find suitable replacements quickly, which wasn't an easy job. I think the old managers never adapted to the new conditions. Back in the old place they more or less did things in their own way and at their own pace. In this new set-up we had professional management control systems and a new impetus. The move brought new pressures to the business. Our overheads were a lot higher. We couldn't afford to operate in the same old way. We needed to do more business more effectively. In this type of situation you just have to find out what has to be done and do it. The new arrangements didn't suit them. As it happens we were lucky. We appointed a new general manager in September 1992 - he came from British Coal and I knew he'd had the right training - and he is doing a good job.

Once again the business was ready to embark on a sales development thrust. Once again, problems were around the corner. On the 13th October 1992, Michael Heseltine made an announcement confirming rumours that the Government planned to decimate the British coal industry by the closure of 31 pits in the near future. The potential damage to Hydro Engineering was only too clear. Jim had expected some of the pits to close and some of the company's business to be lost, but the scope of the closure plan took the company by surprise:

> We were expecting some of the pits to close and some of our business to go with them. However, we weren't expecting the closure programme that was announced. This just blew away the industry. We couldn't find out anything from anybody - nobody in the industry seemed to be talking about what the future would be. Orders just dried up for a period of time. British Coal represented 46 per cent of our turnover last year; now it's less than 20 per cent. I was away at the time of the announcement. I phoned my general manager and we set up a meeting to sort out the options. It was obvious we couldn't maintain our existing cost base without the turnover. We called the men together one morning and explained the situation. They were given a choice of some job losses or a share-out of the pain - short time working. They opted for short time working, three days a week initially, although thank goodness we soon picked up work again and we are now back onto full time working. Nevertheless, wage costs have been reduced by 30 per cent since the pit closure programme was announced.

Personnel Issues

From its four person beginnings, Hydro Engineering new employs eighteen people. Jim demands flexibility, enthusiasm and hard work from his employees:

> They need to be flexible. I sacked someone who could, and would, only machine. I look for enthusiasm. I'd rather have enthusiasm than skill. If you have someone who is enthusiastic, you can help them to develop skills. People who don't come here to work can go.

Employees are paid to industry standards and can earn a small bonus if output has been particularly high. The hours of work are either 7.00 am to 3.30 pm, or 8.00 am to 4.30 pm. Overtime is an accepted part of the job and is used to get orders out on time. Staff must clock in and out of work and are also required to complete the associated documentation before payment is made. Jim has on occasions refused to pay for undocumented claims of work.

An important principle for Jim in his communication and dealing with staff is to be honest and straightforward: "You tell people what's on your mind and what the situation is and they respect you for it." Most training and development undertaken by the organisation is 'on the job', informal training. Jim is not too keen on traditional management development programmes:

> I sent one of my managers on one of these programmes. It seemed to me that he spent most of his time playing at a 'case study'. I'm not too sure about the usefulness of this. So far as I'm concerned, I'm playing at real life. This organisation is a real life case study.

Despite his aversion to particular types of management development programmes, Jim acknowledges the usefulness of a supervisor's training programme he attended during one of his previous occupations. This is the only formal management training he has undertaken, but he continually uses some of the concepts and techniques that were introduced to him on this programme "much more than I ever use material from my engineering background". His managerial philosophy and style, however, are most influenced by his life and work experiences and by his need to be in control.

When asked about his role in the company, Jim says he spends a lot of his time simply 'being around'. His major functional roles are concerned with financial policy and control, quality control, customer attraction and customer service. He lists many of his business associates as friends, but ensures that business and pleasure are not mixed: "If I spend social time with a business associate, we never talk business."

Customers, Marketing and Competitors.

The major occupation of the organisation is the testing and repair of hydraulic machinery. A more precise description of the nature of the company's operations is provided in Appendix One. Many of Hydro Engineering's customers are large corporations and include British Coal, British Steel and BAA. The company has recently achieved 'approved' status with the Ministry of Defence and is awaiting its first orders from the Army. The organisation also carries out work for contractors to these kind of customers. These contractors include big companies such as Feranco, Blue Circle Cementation and Amco.

Hydro Engineering is highly dependent on a small number of clients, some 80 per cent of turnover being generated by 20 per cent of the company's customers. Another problem with the existing customer base is that many of the industries are in states of maturity or decline, particularly in the case of British Coal, and also with British Steel and the Ministry of Defence. Despite this, there is a large total demand for the company's services. As Jim says, "hydraulics is everywhere".

Jim does appreciate the dangers of the current situation and of the associated need to seek out new markets:

We got used to orders coming from British Coal through the post and I suppose life was quite easy. This has changed. We now need to broaden our customer base if we are to maintain turnover and generate the profits that will be important to our moving into new, more lucrative markets. What I tend to do is not to do a big market study or anything like that, but just to keep calling on existing and potential customers periodically, just to let them know that we are still interested and to find out how things are and to let them know that 'this is where we are at'. It's really a matter of talking to them to keep them interested and to let them know that we are still interested.

Jim has recently been exploring the aviation industry and has spoken with buyers from that industry:

Work for this type of industry has to be carried out in an area completely shut off from the rest of the workshop; these type of operations will need quite a lot of capital. I'd like to get into this type of market though, despite the high-capital cost. I see markets as creating a triangle. At the bottom is a broad base of competition, fighting it out over the bread-and-butter work. At the top there aren't so many operators who can deliver what is required. This is where the extra profits are to be earned. I'd like to get us into these areas.

Much of the company's marketing is carried out by word-of-mouth contracts and repeat orders, based on the provision of a high quality service. Jim is the person who spends most time with potential new clients. Two salesmen spend much of their time calling on existing customers.

Work contracts are priced by Jim and the general manager. A sophisticated computer-aided costing system helps them to estimate the likely costs, although Jim believes that cost is not the important aspect of the pricing decision, rather the price the customer is willing to pay. "If I think they will pay a large premium, I'll charge it regardless of whether the cost to us is minuscule." The customers are becoming increasingly cost (and price from supplier) conscious. A recent example of this is a request from a major customer in the steel industry for the company to hold prices at last year's levels.

They are happy with our quality, service and delivery, but they ask 'can we hold our prices?'. I have to go and see them to negotiate. I guess we will have to compromise, ultimately - some prices will hold, some will have to go up.

Service responsiveness and quality of work are key factors in attracting new customers. Jim talks of occasions where customers have placed orders with cheaper competitors only to return to his company to get the job done properly. Again, sophisticated work planning and progressing systems enable the organisation to work to relatively short customer lead times. This responsiveness to customer demands for supply to tight deadlines give the company a competitive edge, but ultimately means extra special effort. Jim sees these type of jobs as important builders of customer loyalty:

> The customer needs us most when his back is against the wall. Last night I took one of our completed jobs to Ollerton colliery. An engineer flew in from Germany and installed the equipment there and then. Others in this industry are only prepared to work nine to five.

Acting quickly to help a customer can cause problems by delaying less-urgent work, but customers are generally understanding, knowing well that they might be the next to require urgent help.

Jim sees Hydro Engineering as a 'national player'. In comparison, many of the company's smaller competitors in the same geographical area see themselves as regional suppliers only, he feels. In contrast to this comparatively wide-ranging perception of the company's market, Jim does not foresee any venture into the European market in the near future. The travel and distribution costs are viewed as a major barrier to entry by Hydro Engineering into this market.

No active monitoring of the company's competitors is currently undertaken. A lot of competition does exist in the form of both large and small companies and the level of competition has been increasing over the last four years. Some informal monitoring takes place, but this usually only amounts to finding out which competitors have taken Hydro's business.

Quality Assurance

Hydro Engineering has the BS5750 quality certification. The primary driving force behind the desire to achieve this standard was the stated intention by British Coal that future dealings would eventually only be with BS5750 approved companies. The intention was that by acting on British Coal's apparent intentions, Hydro would strengthen the trading relationship with British Coal at the expense of unapproved suppliers. So far, however, this quality strategy has not improved trade with British Coal. Recent restructuring of the coal industry has led to a decentralisation of profit accountability by British Coal, so that dealings now take place at colliery level rather than with a central purchasing function. The ensuing colliery level push for profit has meant that many companies without BS5750 have continued to obtain work, particularly if they offer a lower-priced service.

Despite this failure to generate more sales and the initial set-up and maintenance costs, Jim believes that the BS5750 implementation has been worthwhile. The organisation of the firm has been improved by the introduction of the quality system. The system has clarified the processes of the organisation, from order receipt to delivery of the final service and has enabled tighter control of costs, faster speed of delivery and improved service quality. It has also enabled Jim to assess the performance of the company more effectively. The fact that the company has the BS5750 standard is also advantageous in marketing the organisation and its services, as the standard is widely recognised as an indicator of a company that will satisfy the expectations of a customer.

Business Support

Jim Stevens is an effective business-support networker. He uses a wide network of governmental and other support-agency personnel as advisers and resource inputters. If he needs help, he 'rings someone up'. In conversation with one support agency official, it became apparent that agency personnel appreciate his enthusiasm, industry knowledge and his professional approach:

> A key strength of Jim Stevens is his proactive approach to improving the business. He is always looking for something new to do and to take things forward; he doesn't drift.

The tendency of the support people to act as devil's advocates to his projects is one which Jim sees as a challenge. His first response to such challenges is one of proving to them that his ideas will succeed. He also appreciates, however, that the grilling that he receives from these potential resource-inputters is useful in forcing him to think through the issues much more closely and clearly.

For example, the strong emphasis placed by a British Coal Enterprise representative on the need for professional management information systems to be part of the Hydro Engineering operating system from the very beginning was, in hindsight, a key influence toward Jim establishing his business in a controlled manner.

Financial Performance

The organisation's first annual turnover was in the region of £150,000. This grew to around £400,000 in the second year of operation and in its last reported year a turnover of £650,000 was achieved. The estimate for the current year anticipates a fall in turnover to around £600,000. Presently, Jim is seeking to grow his organisation incrementally, rather than to achieve dramatic increases. The present era is seen by him to be a time for consolidation and careful growth. In terms of spare production capacity and workshop space, however, there is much room for growth. The organisation is capable of increasing existing levels of business at least twofold.

Liquidity has been a constant problem as the company has sought to change and develop. Various grants and loans have aided the company's progression to date. Jim recognises that the future of the company will depend on its ability to generate cash and profits. One of Jim's responses to the perceived uncertainty of the markets Hydro services is that of only planning ahead for a period of three months. At this time, he finds it inappropriate to place too much emphasis on forecasts which look further into the future.

Information Processing

One of the main points which becomes apparent when talking to Jim is his inherent need to be aware of the company's situation. He finds it inconceivable that organisations, and more specifically their managers, can tolerate situations where information and control systems are incapable of providing information on important areas of performance. In this context, Jim is proud of his computer based information and control systems. The system has required constant updating as the amount of data processed has increased over the years.

The Impact of the British Coal Pit Closure Programme

British Coal has been a major source of business for Hydro Engineering. The announcement in September 1992 that most of the existing pits would eventually be closed came as a huge shock to the company. The resultant fall in demand for the company's services presented a huge problem to the organisation. How could turnover be maintained at anything resembling the pre-closure- announcement level, when *the* major customer had withdrawn almost all of what was the company's standard work? The problem was tackled in a number of ways.

Firstly, a strategy of market penetration was used. By reducing margins, Hydro Engineering was able to offer a service which was, in relation to its competitors, high in quality and low in price. The desired effect of this strategy was that new customers would be attracted from their existing suppliers to Hydro Engineering. The drive for additional customers has also been advantageous in that the new business consists of a larger number of smaller orders, thus reducing the company's level of dependence on big single customers - one of the reasons, of course, that the British Coal closures have had such a serious effect. The lower-price strategy has been costly, however. The reductions in margins necessary to prise potential customers away from their existing suppliers has had an adverse impact on profitability. Trading during the few months since the closure announcement has produced only small profits and for the year as a whole the company has only just managed to break even.

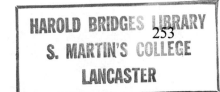

Although contracts with companies that are likely to place repeat orders are preferred, a number of one-off contracts have been taken for obvious reasons:

> I have just accepted job from a company in Scotland. We have agreed in writing what they require and I am insisting on cash 'up front'. The one-off customer is normally too messy. Too often we get problems and disputes with this type of client. We take on this type of work presently, however, because we need work of any type at this moment in time.

Secondly, a stockpile of outstanding orders was dealt with, following the closure announcement, reducing the customer lead time (the time between an order being placed and the job being done) from approximately six weeks to around two weeks. Orders and lead times have subsequently started to build up once again.

Thirdly, what was described by Jim as a 'Godsend' order was attracted from the cement manufacturer Blue Circle. This provided for approximately half of December 1992's turnover. This contract is not a long-term source of income, however. Blue Circle have recently announced a series of cutbacks and redundancies and Jim knows that the contract is unlikely to be renewed after its expiry in March 1993.

Fourthly, in the context of organisational efficiency, controls have been tightened even further. One employee involved in Administration was made redundant, an action which would make a saving of around £10,000 for the year.

A major drive was also undertaken to reduce the time taken for customers to settle their accounts. Jim explains why the debtor turnover rate had become a problem:

> Our customers weren't taking any longer than they previously took to pay us, it's just that before when we were liquid the credit period wasn't a problem. Now, however, because we had overspent on the move to the new premises, because of the downturn in the British Coal situation and, to some extent, because of an increasingly competitive market place, we didn't have the liquidity to finance long credit periods.

A large amount of effort was made to achieve this aim. For example, more time was given to reminding customers that payments were due. Jim was particularly active too: "Only yesterday I drove all the way to Cheltenham to pick up a cheque." In trying to become more efficient in this credit-control aspect of the business, however, it is important that the relative power of the customer and the firm's debtor turnover policy as an ingredient of competitive strategy is understood.

> Last week, one of the girls told an important customer from the stainless steel sector that he couldn't have any more supplies until he paid his account. I told her that it

only requires that customer to put his finger on the 'delete' button of his computer and we are wiped off his 'preferred supplier' memory.

Jim continually exhorts his staff to be sensitive to every aspect of the customer service process. By getting everything 'right first time', including clear communications with customers, the organisation should be able to avoid disputes over payment. Monitoring of the financial and work-flow situation has been further improved so that information is now available on a daily basis. A year previously the system provided updates on a three-monthly basis.

Problems with the Bank

Despite the efforts made to streamline the company, to attract new business and to improve liquidity, the company's bank has been less than understanding, in Jim's opinion:

To say that I am disappointed with my bank's attitude is an understatement. They sent someone from the regional head office to see me. He was arrogant and he treated me as though I was a schoolboy. He gave me no credit for getting out into the market place, working hard and keeping turnover up despite the British Coal situation. Neither did he seem to understand the reality of what you have to do to win business in this sort of situation.

We had two major reasons for going after work on a price-cutting basis. The first was so that we could survive and the second was so that we could gather customers to develop our future. We expect to gain more orders, at better prices, from some of the clients we have attracted. They are ours now, to be worked on.

All the bank guy seemed to ask, however, was 'Why had we taken on low-priced, low-profit- margin work?'. He said I wasn't giving him any confidence for the future. I'd spent a lot of time creating a document which sets out our strategic position, explains why we have problems and what we are going to do about them, but he didn't seem interested or impressed by this. I suppose he is thinking about whether we are making enough profits at this time to pay back our loans. Since the regional guy's visit, I have 'phoned my bank on four different occasions, just to let the manager know how things are going and what we are doing. He hasn't taken my calls and he hasn't 'phoned me back. At the moment, we are operating just below our overdraft limit. I think the bank is adopting a very short term view. What I particularly don't like is that they were only too pleased to help me when I had a lot of money on personal deposit but, now that I really need help, they don't want to know.

Recent Developments

After taking advice from his bank, Jim believes that, in order to make a full recovery from these recent problems and to strengthen the company for the future, he must change the ownership structure of the company:

> It is not what I want to do. I wanted this business to be mine exclusively ... This can't be, however. I won't let my heart rule my head. At a time like this, you have to decide what is really important... What is really important for me right now is that my business survives. I'll do anything I have to in order to make sure this happens.

Once again, it seems, Jim Stevens needs to respond to change - and to create it - quickly.

Appendix 1

HYDRO ENGINEERING SERVICES
Hydraulic, Mechanical and Agricultural Engineers

Hydro Engineering Services specialise in the repair and testing of all types of hydraulic equipment such as pumps, motors, valves, cylinders, and actuators. We have an expanding customer base covering most industries, in particular large National and Public Limited companies such as British Coal, British Steel, British Gypsum, British Rail, Blue Circle Industries, Cementation, etc.

We employ a staff of 20 and are able to offer a wide variety of services associated with all aspects of fluid power generation and control.

Our premises offer some of the most modern, up-to-date, repair and test facilities such as:

A) A 420 Horsepower Power Pack

The test facility is based around a 420HP, 12 cylinder Duetz Diesel engine. This Drives a Hydraulic piston pump capable of developing 500 litres/min at a pressure of 300Bar. The utilisation of a power pack gives the advantage of being able to run the unit under test at any speed and in each direction.

B) A Computer Controlled Test Rig

1) The Test rig is interfaced to our Main process control computer via a microprocessor within the control panel. This microprocessor is responsible for:

   i. The calibration of the FOUR Flow Meters that we have. The Flow meters are able to measure flows in the range from 0-680 litres/minute.

   ii. The assignment of the Flow Meters enables the read-out of any one of them to be displayed at any one of four Digital displays on the control panel.

   iii. Providing corrected test data of a unit's performance. This is done by measuring the number of pulses generated by the flow and speed sensors. In the case of the flow meters it checks the number of pulses per litre within the look-up tables in the processor at the test temperature. Knowing the number of pulses and of the number of pulses/litres an accurate, repeatable value of the total number of litres which passed through the Flow Meter during the test period can be established. Since we have established the total number of litres and we know the test time the computer can establish the precise averaged flow rate for the test period. The processor also provides other averaged data such as pressure, temperature, torque.

The control panel also houses the controls for the engine, "off-line" filtration unit, and pump loading system.

2)   The test facilities on our main computer system are interfaced via the serial port to the control panel. A terminal within the control room enables the operator to search and locate the unit to be tested for the sales order data base. This information is then displayed on the relevant test screen. Details of the acceptable efficiency and geometric displacement of the unit are typed on the screen. When the type of test is selected and the test commenced the information is transferred from the control panel to the computer which uses the information to establish the efficiency of the unit at a particular test pressure. The starting and stopping of the test period is controlled from the control panel. After completing a test at the required pressure subsequent tests may be continued from the computer, which has frozen the corrected data in the previous column. The unit is further loaded and the test continued. After completing the test the computer reads the test results. If at any stage the actual efficiency of the units falls below that of the acceptable the choice of either a Non-conformance or External Concession are the only options available. In this case a Test Certificate cannot be raised. Only if the actual efficiency of the unit exceeds that of the acceptable will a Test Certificate be issued. Examples of Test Certificates and Test Results can be found attached. It should be noted that this information is readily available to customers and clearly indicates all test parameters employed throughout the test. In addition the test results are provided in graphical form.

3)   The testing of hydraulic motors is undertaken in a similar manner to that of pumps. In addition we are able to measure the output torque (0-20000Nm), case leakage and establish the overall and mechanical efficiency of the unit under test. The motor is subjected to full dynamic shaft loading.

4)   Rotary flow dividers are tested by monitoring both input flow and pressure as well as the output performance of each section in turn. The computer is able to establish

the percentage split of each section and thus display the efficiency of each at the various test pressures.

5) In addition to the FOUR flow meters the control panel houses NINE digital pressure displays and ONE digital torque display.

C) Cylinder Test Rig

The cylinder test rig enables single and double acting cylinders to be pressurised up to 600 BAR and in an INFINITE number of positions in the stroke. This being extremely useful for detecting "BARRELLING" of the cylinder tube.

D) Value Testing

Valves of all types IE Flow - Pressure - Direction can be repaired and tested on purpose built manifold and sub-plate mounted assemblies. Our test capacities are up to 300 litres per minute at 300 BAR.

E) Flushing and Filtration

The flushing rig enables all units to be flushed out with clean oil prior to testing to 6 Micron Absolute using absolute rated filters and air breathers on the reservoirs.

In the present economic climate fully utilising equipment is essential and in order to save money on uncalled for repairs we operate a system of "Flush and Test". We are prepared to undertake the flushing and testing of a customer's equipment without stripping the unit down. If the unit exceeds the acceptable efficiency it may be quite suitable to perform satisfactorily. Although the test results are supplied no warranty is available with this service.

F) Quality Assurance

On 31 October 1990 we were successful in the assessment of our Quality Manual to the requirements of BS5750 1987 : Part 2 and ISO 9002. The scope of the assessment covered the activity of The Repair and Maintenance of Hydraulic and Pneumatic Equipment such as Pumps, Motors, Valves and Cylinders. The assessment was carried out by BSI. A copy of our Quality Policy and other relevant extracts from our manual are enclosed.

G) Warranty

All items repaired or overhauled are subject to our standard 6 month parts and labour warranty. Further details being outlined in our warranty terms, a copy of which can be found enclosed.

H) Hydraulic and Pneumatic Training Courses

We are able to stage specialised hydraulic training courses which are designed to meet your specific requirements. The courses are approached in a practical "Hands On" manner. Full course and tuition notes are provided. Training rigs are available which enable students to develop fault location and diagnostic skills. Courses have been staged for The Agricultural Training Board, Blue Circle Industries plc, and British Steel Corporation.

I) Other Services

In addition to the services outlined above we are able to offer the customer other specialist facilities such as:

ON-SITE SERVICING, INSTALLATION, FAULT LOCATION AND DIAGNOSIS,

SYSTEM FLUSHING, LOOP FILTRATION AND FLUSHING UNIT HIRE

By choosing Hydraulic Engineering Services the customer has the security of knowing that:

EVERY ITEM HAS UNDERGONE A FULL AND EXHAUSTIVE TEST

THE OVERHAUL OF EQUIPMENT IS CARRIED OUT AND COMPLIES WITH THE REQUIREMENTS OF RECOGNISED QUALITY STANDARDS

WE SEEK TO ATTAIN STANDARDS OF QUALITY AND SERVICE WHICH MEET THE REQUIREMENTS OF THE CUSTOMER

WE SUPPLY GOODS AND SERVICES THAT DO NOT COME BACK TO CUSTOMERS THAT DO!

MANAGEMENT AND SUPPLY CHAIN ADJUSTMENT IN THE DEFENCE INDUSTRY

Gary Graham and Brian Kenny, Huddersfield Business School

Introduction

The UK defence industry is struggling to reorganise itself for growth, if not survival. The disappearance of the communist threat and the desperate need to revive the UK economy have taken the defence industry for a roller coaster ride, from the unprecedented Thatcher administration build-up in the early 1980s to recent deep cuts in the Ministry of Defence (MoD) budget.

Debate is now centred upon the future size and structure of European armed forces. Increasingly, the consensus is that the post-war security model, and particular conventional forces on the European continent, are no longer necessary or relevant.

Already, changes in the European political climate are providing a rationale for cuts in procurement levels of existing development programmes in Britain (see Cmnd 2270, *Defending our Future*, 1993). This paper is concerned with the industrial implications of cuts in military spending and changes in force structures - especially the question of industrial adjustment to the shrinking UK market.

Market Decline

The problem of defence contraction did not arrive with the fall of the Berlin Wall in 1990 and the end of the Cold War. The fall in demand can be traced back to the mid-1980s, when UK spending peaked. In the UK, tight control of public expenditure was applied to defence spending from 1985 and thereafter military spending fell. The increased use of fixed price contracts and competitive tendering also increased contractor risks and reduced profit margins.

Policy For Prime and Sub-Contractors

In the interests of efficient project management, the MoD have placed most defence contracts in the hands of a single prime contractor. In such cases, the Ministry's role in the day-to-day management of the contract is a limited one; the general rule is that it is for the prime contractor to choose his own sub-contractors. Given this devolution of power to the defence primes and the non-interventionist policy of MoD, it is the purchasing policies of the primes who control the distribution of defence sub-contracts.

A Strategic Management Framework

The subject of business strategy is the management of the relationship between the firm and its external environment- its customers, its suppliers, its competitors and the governments of the countries within which it operates (Kay, 1993, p.335). Many authors (Ansoff, 1965; Boston Consulting Group, 1968; Miles and Snow, 1978) have offered taxonomies of generic strategies - checklists from which corporations could choose the most relevant objectives for particular markets. Porter's (1980) framework has been well received in the literature (see Miller and Dess, 1993). In Porter's framework there are two dimensions of choice. Firms can pursue either cost leadership - the same product as competitors but at a lower cost - or differentiation. They can range narrowly or broadly, thus generating a range of alternatives encompassing cost leadership, differentiation, and focus.

Supply Chain Implications

The work of Porter implies that a buyer pursuing a strategy of 'cost leadership' or 'cost reduction' must effectively apply this strategy at all levels of the value chain such that all 'players' (for example, sub-contractors and parts-suppliers) are beneficiaries via the mechanism of minimising total costs over a reasonable planning horizon (Towill and Naim, 1993, p.39).

Adjusting to Change

Many corporations in Europe and the USA are dependent on the defence markets for large or significant proportions of their sales and profits. Most have attempted to adjust to decline in the defence markets which provides a clear commercial incentive for diversification into the civil sector (NEDO, 1991). This adjustment has primarily taken the form of acquisitions of civilian oriented companies (as in the case of British Aerospace) and/or consolidation in the defence markets through acquisitions, mergers and strategic alliances (as in the case of GEC). SYSTEMCO is engaged in a mix of businesses. The company's product fields include; radar based air defence systems, sensor management of sea, land, and air systems, electro optics and command and control systems. The consensus view at SYSTEMCO was that the collapse of the Cold War and subsequent world-wide reductions in expenditure had led to a greater emphasis on competition and in particular, an increased introduction of fixed-price contracts. This had forced the company to act as a 'managing contractor' sharing out any work that could not be performed cost-effectively on-site.

Subcontractor Strategy

Having itself undergone a very painful rationalisation period, resulting in the displacement of thousands of personnel across the South East, SYSTEMCO was now achieving the necessary flexibility, in adjusting to changing market conditions, through modification of its sub-contractor business. Faced with falling orders, the decision-maker at each level attempts to 'shove the pain down the system' as one participant in the study put it. This is achieved through a process of reducing the sub-contract orders, squeezing the margins on those orders given out and demanding extended credit facilities from suppliers.

SYSTEMCO's purchasing strategy was based upon:

i.   tight cost control
ii.   frequent detailed control reports
iii. structured organisation and responsibilities
iv.   incentive payments based on meeting strict quantitative targets.

The view of SYSTEMCO was that it was up to the sub-contractors to 'put their house in order' to survive in the new environment of the 1990s. Recent changes initiated by the Levene reforms in the early 1980s had compelled SYSTEMCO to reduce its costs and increase efficiency to win MoD contracts. It felt that it was incumbent upon the sub-contractors to respond in a similar fashion to meet the price, quality and delivery times expected of them. Throughout the tendering process, SYSTEMCO continually used competitive bidding, negotiation and firm-price contracting to drive down the price quotations of prospective subcontractors. Using budgeted costs as a basis for firm-pricing was seen as an incentive to get suppliers to cut their costs.

The major Sub-Contracts Manager highlighted this as follows:

Suppliers of a given purchased input will often vary in relative cost position, and identifying the lowest cost source may lead to lower unit purchasing costs in the long term if SYSTEMCO can exercise its bargaining power. Firms have recently being trying to 'buy' business by dropping prices to an unsustainable level. Ultimately we try and avoid this type of supplier as past practice indicates a tendency to increase prices sharply or to compromise on quality in order to recoup its losses.

A supplier's costs are to a great extent fixed by SYSTEMCO's technical requirements. Understanding the cost behaviour of key suppliers has enabled SYSTEMCO to establish better purchasing policies as well as to recognise and exploit linkages. The company identified that in the 1990s it was no longer sufficient for sub-contractors to have the right skills. They also had to offer lower prices, better products and better service. SYSTEMCO expected its key suppliers to have an excess of production and engineering capacity. Traditionally, the base was largely paid for by the MoD through contract R&D or procurement assignments.

Desperate to win contracts, SYSTEMCO has noted a trend for subcontractors to bid at levels far below those needed to sustain their high cost structures, technical workforces and idle plant. Although very much in its infancy, SYSTEMCO was beginning to set up longer-term co-operative relationships between itself and suppliers. However, this was being tempered by the MoD's 'hands-off' approach with its greater emphasis on competition and, in particular, the introduction of increasingly fixed-price contracting. The all-pervading importance of cost control is reflected in the avoidance of sole source procurement, fierce bidding, stringent penalties and the sharing of risk throughout the buying process.

While project complexity may increase the extent of subcontracting, SYSTEMCO has to balance this against corporate procedures to direct work to other divisions, even when it may not be strictly economic. In emphasising market consolidation, SYSTEMCO has structured the company's core businesses to gain pre-eminence in its market segments. SYSTEMCO has modified its strategy. First, the company is placing greater emphasis on growing international sales. Second, SYSTEMCO is changing its R&D and capital investment strategy, putting money where risk is low and procurement more certain. Third, despite SYSTEMCO's insistence on maintaining its defence identity, the company is exploring commercial applications for some of its defence technologies.

Strategy Towards Buyers

In order to illustrate better the experience of sub-contractors and their processes of adaptation, both current and projected, three in-depth case surveys are outlined below. COMMUNICO has over twenty five years experience and expertise in the design, development and manufacture of VHF and UHF systems and equipment for civil and defence applications in ground-to-air, ship-to-shore and surface-to-surface communications. MICROCO was founded in 1977 by a University of Leeds professor to undertake research, development and manufacture of microwave components and subsystems. MICROCO's achievements have been recognised with the award of the Queen's Award for Technological Achievement in 1985 and 1992 and the Queen's Award for Export Achievement in 1988. The company has grown to become one of the world's leading companies in this field with a reputation for quality, innovation and reliability. Since its foundation in 1969 PRECISCO has earned a reputation for quality and reliability in the production of machined components and mechanical assemblies. The firm services leading edge technology industries including aerospace, medical and machine tool producers.

Alter the Balance of Customers as Market Conditions Change

In the face of a shrinking defence market, all three companies identified that the majority of future work would involve smaller orders and the upgrading of current platforms. The firms were responding to this by the vigorous pursuit of export business, and in particular collaborative 'offsets' and attempts at broadening the portfolio of civil customers. The learning process of many export customers had led to their becoming more cost-sensitive and more demanding of the technical performance of the defence equipment supplied.

These three businesses have perceived the need to change product mix and to reduce their ratio of military to civil business over the next five years. At MICROCO the company intended to do this through product development. The company had been reorganised into four operating companies. The engineering and R&D capability developed in the holding company had been successfully transferred to the civil sector. COMMUNICO had originally being set up as a supplier of civil airborne communication equipment. Its military side had largely developed through the award of a large UK naval contract in the early 1980s for a standard civil product that had been adapted to a military specification. PRESICO had the highest military dependence (about seventy per cent of turnover and employment depended on defence expenditure). The future survival of the company was perceived to be dependent on the company's ability to identify new commercial markets. PRESCICO had set itself a long-term strategic objective of having a balanced portfolio of customers, with thirty per cent from civil aerospace, twenty per cent commercial customers (for example, medical equipment) and fifty per cent military.

External Relations

The respondents at MICROCO highlighted that the 'value for money' approach, popular in the 1980s, encouraged price competition and a more adversarial or arms-length relationship in order to force price reductions onto suppliers. There was a high coincidence of views that the collapse of the Cold War and subsequent world-wide reductions in expenditure had led to more collaborative and closer relationships.

Both customer and supplier were mutually aware that quality, reliability, service, risk and lifetime costs were becoming dominant criteria in the award of military tenders. The increasingly close relationship between the larger companies and their sub-contractors is evidently filtering down through the supplier chain via the emergence of preferred supplier lists, vendor certification and moves towards Total Quality Improvement, partly inspired by the MoD's and DTI's drive for high product quality (especially through BS 5750).

Supplier Selection

The dominant factor in supplier selection emerges as the 'buyer's confidence in the supplier' and the provision of sufficient reassurance to buyers to justify their risk. The survey confirmed that the key targets - the decision makers actually reachable by subcontractors - are the buyers, the technical departments and quality inspectorates. In the high technology areas, engineers are very influential in the buying process but often buyers and quality assurance staff have overriding powers.

In military markets, the contract determines the terms and conditions and provides the environment within which the desired product or service must be provided. Thus, strategy seems to be focused upon those factors that are given heavy weighting by the decision maker.

Within this context the three companies simultaneously compete via cost and differentiation strategies (Porter, 1980). For example, COMMUNICO competes for fixed-price MoD contracts on the basis of cost leadership. But the company were recently awarded a contract to supply communication equipment to the MoD in Cyprus because of superior quality and durability and the provision of comprehensive guarantees. In essence, COMMUNICO's success is based on its adaptibility to the technical and commercial specifications of the military customer.

In considering the 'successful approach', the survey emphasised the need for substantial pre-bid work. This tends to be undertaken 6 to 12 months prior to the tender invitation stage. The costs of bidding are sizeable. Thus it is the marketing and sales department's task to find out as much information about the tender as possible.

At MICROCO, one of the key functions is to negotiate with customers in order to align their budgets within the range of costs and prices discussed. The marketing and sales department will consult technical staff to arrive at a rough costing. In addition, it will look at the customer's budget and the follow-up costing of the bid. If there is deviation between the customer and MICROCO it will try and influence the customer to consider a less sophisticated but cheaper solution.

Throughout this stage the marketing and sales department is continuously trying to identify and constrain potential technological risk. The marketing and sales department will try and discover information about the customer's budget and the quoted prices and costs. On the technical side, attempts will be made to influence the customer's requirements into conformity with MICROCO's engineering and technical capabilities, and to demonstrate its capability to perform successfully.

Conclusion

This paper has examined some aspects of the process of industry structural change on the strategy of defence contractors. Specifically, it has revealed that Porter's framework for buyer strategy and subcontractor selection raises as many questions as it answers. Regarding the bidding strategy of suppliers, Porter's framework may be a useful checklist, but a strategic alignment to the customer's capabilities relative to competition is still needed in order to choose target buyers.

Suppliers need to allocate their technical and marketing resources carefully between different parts of their customers' portfolio; to change the market conditions, and to look for specialist niches where they can develop products which are both innovative and cost competitive.

References

Ansoff, H. (1965) *Harvard Business Review, 43* (5) pp.162-78.

Boston Consulting Group (1968) *Perspectives on Experience* (Boston Consulting Group).

Kay, J. (1993) *Foundations of Corporate Success: How Business Strategies Add Value* (OUP).

Miller, A. and Dess, C. (1993) 'Assessing Porter's Model in Terms of its Generalisability, Accuracy and Simplicity', *Journal of Management Studies, 30* (4) pp.554-585.

Miles, R. and Snow, C. (1978) *Organisational Strategy, Structure and Process* (McGraw Hill).

NEDO (1991) *Diversifying from Defence: Case Studies and Management Guidelines* (National Economic Development Office).

Porter, M. E. (1980) *Competitive Advantage: Creating and Sustaining Superior Performance* (The Free Press).

Smith, D. and Smith, R. (1992) 'Corporate Strategy, Corporate Culture and Conversion: Adjustment in the Defence Industry', *Business Strategy Review* (Summer).

Towill, D. and Naim, M. (1993) 'Partnership Sourcing Smoothes Supply Chain Dynamics', *Purchasing and Supply Chain Management* (July/August).

In accordance with signed agreements of confidentiality, fictional names have been assigned to the contractors.

THE HARD CELL? THE PRIVATE MANAGEMENT OF PRISONS

Peter Moran, Bolton Business School.

Introduction

Against the backdrop of a burgeoning public sector borrowing requirement and a government committed to the pursuit of laissez-faire polices, the extension of free market principles to hitherto sacrosanct functions of the state is a predictable extension of an established strategy previously applied to other institutions. However, unlike previously privatised public utilities, where demand for their products and services is arguably affected by the policies of the state only at the margins of their business, the demand for prison accommodation is more directly linked to the 'law and order' elements of government policy.

Notifiable offences recorded by the police in Great Britain have risen from roughly 4.7 million in 1986 to roughly 6.6 million in 1992 (CSO, 1993). Whilst sounding a cautionary note in connection with reporting changes, or changes in the extent and manner of recording by the police of offences reported to them, the 1992 British Crime Survey (Mayhew, Maung *et al*, 1993, p.20) still indicated a rise in crime of 14 per cent between 1987 and 1991. The Prison System's official capacity is roughly 46,600, but rose from around 41,000 in February 1993 to over 47,000 in November 1993. It is anticipated that the prison population will rise to 50,000 by 1994, and that the government policy of renewed reliance on imprisonment as a deterrent will exacerbate the gap between rising demand and available places.

Although a building programme to provide 2,000 more prison places was announced in November 1993, building work will not commence until 1994. In the short term, the Home Office may meet the demand for additional places by utilising a disused army camp, a disused detention centre and a floating barge. More controversial options, which the Home Office have not confirmed, revolve around the possibility of allowing private jails to take

269

additional prisoners in excess of their current capacity or permitting private jails to accommodate different categories of prisoner by mixing remand and convicted inmates.

The pressure on prison places has been intensified by the riots at Strangeways, Wymott and Haverigg. Although Strangeways has partially re-opened, it will be unable to accept its full complement until refurbishment is completed at the end of 1994, and Wymott and Haverigg will be closed for some time. The closure of three penal institutions, all in the North West of England, has skewed the distribution of pressure on the total system.

In the wake of disturbances at Strangeways and other jails in 1990, Lord Justice Woolf conducted an investigation into the causes (Woolf & Tumim, 1991). A number of recommendations were made which included the reduction of overcrowding and the ending of 'slopping out' by the provision of integral sanitation. Implementing these recommendations has placed additional burdens on the system as inmates are decanted from cell blocks whilst sanitary facilities are installed.

The current context of private prison management incorporates a rising prison population which mirrors an increased political deployment of prison as a deterrent in the face of escalating crime. There are gaps on the supply side which have occurred as a result of both planned and unplanned contingencies, the former as a consequence of improvements to comply with Woolf and the latter due to the loss of prisons wrecked by riot. The entry of the private sector into prison management could be regarded as a timely response triggered by market forces. Indeed, the government has adhered rigorously to the rhetoric of competition throughout the short history of the exercise. There are, however, political agendas which include objectives that do not dovetail with a strictly neutral interpretation of 'competition'.

Government Strategy and The Provision of Accommodation

The speed with which government policy has altered in respect of the contracting out of prison management has been matched only by the breathtaking increase in its scale. In 1987, the then Home Secretary said that 'I do not think there is a case, and I do not think the House would accept a case for auctioning or privatising the prisons or handing over the business of keeping prisoners safe to anyone other than government servants' (Hurd, 1987). Contemporaneously, the Adam Smith Institute published research which suggested that public sector institutions, cushioned from competition, were characterised by inadequate supply, low quality and high cost. 'That is why the move towards private prisons in America holds out so much hope for Britain. By introducing an element of competition into the prison business one should be able to increase supply, improve quality and reduce costs' (Young, 1987, p. 2).

In the same year, the Home Affairs Committee supported the contracting out of prisons. 'The employment of private sector companies in prison management in the USA represents an example which should...be considered in relation to the prisons of England and Wales' (Home Affairs Committee, 1987, p.v). In the committee's view the principal advantages of contract provision of penal establishments were lower initial capital costs borne by tax payers, accelerated building and enhanced architectural efficiency and excellence. The committee went on to propose that 'side by side with the present prison establishment, commercial companies should, *as an experiment* [author emphasis], be allowed to demonstrate the types of custodial services they could provide and at what cost' (Home Affairs Committee, 1987, p.vi).

The Home Secretary's response concluded that an experiment was 'not the best way to proceed at present' and that such a scheme would require 'the resolution to difficult and fundamental issues of principle, law and practice. The degree of political accountability, the interface with other agencies of the criminal justice system and the means of assuring satisfactory conditions for inmates are *only* [original emphasis] some of the most obvious' (Home Affairs Committee, 1988, p.iv). The Home Secretary outlined his plans to publish a Green Paper on private sector involvement 'in all aspects of the remand system. This will cover not only the contract provision of remand facilities, but also arrangements for escorting remand prisoners to and from court and for court manning' (ibid). In conjunction with the Green Paper, consultants would be invited to examine the practicalities of such changes.

The Green Paper, published only twelve months after Douglas Hurd's comments, revealed a volte-face of significant proportions when it stated that 'The government is mindful of the state's special responsibilities towards prisoners, but does not accept that these mean that prisoners must necessarily and at all times be looked after exclusively by Crown servants or police officers' (Secretary of State for the Home Department, 1988, p.8). From the outset, government strategy targeted the remand system. The Home Affairs Committee (1987, p.vi) recommended that 'tenders should be invited in particular for the construction and management of new remand centres, because it is there that the worst overcrowding in the prison system is concentrated'.

The determination of government to dismantle the monopoly of the state in prison management became overt in April 1991. The Home Office announced that it would not compete against the private sector by tendering for the contract to run The Wolds Remand Centre on Humberside. Despite the rhetoric of competition to improve the quantity of prison places, the government was not prepared to risk the possibility that a successful in-house bid would overturn its initiatives to involve the private sector at an early stage. In order to avoid this contingency, the market was 'rigged' to favour players from the private sector.

Consequently, the possibility of privately managed penal institutions became reality in November 1991 when Group 4 was awarded The Wolds' contract.

The private sector gained valuable experience from this tendering exercise and, having gained a 'bye' into the next round, their expertise focused on the next big prize, namely HMP Manchester, a.k.a. Strangeways. To date, this is the only 'brownfield' prison that has been subjected to market-testing and is the single instance in which an in-house bid from the Prison Service has been permitted. Much to the chagrin of Group 4 and other private sector organisations, it was announced in July 1993 that the in-house bid had been accepted for a five-year contract to run the jail. In the single instance in which an in-house bid was not declared *ultra vires* by the Home Office, it was successful. With the benefit of hindsight, the government's earlier strategy to disbar the Prison Service from entering the contest to run The Wolds appears to have been a shrewd calculation by the champions of the right.

In May 1993, a second privately-managed prison came on stream. Blakenhurst, run by United Kingdom Detention Services (UKDS), a conglomerate which includes Mowlem, McApline and the Corrections Corporation of America. Apart from the fact that another private sector company had gained a toehold in the service, perhaps the most salient point is that the population of Blakenhurst is not limited to remand prisoners. A mixture of both remand and convicted prisoners is incarcerated at this establishment. This represents another distinct shift in the policy of the government which was initially intended to relieve the pressure on the remand system.

On 1 April 1993, in line with recommendations made by the Lygo Report (1991), the Prison Service became an executive agency. Commentators have suggested that the idea of agency status is 'to re-package services along commercial lines ready for complete privatisation' (CAITS, 1992, p.2). Accompanying the change in status, a new Director General of Prisons Derek Lewis, was appointed operational from 6 January, 1993. An individual member of the Adam Smith Institute, equipped with managerial experience gained solely from the private sector (Home Affairs Committee, 1993, p.21), Lewis' appointment marked a distinct shift from civil service culture. Although the intentions of the government to privatise elements of the service had become evident prior to his arrival, it now had a new ally to advise on the extent and timing of the process.

In the first half of 1994, a newly-built prison will become operational at Doncaster. Derek Lewis has already announced that the public sector will be excluded from the tendering process. This decision has been defended on the grounds that as Doncaster will have no established management or staff, an in-house bid would be inappropriate. Against the backdrop of government rhetoric couched in terms of competition and the in-house victory at Strangeways, this line of defence is thin to the point of transparency. If this strategy is upheld in the short term, it will involve the private management of new prisons to be constructed at Liverpool and Bridgend in addition to Doncaster. In the longer term, no new jails will be managed directly by Crown Servants. Other key issues may be resolved in part by developments at Doncaster. Will its 'customer base' be limited to remand prisoners or will other categories of prisoners be accommodated? Which of the private sector organisations will win the prize and will this allow them to become the premier force driving prison privatisation, possibly to the detriment of 'competition'?

The longer-term expansion of privately-managed institutions appeared to be dependent on the government's prison building programme and the ability of the Conservative Party to win future general elections, which left the private organisations involved in a dilemma. The outcomes of future elections are unknown and yet, having embarked on their current strategy it is questionable whether the current level of private sector involvement justifies the costs they have incurred. Group 4 is reportedly spending £900,000 per annum on maintaining a development team to bid for contracts, whilst they have only gained the contract to manage The Wolds and the Court Escort Service in the East Midlands.

Of the 130 jails in the UK, only two are privately-managed at the time of writing. Private interests have 'told the government that they want to see at least 30 prisons put out to contract to create a financially viable privatised prison sector...[Group 4] is believed to have told ministers that it needs to run at least six prisons to justify its investment' (Travis, 1993). As has been accurately predicted elsewhere, 'it is a question of big money and, most importantly, with this amount of interplay with private profit interests, even up to the level of private prisons, we are building an important growth factor into the system' (Christie, 1993, p.109).

This 'growth factor', combined with the Treasury's squeeze on public spending has generated momentum for the privatisation process that is disproportionate to its original status as an 'experiment'. Michael Howard has recently announced that the number of private prisons will rise to twelve. In the wake of this crash programme, it is to be expected that older state jails will be transferred to private operators, the large dependence on remand prisoners will be alleviated as a variety of prisons may be targeted (those with maximum security units have not been ruled out) and the design/building and possibly finance of all new jails may be transferred to the private sector. The staff and management in existing prisons will be allowed to tender for the work, but both Howard and Lewis have indicated that whenever an in-house bid is accepted, another institution will be added to the list until there are twelve prisons in the private sector.

The Cost of Imprisonment

Incarceration is an expensive business. 'In 1992-3 some £210 million was spent on the existing estate, including £150 million on major capital projects and £28 million on building repairs...The cost of the integral sanitation programme is estimated to be £70 million, but that excludes facilities provided during general modernisation and upgrading work for which the cost of the sanitation work is not separately identifiable' (Home Affairs Committee, 1993, p.4).

The expected rise in the prison population would require a further six new prisons and new accommodation blocks at fourteen existing prisons, requiring an investment of roughly £332 million. The indication by the Home Office that it will permit the private sector to design, build and finance future jails facilitates Howard's twin objectives of circumventing Treasury resistance to meeting additional resource requirements whilst sending more criminals to jail for longer, and it may further enhance the leanings of the government towards the private sector. Not only can the management of prisons be subcontracted so as to generate savings, but the initial 'up-front' capital costs may also be avoided by the government. However, if the comparative costs are to be the determining factor, how does the state compare with the private sector? An answer is attempted in Table 1 below.

Prison	Cost/Week (£)
Frankland	752
Brixton	535
Norwich	434
Winchester	401
Strangeways	350
Wolds	350
Blakenhurst	310

Table 1
Comparative Costs of State and Privately Managed Jails. (Per Prisoner Per Week).

Source: *The Times* (1993); Lewis (1993); Travis (1993a)

While it cannot be claimed that these statistics are absolutely comparable, they nonetheless shed some helpful light upon the issue of prison costs. As Lewis (1993) points out, 'The average weekly cost in the public sector is £440, but this figure covers a wide range of types of prison, including high security prisons which are more expensive to run'. Frankland Prison, which heads the cost table is a high security prison.

Questioning comparative costs on a per capita basis is supported by evidence from the USA. 'The fallacy of such a comparison is that the government cost is an average cost, i.e. it includes costs related to holding both maximum and minimum security prisoners. Private corporations operate only minimum security prisons which require no...elaborate security precautions and, therefore, are much cheaper to run than maximum security prisons' (Borna, 1986, pp.328-9).

It is notable that Strangeways (where the in-house bid proved successful) matches the cost per prisoner place of the Wolds which is run by Group 4. If this level of competitiveness can be achieved by inviting in-house tenders, then the government's exclusion of the Prison Service from bidding for newly-built jails cannot be defended on economic grounds alone. In addition, Nathan (1993, p.14) cites HM Chief Inspector of Prisons (Judge Tumim) to question whether Group 4's costs are accurately assessed. 'Judge Tumim...also criticised the lack of effective monitoring of the financial arrangements between Group 4 and the Prison Service. Value for money was "impossible to determine". His report also reveals that breaches in the contract were not incurring financial penalties'.

One of the other factors that may influence costs is the age profile of the prison estate. New prisons have been designed and built to incorporate the latest technological and architectural security features with the objective of containing costs. The Prison Service, however, has a large number of older prisons where architectural features reflect the period in which they were built, and in 1993 'forty four of the total of 128 establishments were opened before 1914' according to the Home Affairs Committee (1993, p.1). Another element of the cost structure is salary costs. These will be addressed in the following section concerning industrial relations.

Industrial Relations

If the cost comparison does not clearly favour the private sector (and it is too early to conclude that it does), observers of the industry might suggest a 'hidden agenda', the primary purpose of which is to erode the strength of the Prison Officer's Association (POA). Research published by the Adam Smith Institute contained a barbed attack on the POA whilst simultaneously advocating the involvement of the private sector. 'Political fears about strikes or unemployment lead to lax labour relations and overmanning. Political pressure from the employees diverts resources to current spending (on wages) and away from needed capital improvements' (Young, 1987, p.4).

The consultants appointed by the Home Office to examine the feasibility of private sector involvement in the remand system produced a report (Deloitte Haskins-Sells, 1989) which emphasised the POA's marginal position by failing to consult it. The decision taken by the Home Office not to permit the Prison Service to bid for the contract to run The Wolds and to exclude them from bidding for any contracts for new prisons is clearly an assault on the central position held by the POA within the Prison Service.

Facing what it regarded as a concerted effort by the state to break its power base, the POA was at the forefront of the 'Prisons are not for Profit Campaign', launched in October 1991 and supported by the TGWU, GMB and CPSA among others. However, the unity of the unions' efforts to stop prison privatisation suffered an early blow when the GMB announced that its white collar section, APEX, was poised to sign a single-union deal with Group 4, a leading contender for The Wolds' contract. Roy Grantham, at that time leader of the APEX section, was quoted as taking the pragmatic view that 'If we have to have privatisation then we have to deal with the reality of it...We normally enter into recognition agreements with Group 4 when it wins new work and we would certainly wish to extend the arrangement if it takes this contract' (Cowdry, 1991).

The process of fragmenting the collective bargaining arrangements in the Prison Service has begun. The POA represents prison officers in the state sector, APEX represents custody officers at the Wolds and UKDS has not recognised a union. In addition, it was widely reported that at the time the in-house bid was accepted for the management of Strangeways, the POA accepted a procedural agreement restricting its right to take industrial action. This was later denied by both the POA and Robin Halward, Governor of the prison. They suggest that the deal differs from national procedures only 'in specifying that prison officers will maintain the "standard specified in the service level agreement" in the early stages of a dispute. In conventional state prisons staff agree to maintain the status quo' (*Personnel Management*, 1993, p.8).

The changes in the industry's pay structure reflects this fragmentation of collective bargaining and representation. Table 2 illustrates the current wide variations in remuneration.

Employer	Job Designation	Annual Pay	Hourly Pay*
UKDS	Custody Officer	12,168	5.85
Group 4	Custody Officer	14,500	6.97
Prison Service	Prison Officer	{ 15,264 { 19,034**	7.33 9.15

Table 2
Pay by Employer in the Prison Industry 1993 (£).

Source: POA (1993); Group 4 (1993); Nathan (1993a).

*Based on annual pay divided by 2080. (i.e. 40 hours x 52 weeks).
**After 15 years service.

The Table illustrates a number of key points. In the first place, salaries in (non-union) UKDS can be seen to be lower than in the others. Secondly, there is an incremental scale based on service in the Prison Service that is not adopted by the other two entities. Thirdly, there is a significant variation in the range of salary levels: Prison Officers with more than 15 years service are paid 36 per cent more than custody officers working for UKDS and almost 24 per cent more than those working for Group 4. At the lowest entry point on the

276

prison service scale, prison officers are paid 5 per cent more than Group 4 and 20 per cent more than UKDS.

The POA's attitude to privatisation has hardened considerably. From cooperating with the initial experiment, the pace at which the state has moved to break the monopoly of the Prison Service has transformed its approach from reluctant cooperation to outright opposition. The early threat of a national ballot for industrial action was lifted after the Service won the Strangeways contract. The initial government strategy of limiting the private sector to the management of new prisons has been significantly adjusted to permit the private management of existing state institutions to be put out to tender.

A more recent ballot approved action short of a strike to protest against over-crowding, assaults on officers and the government's market-testing programme. The union's plan to refuse admissions from Group 4's court escort service prompted Derek Lewis to suggest that the action could represent a 'serious threat to the operation of the criminal justice system and law and order' (Pike, 1993b).

The swift response of the Home Secretary was to seek an injunction to prevent the action taking place. Mr Justice May issued an injunction on 18 November, 1993 instructing the POA to revoke its planned action or risk fines or the imprisonment of officials for contempt of court. The legal immunity of the POA and its continued existence as a trade union may be swept away by the Home Secretary's ability to link the prison officers with police officers given that both groups have the same powers under the 1952 Prison Act and the 1992 Trade Union & Labour Relations (Consolidation) Act. This places the POA in the same category as the Police Federation, a staff association which does not have the legal right to strike. Furthermore, although the Transfer of Undertakings (Protection of Employment) Act, 1981, will apply to POA members in established state-run institutions that might become privately managed in the future, and individual officers would, therefore, have pay rates and other terms and conditions protected, there is no obligation on the private sector to continue recognition of the POA in the long term. At the time of writing, the POA is preparing its appeal. If it is unsuccessful then its ability to affect the privatisation process by industrial action will be much reduced and its influence on events that remain under the direct jurisdiction of the state will be much diminished.

Conclusion

The government's rhetoric urging better value for taxpayer's money has not deterred it from protecting the private sector's first tentative steps into prison management. This could have been avoided only if the Prison Service had been permitted to bid for the management of new prisons and been soundly defeated by the private sector. The unwillingness of politicians to gamble on the outcome of this scenario calls into question the amount of faith placed in the private sector to defeat the Prison Service on a level playing field. The success of the Prison Service at Strangeways also provides evidence that the public sector can compete effectively.

The future of the POA is in the balance. A great many industries and unions have already been altered beyond recognition through employers utilising the recent plethora of industrial relations legislation. The POA appears to be boxed in, with few (if any) other options than to fight the injunction of November 1993 through the courts. Even if it is successful in overturning the ruling of Mr Justice May, this may not assist it in the longer term if future private prison operators choose not to grant it recognition. If it is unsuccessful, then its very survival may be threatened.

The fragmentation of representation in the private sector is already a *fait accompli*. Group 4 recognises the GMB, while UKDS do not recognise any trade union. Wage rates and other terms of employment already differ widely. The extension of low pay to custody officers is already demonstrable in that the private sector do not offer the same terms to their employees as are on offer to employees of the Prison Service. Private sector bodies have pushed successfully for more prisons to be market tested commencing this year. Those organisations which have invested resources in the securing of contracts will have a vested interest in keeping the prisons full in order to generate profit. It will be of interest to see what effect, if any, this has upon the ongoing debate between those who believe that prison serves mainly as a school for criminal skills and those who are deeply disturbed by the low proportion of criminals who are given custodial sentences.

References

Association of Chief Police Officers (1988) *Electronic Surveillance* (London: ACPO).

Berry, B. and Matthews, R. (1989) 'Electronic Monitoring and House Arrest: Making the Right Connections' in Matthews, R. (Ed) *Privatising Criminal Justice* (London: Sage) pp. 107-134.

Borna, S. (1986) 'Free Enterprise Goes To Prison', *British Journal of Criminology*, 26 (4) pp. 321-34.

CAITS (1992) *Prison Services Privatisation* (London: Prisons Are Not For Profit Campaign).

Central Statistical Office (1993) *Monthly Digest of Statistics. 573* (London: HMSO).

Christie, N. (1993) *Crime Control As Industry Towards Gulags Western Style* (London: Routledge).

Committee of Public Accounts (1993) *Police Cell Accommodation Costs - Minutes of Evidence*, 24 February (London: HMSO).

Cowdry, Q. (1991) 'Home Office Gives Firms Free Run At Jail Contract', *The Times* (27 April).

Deloitte Haskins-Sells (1989) *A Report To The Home Office on The Practicality of Private Sector Involvements in The Remand System* (London: DHSS).

Group 4 (1993). *Letter to Author.*

Home Affairs Committee Fourth Report (1987) *Contract Provision of Prisons. Session 1986-1987* (London: HMSO).

Home Affairs Committee First Special Report (1988) *Government Reply To The Fourth Report From The Home Affairs Committee. Session 1986-87* (London: HMSO).

Home Affairs Committee (1993) *The Prison Service - Minutes of Evidence* (London: HMSO).

Hurd, D. (1987) *House of Commons Debate* (16 July).

Lygo, R. (1991) *Management Of The Prison Service* (London: Home Office).

Mayhew, P., Maung, N. and Mirlees-Black, C. (1993) *The 1992 British Crime Survey* (London: HMSO).

Moran, P. (1993). 'The UK's Private Security Industry: A Study of Trade Union Issues'. Paper Presented to Employment Research Unit Conference, Cardiff Business School. (September).

Nathan, S. (1993a) 'Privatisation Fact File Three', *Prison Report, 24* (Autumn).

Nathan, S. (1993b) *Letter to Author.*

Personnel Management (1993) 'Strangeways No Strike Deal Denied' (August).

Pike, A. (1993a) 'Strangeways Team Beats Private Sector Bid', *Financial Times* (16 July).

Pike, A. (1993b) 'Howard To Seek Bar on Industrial Action by Prison Officers', *Financial Times* (18 November).

POA (1993) *Notice to Staff.* 166/1993.

Prisons Are Not For Profit Campaign (1991) *Prisons Are Not For Profit* (London: PANFPC).

Secretary of State For The Home Department (1988). *Private Sector Involvement In The Remand System* (London: HMSO).

The Times (1993) 'Crowded Jails Prepare To Send Inmates To Camps' (12 June).

Travis, A. (1993a) 'Riot Jail To Stay In Prison Service', *The Guardian* (16 July).

Travis, A. (1993b) 'Firms Call For More Prisons To Go Private', *The Guardian* (1 September).

Woolf, Rt Hon Lord Justice & Tumim, S. (1991) *Prison Disturbances April 1990* (London: HMSO).

Young, P. (1987) *The Prison Cell, The Start Of A Better Approach To Prison Management* (London: Adam Smith Institute).

THE POLICE FORCE OF THE FUTURE - A SECURITY RISK ?

Peter Moran, Bolton Business School and Alex Alexandrou, Research Officer, Police Federation of England & Wales.

Introduction.

This paper critically evaluates the strategic objectives of the UK government in restructuring the Police Service in England and Wales. It discusses the nature of the changes involved, against a backcloth of Atkinson's (1985) flexible firm model, and comments on some of the risks which attend this strategy and their associated changes. The paper begins by outlining the context in which the Police Service is being restructured in the mid-1990s.

Police Service Restructuring - An Overview

Changes being made to the organisation of police work in the UK should be viewed in the wider context of changes involving a plethora of other public services in a sector characterised by deregulation and competition. Such changes are being propelled by a government which, committed to market forces and manifesting an ideological predisposition towards the private sector, has embarked upon the re-organisation and dismantling of many sacred cows within the public sector. An additional contextual factor is the current struggle by the Treasury to regain control over a burgeoning Public Sector Borrowing Requirement.

Crime levels, too, are on the increase. Crime is an important aspect of the current political agenda and represents an issue of growing concern at individual and community levels, being linked to the public perception of the likelihood of becoming a victim of criminal activity. Notifiable offences recorded by the Police in Great Britain have risen from about 4.7 million in 1986 to roughly 6.6 million in 1992 (CSO 1993). Whilst sounding a cautionary note about the impact of changes to systems for recording and reporting crime, the 1992 British Crime Survey (Mayhew, Maung *et al* 1993, p.20) nevertheless indicated a rise in crime of 14 per cent between 1987 and 1991. Audit Commission figures (1993, p.3) indicate that in England and Wales there were 5.4 million crimes recorded in 1992 (excluding offences of criminal damage of under £20 in value), representing a 74 per cent increase over 1982 figures. The Audit Commission also noted that because of the increase in recorded crime, the proportion of crime solved by the police had declined from 37 per cent in 1982 to 26 per cent in 1992.

Successive Conservative administrations have laid claim to the electoral high ground of law and order, but the rise in recorded crime has undermined this claim and pushed the topic up the political agenda. The 'party of law and order' has been embarrassed to find that it has presided over record increases in crime rates (McLaughlin and Murji 1993, p.96). Although the police seemingly enjoyed favoured status in previous recessions, immune from the policy of retrenchment endured by other public sector organisations, it seems that this cosy relationship is unlikely to survive in the 1990s. Rather, the police, long used to viewing the Conservatives as their natural allies, have now found that they too are under scrutiny.

Public perceptions of the efficacy of the Police Service and other elements of the criminal justice system are largely negative. A Gallup Poll prepared in conjunction with *The Daily Telegraph* (August 30, 1993) suggested that only 55 per cent of the population have confidence in the police and, perhaps more disturbing, 75 per cent thought vigilante action could sometimes be justified. Public confidence is also undermined by miscarriages of justice and the well-publicised but relatively infrequent incidences of dishonesty among police officers. Public angst over sentencing policy, which is beyond the brief of police officers, nevertheless contributes to a lowering of public confidence in the police and frustration among individual officers.

The Government Restructuring Strategy in the Context of Atkinson's Flexible Firm Model

Michael Howard's response to the context in which the Police Service operates is constrained by Treasury pressure to contain spending. There appear to be two strands to his strategy. The first is to reduce expenditure on the Police Service by introducing less expensive personnel to carry out functions once regarded as the sole preserve of the Police. The second is to seek a greater degree of flexibility from the Service as a whole based on the utilisation of non-core police officers.

This section of the paper will examine these types of changes against the backcloth of Atkinson's (1985) flexible firm model. This model is explained next.

The Flexible Organisation.

Atkinson suggests that desirable organisational flexibility is underpinned by a workforce that responds swiftly to change and that can be contracted or expanded in line with economic conditions, and by an accompanying managerial drive to hold down unit labour costs by matching worked time precisely with job requirements. A slack labour market and a weakened trade union movement assists employers in operationalising these flexible pre-requisites. Additionally, Atkinson identifies three different types of desirable flexibility:

(i) *Functional Flexibility* - to ensure employees can be redeployed quickly and smoothly between activities and tasks.

(ii) *Numerical Flexibility* - to facilitate rapid changes in headcount to match even short-term changes in the level of demand for labour.

(iii) *Financial Flexibility* - to allow remuneration costs to reflect the interaction of supply and demand in the external labour market in the short run. Of greater importance in the longer term, pay flexibility may require a shift to new systems of remuneration that facilitate either numerical or functional flexibility (for example, assessment based salary schemes to replace rate for the job systems).

Hence, Atkinson's thesis prescribes the restructuring of the work organisation in order to achieve greater organisational flexibility. An employment model emerges from this prescription which makes it easier for employers to secure all three types of flexibility. Figure 1 indicates a radical departure from orthodox hierarchical organisation structures

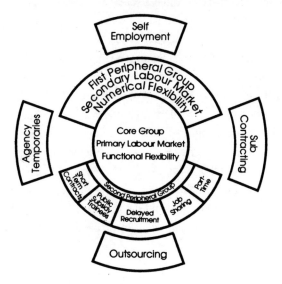

Figure 1. The Flexible Organisation

283

and implicitly enables different employment policies to be applied to different sets of employees. Atkinson's approach involves the division of the labour force into a stable, numerically small core group who conduct the organisation's key operations, and a larger peripheral group of flexible employees. For the core group, functional flexibility is emphasised, whilst numerical flexibility becomes more important for the peripheral groups. The aim is to ensure that tasks and responsibilities change only for the core employees and, as market conditions grow or contract, the number of peripheral workers is adjusted accordingly. Thus the core group is protected from the vagaries of the market and the peripheral groups are more directly exposed to them.

The Flexible Police Service.

Using Atkinson's classification, the groupings of core and peripheral employees in the Police Service can be categorised as follows:

1. Attested Police Officers (Core Group)

Attested Police Officers are employees who have sworn an oath and are officers of the Crown. They have extended powers and can be regarded as the core group of the Police Service. They hold permanent full-time posts and job security is sustained by the acceptance of functional flexibility. The most important characteristic of this group is that they possess the skills and experience necessary to achieve specific organisational goals and that these specific skills cannot be readily bought in from elsewhere. This core group is the highest paid of the employee groupings.

Following the implementation of the recommendations made by the (Edmund-Davies) Committee of Inquiry on the Police (1978), remuneration, recruitment and retention levels of core group personnel increased significantly during the 1980s: "In the period from 1979 to 1992 a constable's pay increased by 41 per cent in real terms. The number of officers increased by 23 per cent and the number of civilian employees by 15 per cent" (McLaughlin and Murji 1993, p.95). This permitted the Service to overcome the recruitment and retention problems it had suffered during the 1970s as a consequence of higher remuneration levels offered by alternative employers. The levels of pay are geared to service for police constables, and are illustrated in Table 1, whilst the growth in establishment rates (the number of officers each force is permitted to employ by the Home Office) is shown in Table 2.

	On Appointment	12,744
After	1 year	13,626
	2 years	16,044
	3 years	16,422
	4 years	16,965
	5 years	17,547
	6 years	18,105
	7 years	18,666
	8 years	19,218
	12 years	20,343
	15 years	21,267

Table 1. Annual Salary for Police Constables (£s)

Note: Excluding all other allowances, from 1 September 1993.
Source: Police Negotiating Board (1993).

Year	Authorised Establishment (And Approved Supernumery)	Actual Strength	Overall Vacancies Over Strength	% Difference
1983	120,447(N/A)	119,514	- 944	-0.78
1984	120,679(N/A)	119,103	-1589	-1.32
1985	120,903(N/A)	119,173	-1782	-1.47
1986	121,785(N/A)	119,825	-1968	-1.62
1987	122,648(N/A)	122,265	- 653	-0.53
1988	123,551(286)	122,907	- 952	-0.77
1989	124,667(310)	124,161	- 842	-0.67
1990	125,646(332)	125,060	- 918	-0.73
1991	126,325(276)	125,066	-1535	-1.21
1992	126,941(395)	125,879	-1457	-1.14
1993a	126,580(456)	125,878	-1158	-0.91

Table 2 Police Officer Establishment Rates in England & Wales. 1983-93

Notes: Investigation of the Home Office authorised establishment and approved supernumery rates clearly indicate that they are altered during the year and this at times can create a false picture of the number of officers that should be included in authorised establishment rates. For example, in January 1993 the authorised establishment figure was 127,374 by August the figure had been reduced to 126,580. Thus, the Police Service in England and Wales could be regarded as 1,442 officers under strength by August 1993.

Latest published figures in respect of 1993

Source: Home Office Statistics.

Table 2 indicates that police numbers have not been maintained at the levels authorised by the Home Office. The statistics also suggest that this trend has become more apparent through the recessionary years 1989-92. Despite this failure, actual strength has risen by 5.3 per cent between 1983 and 1993. However, the demands placed on the Service have risen disproportionately to the increase in numerical strength, as indicated in Figure 2.

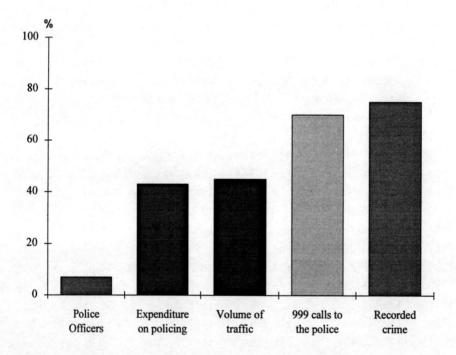

Figure 2

Changes in Police Resources and Demands for Police Services 1982-92

Source: Audit Commission (1993, p.8).

286

The overall picture also obscures the uneven distribution of the shortfall in numeric strength. In October 1993, thirty seven forces were under strength, and of these, eight forces were significantly under strength as illustrated in Table 3.

Force	Authorised Establishment	Number Below Strength	% Difference.
West Yorkshire	5297	292	-5.51
Gloucestershire	1184	40	-3.37
North Yorkshire	1418	69	-4.86
City of London	903	25	-3.13
Cleveland	1502	72	-4.79
Cheshire	1923	65	-3.83
Derbyshire	1850	64	-3.45
Lancashire	3232	83	-2.57

Table 3

Forces Significantly Under Strength in October 1993

The data in Table 3 suggest that officer numbers are contracting in certain forces, a situation exacerbated by the implementation of a freeze on authorised establishment figures for two consecutive years by the Home Office. This undermines the assumption implicit in Atkinson's model that core group employees remain numerically stable and are protected from the vagaries of market forces. Indeed, the Home Office have also mounted an assault on the financial rewards for core group employees in the form of the (Sheehy) *Inquiry Into Police Responsibilities and Rewards* (1993) which recommended a reduction in the overall remuneration package of police officers, through the elimination of allowances and the introduction of performance-related pay and short-term contracts for some officers. Although Michael Howard has not accepted all the recommendations made by Sheehy, he has referred a number of issues highlighted by the inquiry to the Police Negotiating Board (PNB) for consideration. These include pay scales, overtime allowances, assessment-based pay and pensions. The Home Secretary has clearly stated that there is no additional finance for the Service (Howard 1993), and the PNB has made it clear that it is seeking an overall reduction in the pay bill (PNB 1993a).

These developments have put core group officers under pressure, and have been compounded by the proposals contained in the White Paper on Police Reform (Secretary of State for the Home Department 1993) which alludes to the appointment of 30,000 Special

Constables. Furthermore, the Police and Magistrates Court Bill (1993) proposes to allow Chief Constables greater freedom to run their own forces. The most salient feature here is that they will no longer be bound by the establishment rates set by the Home Office. Chief Constables will determine the operational strength of their forces. Procedures governing the amalgamation of forces have also been relaxed, and this could be the precursor to a reduced number of forces with fewer officers. The Home Office has also announced a research study into the core functions of policing with the aim of identifying primary and ancillary functions. The objective is to specialise in the former and divest the latter to other bodies.

In 1992, Her Majesty's Inspector of Constables (HMIC) redefined operational constables as those "who, on a daily basis, come into regular contact with the public, and who may be required to use their powers as constables" (HMIC 1992). It was anticipated that there would be a consequent reduction in the "proportion of officers deemed operational". In order to measure officer and civilian numbers more accurately HMIC sub-divided the Service into three categories:

Category A: roles in which civilians would normally be expected to perform duties.

Category B: roles suitable for civilians but where a recognised need for some police procedures exist.

Category C: roles considered entirely suitable for civilians.

HMIC's redefinition of roles may be interpreted as another attempt by the government to reduce the number of police officers and to hive off their functions to civilians and other bodies. This scenario may be further complicated by the creation of an independent committee of inquiry into the role and responsibilities of the police by the Police Foundation and the Police Studies Institute (Police and Magistrates Courts Bill 1993). One area that may be investigated by the committee is related to those functions of the service which may be privatised or civilianised. Plans to privatise the traffic warden service in Strathclyde are well advanced. It is suspected that the new self-financing system will be privatised through the mechanism of compulsory competitive tendering (Police Review 1993).

2. Full-Time Civilian Employees & Traffic Wardens (First Peripheral Group)

Although there are some exceptions, full-time police employees have jobs rather than careers and these are not, in the main, highly skilled. Turnover is higher in this first peripheral group compared to the core group, which may be linked to a lack of career opportunities. Pepper (1993) emphasises this in his study which indicated that 86 per cent of civilian staff did not believe there was a career structure for them within the Police Service. Civilian employees are more exposed to the external labour market and this assists

288

employers in achieving flexibility in numerical strength and remuneration. This group's activities have been confined to highly specialised tasks or general administrative or maintenance functions.

The Home Office (1983, 1988) had consistently advocated the increased deployment of civilians in the 1980s, in order to release officers to perform operational duties and increase force establishment rates. The growth in civilian employees and traffic wardens is illustrated in Table 4.

Year.	Civilian Full-Time.	Civilian Part-Time.	Traffic Wardens.
1983	34,155	5971	4661
1984	34,763	6402	4891
1985	34,043	5578	4558
1986	35,765	5942	4627
1987	37,910	6158	4820
1988	38,512	6320	4704
1989	39,797	6309	4650
1990	41,493	6239	4609
1991	42,776	6141	4868
1992	44,183	6740	5077
1993	46,191	7625	5068

Table 4
Police Civilian Full-Time, Part-Time and Traffic Warden Establishment Rates in England & Wales. 1983-92

Source: CIPFA Figures.

The data indicate a 35 per cent increase in the number of full-time civilian posts between 1983 and 1993 and that part-time posts increased by almost 28 per cent during the same period. The number of traffic wardens rose by 8.7 per cent. Similar computations applied to the core group in Table 2 indicate that the authorised establishment of police officers rose by 5.09 per cent, whilst actual strength rose by 5.32 per cent during the same period. The process of civilianisation is likely to expand during the remainder of the 1990s as the government seeks to free police officers for operational duty. Both the Sheehy Inquiry (1993) and the Police Reform White Paper (1993) advocate an enhanced role for civilians. Furthermore, the Police and Magistrates Courts Bill (1993) proposes to transfer civilian employees from the employment of local authorities to police authorities, which is likely to increase substantially the degree of direction and control exercised over civilians by Chief Constables. This could prove to be significant in terms of the duties allocated to civilians and the remuneration they receive.

The number of areas in which civilians are now deployed has grown considerably and these now include traffic duties and the enforcement of parking regulations, vehicle pounds, custody suites, control rooms, forensic and fingerprinting services and the functions of finance, communications, personnel and scenes of crime activities. In 1993, traffic wardens were empowered to remove and immobilise vehicles, issue fixed penalty tickets and require motorists to produce driving licences if they considered that a motoring offence had been committed. Longrigg (1993) suggests that by taking over the management of endorsable parking offences, wardens are relieving the police of some of their more boring duties and, more significantly, that wardens now regard themselves as 'mini police officers'.

3. Part-Time Civilian Employees, Special and Parish Constables (Second Peripheral Group)

The second peripheral group has become more prominent in the Police Service during the past decade, as indicated in Table 5. Civilian members of this group are part-time workers, some of whom are on short-term contracts, and job share employment. This facilitates maximum organisational flexibility whilst minimising the organisation's committment to the job security and career development of these employees.

Year	Total	Year	Total
1983	15,331	1988	15,788
1984	16,012	1989	15,589
1985	16,161	1990	15,902
1986	16,070	1991	18,072
1987	16,209	1992	19,243

Table 5
Special Constable Establishment Rates in England and Wales. !983-92

Source: Home Office Statistics and HMIC Annual Force Reports.

Special and Parish Constables are unpaid volunteers who are deployed to supplement the numerical flexibility of the core group. Although specials have existed for more than 150 years, government interest in the Special Constabulary intensified during the mid-1980s. The White Paper on Police Reform (1993) outlines government proposals to increase the number of specials to 30,000, an increase of 55 per cent on current levels.

Not only are there more specials, with numbers up 25 per cent between 1983 and 1992, their duties are also being expanded to include driving police vehicles and taking part in specially targeted operations. Training is offered under the Special Constabulary Development Course, introduced in 1993, with the objective of ensuring that specials achieve the same professional standards as their regular counterparts, and core group police officers may regard the new special as a threat to their position. Pepper (1993) provides some evidence of the inroads being made by the special officers by highlighting the case of the special officer who worked 1,700 hours and the example of the 250 specials in one force who performed 50,000 duty hours. The real and anticipated budget savings that are associated with the employment of specials are large.

In tandem with an increased deployment of specials, Parish Constables are to be resurrected. In modern guise, Parish Constables will have the same powers, training and uniform as the Specials. Parish constables will be unpaid and have jurisdiction only in their own parishes. They will, however, be part of the force structure and under the command of the Chief Constable. The government hoped to have about 20 pilot schemes, involving Parish Constables, running by the end of 1993.

4. Private Security Contractors (External Groups)

In terms of Atkinson's categorisations the external groups that are coming to the fore in traditional Police service markets are private security operators. The 'manned' (sic) services offered by the private sector have traditionally included cash in transit, secure delivery of overnight parcels, store detectives and the guarding/patrolling of commercial premises. For many static guards, pay levels are low and long hours are the norm. The 'trade' body for private security operators is the British Security Industry Association (BSIA). The BSIA survey of security officers' hourly pay conducted in October 1993 shows that:

> The national average has increased to £3.52 from £3.40 in April 1992. Average weekly pay is now £194.63 against £190.92, the highest since October 1991 when guards were working almost a 60 hour week compared to 55 hours now (Professional Security, 1993).

Wide regional variations are disguised by the average. Guards in Central London earn £4.05 per hour and are the highest paid, whilst guards in the North East earn average pay of just over £150 for a 55 hour week (equivalent to about £2.72 per hour). These low-paid employees, on contract, offer the numerical and financial flexibility of Atkinson's model and so are extremely attractive to the consumers of private security services.

The training of security guards has attracted adverse criticism. Mann (1992) examined the recommended minimum training course for security personnel prior to their despatch to clients' premises. This included:

- Introduction to security officer's duties
- Assignment instructions (key registers, passes, safes, etc)
- Reporting routines and 999 calls
- Patrolling and observation
- Types of fire and fire fighting
- Reporting: accidents, hazards, etc.
- Introduction to law: trespass, theft, arrest, search, health and safety, etc.
- Major incidents: bomb threats, etc

With the exception of first aid, this appears to be remarkably comprehensive "until one reads that the BSIA recommended the minimum training period for it all should not exceed two days" (Mann 1992). Very similar induction training is recommended by the British Standards Institute (BSI) for companies seeking registration under B.S.7499 who prescribe that the duration of training should not be less than two days (BSI 1991, p.6). These prescriptions do not bear comparison with the lengthy training undertaken by attested officers in the core group.

The industry's internal arrangements for the vetting of potential employees have also been called into question. The International Professional Security Association (IPSA), a training and educational body, has been calling for legislation to regulate this process for many years. Currently, there are no statutory regulations governing the screening of recruits or employers.

The BSIA code of conduct requires member companies to check the previous 20-year employment history of applicants. However, many of the smaller operators within the industry do not belong to the BSIA and are not constrained by these guidelines. Following the bombing of Deal Barracks, the Defence Committee highlighted the shortcomings of the screening procedures in use at the time. Despite the 20-year screening of applicants outlined by the BSIA code, it emerged that provisional employment (of up to four months' duration) could be offered, based on screening for the previous five years only. The Committee commented that "This form of screening can be completed in two days and strikes us as completely inadequate" (Defence Committee 1990, p.xviii).

Prior to the disaster at Deal, attempts to legislate for the regulation of the industry (George 1977; Dixon 1987) had failed and after Deal a further attempt was made (Wheeler 1989). All were snubbed by the governments of the day. In its response to the Defence

Committee, the government's unflinching adhesion to laissez-faire policies were clearly expressed:

The Government notes that the Committee believe that the security companies' screening of potential employees is often inadequate. This is for the companies themselves to consider and any improvements would be most welcome to the Government (Defence Committee 1990a, p.vi).

The Association of Chief Police Officers (ACPO) has called for an independently regulated industry (ACPO 1988). Sir John Woodcock, Her Majesty's Inspector of Constabulary, echoed the call for regulation in 1991 (Cowdry 1991). Post-Deal, the BSIA itself called for regulation, but successive Home Secretaries have ignored these supplications. The BSIA has attempted to strengthen its framework for self regulation. B.S.7499 is the tangible output of these exertions, and includes guidance on vetting and training similar to that established in the BSIA code. The most significant difference is that companies registered under B.S.7499 are inspected by an independent third party, the Inspectorate of the Security Industry (ISI), which was established in 1992. Although this is an initiative to be welcomed, by the end of 1992 the number of companies holding inspected status was only 45 (Sanderson 1993) and this number consisted of the established reputable companies. As has been noted elsewhere, "Without the force of law to impel companies to join the scheme, many have not done so. As a result the ISI are inspecting a fraction of those operating within the industry" (Moran 1993).

Many of the more reputable companies exceed the BSIA and BSI training and vetting minima by substantial margins. In 1988, Securicor was reportedly spending in excess of £1,200 per person on these activities (Raphael & Hyder 1988). Group 4 personnel employed in the privately managed prison and court escort services are subject to far more scrupulous vetting and rigourous training than is laid down by the BSIA. Schedule 3 of the Operational Specification for the Court Escort Service (Home Office 1992) outlines a core training requirement for Prison Custody Officers of 152 hours in duration and particular 'defined functions' attract further training. Group 4 indicates that at The Wolds Remand Centre:

All operational staff (prison custody officers) receive a minimum of 315 hours of training. The content of the training has been agreed by the Home Office and is defined in the contract...all personnel are security screened by the Home Office. This is required by law and is the same screening as is required for Prison Officers (Howard League 1993, p.11).

The state is duplicitous in setting high standards of vetting and training which have to be met by contractors bidding for work in the fields of private prisons and escort services whilst simultaneously refusing to legislate to set equally high benchmarks for other clients of security contractors. In preferring to rely on the operation of market forces to regulate the allocation of contracts, the government facilitates a market place wherein the adage *caveat emptor* assumes greater significance.

The Growing Involvement of External Groups

The gap between demand for, and availability of, police services, illustrated in Figure 2, has generated a vacuum strong enough to propel the private sector to growing prominence as an alternative provider of functions in an area once regarded as the sole domain of the Police Service.

As has been noted elsewhere, there exists an overlap in, and a demarcation between, the services offered by the police and the private sector:

> Public officers have a relative monopoly over tasks such as interrogation, whilst private security personnel enjoy similar control over locks and keys. In between, however, there is a continuum of activities, many of which cut across the public-private divide; alarm responses, escort duties...control of access and movement (Johnston 1991, p.26).

It is the balance between public and private provision that is changing, reflecting a market oriented laissez faire approach by government.

In the past few years there have been calls from the BSIA and individual security firms for a closer working relationship with the Police, couched in terms of relieving the police of their more mundane duties, extending cooperation, maximising resource utilisation and so forth. These calls mask an encroachment into operational territory that was once theirs alone. This has been exemplified in David Fletcher's (Chief Executive of The BSIA) address to the 1992 ACPO conference, during which he proposed that private organisations should deal with speeding motorists, the issuing of firearm certificates and the escorting of abnormal loads (Campbell 1992). Fletcher intertwined these proposals with calls for access to criminal records in order to tighten the vetting of potential employees.

Reports (*Sunday Times*, 13 June 1993) that the Home Office planned to allow private sector organisations to deploy marked cars on motorways to catch speeding motorists were later denied (Joshi 1993). However, the same source confirmed that the Home Office was in the early stages of examining ways in which the escorting of heavy loads on motorways could be transferred to the private sector. One motorway control room in Kent is already run by a private sector organisation, the Automobile Association (Police Federation 1993).

Similarly, David Dickinson, Group 4's Sales and Marketing Director, whilst stressing the need for some kind of accreditation of private security companies, has suggested that the first response to intruder alarm calls (98 per cent of which are false) could be dealt with by the private sector, saving the Police Service in excess of £100 million per annum (Dickinson 1993).

The Home Office has already subcontracted the guarding of their residental and training establishments to private concerns. The Immigration Detention Centre at Harmondsworth has been managed by the private sector for twenty years. The deportation of illegal immigrants is now also being handled by the private sector. In the case of Dorothy Nwokedi, the Home Office employed Airline Security Services, despite the fact that at that time the company was not ISI registered. An ISI spokesperson was quoted as suggesting that "It is surprising that the Home Office does not demand in its contracts the basic standards that it has recognised as one of the cornerstones of self regulation in the industry" (Pilkington 1993). The Home Office has already subcontracted the escorting of prisoners and those on remand in the East Midlands area to Group 4, and Securicor will assume this role in the London Metropolitan area on a phased basis commencing in July 1994. Group 4's difficulties in this area have been widely reported. There were eight escapes in the first two weeks from either the privately managed prison or the privatised escort service. Shortly after, Group 4's reputation suffered further when an inquest jury returned a verdict of lack of care in connection with the death of Ernest Hogg while he was in Group 4's custody (Travis 1994).

In November 1992, when Kenneth Clarke announced that Group 4 had won the court escort contract, he said:

> The new escort service will lead to far more efficient use being made of the valuable time of police officers...those officers...previously involved in escorting work will in future be free to concentrate their skills on the police... jobs for which they were trained (Prison Service 1992).

A subsequent report from the Prison Reform Trust (1993) suggested that the involvement of the private sector jeopardized core group posts in that sixty three police posts were identified for loss in the East Midlands Police in anticipation of the contract. Derek Lewis, Director General of Prisons, reportedly remarked that "To suggest that a new service costing tens of millions of pounds should be set up without looking at the police or prison service to shed any posts is unrealistic" (Travis 1993).

The impact of the Securicor contract on the establishment of the Metropolitan Police has also been queried by Richard Coyles, the chairman of the Police Federation. Coyles has suggested that:

> ...almost 300 Metropolitan Police officers currently engaged on these duties will cease to be so engaged...But that does not mean that nearly 300 officers will be released for duty on the streets. Because, of course, that £96 million will be paid to

Securicor by the taxpayers and those 300 posts will disappear from the establishment of the Metropolitan Police (Coyles 1994).

Thus, to a large extent, the expansion of the use of private security has been propelled by the policies of the state. Citizens have also banded together and hired security guards to perform street patrols, a key function of the police service. Precise figures for the number of private patrols are not available, but one survey suggests that "there may be as many as 1000 of these throughout the country. Some are carried out by municipal employees and groups of concerned citizens, but the vast majority are undertaken by private security companies" (Boothroyd 1989). Some of this deployment of private security patrols in residential areas is indicated in Table 6 below.

District.	Security Company.
Stoke Bishop (Bristol)	System And Security
St. Anne's (Bristol)	Knighthawk
Wyke Regis (Dorset)	N/A
Goose Green (Wigan)	Property Watch
Winstanley (Wigan)	Property Watch
Hightown (Crosby)**	N/A
Hylton Manor (Sunderland)*	Delta One
Fulford Grange (Sunderland)*	Delta One
Wentworth (Surrey)	Executive Security

Table 6
Uniformed Private Security Patrols in Residential Areas

Notes: * Defunct after residents discontinued payment.
       ** Pilot scheme, ran for ten months.

Sources: *The Guardian* (16 July 1993 and 21 June 1993).
         Sunday Times (22 June 1993).
         Beatt (1992)
         Elliott (1989).

In addition, some local authorities employ uniformed security guards to patrol housing estates as part of their duties. These authorities include Wandsworth, Camden, Livingston

(Elliott 1989) and Sedgefield (*The Guardian*, 28 September 1993). Michael Howard has suggested that the general public should patrol the streets within the auspices of schemes run by Neighbourhood Watch and is currently drawing up a code of conduct with ACPO to facilitate this development (Vervier & Dixon 1993). It has been reported that Group 4 has already made formal approaches to a number of Chief Constables. Group 4 is seeking to draft a national code of practice for those involved in street patrols in the hope that the government will support the establishment of an official register of security firms which could be appointed by either local authorities or the police (Purnell 1993).

In the context of our railways, the future role of the British Transport Police in protecting the passengers and property of British Rail is highly uncertain. If BR is privatised, then it is questionable whether the Transport Police will retain all their present duties. Johnston (1992, p.104) indicates the growth of private security in the field of transport. In 1989, Sealink ended its contract with the British Transport Police, recruiting in their place Protective Security Systems to police Parkstone Quay in Harwich.

The prevention of terrorism has also expanded the private security industry's role in the sphere of transport. The Aviation and Maritime Security Act (1990) requires Port Authorities to search ships, harbours, persons and property and gives powers of search to constables and 'other persons' specified by the Secretary of State. Private security guards have had the powers to search airline passengers and their luggage since 1973. The anti-terrorism theme was echoed by Lord Caithness during the House of Lords Committee stage debate on the Railways Bill, suggesting that ministers could require railway companies to "employ specified numbers of suitably trained staff for the purpose of preventing the occurrence of acts of violence" (*Financial Times*, 20 July 1993). This may generate further opportunities for security contractors.

The devolvement of Police Service budgets to Chief Constables may also help tip the balance in favour of the private sector in certain functional areas. As suggested by Pirie, (1992, pp.15-16):

> The discretionary power available to local budget holders should include the ability to hire private security under contract ...The power should also convey the right to contract out other police services including, for example, driver training and fleet management. Police communications and associated training might be contracted out, as might certain traffic duties.

Pirie points to the US example, where some Forces use civilian drivers, radio and telephone operators and contractors to visit the scenes of burglaries in order to record the circumstances of the crime including details of missing property.

Future Policing and Risk.

There can be little doubt that creeping privatisation of police functions is taking place with the tacit assent, if not active encouragement, of the Home Office. There are risks associated with this process. Attested police officers are a homogenous group with regard to training and vetting; private security guards are not. The roles and activities of police officers are largely prescribed by statute and the internal procedures of the service. Private security operators are largely unregulated.

Some advocates of the enhancement of private sector involvement in the provision of Police Services resist the pressure for regulation of the industry by suggesting that regulation would act as a barrier to entry and thun protect existing operators to the detriment of service effectiveness. Elliott (1989, pp.6-7) makes this point and suggests that although most residents employing private firms are unfamiliar with the market:

> ... it is perhaps not surprising that their choices of firm are not always well informed. But this may be a problem that can only be alleviated over time. As they become more practised at dealing with security firms, residents will probably become more discerning and "cowboys" will be weeded out through competition.

However, the nature of problems that residents may encounter and the consequences of these problems for them are not addressed in Elliott's work. In the security industry, "cowboys" should be weeded out by the state, not by trial and error on the part of consumers.

The reliance on market forces may generate risks for society in general rather than for just those who hire private security patrols in residential areas. Sir John Smith, Deputy Commissioner of the Metropolitan Police, has warned that the creeping privatisation of police functions is becoming socially divisive. Sir John warned that "the philosophy of free market thinking may affect safety in the community" (Campbell 1994). Sir John suggested that those people that were already on the margins of society were becoming even more marginalised and that a two tier system of policing was evolving. Criminal activity may be displaced from privately patrolled estates to areas that are unable to afford additional security provision. In addition, the proliferation of private street patrols places further strain on police resources through their being frequently called to affluent areas that employ private guards. The Police are obliged to answer these calls and this detracts from their ability to perform duties in other, less affluent areas.

Community policing is a multiple goal activity intended to increase police effectiveness. Clarke and Hough (1984, p.15) suggest that such initiatives have a number of aims which include the improvement of relations with the public; the instilling of a greater committment to law and order; the improvement of the flow of information coming to the police about crime; and the encouragement of community crime prevention. Private security guards patrolling residential areas may well undermine several of these objectives and although this is difficult to quantify, the loss of information to the police may be significant.

There are also risks which attract to security guards involved in street patrols. For example, they may be tempted to 'have a go' at apprehending suspects and in so doing might exceed their limited powers. In this scenario, those hired to contribute to crime prevention may themselves be the subject of litigation. In some areas the streets are dangerous places to work in and the number of police officers assaulted per annum is around 17,000 (Humphrey 1992, p.115) - about 13 per cent of the total Force. It is unlikely that members of the criminal fraternity would discriminate between police officers and security guards when resorting to violence.

Less tangible, but of equal concern, is the issue of accountability. Although the mechanisms for ensuring police accountability have been criticised, they are, at least, in place and do provide a backstop for citizens affronted by police activity (or lack of it). The issue of accountability of the private patrols has yet to be addressed fully. To whom are the companies that employ private security guards accountable, the shareholders of the company which employed them or the citizens which pay for the service? What of those who lack the economic means to hire them. Are they to be taken out of the the equation of accountability? Is the key control mechanism for those who do hire them the threat of awarding the contract elsewhere in the event of disatisfaction with the level of service provided? Market forces do not provide a range of accountability devices beyond the single measure of withdrawing from the contract.

Conclusions.

Although Atkinson's model has its critics such as Pollert (1986), it is a useful tool for analysing the current changes being made to the work organisation of the Police Service. The evidence provided indicates that the role of attested police officers is being eroded by other (peripheral) groups within the service and by the private sector. Indeed, Lyn Williams, General Secretary of the Police Federation estimates that the Home Office's internal review of police functions could result in 46,000 fewer officers (Brown 1993).

It is also apparent that the Home Office has not maintained the number of serving officers at the levels of authorised establishment, and that this has been more detrimental to some forces than others. The number of civilians working in the service and the number of Special Constables have also increased dramatically, and it is likely that the number of Parish Constables will rise substantially. Not all of these peripheral groups have the same powers or transferability of the core group of full-time Police Officers.

The subcontracting of police functions to external groups is also accelerating. Although there has been an overlap between the police service and private operators for some time, the balance between them is changing in favour of the latter. In its wider context, a highly-trained, highly-regulated group is being diluted by one which is reliant on self regulation to only a limited degree and which is not uniform in its approach to training and vetting. This alteration in the balance between the two groups is driven partly by ideological and partly by economic considerations, and is taking place without the level of debate necessary to consider the risks attendant on such a strategy. This is all the more incongruous as senior figures in the Institute of Directors (IOD) are urging that security be pushed up the agenda and should be a "major boardroom issue" (Morgan 1993).

The expanding role of the private sector also marks a shift in the motivation underlying the provision of these services. As profit replaces the ethos of public service, does this in itself generate risks? Although advocates of private street patrols acknowledge that consumers may be unfamiliar with the market and that "cowboys" do exist, the risks are not analysed. Rather they are assumed to be treatable by recourse to market forces which do not arm the consumer with rights of redress via explicit channels of accountability. If this is the nature of the police force of the future, the security risks may be higher than initially calculated by those who have the ability to change its development.

References.

ACPO (1988) *A Review of the Private Security Industry*, North Wales Police.

Atkinson, J. (1985) *Flexibility, Uncertainty and Manpower Management (Brighton:Institute of Manpower Studies).*

Audit Commission (1993) *Helping With Enquiries: Tackling Crime Effectively* (London: HMSO).

Beatt, A. (1992) 'Market Forces', *Police Review* (4 September) pp. 1628-29.

Boothroyd, J. (1989) 'Nibbling Away At The Bobby's Patch', *Police Review* (13 January) pp.664-5.

British Standards Institute (1991) *Manned Security Services Part 1. Code of Practice for Static Guarding and Mobile Patrol Services* (Milton Keynes: BSI).

Brown, C. (1993) 'Police Warn Howard Over Job Cuts', *The Independent* (28 December).

Campbell, D. (1992) 'Private Firms Eye Speeding Drivers', *The Guardian* (12 June).

Campbell, D. (1994) 'Police Chief Warns of Two Tier System', *The Guardian* (10 January).

Central Statistical Office (1993) *Monthly Digest of Statistics 573* (London: HMSO).

Clarke, R. and Hough, M. (1984) *Crime and Police Effectiveness. Home Office Research Study 79 (London: HMSO).*

Cowdry, Q. (1991) 'Security Firm Growth Should Be Checked Police Watchdog Say', *The Times* (20 September).

Coyles, R. (1994) 'We Fear Private Takeover', *Police* (February) p.17

Defence Committee Sixth Report (1990) *The Physical Security of Military Installations in the United Kingdom. Session 1989-90* (London: HMSO).

Defence Committee Fourth Special Report (1990a) *Government Reply to the Sixth Report from the Defence Committee. Session 1989-90 (London: HMSO).*

Dickinson, D. (1993) 'When The Police Are Not There!', paper presented to the *Policing...Private or Public Conference*, Manchester Metropolitan University.

Dixon, D. (1987) *Private Security Bill [Bill 40]* (London: HMSO).

Edmund-Davies, Lord (1978) *Committee of Inquiry On The Police* (London: HMSO).

Elliott, N. (1989) *Streets Ahead* (London: Adam Smith Institute).

George, B. (1977) *Private Security (Registration) Bill. [Bill 114]* (London: HMSO).

HMIC (1992) *Statistical Analysis of Force, Officer & Civilian Strength* (London: HMSO).

Home Office (1983) *Circular 114/1983.*

Home Office (1988) *Circulars 105/1988 and 106/1988.*

Howard League For Criminal Reform (1993) 'The Facts About The Wolds', *Criminal Justice, 11*(2) p.11.

Howard, M. (1993) Letter to Prof L.Hunter, Chair of the PNB. 29 October.

Humphrey, C. (1992) 'The Police Service and the Management of Crime: A Case of Efficiency Gone Mad?', in Wilkinson, C., Brown, D. and Otley, D., *Case Studies in Management Control* (Hemel Hempstead: Prentice Hall).

Johnston, L. (1991) 'Privatisation and The Police Function: From "New Police" to "New Policing" ', in Reiner, R. and Cross, M., (eds), *Beyond Law and Order: Criminal Justice Policy and Politics into the 1990s* (Basingstoke: Macmillan) pp.18-40.

Johnston, L. (1992) *The Rebirth of Private Policing* (London: Routledge).

Joshi, S. (1993) *F8 Division*, Home Office, Letter to P.Moran (7 July).

Longrigg,C. (1993) 'All Power To The Wardens', *Independent Magazine* (16 October).

Mann, T. (1992) 'Security Services Under Fire', *Management Services, 36*(1) pp.28-30.

Mayhew, P., Maung, N. and Mirlees-Black, C. (1993) *The 1992 British Crime Survey* (London: HMSO).

McLaughlin, E. and Murji, K. (1993) 'Controlling The Bill: Restructuring the Police in the 1990s', *Critical Social Policy,13*(1) pp.95-103.

Moran, P. (1993) 'The UK Security Industry - A Study of the Trade Union Issues', paper presented at the *Employment Research Unit Conference*, University of Cardiff (September).

Morgan, P. (1993) 'Protecting Business Assets', *Director's Guide To Security* (London: Institute of Directors) p.4.

Pepper, S. (1993) 'Special Effort', *Police Review* (6 August) p.23.

Pirie, M. (1992) *The Radical Edge* (London; Adam Smith Institute).

Pilkington, E. (1993) 'Deportation Used Unregulated Firm', *The Guardian* (1 September).

Prison Reform Trust (1993) *Court Escort Services. The Case For A National Publicly Run Escort Service* (London: PRT).

Prison Service (1992) *News Release 282/92.*

Professional Security (1993) 'Plenty or Pittance?', *Professional Security, 3*(6) p.27.

Police & Magistrates Courts Bill (1993).

Police Federation (1992) Letter To P. Moran.

Police Negotiating Board (1993) *PNB Circular 93/7.*

Police Negotiating Board (1993a) *Official Side's Response to the Sheehy Report.*

Police Review (1993) 19 November.

Pollert, A. (1986) 'The "Flexible Firm" A Model in Search of Reality (or a policy in search of a practice)?', *Warwick Papers in Industrial Relations.*

Purnell, S. (1993) *Daily Telegraph* (25 October).

Raphael, A., and Hyder, K. (1988) 'Private Force That is a Law Unto Itself', *The Observer* (21 August).

Sanderson, I. (1993) 'Inspector General, ISI'. Letter to P.Moran (9 February.)

Secretary of State For the Home Department (1993) *Police Reform: A Police Service for the Twenty First Century* (London: HMSO).

Sheehy, Sir P. (1993) *Inquiry into Police Responsibilities and Rewards* (London: HMSO).

Travis, A. (1993) 'Police and Prison Jobs Lost to Group 4', *The Guardian* (16 July).

Travis, A. (1994) 'Prisoner's Death From Lack of Care', *The Guardian* (16 February).

Vervier, C. and Dixon, C. (1993) 'Howard Backs Street Patrols To Cut Crime', *Sunday Times* (5 December).

Wheeler, J. (1989) *Security Industry Bill [Bill 214]* (London: HMSO).

THE STATE OF ITALY, CORRUPTION AND PRIVATIZATION

Peter Curwen, Sheffield Business School

Introduction

There is a country where the national debt exceeds 110 per cent of GDP, the Budget deficit is roughly 10 per cent of GDP, the unemployment rate is officially 10.5 per cent but large numbers are additionally laid off temporarily and the country is politically unstable and riddled with corruption. That country is the state of Italy.

At present, Italy's foreign debt is so large that it can only be brought under control through a tight fiscal policy. In this respect it is important to distinguish between the primary balance and the overall budget balance which includes interest payments on the outstanding debt. Throughout the 1980s, Italy ran a continuous series of primary deficits. However, since 1985 the size of this deficit has been shrinking, and the deficit became a surplus during the 1992-93 financial year. Unfortunately, the build-up of debt during the 1980s generated an ever-rising interest bill. By implication, it is necessary to run a sizeable primary surplus in order to make any real inroads into the debt, yet that in turn implies tax increases and/or spending cuts on a scale unprecedented in modern Italian history.

A root cause of this fiscal malaise both was, and largely remains, the ingrained habit of political patronage, of which one particular manifestation is the 'allocation' of loss-making state industries to political parties such that, for example, votes can be 'bought' with the offer of wholly unnecessary jobs.

By the early 1990s it had become clear to the whole of Italian society that this situation could not go on for much longer, and indeed the four-party coalition elected in April 1992, led by Guiliano Amato, was given a mandate to tackle the problem which initially it did with some success. However, higher taxation is never electorally popular, and it soon became clear that a programme of privatization would provide the theoretically least-painful way to shrink the deficit. This paper addresses whether Italy has the capacity to set in motion and sustain such a programme.

The Early History of Italian Public Enterprise

The nationalized industry format has almost never been used in Italy, with the exception of the electrical industry, part of the state agency ENEL (*Ente Nazionale per l'Energia Elettricà*). Instead, there is a wide variety of formats, ranging from joint stock companies (*Società per Azioni*) to foundations and public law entities.

One of the main ways in which the state exercises direct control over ownership is through autonomous state entities such as the FFAS which operates the railways and the ANAS which operates and leases the road network. However, the system of state shareholdings (*Partecipazioni Statali*) is much more common, and dates back to 1933 with the creation of IRI (*Instituto per la Ricostruzione Industriale*). During the Great Depression the banks found themselves acquiring large industrial shareholdings, and these were passed over to the IRI in order to stave off bankruptcies. These were not returned to the private sector, and indeed the banks themselves ended up under the umbrella of the IRI (Vigliano, 1988).

This could partly be ascribed to a lack of private capital available to repurchase these shareholdings (Bianchi *et al*, 1988). Hence, whereas there were a significant number of denationalizations during the latter half of the 1930s, the major industrial concerns remained in state ownership as part of IRI which in June 1937 became a state holding company, owned in its entirety by the state and controlled by the Ministry for State Holdings. Until 1953, IRI and industrial policy were synonymous. However, in sectors such as oil and chemicals the authorities considered that the existence of private monopolies and foreign companies was destroying competition, and in order to offset this the state created the ENI (*Ente Nazionale Idrocarburi*) in 1953. This was followed, in 1962, by the creation of EFIM (*Ente Partecipazione e Finanziamento Industria Manifatturiera*) encompassing primarily the engineering and metal-working sectors.

Each holding company (*ente autonomo di gestione*) has access to an endowment fund with which to acquire majority holdings in companies. Commonly, the actual acquisition has been made by an intermediate level concern such as Finmeccanica and Finsider. As agents of industrial policy IRI, ENI and EFIM increasingly found themselves involved in the creation of manufacturing concerns in southern Italy where, as in the case of cars, conditions were less propitious than in the north. As a result, their portfolio of companies became increasingly weighed down with loss-making concerns, especially in the period subsequent to the first oil crisis in 1974. Eventually, IRI was to become the world's largest state-owned enterprise, with roughly 1,000 companies under its control. It also came to account for 5 per cent of Italian GNP.

Barriers to Privatization

The use of state-owned concerns to promote industrial policy is deeply ingrained. It is undoubtedly the case that the unusually large disparity in economic development between the industrial north and rural south could not have been even partially resolved in the absence of a deliberate attempt to use state-owned concerns as a vehicle for investment in the south. In this respect, account has to be taken of the underdeveloped stock market in Milan. There are no large institutional investors in Italy, and savings have tended to be sucked into the market for government securities because of the need to finance ongoing, sizeable fiscal deficits. In any event, the system of political patronage (*lottizzazione*) necessitates sufficient state-owned resources to be spread around.

During the 1980s some privatizations did take place, although these were invariably semi-privatizations which left the state with a controlling interest (Bianchi *et al*, 1988). In aggregate, they made barely any inroads into the accumulation of losses in the public enterprise sector. This, in turn, meant that the public finances were almost unaffected by revenue raised through asset sales. As a consequence, ever-larger numbers of government securites needed to be sold in order to finance the fiscal deficits, which itself drove up interest rates and deprived the equity market of essential liquidity. Higher interest rates meant an increasing burden on the budget, and also served to maintain the exchange rate at a higher level than was desirable for competitiveness in international trade. What was needed was a boost to confidence on the back of which further asset sales could be launched. What transpired was the stock market crash of 1987 which largely put paid to any lingering hopes of popular or people's capitalism. However, it is also worth noting that the general public, unlike in the UK, were never offered any opportunities to buy shares in the public utilities. Nor were administrative and legal arrangements such as to facilitate sales (Bianchi *et al*, 1988).

New Directions in Policy

Nevertheless, during the early 1990s, it finally began to sink in that a fiscal disaster was impending. The election of the Amato government, albeit as yet another coalition between the established ruling parties, also indicated that a new sense of reality was pervading the body politic. Accordingly, in mid-July 1992, IRI, ENEL, ENI and INA (*Instituto Nazionale delle Assicurazioni*), the national insurance institution, were converted into joint stock companies under the control of the Treasury as a preliminary step towards their privatization.

The government declared its intention to cut the budget deficit by L30,000bn (£120bn) by the end of the 1992-93 financial year. The threatened cuts in public spending brought the citizenry out on to the streets, so the government hurried through plans to raise revenue through asset sales. These plans, which involved the creation of two new super-holding companies, were universally criticised and had to be dropped almost immediately. A critical issue was the uncertainty surrounding where responsibility would lie for the extensive foreign debts of IRI, ENI and ENEL. Foreign creditors were worried about this, and, as it turned out, rightly so since on 20 July the government issued a decree to the effect that EFIM had gone into liquidation.

EFIM was created essentially as an industrial hospital to sustain companies committed to expansion in the Mezzogiorno. From the outset it was loosely managed and politically manipulated. During the 1980s, billions of lira of public money were poured into EFIM in order to make aluminium and glass at a loss. Losses at Alumix and its defence subsidiaries accelerated at the beginning of the 1990s, and by mid-1992 the holding company's debts amounted to L8,500bn, of which L2,300bn was owed to foreign banks. The government initially contemplated writing off EFIM's debts, but subsequently agreed that interest would be paid though not necessarily for some considerable time. However, creditor banks refused to accept the government's excuse that EFIM's financial problems were public knowledge and that the banks had received especially high interest rates on the debt in previous years. They argued that they had regarded EFIM as a *de facto* arm of the Treasury, and that they would take legal action were the government to default on its quasi-state debt.

The government accordingly passed a number of decree-laws which introduced measures to assist EFIM. These included an advance of ECU120mn from the Cassa dei Depositi e Prestiti, a guarantee for the totality of the group's debts and a reduction in electricity tariffs for Alumix. These were notified to the European Commission who were particularly concerned that they did not include any indication as to how transparency would be ensured in the liquidation process. The Commission ruled that since EFIM was in liquidation when the assistance was granted, the measures amounted to a form of aid. Consequently, due to the lack of information with which to assess the measures' compatibility, the Commission decided to initiate Article 93(2) proceedings in December 1992 (CEC, 1993, pp.259 and 471).

In late October, the Treasury minister signed a special decree authorising the payment of a first tranche of L2,170bn in the form of government bonds, primarily to Italian banks, although even this tranche was delayed, partly on account of the Commission and partly on account of new revelations about financial irregularities at EFIM subsidiaries. Some foreign bank creditors received repayments in December equivalent to the outstanding capital plus 70 per cent of the interest. Repayments relating to subsidiaries not wholly-owned by EFIM remain in dispute.

The prospects for disposing of EFIM's 120 subsidiaries are fairly grim. At the time of EFIM's liquidation, only 33 of these were profitable. In addition, there is a recession, the need to bring together three ministries (Treasury, Industry and State Shareholdings), to satisfy the Commission and to deal with corruption at Nuova Safim (finance) and Agusta. There is anyway little expertise in Italy in dealing with liquidation. In July 1993, Pilkington and Techint jointly offered to buy SIV, the glass maker which lost L61bn pre-tax in 1992, for L210bn plus taking on L250bn of its debt, but even if further asset sales take place, the sums raised will nowhere near cover the outstanding debts.

The Way Forward?

There is considerable disarray in the government concerning the appropriate way to proceed with the privatization programme. This arises primarily from controversy about the techniques to be employed. On the one hand, Romano Prodi, the head of IRI, champions the 'public company' route involving a public offer for sale which transfers ownership into dispersed private hands. On the other hand, Paolo Savona prefers the creation of a 'hard core' of large shareholders as adopted in France. The government passed a decree in late September 1993 covering the flotation of shares in banks, insurance companies and utilities. This authorised the creation of a 'hard core' if appropriate, and also the creation of a 'golden share'. This latter mechanism was widely seen as a means for ensuring that the Christian Democrats would be able to retain at least some political patronage.

Meanwhile, the opposing camp are keen to back the ambitions of Mediobanca, the Milan merchant bank, which is anxious to create a major financial force in northern Italy through, for example, a merger with Banca Commerciale Italiana (BCI). Its anxiety stems in part from the fact that a controlling interest is held by three IRI subsidiary banks, BCI, Credito Italiano and Banca di Roma, and their privatization would cause this to pass into potentially less-friendly hands.

The Need For Progress

The controversy over EFIM has left the Italian government in something of a cleft stick. On the one hand, it cannot afford to alienate foreign creditors given that it needs to raise such huge sums on the bond markets in order to finance its borrowing requirement. Equally, it does not want to behave in such a way as to prejudice the success of its privatization programme. On the other hand, it is reluctant to pay-off all of the creditors of state-owned concerns at a time when it is trying to cut public spending. It has made a good deal of progress in the latter respect insofar as it has taken a number of deeply unpopular decisions, most notably to cut pensions and to terminate the *scala mobile* wage indexation system. However, progress is also clearly needed on the revenue side of the budget, and hence the need for asset sales.

In principle, the list of potential candidates for privatization is long. Indeed, some have already come to market. For example, Crediop, the Treasury-controlled long-term lending bank, was sold in 1992 for L2,100bn to San Paolo di Torino and, in December 1992, Agippetroli, the petroleum refining and distribution arm of ENI, sold fifteen motorway hotels for L185bn to the National Westminster Bank of the UK. This was followed in 1993 by

The situation for the holding companies is as follows:

IRI: IRI recently reappointed as chairman Romano Prodi, previously chairman from 1982-89 during which time he brought IRI back into profit. IRI's financial situation is very serious. Group debt is roughly L80,000bn. The net loss for 1993 was roughly L10,000bn. Any revenue accrued from asset sales must accordingly be used to shore up its balance sheet rather than be passed over to the government. It has received no government funds since 1991, and in September 1993 Parliament refused to approve L2,000bn in unpaid tax credits. The banks have cut lending, fearing a repetition of EFIM. At least L20,000bn accordingly needs to be raised from asset sales in the near future.

In February 1992, IRI disposed of its 52 per cent stake in Cementir, a quoted subsidiary, for L480bn, and various small stakes in bank and telecommunications operations have been sold. It has made progress in selling-off SME, beginning with the 62 per cent stake in Italgel, the frozen foods division, to Nestlé in July 1993. In September it failed to find a buyer for the GS (supermarkets) and Autogrill (catering) divisions, but in October it sold its 62 per cent stake in Civio-Bertolli-De Rica (CBD) to FSVI for L307bn.

Finmeccanica, the quoted sub-holding 85 per cent owned by IRI, has offset its first-half pre-tax loss of L160bn with two public offerings on the New York stock exchange in November. The first involved 35 per cent of Elsag Bailey Process Automation which raised $150mn. The second comprised 40 per cent of Union Switch & Signal, sold for $49mn. It is also in the process of reducing its holding in quoted subsidiary Ansaldo Trasporti to 50.1 per cent.

More positively, the main prospects lie in two sectors. The first, financial services, is discussed below. The second relates to IRI's 53 per cent stake in Stet, the holding company for the telecommunications sector which made a group profit of L1,788bn in 1992. Stet presides over a collection of separate companies which include Finsiel, 60 per cent of Sip, 53 per cent of Italcable, 33 per cent of Telespazio, 49 per cent of Sirti and 80 per cent of Italtel.

Each company has its own costly, sometimes overlapping structure, a reflection of the customary practice of sharing out jobs between coalition parties anxious for patronage. However, the government has approved a rationalisation which will create a single company. This will incorporate Italcable, Iritel, Telespazio and Sirm into Sip provided this is agreed at a shareholders' meeting in May.

Progress towards privatisation is also being made in respect of Ilva, the steel group which has been ordered by the European Commission to cut output as part of a Community-wide restructuring plan. Ilva is in the process of being split into two parts, comprising flat products based around Taranto, and special steels. Two phases in the bidding process have been completed so far, and the process is expected to be concluded during 1994.

ENI: ENI is primarily an energy and chemicals group, and in the latter respect has suffered badly during the recession. Its subsidiary EniChem, for example, is expected to lose L2,200bn in 1993, its third successive year of loss since it took over Enimont, a joint-venture between ENI and Ferruzzi, which cost ENI L4,000bn and which led to corruption charges. It badly needs to be recapitalised by ENI under Italian law, but it must first be restructured and there is the additional difficulty of persuading the European Commission that new finance does not represent illegal state aid.

It is planned that 10,000 workers will be shed over four years, during which time ENI is prepared to sell or joint venture all but core ethylene production. This will not be easy, judging by the attempt in September 1993 to dismiss workers at Crotone in depressed Calabria, Italy's only phosphorous plant, which was shut down in 1992 after losing L24bn. This closure of the first of ENI's forty sites led to riots, and politicians from the prime minister downwards promptly insisted on a policy of no redundancies. EniChem accordingly had to keep all of the workers on its books, albeit with their salaries paid by the state.

The new managing director has so far managed to sell some thirty small companies, including ENI's hotel and coal interests, and a further fifty are under negotiation. The sale of Nuovo Pignone in December 1993 raised the more substantial sum of roughly L1,100bn. However, these sales are modest in relation to the losses at EniChem. It was accordingly proposed in September 1993 that 'Super Agip' would be created which would incorporate Agip upstream and downstream, Snam, Snamprogetti and the quoted Saipem. Agip's stake in EniChem will have to be expunged before the new company can be floated either whole or in part, but advisors have been appointed with a view to a flotation by 1995. In the meantime, a European cross-border alliance is being actively sought, possibly with France's Elf-Aquitaine.

ENEL: In many ways, the problems of ENEL (electricity generation) are relatively straightforward. It is profitable, though insufficiently so, and is carrying debts of L30,000bn. Before it can be sold its legal monopoly and tariff structure need to be reformed. There is unlikely to be much progress towards a partial flotation until well into 1994.

Privatizing Financial Services

The most urgent need for some time has been to privatize the main state-owned purveyors of financial services, in particular BCI, Credito Italiano and Instituto Mobiliare Italiano (IMI), the latter a state-controlled financial services group 50 per cent owned by the state and 9.3 per cent by INA. IMI's diversified activities leave it less vulnerable than the banks to the much increased need for provisions against bad debts. Indeed, if anything, it is over-capitalised. The decision by the government to float an opening tranche of roughly one third of its capital at the end of January 1994 reflected the failure during 1993 to sell IMI to a group of large savings banks led by Cariplo of Milan. Of the 218.75mn shares on offer, 75mn were reserved for the public in Italy (topped up to 93.75mn), 25mn for Italian institutions, 35mn for the USA and 65mn for other foreigners. The public tender offer at the L10,900 offer price (a 6 per cent discount to the market), involving 375,000 individuals, was five times subscribed and had to be closed ahead of schedule with most applications scaled back to the minimum 250 share level. Total receipts amounted to L2,384bn (just under £1bn). The first-day premium was 23 per cent.

BCI reported a net profit of L387bn for the first half of 1993, a much better performance than in previous years. Although its involvement with Ferruzzi cast a cloud over its attractions as an investment, its flotation was announced on 11 February 1994, at a time when the share price was L5,491, to take place commencing on 28 February. IRI held 482.1mn shares to which were added a further 88.6mn once savings shares were converted (54.35 per cent of the issued capital in total). 260mn shares were initially reserved for the public and most of the rest for institutions in Italy and abroad. The offer price, at L5,400, was set at only 5.3 per cent below the market price ruling at the time and valued BCI at roughly its net worth. Despite this the public offer was heavily oversubscribed and closed three days early.

This tight pricing reflected, in part, the experience of floating Credito Italiano. During 1993, Merrill Lynch, the US investment bank, failed to identify either a trade buyer or a suitable pool of domestic and foreign institutions willing to buy the state's 67 per cent stake in Credito. Accordingly, 879.06 million shares were put on offer on 6 December. The general public were not expected to express much enthusiasm, given a fall of over 30 per cent in the share price during the year, but in practice 295,000 individuals applied and, overall, the offer was six times subscribed causing it to be closed three days early. Individual investors were undoubtedly influenced by the offer price of L2,075 compared to the market price of L2,300 and the existence of loyalty bonus shares after three years. Unhappily, some 100,000 received no allocation at all and successful applicants were limited to 2,500 shares. The sale raised roughly L1,750bn (£697.1bn).

The Body Corrupt

The issue of corruption not only has a bearing upon the state of Italy, but its tentacles have reached deeply into many state-owned companies. The legal battle over the ownership of the chemicals company Enimont in 1990 led, in March 1993, to the arrest of the then chairman of ENI and the heads of three subsidiaries on corruption charges. In September 1993, the deputy head of the Milanese courts was arrested, accused of having accepted L400mn as a bribe to influence the outcome of the battle.

Meanwhile, the Milan corruption inquiry, *mani pulite* (clean hands), has issued a warrant for the arrest of the former chairman of BCI who faces charges of conspiring with the head of Ferruzzi who lost the battle for Enimont, and in October a senior officer of Credito Italiano was arrested on fraud and bankruptcy charges in connection with the collapse of Federconsorzi.

In March 1993, the deputy chairman of EFIM was arrested on charges of alleged fraud. The then chairman of IRI, Franco Nobili, was arrested for alleged corruption in May. In June, Saipem and Nuovo Pignone admitted paying almost $160mn in kickbacks and bribes to win new business over a six-year period. The chairman of Saipem was duly arrested. At the same time, the managing director of Stet followed the managing directors of the Sirti and Italtel into custody.

So far in 1994 the former chairman of EFIM has been arrested for fraud and false accounting, a warrant has been issued for the former chairman of Alumix and the head of ENEL, Franco Viezzoli, together with ten other executives have been arrested in connection with the alleged rigging of bids and connections with the Mafia. All of this activity certainly suggests that 'new brooms' will be left in charge of privatized concerns, if only by default, but there are obvious question-marks over the viability of concerns under constant investigation for corruption.

Conclusion

At the beginning of July 1993, prime minister Ciampi announced that a high-powered five-man committee headed by the Treasury director-general was to be set up to oversee the privatization programme. The two banks, IMI, INA, ENEL, Agip and Stet were to be sold by some time in 1995. At the time, there was little reason to expect that there would not merely be yet another general election in 1994, but that it would bring down the fifty-second postwar coalition government. The new government, once it is formed, will be relatively untainted by corruption and relatively free from fingers in the patronage pie. However, it will contain groups with somewhat differing views about the virtues of privatization, with unpredictable consequences for the programme as currently set out.

What all these groups share is the realisation that the fiscal situation demands harsh remedies. Unfortunately, it is one thing to throw out the ruling coalition because it was riddled with corruption, quite another to assume that the incoming government will immediately turn upon many of those who elected it with an offer of cuts in public spending and higher taxes. Indeed, Silvio Berlusconi, nominal leader of the victorious Freedom Alliance which obtained 366 of the 630 seats in the March 1994 general election, shamelessly promised tax cuts and jobs during the election campaign, and the inheritors of the communist mantle in the south will scarcely want to support any policy that will result in widespread redundancies. The Alliance will have to renege on its promises, with unpredictable results, if it is to retain any credibility. Meanwhile, asset sales remain a necessary but by no means a sufficient condition to resolve the crisis, but in spite of the successful start to the privatization programme, Italy may not have the capacity to pursue them to the point at which they will make a significant contribution to the resolution of the difficulties with which it is beset.

References

Bianchi, P. (1986) 'The IRI in Italy: Strategic Role and Political Constraints', *West European Politics, 10*(2), 269-90.

Bianchi, P., Cassese, S. and della Sala, V. (1988) 'Privatisation in Italy: Aims and Constraints', *West European Politics, 11*(4), 87-100.

Brady, S. (1992) 'Is Italy Going Down?', *Euromoney* (October), 26-30.

Commission of the European Communities (1993) *XXIInd Report on Competition Policy 1992* (Brussels:CEC).

Curwen, P. (1993) 'Privatization, the Italian State and the State of Italy', *International Review of Administrative Sciences, 59*(3), 463-476.

Stefani, G. (1988) 'Privatising Italian State Holdings', Rivista Internazionale di Scienze Economiche e Commerciali, 35(10-11), 935-50.

Vigliano, F. (1988) 'Privatisation in Italy', *International Financial Law Review* (April), 19-21.

RAIL SERVICES IN JAPAN: (MIS)MANAGING THE PRIVATISATION OF JAPANESE RAILWAYS

Tetuszo Yamamoto, Waseda University, Tokyo, Japan

Introduction

The period from 1981 to 1987 is often referred to as the age of administrative reform in Japan. This period began with the creation of the second *ad hoc* Council on Administrative Reform (Rincho) and ended with the privatization of Japan National Railways (JNR).

In the Third Report of Rincho it was pointed out that public corporations faced major difficulties such as government interventions, the ambiguity of managerial responsibility and the inability to deal with labour problems. Secondly, there existed a lack of self-awareness on the part of the workforce as to their role as public servants. Thirdly, excessive demands were made upon public corporations by the general public. Finally, mangerial control was problematic due to the large scale of organizations.

The Report insisted that the public corporations could not control themselves or promote needed reforms within the existing framework. It went on to recommend that they should accordingly be privatized and effective competition introduced. It highlighted JNR's problems, which were identified as external interference, a centralised management which disregarded differences in regional conditions and the unstable relationship between management and the workers. To remedy these faults, the Report suggested that government intervention should be abolished and that government regulations should be reduced to the same level as those affecting the private sector. It concluded that JNR should be divided into seven special corporations and privatized in its entirety via a public offer of its shares some five years later.

With regard to the burden of the huge outstanding liabilities, the Report suggested that Japan Railways (JR) should inherit a level of debt consistent with being able to repay capital plus interest once rationalisation and cost reduction had taken place. It further suggested that the remaining debts should be retained by the JNR Settlement Corporation and subsidized by the government.

The JNR Reconstruction Supervision Commission was set up in 1983 in order to address the mechanics of privatization and the problems of JNR's indebtedness and inefficiency. This process is discussed elsewhere (see, in particular, Yamamoto 1993) and does not directly concern us here. We need merely note that the JNR was duly split up and privatized in 1987. The regional division was determined on the following criteria: to achieve an appropriate scale of management; to respond to the needs of the regions; to introduce competition; and to guarantee accountability in each region.

Seven years have now passed, and the shares of JR East (Japan Railway Company Higashi, the largest of the six passenger companies), were finally sold in October 1993 transferring it from the JNR Settlement Corporation to the private sector. These years could be said to have witnessed considerable progress in transforming the fortunes of the railway companies insofar as there has been a distinct improvement in the competence of management, and the three inland companies and the Japan Freight Railway Company have recorded operating profits, although even after subsidisation the three island companies have struggled to keep their heads above water as shown in Table 1.

	JR Hokkaido	JR East	JR Central	JR West	JR Shikoku	JR Kyushu	Total (passenger companies)	Freight Company	Overall total
(A) Part of ordinary revenue and expenditure									
(A.1) Section of operating account									
(1.1)	80.9	1672.8	999.5	823.1	41.0	129.7	3747.0	192.1	3939.1
(1.2)	131.7	1395.5	887.1	734.4	51.1	152.9	3352.7	182.2	3534.9
(1.3)	- 50.7	277.3	112.4	88.6	- 10.0	- 23.2	394.4	9.8	404.2
(1.4)	18.9	62.6	3.6	11.2	2.8	14.2	113.3	-	113.3
(1.5)	20.8	58.8	2.3	8.9	4.4	19.7	114.9	-	114.9
(1.6)	- 1.9	3.7	1.3	2.2	- 1.6	- 5.5	- 1.8	-	- 1.8
(1.7)	- 52.7	281.1	113.7	90.9	-11.6	-28.7	392.7	9.8	402.5
(A.2) Section of non-operating account									
(2.1)	3.4	- 177.6	- 5.3	- 50.6	2.5	4.4	- 223.2	- 3.4	- 226.6
(2.2)	49.5	-	-	-	15.1	28.2	92.8	-	92.8
(A.T.)	0.2	103.4	108.3	40.2	6.1	3.8	262.0	6.4	268.4
(B) Part of extraordinary revenue and expenditure									
(B.1)	0.0	1.7	16.6	1.9	0.0	0.7	20.9	0.1	21.0
(C)	0.3	105.2	124.9	42.1	6.0	4.5	283.0	6.5	289.5
(D)	0.1	47.9	58.2	16.4	2.4	0.7	125.7	3.5	129.2
(E)	0.2	57.2	66.7	25.7	3.6	3.8	157.2	2.9	160.1

Table 1

Japan Railways: Revenue and Expenditure in 1989 (billion yen)

Source: The White Paper on Transportation

Notes:

(1.1)   operating revenues of railway business

314

(1.2)   operating expenses of railway business

(1.3)   operating revenue and expenditure of railway business

(1.4)   operating revenues of the other businesses

(1.5)   operating expenses of the other businesses

(1.6)   operating revenue and expenditure of the other businesses

(1.7)   Total operating revenues and expenditure

(2.1)   non-operating revenues and expenditure

(2.2)   revenue and expenditure from employing fund for stabilizing management

(A.T.) Total ordinary revenue and expenditure

(B.1) extraordinary revenue and expenditure

(C)   income for this term before taxes

(D)   corporation tax and like

(E)   income for this term

This is less than surprising given the recent depressed state of the Japanese economy, but a number of problems clearly remain to be addressed. These include, in particular, the ongoing difficulties in strengthening the management of the companies, the problem of rail fare review and the institutional changes affecting the companies.

A Catalogue of Problems

It is indisputable that the companies are vulnerable to the economic cycle because their most important customers are the *Shinkansen* (business customers) and commuter passengers in urban areas. Equally, in terms of internal efficiency, the companies have not caught up with their competitors. Though their average operating cost (per vehicle/kilometre), which was estimated to lie between a minimum of 602 yen (JR Kyushu) and a maximum of 1,020 yen (Central), has got closer to the average of the big fourteen private railway companies (513 yen), it remains excessive in comparison with the latter. The companies remain at a disadvantage when competing directly with private railway or bus companies.

Although the three Honshu JRs (East, Central and West) make operating profits, they are lower, when expressed as a percentage of turnover, than the average rate of the big fourteen private companies (14.6 per cent in 1991) except in the case of JR East (16.1 per cent). If the details of their operating costs are inspected closely, it can be seen that personnel expenditure (30.9 per cent) and transportation costs (50.7 per cent including rental charges of *Shinkansen*) account for the greater part of operating cost. It is apparent that more must be done to reduce the ratio of personnel expenditure and to improve efficiency. The companies have developed various rail-related activities such as car rental, property, cruises, travel agencies and warehousing since their privatisation. However, these revenues account for a smaller share of their total operating revenues than those of the private companies. It seems that the JRs must enlarge their related activities and increase revenues by utilising their assets and manpower effectively, while raising traffic demand for them. This necessitates consideration of more than just local business interests or political interests.

Furthermore, almost none of the JRs have yet made long-term management plans with regard to capital expenditure and the allocation of resources, including employees and finance, in order to strengthen their managerial bases. In the longer term, they will be required to follow strategies to become more competitive and hence able to increase their market share at such time as demand once again begins to enlarge. This implies allocating resources effectively, and at the same time cutting operating costs, especially personnel expenditure, by pursuing the rationalisation of existing managerial structures.

Managerial Problems in the Short Term

The recent investigation by the Office of Administrative Supervision suggested that JRs should promote the following measures to ensure stability:

- Develop new customer based services such as discounted return tickets, particularly on the lines which overlap with their competitors.
- Strengthen and secure competitiveness by cutting costs, raising demand or speeding traffic service for their scheduled trains.
- Adjust the number of coaches on express train services which would otherwise make a loss due to the level of passengers.
- Increase the revenues from related activities and restructure the loss-making activities such as travel agencies.
- Make more use of their station sites by sharing them with tenants such as hotels, shops or by using ground under overhead lines for parking.
- Promote working efficiency and reduce surplus workers on the loss-making lines by modernising facilities or equipment (for example, by introducing auto-ticket sales machines, auto-ticket examining machines, and one-man train operation).
- Review the number of employees needed and their allocation, along with a review of the structure of field organisations, possibly integrating divisions.
- Take back some contracted-out activities and manage them directly in order to revitalise idle assets or surplus workers.
- Improve procurement methods and promote stock control.

It should be noted that most of these measures cannot be achieved without stable and reliable relationships between management and employees. There are two concerns, however, in this respect. One relates to the difficulty for management to restrain wage levels. Rising wages seem to have been one of the conditions in the trade union's agreement to co-operate

316

with management and to be their reward for increasing efficiency. In practice, personnel expenditure in JRs has not only risen faster than total operating costs, but it has also increased more rapidly than that of the private railway companies since privatisation. The other concern is that the trade union is likely to split into two. This seems likely to destabilise the future relationship between management and workers. It can be said that improvements in JRs' internal efficiency will depend upon whether management can control rising personnel expenditure within total operating cost.

In order that JRs can pursue the above measures, the other problem to be overcome is to promote deregulation, or at least to simplify getting approvals from the transport authorities. The Railway Activity Act was passed in 1987 as a fundamental law to provide the same regulations for JRs and private railway companies. It replaced the three existing laws concerning JNR and the Local Railway Act which laid down the regulations for supervising private companies. The 1987 law gives the regulator (the Department of Transport - DoT) many rights and discretionary powers to regulate JRs' management. Altogether, there are 93 items including approval of changes in rail facilities, passenger fares, pre-notified discounted fares, timetables and constraints on maximum speeds. In addition, a Railway Operating Act lays down the regulations which cover 32 items such as approvals for railway facilities and equipment, special vehicles' structure and overall network requirements.

Surprisingly, the number of approvals given by DoT has only increased a little since privatisation. The government should abolish some regulations that are unsuited to the needs of current service provision and simplify the complicated regulatory system which prevents JRs from operating their activities smoothly. This can be illustrated by the fact that:

- JRs find it burdensome to get the DoT to approve changes to their passenger fare structure. If they wish to introduce new fares, it takes time and can be costly administratively, even though the regulations about fares and tariffs under the legal price system were transformed into the approval system (see Table 2).
- JRs have to send their application papers to several local transport authorities and get permission from each of them if their fare structures involve the lines controlled by more than one authority.

Item	Old System	New System
Management form	Public corporation	• Special companies (six passenger companies, one freight company • Shinkansen Holding Corporation • The other private successors of JNR's businesses • JNR Settlement Corporation
Investment	All capital invested by the government	As for special companies, the capital of which was invested in kind by JNR Settlement Corporation. However, JR will be transformed into purely private companies through share-sales to the public as soon as the management is stabilized.
Scope of business	• Railway business • Ferry business connected with railway • Oil-pipeline business where JNR made use of its railway lands • Generation and transmission of electric power • Incidental business	• Passenger (Freight) railway business • Incidental business • Transportation by automobile (bus) • Travel agent • Other business Some businesses related to JNR were transferred to the private sector through divestment
Regulation	• Budget decided through the Diet • President of JNR was nominated by the Prime Minister, and commissioners of JNR-RSC were appointed by the Secretary of the Transport Ministry • Authorization for constructing the new railroad etc. came under JNR Act.	• Approval of business plan • Approval of election of a representative director and inspectors • Approval of the businesses and activities under the Railway Activity Law Regulation for JR is to be at the same level as that of private railway companies.
Fares and Tariffs	Principle of legal price system (by 1977)	Approval system
Labour relations	Application of National Public Service Law	Application of the so-called Three Labour Laws (the Labour Standard Law, the Trade Union Law and the Labour Mediation Law

Table 2

Differences Between the Old System and the New System of Japan National Railways

Source: Kotsu Nenkan (1991)

Managerial Problems in the Long Term

One of the most pressing problems for the three Honshu companies (East, Central and West) is wipe out their liabilities. These companies started their new management with total liabilities of almost 4,300 billion yen as a result of a government decision to limit liabilities to an amount within their ability to repay. In so doing, the government attempted to help with privatising the JNR. The large residual part of the liabilities was inherited by the JNR Settlement Corporation. As a result of their efforts, the total liability of the three companies had decreased to around 3,465 billion yen by 1990. However, these efforts to reduce liabilities halted in 1991 when the privatised companies bought *Shinkansen* lines which were owned by the Shinkansen Holding Corporation (SHC), for which they had to pay about 9,200 billion yen. As a result, their now huge liabilities may prove extremely restrictive and deter capital investment if they cannot be repaid as intended. It may be noted that JNR could not invest enough capital in infrastructure and R&D because of its accumulated debts, and its investment did not simply decrease in volume year by year but was also restricted to maintenance of facilities and was rarely innovatory. In practice, capital investment began to decrease after 1991 whereas it had increased in the years following privatisation. Taking into consideration the recent recession in the Japanese economy, this raises doubts whether JRs will invest enough towards strengthening their managerial bases or consolidating infrastructure.

In contrast, the three island companies (JR Hokkaido, JR Shikoku and JR Kyushu) are incapable of generating profits by themselves even though they were exempted from inheriting liabilities at the time of privatisation. As they rely on the stabilisation funds supplied by government, they are more vulnerable to the business cycle, and especially conditions in the financial markets. If additional funds are not supplied, the situation will deteriorate further. Far from being able to sell their shares, they will remain as special companies if they are left as they are. Without being transformed into pure private companies, they are unlikely to utilise their assets optimally.

In conclusion, it can be said that with regard to the three island companies, alternative policies or measures to support their independence have to be devised in order to improve prospects for a future sale of their shares.

Reviewing Fares

The problems facing JRs mentioned above can be regarded as commonplace matters in the aftermath of privatisation in many countries. Even though these matters have been approached positively by JRs, it is doubtful whether they can restore their financial position since one of the most important problems relating to the largest source of JRs' revenues has been neglected.

Naturally, JRs have attempted to raise demand and increase revenues by introducing various kinds of discounted tickets, especially those issued for tourists and students. They can get an approval from the transport authorities in principle if the discounted fares would produce more revenue than before. Whenever they have received an application from JRs, transport authorities have proved willing to allow the proposed discounted tickets. In spite of this, they have failed to introduce discounted fares because they have been unable to estimate the price elasticity of demand involved or to forecast trends in demand.

The problem highlighted here is different from these proposals. It relates to the fundamental issue of fixing fares at an appropriate level. Surprisingly, JRs have not revised their fares since privatisation except for the introduction of value-added tax (VAT) of 3 per cent. They could potentially increase their revenues without a fundamental review of fares, but it may be difficult to maintain their profit levels unless they do revise their fares overall. It now appears that JRs will be obliged to revise them, because the successful sale of shares in the other five JRs will require the JRs concerned to achieve good performances in order to secure high levels of profits and dividends.

The issue is what system of prices JRs should adopt. Although existing procedures were transformed into the approval system, it was doubtful whether JRs would adopt a fare scheme such as one related to demand elasticity by line and region, or whether the DoT would replace the existing price regulation by a new one such as incentive regulation along the lines of RPI-X in Britain.

Before privatisation, the DoT had adopted a 'total cost-plus' formula. This formula had established fares aimed at meeting public demands for 'equity' and 'universal service'. On the basis of this formula, the principle of securing 'the same price per kilometre' all over the country was adopted in the name of equality, and seems to have been maintained after privatisation due to JRs' lack of experience of price revision.

The 'total cost-plus' formula should be seen in terms of a kind of rate-of-return regulation where various costs, including interest payments, should be taken into account.

If acting as a monopolist, the JNR would have set out to equate marginal cost with marginal revenue in order to maximise its profit and determine the price corresponding to it, thereby fixing the optimum amount to be supplied. In practice, the JNR had been far from a monopolist in the urban areas, and its fares had also been regulated under the legal system. The JNR had been forced to adopt the price yielding only a break even, set at the point where average cost equalled average revenue. Although JRs were expected to raise fares and reduce the quantity supplied, in fact they did not do so. It seems that they adopted a strategy of leaving fares unchanged. They hoped that it would enable them to recapture their lost customers.

The problem which this price strategy causes to JRs is that it has resulted in cross subsidisation. Let us suppose that there are two railway lines in order to simplify the discussion. One is a heavily used line typically associated with urban areas, while the other is a lightly used line associated with rural areas. The demand curves can be seen as parallel to each other where the urban line represents greater output capacity than the rural line. For the sake of simplification, let us suppose that the cost functions are the same in both cases. In order to balance costs and revenues by means of a common fare applied to the two lines, the fare should be set at the level where the profit in the urban area is offset by the loss in the rural area. JNR's privatisation was expected to reduce or end these cross subsidies. If JRs were to attempt to achieve a profit on a line-by-line basis, fares would need to be set at levels that reflect the relevant demand elasticities and costs. As a result, the fare in the rural area would rise while that in the urban area would fall. However, the fare system did not change substantially after privatisation. As noted, JRs chose to freeze the fare level, taking account of public opinion and competition in the urban areas.

In spite of this, privatisation with regional division seems to have brought some reduction in the extent of cross subsidies. One reason is that 83 local lines which recorded considerable losses were abolished at the time of privatisation. Another is that the regional structure has limited the scope for cross subsidy and narrowed the gap between the profitable and loss-making lines.

The recent decline in profits of JRs in association with the recession seems likely to force JRs to improve internal efficiency, especially allocative efficiency, by reviewing their existing fare systems more thoroughly. However, this may conflict with securing 'equity' or universal service. Thus, attention should be paid to the choice of price strategies and the policies to be adopted by JRs and the DoT when the renewal of fares falls due.

The Institutional Problems Surrounding JRs

It can be said that the prospects for JRs are influenced by the managements of the JNR Settlement Corporation and the Railway Development Fund (RDF) which were established to replace the Shinkansen Holding Corporation in October 1991 in order to supply funds to aid the consolidation of the railways (both in respect of construction and maintenance). The issue is whether the managements of the two organisations either have succeeded or will succeed in the future.

With regard to the former, it should be noted that the Corporation has failed to repay all of the liabilities which it inherited at the time of privatisation. The main reason why it could not reduce the liabilities on schedule was that it was not permitted to sell its assets. The Corporation has been constrained by government in selling railway land to private companies or local authorities because such sales might accelerate the inflation of land values, especially in urban areas. In the late 1980s, land values in Japan rose rapidly in the big cities due to the so-called bubble economy. In response to complaints by the general public, the government required the Corporation to postpone or cancel land sales via competitive tendering.

The Corporation was also unable to sell its holding of JR shares because it missed the best opportunity for such a sale. It was accordingly obliged to wait until the results of other privatisations had become clear. Unfortunately, after a few years the share price of Nippon Telephone and Telegraph, which was sold in two tranches in 1987 and 1989, fell rapidly below the first and second offer price due to the pricking of the bubble economy in Japan. Many individual investors were disappointed and stayed away from the stock market. Hence, if JR shares were to be floated, they would be unlikely to attract investors. Obliged to take action by the financial pressures which resulted from huge interest payments, the shares of JR East were at last floated in October 1993. Although its share price (offer price: 390,000 yen per share) rose considerably to a peak of 640,000 yen, an improvement on a scale rarely seen recently in the Tokyo stock market, even this was insufficient to revitalise the stagnant stock market as it seems to have resulted from stock switching alone. Many investors sold their holdings of shares which were judged to be unprofitable and purchased the shares of JR East expecting to make a capital gain.

In order to reduce its accumulated liabilities, the Corporation must:
- Dispose of railway lines by adopting various methods such as a system of land trusts in order not to raise land values again.
- Calculate the timing of other JR share sales in order to maximise their proceeds.
- Review the pension fund schemes in order to reduce their deficits.

In short, whether the Corporation can achieve its objective of repayment of its liabilities will depend upon the extent to which it can sell the assets it holds.

Turning to the second institution, it is feared that the RDF will require an increased level of government subsidies in the future. The RDF was established as a special company in order to aid such railway activities as construction and maintenance of the new Seibi-Shinkansen lines, major railway lines in the national network and main lines in the big cities; to promote R&D in new railway technologies, including the linear motor car; and to secure safety and prevent natural disasters. The company's fund is composed of money from the transfer of Shinkansen lines to JRs, finance from the Special Account for Industrial Investment in the public sector (NIT-B Fund) and various subsidies from the government's general budget.

Establishing the RDF has arguably created a number of ambiguities, such as who should inherit the burden if it fails to supply funds properly. Although its creation seems to have been necessary in order to promote long-term investment and to contribute to the capital expenditure schemes of JRs, at the same time it involves various risks. For example, there are doubts about whether its funding through Japan's Development Bank could be frozen. It is unclear whether the Seibi-Shinkansen lines are really needed, and in any event JRs will not make profits if they were to be constructed. Furthermore, in these big projects the funding set aside at the beginning is likely to run short. If the financial position of the RDF were to worsen, the public would have to shoulder the burden by paying more tax.

Conclusions

Overall, the rail service in Japan must be analysed as part of the nation's transport policy problems currently facing consumers and policy-makers. JRs have increased the volume of traffic and have grown more rapidly than private railway companies since privatisation. In spite of their efforts, however, the market share of JRs in the whole transport market has diminished gradually and seemingly will continue to diminish. This is also the case for the freight company. They cannot compete with aviation and road transport for private use.

Although it is expected that the introduction of the linear motor car will recapture some customers who changed their preference to other means of transport, the possibility for JRs to recover market share seems to be limited. Competing transport policies such as the Fourth Plan for Cultivating the Country (extending the highway system to 14,000 kilometres) and the scheme for constructing an airport in each prefecture are currently being promoted by government and the local authorities.

These matters are not directly the concern of the managements of JRs, but there can be no doubt that the time has arrived to consider seriously how JRs should be placed in the transport market.

Bibliography

Calder, K. (1990) 'Public Corporations and Privatization in Modern Japan', in E. Suleiman and J. Waterbury (eds) *The Political Economy of Public Sector Reform and Privatization* (Boulder, Colorado: Westview Press).

Gow, I. (1989) 'Government-Industry Relations: Japanese-Style Public Corporations and Privatization', *Japan Forum, 1* (2).

Hurl, B. (1988) *Privatization and the Public Sector* (London: Heinemann).

Kotsu Nenkan, Kotsu Kyoryyokukai, 1987 onwards.

Seizaburo Sato (1985) *The Experience of Japan's Privatization: Policies, Methods and Procedures* (Manila: Asian Development Bank).

Unyusho, *Unyu Hahusho* (The White Paper on Transportation) 1987 onwards.

THE POLITICS AND ECONOMICS OF PRIVATISATION IN NIGERIA

Sonny Nwankwo, Sheffield Business School.

Introduction

The 1980s witnessed a dramatic re-orientation of, and reforms in, the political economy of many Sub-Saharan African Nations (IMF,1989). These reforms were primarily aimed at restructuring the countries' economies towards market responsiveness; trimming budgets, reducing subsidies, rescheduling foreign debts, devaluing currencies and re-organising state-owned enterprises.

Nigeria's experiment in privatisation is an important case study because of the country's strategic position in the Sub-Saharan African Nations (SSAN). Nigeria is reputed to be the most populous (and the richest?) Black nation on earth. The country's population is estimated at over 112 million people and occupies an area in Western Africa of approximately 923,770 square kilometres (about 4 times the size of UK). With a GDP of £37.5 billion, a per capita income of £329, and a real growth rate of 3.4 per cent, it is the most attractive market among SSANs (Okoroafo, 1992). In a recent *Financial Times* survey, Nigeria, described as "a powerhouse waiting to happen", emerged as Africa's fastest growing market (*Financial Times*, 1994, p.14). Nigeria is a member of OPEC and is Africa's leading oil-producing nation. As shown in Table 1, oil exports account for about 96 per cent of export earnings and 70 per cent of government revenues. The agricultural sector accounts for 28 per cent of GDP while the manufacturing sector accounts for 12 per cent (Sawyer, 1993).

Year	Total Export Earnings (TEE)	Total Oil Export Earnings	Total Non-Oil Export Earnings	Proportion of Oil to TEE (%)	Proportion of Non-Oil to TEE (%)
1970	88.6	509.6	376.0	57.6	42.2
1971	1,293.2	953.0	340.4	73.7	26.3
1972	1,434.2	1,176.2	258.0	82.0	18.0
1973	2,277.4	1,893.5	383.9	83.1	16.9
1974	5,794.8	5,365.7	429.1	92.6	7.4
1975	4,935.5	4,629.9	295.6	94.0	6.0
1976	6,751.1	6,196.2	554.9	91.8	8.2
1977	7,630.7	7,080.4	550.3	92.8	7.2
1978	6,064.4	5,652.9	411.5	93.2	6.8
1979	10,836.8	10,166.8	670.0	93.8	6.2
1980	14,186.7	13,523.0	663.7	95.3	4.7
1981	10,876.8	10,680.5	196.3	98.2	1.8
1982	8,722.5	8,601.6	120.9	98.6	1.4
1983	7,502.5	7,201.2	301.3	96.0	1.0
1984	9,088.0	8,840.2	247.4	97.3	2.7
1985	11,214.8	10,890.6	324.2	97.1	2.9
1986	8,513.0	8,273.0	240.0	97.2	2.8
1987	30,360.6	28,208.6	2,152.0	92.9	7.1
1988	31,192.8	28,435.4	2,757.4	91.2	8.8
1989	57,971.2	55,016.8	2,954.4	94.9	5.1
1990	109,886.1	106,626.5	3,259.6	97.0	3.0
1991	121,533.7	116,856.5	4,677.2	96.2	3.8

Table 1:

Nigeria's Exports 1970-1991 (Naira million)

Source: Central Bank of Nigeria Annual Reports

Nigeria was instrumental in establishing the Organisation of African Unity (OAU), spear-headed the creation of the West African regional economic bloc (Economic Community of West African States - ECOWAS) and provides the 'African voice' in the international forum. In aspiring to live up to its leadership role in Africa, Nigeria invested heavily in the economies of most of the SSANs in the 1970s. Popular opinion has it that Nigeria's privatisation experiment will provide a useful insight into patterns of economic reform in the SSANs. The international community, especially lenders/financiers to debt-ridden developing nations, are keenly watching the developments at the Nigerian front. Other countries in African are already following the direction set by Nigeria as one of the earliest 'pioneers' in privatisation (Drum, 1993).

326

Background to Privatisation in Nigeria

Privatisation has surfaced as another fad to capture the national consciousness. Two previous popular ones were 'Nigerianisation' and 'Indigenisation' (Odife,1988). Nigerianisation was the clarion call prior to, and immediately after, wrenching independence from Britain in 1960. The nationalist politicians at the time felt that national independence would become a smoke screen if the colonialists continued to control the nation's political institutions such as the Civil Service. It would be more meaningful for Nigerians to run the affairs of Nigeria - total political emancipation.

Again in the 1970s, the popular maxim was that political independence without economic independence is a farce. Ownership of economic infrastructure was equated with control and it was felt that Nigerians would not gain control of their economic destiny unless they became majority owners of the shares of companies set up by foreigners in Nigeria. Indigenisation was to ensure that this happened. Unwittingly, the exercise drew the government squarely into the economic marketplace as a major player. This was made possible because of the enormous 'windfall' to the State treasury resulting from the 'oil boom' of the 1970s.

The 'oil boom' of the 1970s turned into a glut by the 1980s. Oil prices fell drastically as the international oil market edged towards a collapse. In a bid to contain the crisis, OPEC imposed restrictive production quotas on member countries. Oil, the 'black gold', was quickly turning into a 'black dust'. Concomitantly, the 'wealth of the nation' took a tumble; federally collected revenues and external reserves fell dramatically and payments in arrears of imports rose. As the economy degenerated into something of a crisis, the fragile civilian government of Shehu Shagari introduced the 'economic stabilisation programme' which aimed at reducing internal and external deficits through demand management - import restrictions were among the measures imposed. The programme did not help very much partly because the world economy, in general, was beginning to 'heat up'. The government, in a desperate attempt to contain the worsening situation, applied to the International Monetary Fund (IMF) for a loan facility of N2.4 billion. The IMF, in the characteristic manner it uses to deal with developing countries, imposed its *conditionalities*; curbs on government spending, privatisation and commercialisation of parastatals, trade liberalisation, rationalisation of tariff structures, introduction of sales taxes, phasing out of subsidies, an increased share of the private sector in credit issues and a vigorous expansion of the non-oil sector (Bangura, 1987; Abdulraheem *et al,* (1986).

It was against this emerging background that the government appointed a Presidential Commission on Parastatals in 1981 - the first serious attempt to examine the role of the state in the marketplace. The Commission painted a very negative picture of the parastatals; poor financial performance, overstaffing, dependence on subsidies and unilateral budget transfers, highly centralised and politicised organisations, and mismanagement (Yahaya, 1993; Lieberman, 1993). The civilian government was dismissed at the end of 1983 before it could 'make up its mind' on the report.

Although the argument for privatisation was overwhelmingly persuasive from an economic point of view, the new government (Appendix 1) resisted it, supported by the short-term vested interests of certain powerful groups. As aptly noted by Odife (1988, p.33), "Nigerians always put politics rather than economics in the forefront of their priorities". A number of diversionary tactics were tried (including counter-trade, gagging of the press, and social repression) to stem the tide of the downward spiralling economy, but to no avail. In August 1985, a new military administration took over the reins of government and called for a national debate on the IMF. While the nation was gripped in the furore of the debate, the government, in July 1986, launched a two year Structural Adjustment Programme (SAP) by which it accepted most of the IMF conditionalities - through the 'back door'. Yahaya (1993, p.19) commented that the SAP programme "in totality was enunciated within a perspective that endorsed the free market as the framework for a major restructuring of the Nigerian economy". In the 1988 budget, the government issued a list of state-owned enterprises (SOEs) grouped into four schedules according to whether they are to be fully or partially privatised (Appendix 2).

Schedule I: (full privatisation) included 13 insurance companies in which the federal government had a 25 per cent to 40 per cent shareholding, 10 medium-to-large scale manufacturing firms, 2 hotels, 4 companies in the transport sector and 15 agricultural and agro-allied firms. The total value of the shares which the government expected to sell in these firms was estimated at about N150 million.

Schedule II: (partial privatisation) Enterprises in this category were made up of 27 commercial and merchant banks, 27 major manufacturing companies spanning cement production, trucks, commercial vehicle and car assembly plants, fertilizer factories, newsprint and paper mills and engineering and electricity component plants. They also included 3 steel rolling mills, newspapers, oil companies, shipping and air line companies. The total value of the government's holdings in these firms was put at over N21.1 billion.

Schedule III: (full commercialisation) - Appendix 2
Schedule IV: (partial commercialisation) - Appendix 2

In July 1988, the government promulgated a decree setting up the Technical Committee on Privatisation and Commercialisation (TCPC) to oversee the implementation of the exercise. By the end of 1989, the TCPC had arranged for the sale of 16 firms, including 2 petroleum firms and 13 insurance companies (Yahaya, 1993). The goal was to complete the programme by late 1992.

The main aims of Nigeria's privatisation programme (Drum, 1993) are to:
- improve enterprise performance and viability
- reduce the levels of unproductive public sector investment
- encourage recourse to the private capital market rather than recourse to the Treasury for finance
- transfer to the private sector those activities it can best manage
- created a favourable investment climate for foreign and local investors
- reduce debt by debt-equity swaps

Arguments for Privatisation

All sorts of arguments have been put forward to underpin Nigeria's privatisation programme. In general, the arguments contain a mixture of strands and parallel those offered in the Thatcherite era (Richardson, Nwankwo and Curwen, 1993). For example, Odife (1988) justified the programme on the following grounds:
- the need to deregulate the economy and reduce governmental control
- the need to encourage productive efficiency
- enhancement of allocative efficiency in the economy
- economic mass mobilisation

A close observation will reveal that the arguments revolve around two principal issues: (1) internal crisis and (2) external pressures.

Internal Crisis

It has been argued that Nigeria in the 1980s experienced the most severe economic crisis since its creation as a nation state. The collapse of the world oil market resulted in a drastic fall in Nigeria's oil earnings; from N10.1 billion in 1979 to N5.16 billion in 1982. The country's light grade crude oil fluctuated from less than $4 a barrel to about $42 in 1980 and down to about $17 in the mid-1980s. At this time, the country's external reserve estimated at $8.50 billion in 1981 could no longer support 6 weeks of import even at the diminished level of the period (Oloukoshi, 1993).

This triggered a major crisis in the rest of the economy; a run-away inflation, shortages of industrial and consumer goods, capacity under-utilisation in the manufacturing sector, retrenchment and industrial shut-downs, massive national debt (internal public debt rose from N4.6 billion in 1979 to N22.2 billion in 1983), decay of infrastructural facilities, and a massive reduction in public spending (education, welfare, etc). The Naira (the national currency unit which exchanged at $1 = N0.74 at the peak of the oil boom) nose dived. This sort of crisis not only provided the immediate domestic context but also the rationale for privatisation. Against this background, three factors speeded up the march towards privatisation; (a) the poor performance of the SOEs, (b) the government's liquidity problems and (c) the growth of an entrepreneurial culture.

I. *Poor performance*: The poor financial performance of the SOEs is, perhaps, the most influential argument for Nigeria's privatisation programme. This was revealed as far back as 1985 by the then military Chief of General Staff, Commodore Ebitu Ukiwe. He announced that of a total investment of over N23 billion in SOEs, equity returns amounted to a paltry N933.7 million. Similarly, of the more than N10 billion lent out to various SOEs, only N67.9 million had been received as loan repayment. The abysmally low return on government investment in SOEs made the move to privatisation a matter of necessity.

> It is clear from the foregoing that the rate of return on government investments in parastatals and companies in respect of both equity and loans are not satisfactory and for that reason, this administration is reviewing the situation with a view to formulating a policy of 'privatisation' and/or 'commercialisation' of some of these parastatals and companies (Ebitu Ukiwe, *Business Times*, 16 December 1985).

II. *The Government's liquidity problems*: The government's move away from unmitigated support for SOEs in the mid-1980s was not due to a change in ideology or political orientation but necessitated by the economic realities of the day. Prior to this period, the government guaranteed both local and foreign loans to SOEs - in addition to direct investments. In 1985, total recorded subventions to these enterprises stood at over N11 billion, in addition to over N10 billion in lending. Also in 1985, the government significantly stepped up the servicing of the country's external debts, devoting a staggering 44 per cent of the total foreign exchange earnings accruing to the state to that purpose.

As the government became more hard pressed to fund national budgets, privatisation gathered momentum as the solution to effect economic adjustment and mobilise sorely needed investment capital. With the collapse of oil prices and OPEC's restrictions on production, the government found itself unable to continue to prop up ailing SOEs. Thus, shortage of funds forced the government to begin, in a more serious way, to review ways of allocating dwindling resources more prudently and its relationship with SOEs.

III. *Growth of local entrepreneurship:* Some Nigerians emerged from the 'Indigenisation' exercise of the 1970s with enormous financial clout and, consequently, power. It is sometimes said that some individual Nigerians are in a better financial shape than the Nigerian state. Their wealth and visibility provided them with a platform to challenge vociferously the government's intervention on behalf of their 'competitors' and to shape public opinion against 'wasteful spending'. Some of these individuals owned large organisations in areas such as airline, shipping, communications, construction, real estate, commerce and distribution, often in partnership with foreign states and/or capital. These privately owned enterprises provided a benchmark for appraising related SOEs and, inadvertently, crystallised their inefficiency.

Anecdotal evidence shows that the bulk of the shares of the already privatised enterprises were bought up by these powerful entrepreneurs.

External Pressures

External pressures were clearly evident from the following sources: (a)international financial institutions (b) the 'New Right' and (c) newly industrialised countries.

I. *International financial institutions*: Yahaya (1993) argued that the most significant impetus for privatisation emanated from the pressure of international financial institutions and cartels such as the IMF, the World Bank, the 'Paris/London club' - a cartel of banks with debt/equity interests in the Nigerian economy, and bilateral donors in the industrialised countries such as the United States Agency for International Development (USAID). Mismanagement, inefficiency and incorrect economic policies were identified by most of these agencies as the root cause of Nigeria's economic problems. In particular, government ownership of enterprises was emphasised as a prime cause of market distortion. The correction of these distortionary policies has therefore been at the core of conditionality clauses which are attached to loans from the international financial community. The tough pills of market liberalisation were forced down the throats of debtor nations like Nigeria. Privatisation became a major string usually attached to loans and aid on which many developing economies depend.

II. *The 'New Right'*: With the collapse of the 'iron curtain' and the demonstrated weaknesses of socialism as an economic development model, conservatism emerged as a dominant world ideology. Powerful 'right-wing' regimes - the New Right (Wiltshire, 1987) - especially in the USA and UK forcefully preached market liberalisation and de-control as the panacea for the economic turmoil which bedeviled developing economies. The role of prominent Western leaders such as Mrs Thatcher in propagating privatisation and market competition has been well reported in the literature (Richardson, Nwankwo and Curwen, 1993).

III. *The Newly Industrialised Countries* (NICs): The philosophy of state control of the 'Commanding Heights of the Economy' as the main vehicle of economic development was popular in the 1960s. In the early 1970s most developing countries following the state-interventionist framework for economic development began to suffer economic crises while the NICs, presented as the model of 'third world' market capitalism, were enjoying a boom and were doing much better (Yahaya, 1993). In the 1980s, a decisive swing in the dominant intellectual attitudes and development strategy was discernible. The swing has been primarily towards rolling back the frontiers of the state in industrial investments.

Obviously, this was stimulated by the perceived success of the NICs in contrast to low or negative growth in most 'less developed countries'.

Opposition to Privatisation

Privatisation is an emotive topic in Nigeria. Some people oppose privatisation on philosophical or ideological grounds while others do so as a result of the untoward aftermath of the indigenisation exercise (Odife, 1988, p.31) whereby:

- a few privileged people buying up most of the shares
- some sections of the country cornering the bulk of the shares
- a few people being chosen by the expatriates to serve on the board of most companies
- some Nigerians fronting for expatriates or for other Nigerians
- some people paying for their shares out of dividends
- many of those who became captains of industries set up by aliens did not bother to share their own companies with other Nigerians

The most common arguments against privatisation included:

- domination of the economy by a few people who currently dominate the private sector
- creating capitalism without capital
- assets of most parastatals may suffer significant write-offs before quotation thereby enriching a few people.
- privatisation would lead to unemployment
- workers would suffer when parastatals are privatised
- all means of production should be controlled by the government as provided by the Federal Constitution:
  economy to be controlled in order to ensure maximum welfare, freedom and happiness of every citizen on the basis of social justice and equality of status and opportunity (1979 Federal Constitution, section 16(1))
- 'Federal character' will suffer in privatised parastatals
- privatisation is no guarantee of profitability
- privatise only unprofitable enterprises.

Regardless of opposition from vested interests such as labour groups, the programme started very well and has received commendations from international observers (Drum,1993; *Financial Times*, 1994). This is not to say that the implementation is not without problems. Problems experienced have included:

- delays in processing application forms and in returning monies for over-subscribed issues
- over-concentration of shareholdings in certain geographical areas

- problems of small investors obtaining credit from the banking system
- some degree of frustration on the part of larger investors as priority in allocation has been given to small investors.

Conclusion

It is possible to draw some parallels and, perhaps, set out certain generalisations on the basis of the on-going programme in Nigeria in relation to the UK's experience. Such generalisations may provide the basis for constructing a general model of privatisation.

A synthesis of the literature reveals that there are characteristics which are common to privatisation approaches whether in the predominantly market economies or the socially planned economies. Those characteristics such as the ones discussed by Cameron (1992) may be given as the preconditions for privatisation:
- sluggish or negative growth in output
- relatively high inflation
- relatively high unemployment
- burdensome level of national debt
- monopoly power in some industries and relatively high cost of SOEs
- subsidisation of agriculture and other industries
- strict regulation of the financial sector

Once an economy is characterised by these features, the question will then no longer be 'when' but 'how' to privatise. Successful privatisation needs to be methodical in approach and carefully thought through. Again, a general trend which underpins a successful implementation is observable:

The soft option approach: The first set of privatisation 'casualties' are usually the 'easily saleable enterprises' often in sectors such as transport, food, leisure and finance. Such enterprises neither provide 'collective goods' nor operate under conditions of market failure. UK examples are given in Table 2 (contrast this with schedule 1 of Appendix 2).

Company	Period of Privatisation	Method of privatisation
British Petroleum	1977-1987	public offer
ICL	1979	private sale
Fairey	1980	private sale
Ferranti	1980	private sale
British Sugar Co.	1981	private sale
National Freight Co.	1982	private sale
British Rail Hotels	1983	private sale
Sealink	1984	private sale
Wytch Farm	1984	private sale
Jaguar	1984	public offer
Inmos	1984	private sale
National Bus Co.	1986-88	private sale
Unipart	1987	private sale
Rolls Royce	1987	public offer
Istel	1987	private sale
Rover Group	1988	private sale

Table 2:

Source: Price Waterhouse (Various).

The Sweetener Effect: It has become a common practice both in the developed and developing economies to 'fatten up' enterprises earmarked for privatisation. The reason is obvious - to make such enterprises attractive to potential investors. In the case of Nigeria, the government made known its intention to provide financial injections in the form of debt cancellations or increased user charges to commercially unattractive SOEs. Parastatals with very low equity/debt ratios would be revived with the injection of more equity or conversion of some of their loans to equity.

Further pre-requisites for successful privatisation have been discussed by Ivanov *et al* (1994) and include:
- strong political leadership - a champion with power and zeal
- a strong strategic position, an attractive market situation and a sound competitive strategy
- a systematic and incremental process of implementing the privatisation programme
- a national culture which incorporates free market principles, structure and systems and behaviour
- skilled manpower.

In spite of these generalisations, it is intellectually flawed to assume that a generic model of privatisation is a reality. There are obvious contextual differences and national peculiarities which will need to be considered and designed into privatisation strategies. This is a truism and derives empirical support from several cross-national comparative works such as those conducted by Cameron, (1992); Drum, (1993); and Ivanov *et al* 1994. Each country has to adopt methods best suited to its characteristics and will need to tailor privatisation strategy to the particular circumstances of the country. The Nigerian experiment, for example, is predicated on economic exigencies rather than the oft repeated ideological justifications. Consequently, the arguments that have been used to rationalise privatisation in the UK, for example, could quickly collapse if applied to Nigeria because of the different underlying motivations. It may be that some of the implementation difficulties being experienced by many developing nations arise from the blind application of models developed in different contexts. For example, the 'big bang' approach can create social problems, with long-term political implications, for countries where the government has traditionally played the role of the 'ultimate provider'. The real worry is that many of such countries have little or no choice other than to 'swallow the pill' no matter how bitter it may be.

References

Abdulraheem, T., Olukoshi,A., Mustapha, A. & Williams, G. (1986) 'Nigeria: Oil, Debts and Democracy'. *Review of African Political Economy*, 37 (December).

Bangura, Y. (1987) 'IMF and World Bank Conditionality and Nigeria's Structural Adjustment Programme', in Havnenik, H. (ed.), *The IMF and the World Bank in Africa: Conditionality Impact and Alternatives* (Uppsala: Scandinavian Institute of Africa Affairs).

Cameron, C. (1992) 'A Comparison of Privatisation in Capitalist and Socialist Countries'. *International Journal of Social Economics*, 19, pp.55-60.

Drum, B. (1993) 'Privatisation in Africa'. *The Columbia Journal of World Business*, (Spring), pp.144-149.

Financial Times, (1994) 'Financial Times Survey: Emerging Markets'. (February) 7.

IMF (1989) 'Countries Are Adopting Reforms'. *IMF Survey*, 18(6).

Ivanov, D., Montanheiro, L., Nwankwo, S. & Richardson, B.(1994) 'BT and Bulgaria: A Specific to General Comparison of Privatisation Success Ingredients'. Paper presented at the 2nd Annual conference on *Managing in Enterprise Contexts*, Easingwold, Nr. York, 5-7 January.

Lieberman, I. (1993) 'Privatisation: The Theme of the 1990s'. *The Columbia Journal of World Business*, (Spring), pp.8-17.

Odife, D. (1988) *Privatisation in Nigeria*. (Lagos: Alkestis Books).

Olukoshi, O. (1993) 'From Crisis to Structural Adjustment in Nigeria', in Olukoshi, O. (ed.), *The Politics of Structural Adjustment in Nigeria*. (Ibadan, Nigeria: Heinemann Educational).

Okoroafo, S. (1992) 'Economic Reforms Create Opportunity in Africa'. *Management Decision,* 30 (7).

Okugu, B. (1986) 'The Outlook for Oil: 1985-2000: Four Scenarios'. *Review of African Political Economy*, 37, pp.11-23.

Richardson, B., Nwankwo, S., & Curwen, P.(1993) 'Regulating Consumer Responsiveness in Public-to-Private Organisations in the United Kingdom'. Paper presented at the Annual Conference of the *International Institute of Administrative Sciences*, Toluca, Mexico. July 27-30.

Sawyer, O. (1993) 'Environmental Uncertainty and Environmental Scanning Activities of Nigerian Manufacturing Executives: A Comparative Analysis'. *Strategic Management Journal*, 14, pp.287-299.

Wiltshire, K. (1987) *'Privatisation: The British Experience* .(Melbourne: CEDA/Longman).

Yahaya, S. (1993) 'State Versus Market: The Privatisation Programme of the Nigerian State', in Olukoshi, O. (ed.) *op cit.*

APPENDIX 1:

Political History of Nigeria Since Independence

October	1960	Attainment of independence and instalment of civilian government.
October	1963	Adoption of republican constitution
January	1966	Coup d'etat, overthrow of civilian government by military and ban on political activities
July	1966	Coup d'etat
July-1967Jan-1970		Civil war, military in power
July	1975	Coup d'etat
February	1976	Coup d'etat
September	1978	Ban on politics lifted and constitution foe Second Republic written
October	1979	Installation of civilian government and adoption of US presidential style government
December	1983	Coup d'etat, overthrow of civilian government by military, ban on political activity
August	1985	Coup d'etat
Spring	1989	Ban on politics lifted, Constitution for Third Republic written
April	1991	Attempted Coup d'etat
October	1992	Planned transition to civil administration stalled
June	1993	General election held and the result annulled by the military government.

APPENDIX 2:

Privatisation and Commercialisation of Government Enterprises in Nigeria (Decree No. 25 of 6 July, 1988. Also, Official Gazette Extra-ordinary, Vol.75, No.42, 1988)

Schedule I: (Full Privatisation - in which 100% of equity held by the Federal Government shall be fully privatised).

1. Nigerian Hotels Limited
2. Durbar Hotels Limited
3. Aba Textile Mills
4. Central Water Transportation Company Limited
5. National Cargo Handling Limited
6. Nigerian Dairies Company Limited
7. Nigerian National Fish Company Limited
8. Nigerian Food Company Limited
9. National Grains Production Company Limited
10. National Poultry Production Company Limited
11. National Root Crops Production Company and other such food production companies
12. Nigerian National Shrimps Company Limited
13. New Nigerian Salt Company Limited
14. National Fruit Company Limited
15. National Salt Company Limited, Ijoko
16. Specomil Nigerian Limited
17. South-East Rumania Wood Industries Limited, Ondo
18. Nigeria-Rumania Wood Industries Limited, Calabar
19. Nigerian Yeast and Alcohol Company Limited, Bacita
20. Nigerian Film Corporation
21. National Freight Company Limited
22. National Animal Feed Company Limited
23. Opobo Boat Yard
24. Madara Dairy Company Limited, Vom
25. Ore/Irele Oil Palm Company Limited
26. Okumu Oil Palm Company Limited
27. National Livestock Production Limited
28. Road Construction Company of Nigerian Limited
29. National Film Distribution Company Limited

30. Nigeria Ranches Company Limited, Kaduna
31. Impressit Bakalori Nigeria Limited
32. North Breweries Limited Kano
33. Nigerian Beverage Production Company Limited
34. West African Distilleries Limited
35. Nigerian Engineering Construction Company Limited
36. Tourist Company of Nigeria Limited
37. Electricity Meters Company Limited
38. American International Insurance Company Limited
39. Guinea Insurance Company Limited
40. Sun Insurance Company Limited
41. United Nigeria Insurance Company Limited
42. United Nigeria Life Insurance Company Limited
43. Niger Insurance Company Limited
44. Mercury Assurance Company Limited
45. Crusader Insurance Company Limited
46. Royal Exchange Insurance Company Limited
47. NEM Insurance Company Limited
48. Law Union and Rock Insurance Company Limited
49. Prestige Assurance Company Limited
50. British American Insurance Company Limited
51. West African Provincial Insurance Company Limited
52. Manchok Cattle Ranch
53. Mokwa Cattle Ranch
54. Poultry Production Units, Jos, Ilorin & Kaduna
55. Kaduna Abatoir and Kaduna Cold Meat Market
56. Bauchi Meat Factory and Galambi Cattle Ranch
57. Minna Pig Farm
58. Kano Abattoir Company Limited
59. Umuahia Pig Farm
60. Giant Cold Store Kano
61. Ayip-Eku Oil Palm Company
62. Ihechiowa Oil Palm Company Limited
63. Sokoto Integrated Livestock Company Limited
64. Motor Engineering Services Company Limited
65. Flour Mill of Nigeria Limited

Schedule II: (Partial Privatisation - Enterprises in which equity holding by the Federal government shall be partially privatised).

Enterprise	Present Federal Gov't Holding %	Maximum Federal Government Participation as % of Equity (post privatisation)
Commercial Banks:		
Savannah Bank of Nigeria Ltd.	51.34	Present holding to be maintained
Union Bank of Nigeria Ltd.	51.67	Present holding to be maintained
United Bank for Africa Ltd.	45.76	Present holding to be maintained
International Bank for W/A Ltd.	50	Present holding to be maintained
Allied Bank of Nigeria Ltd.	51	Present holding to be maintained
Continental Merchant Bank Ltd.	51	Present holding to be maintained
International Merchant Bank Ltd.	60	Present holding to be maintained
Nigeria Arab Bank Ltd	60	Present holding to be maintained
Nigeria Merchant Bank Ltd.	60	Present holding to be maintained
First Bank of Nigeria Ltd.	44.8	Present holding to be maintained
NAL Merchant Bank Ltd.	20	Present holding to be maintained
Merchant Bank of Africa	5	Present holding to be maintained
Federal Mortgage Bank of Nigeria	100	Not more than 70%
Nigerian Industrial Devpt. Bank	100	Not more than 70%
Nigerian Bank for Comm & Industry	100	Not more than 70%
Federal Savings Bank	100	Not more than 70%
Oil Marketing Companies:		
Unipetrol	100	Not more than 40%
National Oil & Chemical Co. Ltd.	60	Not more than 40%
African Petroleum Ltd.	80	Not more than 40%
Steel Rolling Mills:		
Jos Steel Rolling Mill	100	Not more than 40%
Kastina Steel Rolling Mill	100	Not more than 40%
Oshogbo Steel Rolling Mill	100	Not more than 40%
Air and Sea Travel Companies:		
Nigeria Airways Ltd.	100	Not more than 40%
Nigeria National Shipping Line	100	Not more than 40%
Fertilizer companies:		
Nigerian Superphosphate Fert.Co.	100	Not more than 40%
National Fertilizer Co. Ltd.	70	Not more than 40%
Paper Mills:		
Nig. National Paper Manuf. Co.	64.3	Not more than 40%
Nigeria News print Co. Ltd.	100	Not more than 40%
Nigeria Paper Mills Ltd.	100	Not more than 40%
Sugar companies:		
Savannah Sugar Co. Ltd.	75.4	Not more than 40%
Sunti Sugar Co. Ltd.	90	Not more than 40%
Lafiaji Sugar Co. Ltd.	70	Not more than 40%
Cement companies:		
Ashaka Cement Co. Ltd.	72	30%
Benue Cement Co. Ltd.	39	30%
Calabar Cement Co. Ltd.	68	30%
Cement Co. of Northern Nigeria	31.53	30%
Nigeria Cement Co. Ltd. Nkalagu	10.72	10%
Motor Vehicle and Truck Assembly Companies:		
Anambra Motor Manuf. Co.Ltd.	35	Present holding to be maintained
Leyland Nigeria Ltd.	35	Present holding to be maintained
Nigeria Truck Manuf.Co.Ltd.	35	Present holding to be maintained
Peugeot Automobile of Nigeria	35	Present holding to be maintained
Volkswagen of Nigeria Ltd.	35	Present holding to be maintained
Steyr Nigeria Ltd.	35	Present holding to be maintained

Schedule III: (Full Commercialisation)

1. Nigerian National Petroleum Corporation
2. Nigerian Telecommunications Limited
3. Associated Ores Mining Company Limited
4. Nigerian Mining Corporation
5. Nigerian Coal Corporation
6. National Insurance Corporation of Nigeria
7. Nigeria Re-Insurance corporation
8. National Properties Limited
9. Tafawa Balewa Square management Committee
10. Nigerian Ports Authority
11. African Re-Insurance Corporation

Schedule IV: (Partial Commercialisation):

1. Nigerian Railway Corporation
2. Nigerian Airport Authority
3. National Electric Power Authority
4. Nigerian Security Printing and Minting Company Limited
5. All the River Basins Development Authorities
6. National Provident Fund
7. Ajaokuta Steel Company Limited
8. Delta Steel Company Limited
9. Nigerian Machines Tolls Limited
10. Federal Housing Authority
11. Kainji Lake National Park
12. Federal Housing Authority
13. Nigerian Television Authority
14. News Agency of Nigeria

PRIVATISATION IN FRANCE: ANOTHER FALSE DAWN?

Peter Curwen and David Holmes
Sheffield Hallam University

Introduction

During the postwar period governments in France have been extremely ambivalent about the desirability of public ownership of financial and industrial assets. Briefly, commencing in 1986, it looked as though the then government was embarked upon a programme of privatisation to rival that of the UK. In the event, the programme rapidly ground to a halt, and it is only recently that a further programme has been initiated. In particular, this new programme is intended to be attractive to individual investors who are known to hold rather negative views concerning the previous round of sales. However, little attention appears to have been paid to discovering whether such views are justified, even though that is bound to have some bearing upon how the new issues are received. This article accordingly outlines the two programmes and their respective treatment of small shareholders, calculates the returns to small shareholders during the earlier round of sales and assesses the prospects for the current round.

The 1986-88 Programme: Background

The privatisation programme of 1986-88 can itself at least partly be attributed to a reaction to the programme of nationalisation introduced under the Public Law of 11 February 1982 following the election of President Mitterand on a Socialist/Communist ticket. Altogether, 47 companies passed into public ownership. However, in March 1986, a right-wing government was elected, with Jacques Chirac as Prime Minister, with an explicit commitment to privatise as much as possible of the state's corporate holdings.

The new government passed the Public Law on 2 July (operational from 6 October) which would enable it to privatise a total of 65 companies over a five-year period (to which was added TF-1, the television company). Although the list was wide-ranging, it excluded two major categories of company, namely public service utilities and monopolies and companies with a poor financial performance (Bauer, 1989, p.51).

Even though most of the 66 companies were ultimately left unaffected, the programme nevertheless proceeded with great speed. This reflected the fact that even those companies nationalised in 1982 were public limited companies with their shares owned either by the government or other public sector bodies. Furthermore, most were in sound financial health (Andreff, 1992, p.146).

The privatisation law was vague on technicalities, and the government effectively had complete freedom to decide the shareholding structure of privatised companies (Bauer, 1989, p.53). In practice, all of the major privatisations were accomplished in a similar manner (see, for example, Delion, 1990, pp.67-8). French citizens and residents were initially promised 10 shares apiece and allocated overall roughly one half of the available shares; a further minimum of 10 per cent were offered at a preferential rate to employees; 15 per cent were offered to foreigners; and between 15 and 30 per cent (typically 25 per cent) were offered to a 'stable nucleus' or 'hard core' (*noyau dur*) of industrial and financial concerns, each entitled to hold between 0.5 and 5.0 per cent of the shares.

Fewer than ten foreign companies were permitted to join any *noyau dur*, as compared to a total of 45 French concerns. Many among the latter were state-owned (Andreff, 1992, p.148), which effectively 're-nationalised' some assets. However, some of these assets were privatised once again as a result of the flotation of the company which had acquired them.

The choice of the *noyau dur* lay in the hands of the Minister of Finance. This choice was widely perceived as a form of political patronage, and it is indeed striking how many of the chosen concerns were either state-owned or recently privatised. In general, the *noyau dur* were obliged to pay a premium over and above the official flotation price in return for a guarantee that they would receive a stated minimum allocation of shares which they undertook to retain for some time, usually two years.

Whereas the existence of the *noyau dur* served to prevent the excessive dispersion of ownership noted as a characteristic of UK privatisations, the government also set out to attract a large number of new individual shareholders, in most cases by offering a series of incentives. Applications for no more than ten shares were to be met in full (the small number reflecting the high value of individual shares); payment could be made by instalments (though shares were in fully-paid form and could not be sold until fully paid for); one free share was to be given as a bonus for every ten bought and held for eighteen months (subject to a maximum bonus of fifty shares); payments and bonus shares were free of income tax; and the shares were sold at a discount to the market price, where quoted. Employee participation in the substantial shareholding reserved exclusively for them was also fostered through a 5 per cent discount on the issue price.

The 1986-88 Programme: Cases

Strictly speaking, privatisation did not begin in 1986 since between 1983 and 1986 the government allowed certain state-owned concerns to sell their subsidiaries to private companies (Bauer, 1989, p.51). However, it should be noted that we are concerned here only with cases involving a public offer for sale (*offre publique de vente*). In addition to the public offers discussed below there were at various times during 1986-88 private (trade) sales, sales by special state decree and sales to regional and local affiliates.

The programme commenced with the sale of 11 per cent of Elf-Aquitaine in September 1986. This is often omitted from accounts of the programme as it preceded 6 October and the state was left with more than 50 per cent of the shares, but it shared the characteristics of subsequent sales noted above. The public offer was more than four times subscribed at Ff305 per share, with 300,000 small investors attracted by a price fixed 10 per cent below the market level and a 1 in 10 bonus, and modest (stagging) gains were made if shares were sold during the first day of official trading.

In November came the sale of the glass-maker St Gobain which attracted five times as many individual applications and was 13.7 times subscribed. The offer price, at Ff310, was slightly above the market price ruling at the time of its fixing, but it subsequently rose fairly steadily for three months as institutions built up their holdings. Holders of *Certificats d'Investissement*, a form of non-voting shares first introduced in 1984 (Redor, 1992, p.159), were entitled to exchange them, together with a payment of Ff10, for voting shares.

The first bank privatisation came in January 1987 with the flotation of the government's residual stake in Compagnie Financiere de Paribas (Paribas), a holding company which had been nationalised in 1982. The state initially disposed of 18 per cent of its holding via a placement. The subsequent offer for sale to the public was manifestly underpriced at Ff405 given a grey market value of Ff470, and as a result was 39 times subscribed. Private applications were heavily scaled down, and the minimum allocation was reduced to four shares. Institutional investors received nothing at all and even employees had their allocations scaled down, whereas the *noyau dur* were obliged to pay only a 2.5 per cent premium at Ff415. The first day stagging gain, at 24 per cent, was large by French standards, though often exceeded in the UK, but the price was nevertheless back at its issue level prior to the October 1987 crash.

In March, 47 per cent of the largest French regional bank, Société Générale Alsacienne de Banque (Sogénal), also nationalised in 1982, was sold off at Ff125 per share. Compared to the previous two sales this raised little revenue, and although there were only 850,000 individual applications, the scarcity of the shares meant both that allocations were very small (a maximum of 6 shares) and that the stagging gain was very large at 36 per cent.

Almost the entire state shareholding in the Banque du Bâtiment et des Travaux Publics (BBTP) was sold off early in April 1987 at Ff130 per share. The *noyau dur* were allocated 51 per cent of the 3 million shares on offer. One million individuals applied for just over one million shares in the public offer. As a result they were 65 times subscribed and the minimum allocation was reduced to one share only, in relation to which there was a 23 per cent stagging gain. In the same month, one third of the equity of the Banque Industrielle de Mobilière Privée (BIMP) was also sold off at Ff140 per share. This disposal attracted only half a million individual applications for, once again, comparatively few shares, and the stagging gain was 21 per cent. In this case, most unusually, the price subsequently rose sharply and then remained steady through to October.

A third bank, Crédit Commercial de France (CCF), was sold off in stages, commencing at the end of April. The shares were inexpensive at Ff107, and individuals were guaranteed a minimum allocation of twelve. One and a half million applications were made, and the stagging gain was 17 per cent.

The international advertising agency, Agence Havas (Havas) followed in May when 19 per cent of its equity was sold to individual subscribers at a price of Ff500, which meant that the outlay was quite large even for a few shares. Roughly 40 per cent of the company was already quoted on the Paris Bourse, and the price rose by only 8 per cent on the first day to the Ff540 price paid by the *noyau dur*. In the same month the residual state holding in Compagnie Générale d'Electricité (CGE - now Alcatel), nationalised in 1982, was sold off at Ff290 per share together with roughly the equivalent number of new shares and converted *Certificats d'Investissement*. Two and a quarter million individuals applied for the 28 million shares in the public offer, producing a stagging gain of 11 per cent. Each applicant was guaranteed a minimum of 10 shares, but beyond that limit all applications were heavily scaled down.

Société Générale, the fourth largest bank in France, was wholly privatised in June. It broke new ground insofar as it was the first sale of state assets in a bank nationalised before 1982. The shares were worth more in aggregate than in any other case. They were also individually expensive at Ff407 and the public offer attracted only 2.3 million applications, resulting in a stagging gain of 6 per cent. This sale was followed immediately by that of 50 per cent of TF-1, the television channel. Individual applicants had only to pay Ff165 (whereas Bouygues paid Ff285 for a 25 per cent holding). The flotation attracted 416,000 applicants, and their stagging gain was 8 per cent.

This rapid sequence of privatisations came to a grinding halt with the flotation of Compagnie Financière de Suez (Suez), the holding company controlling the Indosuez banking group, only days before the October stock market crash. 1.6 million individual subscribers paid Ff317 per share only to see the price fall back by 18 per cent to Ff261 when the shares were first quoted on the Bourse. As a consequence, the sale of the state's 51 per

346

cent stake in Matra, the aerospace and motor engineering group, was postponed until the end of January 1988, priced at Ff112 per share after a 12 for 1 share split. Only 300,000 individuals applied for shares, but the issue was deliberately under-priced and there was nevertheless a stagging gain of 14 per cent. Interestingly, this was one of only two occasions, of which the other was Havas, where the government acquired a special 'preference' share entitling it for a period of five years to veto any individual holding in excess of 10 per cent.

Events Since 1988

Post-Matra, the mood changed with the election of a Socialist government under Michel Rocard. President Mitterand then proposed that no further privatisations or nationalisations should take place (the 'ni-ni' policy) for the time being, and the uncovering of misdemeanours in the state-owned sector, including insider dealing scandals implicating senior figures in the Socialist Party, gave cause for concern. As a consequence, no further privatisations took place during 1989.

When it was subsequently decided, in March 1990, to undertake a partial privatisation of Union des Assurances de Paris (UAP), previously postponed at the end of 1987, it proved to be a fiasco. Lack of interest on the part of individual subscribers at the Ff625 issue price left the French underwriters with excess shares, which were then offered to UK institutions at Ff10 less than the issue price at which they had previously oversubscribed their 10 per cent allocation.

Not surprisingly, therefore, no further attempts at a public offer took place until that of 20 per cent of Crédit Local de France (a partial privatisation) at the very end of 1991, at an issue price of Ff210. Although this got off to a poor start, with the price dipping below Ff200, it rose again almost immediately above the issue price.

Returns to Small Shareholders

In 1986, the general public was invited to participate in a privatisation programme more or less as a gesture of faith in the virtues of private ownership, although they were probably mostly aware of what had taken place previously in the UK. They could instead have put their money in a risk-free investment, or simply bought a cross-section of shares already trading on the Bourse. It is accordingly important to analyse whether they should or should not have participated in the programme, to be assessed primarily in relation to the returns on an arbitrary portfolio as proxied by the performance of the French stock market in general.

The approach adopted has been to calculate gross returns, firstly for a complete portfolio of privatisations via public offers for sale and secondly for the stock market as a whole, with the two portfolios being compared both on an annual basis and averaged over the period 1986 to 1993.

The annual return was obtained making use of the formula:

$$\frac{P(a) - P(a-1)}{P(a-1)} + D \quad \text{where:}$$

P(a)   is the average value of a privatised share or the Datastream French Index during the relevant year (or end-September in the case of 1993).

P(a-1) is the average value of a privatised share or the Datastream French Index during the previous year.

D   is the average gross dividend yield pertaining to the individual share or the market as a whole for the relevant year.

The decision was made to use average prices and dividend yields in the yearly calculations rather than price changes during a particular calendar year or dividend yields on a specific day, on the grounds that the latter statistics are very much determined, not to say distorted, by prices ruling on just two days of the year, namely 31 December and 1 January.

The calculations to obtain average annual returns over the period under consideration involved the use of both arithmetic and geometric means. The advantage of using a geometric mean is that it provides a better indication of the rate of growth of returns whereas returns using an arithmetic mean may, under certain circumstances, bear little relationship to the actual returns achieved. It should, however, be noted that in a rising stock market a geometric mean produces slightly lower returns than an arithmetic mean.

In the case of the portfolio of privatised shares it was considered to be desirable to present the arithmetic and geometric means in both weighted and unweighted forms. Weighting was considered to be desirable on account of the differing number of companies in the portfolio in different years. Although it might have been appropriate to have determined the relative weights according to market capitalisation as of September 1993 in order to facilitate an accurate comparison with market indices, this was not undertaken because a number of the sales were of shares in companies which were already listed on the Bourse. Instead, weighting was done according to the number of companies which had been privatised in any particular year.

The returns to shareholders are presented in the form of two tables. Table 1 illustrates returns in an annualised format. This normally results in a distorted picture in the year of privatisation of the relevant company, especially where the flotation occurs towards the end

348

of the year and in the case of the period ending in September 1993. In order to offset this problem the data have also been presented in Table 2 such as to display the compounded annual returns achieved both for individual shares and for the portfolio as a whole.

It should be observed that certain difficulties arise in making valid comparisons between the returns on the privatisation portfolio and that on the stock market at large. In the first place, the tax position of the investor has been ignored. In France, there is a distinction between the rate of taxation on capital gains and that on dividend income, with discrimination in favour of the former except insofar that when companies reinvest their income, their tax liability is either reduced or commuted. Strictly speaking, it would have been desirable to calculate net-of-tax returns to investors, but given the complex nature of the French tax system and the differing dividend strategies adopted by companies this was not feasible.

Secondly, a number of the issues were accompanied by incentives designed to encourage shareholder loyalty, generally in the form of bonus issues at the end of a qualifying period. These obviously enhance the returns achieved by long-term shareholders, but the difficulties of modelling their effects have precluded their inclusion. Finally, although it would have been desirable to have utilised the well-known CAC40 or the CAC General market index for purposes of comparison, these do not appear to have an associated dividend yield index. As a consequence, the Datastream price and yield index has been employed instead, and appears as Table 3.

Despite these reservations the picture represented by Tables 1-3 is unambiguous - the privatisation portfolio performed poorly in comparison to the French stock market as a whole. The geometric mean for the privatisation portfolio averaged 14.8 per cent whereas that for the Bourse over the comparable period averaged 20.9 per cent. The use of an arithmetic mean serves only to accentuate this difference.

A comparison of Tables 1 and 3 reveals that whereas the two portfolios performed similarly in most years, the privatisation portfolio performed extremely badly in 1988 (although it caught up somewhat in 1989). It also suffered an unusually large loss in 1991. It is notable that over the period since the beginning of 1991 it has been trailing the Bourse by a significant margin. The reason for this can clearly be seen in Table 1, which shows firstly that 11 of the 15 privatised companies made losses in 1991 and 6 among them in 1992. Even in 1993, 3 were still making losses, two on a large scale, despite the upturn in the financial markets. Secondly, it may be observed that among the 12 companies privatised since 1987, only one has avoided a loss in every year, and that the overall profile is extremely volatile.

349

The New Programme

At the beginning of 1992, the government made two further partial privatisations in respect of Total and Elf Aquitaine, raising a total of Ff10 bn. It was announced in October 1992 that the state's direct and indirect shareholding in Rhône-Poulenc would be reduced from 56.9 per cent (representing 77.5 per cent of the voting rights) to 46.3 per cent before the year end, the first time that this government ostensibly stood ready to let its stake fall below 50 per cent. This was, however, deceptive in that a further 20.8 per cent was held by Crédit Lyonnais, AGF and other concerns under state control.

It was intended that *Certificats d'Investissement* would be convertible into ordinary voting shares at no charge, thereby valuing the shares to be sold in the region of Ff3-4 bn, all of which was to be used to create jobs and fund other public sector companies. However, the erratic state of the Paris Bourse caused the sale to be postponed in December, and the sale was eventually executed on 2 February, 1993.

In April, Total announced the sale of 4.3 per cent of its equity to Cogema, the state-controlled nuclear group, 2 per cent to Société Générale and 1 per cent to Lyonnaise des Eaux-Dumez as a prelude to creating a *noyau dur* of 12 per cent. Total would take reciprocal stakes, but be left with a net Ff2.5 bn of proceeds.

At the end of May, after eight weeks in office, the new centre-right administration led by M Balladur announced that it intended to raise Ff40 bn during 1993 through the partial privatisation of all state holdings bar the utilities, telecommunications, munitions and gaming concerns. As this had been included in the government's election manifesto it was a surprise only in that it proposed to issue Ff40 bn of 'Balladur bonds' which would be convertible into shares in privatised companies if the holders so wished. From a philosophic viewpoint the proposed list of privatisations, set out in Table 5, did not indicate a sea change in that, like the Socialists, the government still appeared to believe that companies should rely on private sector capital but be subject to state influence.

An ostensibly important change from policy in 1986-88 was the stated intention to permit non-EC investors to buy more than 20 per cent of a newly-privatised company's shares, but as this was anyway possible once the shares were listed it was of little consequence. In any event, the government intended to retain a golden share where appropriate in order to prevent an unwelcome foreign take-over bid.

At the same time, the government announced that it would be selling off 30.5 per cent of Crédit Local before the end of June. The company was not on the list of proposed privatisations because its privatisation was already authorised. The first sales from the list would comprise Rhône-Poulenc, Banque Nationale de Paris, Banque Hervet and Elf-Aquitaine, all of which were already quoted on the Bourse. In the event the CLF offer, which raised Ff4.2 bn (of which Ff2.4 bn was taken by the government and Ff1.8 bn by the

Caisse des Depôts), was heavily over-subscribed with domestic applications for 113 mn shares compared to the 6.5 mn on offer and international applications for seven times the 4.4 mn shares on offer.

This augured well for the main privatisation programme, but the general public, only 10 per cent of whom owned shares, remained unenthused, so various incentives were proposed such as a 20 per cent discount for employees, enhanced dividends as a loyalty bonus and payment by instalments in addition to the conversion of Balladur bonds launched in late June.

Early in July, the government was forced to accept an amendment by the French Senate to the privatisation bill restricting non-EC foreigners to 20 per cent of newly-privatised companies shares. As noted above, this was not a vital issue, and *partenariats* - companies involved in joint ventures with companies due to be privatised - were anyway exempt. The Privatization Law became operational on 19 July.

On 11 July, it was announced that the Balladur bonds had raised a total of Ff110 bn, nearly three times the target figure. Meanwhile, the chosen four companies prepared themselves for privatisation, with Rhône-Poulenc selling-off its stake in Roussel-Uclaf for Ff4.5 bn and announcing a proposed four-for-one share split, Elf-Aquitaine reducing the number of shares that investors could buy from 100 to 10 and BNP proposing a two-for-one share split to be authorised on 17 September.

Banque Nationale de Paris

The first flotation in the new programme was France's third-largest bank, Banque Nationale de Paris (BNP), of which at the time 72.9 per cent was owned by the state. Roughly 72 million shares were on offer, of which 37.5 mn (52 per cent) were initially reserved for individual investors and 34.6 mn (48 per cent) for institutions (17 per cent French and 31 per cent foreign), with a clawback provision to raise the share of the general public to 47 mn shares (65 per cent) given a sufficiently large subscription. The value of the offer, priced at Ff240 per share, was Ff28 bn and the value of the entire company Ff43 bn. The offer was set to close on 12 October 1993.

At the time the price was announced the only tradeable shares in BNP, the non-voting *Certificats d'Investissement*, were valued at Ff282, which, given a Ff5 cost to acquire voting rights, implied a flotation price of Ff277, significantly above the figure set. Although this price was set by an avowedly independent body, the privatisation commission, it appeared to be influenced by a desire to ensure a successful start to the privatisation programme. In the event it was so successful that within two days the institutional issue was 12 times over-subscribed and had to be terminated on 6 October.

The general public were initially promised 40 shares apiece, with an additional 40 for individuals converting their Balladur bonds into BNP shares. Roughly 1 mn individuals were expected to apply, but in the event there were 2.8 mn applications for five times the number of shares on offer, so the allocations had to be restricted to 15 shares even after the clawback provision was triggered.

In addition to Union des Assurances de Paris (UAP), the state-owned insurer with a pre-existing 9.8 per cent stake which was set to rise to 15 per cent, the *noyau dur* comprised a further 15 companies which, subject to clawback, were allocated a further 15 per cent of the total shares in BNP. Not all of these were French, and the foreign companies were participating either as a guaranteed way of obtaining shares or in order to be favoured in future offers. The Dresdner Bank had a pre-existing commercial partnership and had negotiated a cross-shareholding agreement whereby each bank would take up to 10 per cent of the other's equity subject to authorisation by the European Commission. Once this is transferred to Dresdner the state will be left with a 5 per cent holding to cover free shares to employees and bonus shares to individuals. No *action spécifique* (golden share) was created on this occasion.

On 19 October, the first day of official trading, the shares closed at Ff283.90 having earlier breached the 15 per cent increase limit set for first day sales on the Paris Bourse. Roughly 4 mn shares were traded (3.4 per cent of BNP equity) as institutions topped up their holdings. However, given their small allocations, stags did not make much of a killing.

Rhône-Poulenc

The sale of 25.8 mn shares in February was followed by a series of Capital Transactions which had the effect of leaving the state with a 43.4 per cent direct holding, Crédit Lyonnais and AGF each with roughly 7.5 per cent and the state with a total direct and indirect holding of 59.6 per cent. Immediately the BNP sale was concluded it was announced that the state's 43.4 per cent direct stake, worth roughly Ff13 bn, would comprise the next privatisation with all proceeds accruing to the state. The reservation of shares commenced on 28 October.

Of the 88.1 mn shares on offer, 47.6 mn (60 per cent) were allocated to the public offer for French and EC citizens and 31.7 mn to institutional investors, with a clawback provision in respect of 15 per cent of the latter which was exercised. Private investors were given priority on up to 60 shares, and on a further 60 shares if converting Balladur bonds. Employees were offered 8.8 mn shares at a 20 per cent discount, a certain number of additional free shares in proportion, subject to a cap, and delayed payment and other preferential terms. A *noyau dur* was formed initially comprising Crédit Lyonnais (7.4 per cent), AGF (6.62 per cent), Société Générale (2.83 per cent) and BNP (1.15 per cent). These signed a *protocole* obligating them to hold all of their shares for three months and 80 per cent of them for a further 15 months, and to offer 80 per cent of any sold during the subsequent three years to other members of the group. They were later joined by Fiat and Axa with the intention of an overall *noyau dur* holding of 24 per cent of the post-privatisation capital.

The price in the public offer was fixed at Ff135, a substantial discount compared to the then ruling price of Ff154. The institutional price was to be fixed via a book-building exercise. The flotation was executed on 25 November, with the institutional and public offers both over-subscribed, the latter roughly three times subscribed. The shares ended the day at just under Ff154. As a result of the over-subscription individual investors received only 17 shares, together with a further 16 shares if converting Balladur bonds.

Recent Developments

On the same day the economy minister, Edmond Alphandéry, confirmed that the state's 50.8 per cent stake in Elf-Aquitaine, worth roughly Ff50 bn, would be the next to be privatised via a public offer. At the end of November, Elf issued a warning that 1993 profits were expected to be little more than Ff1 bn compared to Ff6.2 bn in 1992. Subsequently, UAP was confirmed as the fifth candidate for sale. Meanwhile, a tender offer was launched for the state's 89 per cent stake in Banque Hervet, expected to raise Ff1 bn early in 1994. The government also reduced its stake in Total from 8.17 per cent to 5 per cent through a market placing in September 1993 at Ff296 a share, raising Ff2.06 bn.

In mid-December it was announced that, despite the breakdown of the planned merger with Volvo, the privatisation of Renault would still proceed in the latter part of 1994. In January 1994, the government launched the privatisation of Framatone, the nuclear power station group which had not been on its original list of candidates. The state's entire 51 per cent holding was to be sold off via a limited tender offer.

Meanwhile, the privatisation of Elf-Aquitaine moved on apace with the announcement that the government would retain a golden share of unlimited duration which would require government approval for other investors, either acting individually or in concert, to raise their shareholdings in Elf above the limits of 10 per cent, 20 per cent and 33.3 per cent. The *noyau dur* would consist of UAP with 1.5 per cent plus other companies with 8.5 per cent in total as a result of a tender. The government would retain roughly 13 per cent of the shares through the state holding company, Erap.

All told, 66.5 mn shares would be offered with 33 mn reserved for individual investors, 27 mn for institutions and 6.5 mn for employees on preferential terms. Up to 20 per cent of the institutional tranche would be subject to clawback, but additional shares might then be made available to institutions through Erap.

Conclusion

Taken as a whole, the privatisation programme has apparently achieved one of its primary objectives. Before the Socialists came to power in 1981, France had roughly 1.5 million shareholders. By early 1988 that figure had grown to 8 million (Bauer, 1989, p.58). This does not imply, however, that the experience of direct personal shareholding has been an altogether happy one.

Judging by the flotations of BNP and Rhône-Poulenc, the French government is as determined to make a success of its privatisation programme as was the case in 1986. On the face of it, ensuring a success is the least of its problems if success is to be judged by an over-subscription for the shares, since they can be (and have been) deliberately underpriced. From the point of view of the small individual shareholder this guarantee of a capital gain may represent an offer he or she cannot refuse. However, as has so often been the case in the UK, once trading costs are netted out the tiny allocations to individuals are barely worth the effort of stagging the issues (unless families obtain multiple allocations), and in practice roughly 80 per cent of individuals have held on to their shares.

If the individual investor buys the shares as a long-term investment then the evidence from the 1986-88 privatisations is that this is a risky way to build up a portfolio, since individual issues may well perform badly and allocations in each new issue will almost certainly be small.

This conclusion appears to contradict evidence from the UK where investors in privatised shares have fared better than the stock market as a whole (Curwen and Holmes, 1992). It may, however, be noted that there have been successes and failures among privatised concerns even in the UK, and particularly that the successes have mostly been the utilities (telecommunications, gas, electricity and water) whereas the failures have comprised industrial companies vulnerable to recession. In addition, there have been no privatisations of financial intermediaries in the UK.

The combination of industrial and financial companies on offer in France both in 1986-88 and currently hardly represents the kind of package which should be attractive to 'widows and orphans'. Just prior to the announcement of the flotation of Rhône-Poulenc, for example, its chairman noted that it faced the most difficult chemicals market since the second world war together with depressed demand for fibres and polymers. For the individual shareholder, the new programme of privatisation in France may well prove to be another false dawn.

References

Andreff, W. (1992) 'French Privatization Techniques and Experience: A Model for Central-Eastern Europe?', in F. Targetti (ed) *Privatization in Europe. West and East Experiences* (Dartmouth) 135-53.

Bauer, M. (1989) 'The Politics of State-Directed Privatisation: The Case of France, 1986-88', in J. Vickers and V. Wright (eds) *The Politics of Privatisation in Western Europe* (Frank Cass) 49-60.

Bizaguet, A. (1988) 'Le Secteur Public Francais et les Privatisations', *Revue Internationale des Sciences Administratives, 54* (4)

Bizaguet, A. and Sirel, F. (1988) 'Privatisation Schemes in Europe', *The World of Banking* (July-August) 14-16.

Curwen, P. and Holmes, D. (1992) 'Returns to Small Shareholders from Privatisation', *National Westminster Bank Quarterly Review* (February) 41-57.

Delion, A. (1990) 'Public Enterprises: Privatisation or Reform?', *International Review of Administrative Sciences, 56,* 63-78.

Fraser, R. and Wilson, M. (1988) *Privatisation: The UK Experience and International Trends* (Longman).

Graham, C. and Prosser, T. (1991) *Privatising Public Enterprises* (Oxford: Clarendon Press).

Jacquillet, B. (1988) *Nationalization and Privatization in Contemporary France* (Stanford: Cal., Hoover Institution Essays in Public Policy 10).

Jenkinson, T. and Meyer, C. (1988) ' The Privatisation Process in France and the UK', *European Economic Review, 32,* 482-90.

Pint, E. (1990) 'Nationalization and Privatization: A Rational-Choice Perspective on Efficiency', *Journal of Public Policy, 10* (3) 267-98.

Redor, D. (1992) ' The State Ownership Sector: Lessons From the French Experience', in F. Targetti (ed) *Privatization in Europe. West and East Experiences* (Dartmouth) 155-65.

Suleiman, E. (1990) 'The Politics of Privatisation in Britain and France', in E. Suleiman and J. Waterbury (eds) *The Political Economy of Public Sector Reform and Privatisation* (Westview Press).

Company	1986	1987	1988	1989	1990	1991	1992	1993 (End Sept)
BIMP		27.1	(14.6)	43.7	78.9	(27.0)	(34.6)	(31.2)
BTP (LACIE)		(3.5)	(13.6)	10.6	(4.8)	(15.7)	(6.5)	(29.0)
ALCATEL ALSTHOM		3.4	2.5	53.9	31.6	8.1	12.0	9.7
CRED. COMM		54.6	3.6	59.7	2.7	(37.5)	18.9	29.4
CREDIT LOCALE							29.8	58.3
ELF	42.0	22.3	(1.1)	64.2	37.6	16.6	5.7	12.3
HAVAS		32.0	19.0	66.5	48.9	(11.5)	0.3	(2.1)
MATRA			(0.7)	100.0	(2.9)	(26.4)	(12.1)	74.3
PARIBAS		10.0	(11.3)	40.6	14.9	(22.2)	(11.3)	24.2
ST GOBAIN	102.2	24.5	11.6	33.7	(15.1)	(8.5)	26.1	2.4
SOGENAL		(6.4)	2.4	14.6	(11.7)	(17.7)	2.4	41.6
SOC GENERALE		(9.8)	(1.7)	37.6	5.7	(9.7)	25.4	22.0
SUEZ		15.4	(3.0)	35.9	13.9	21.6	(7.0)	11.1
TV FSE 1		17.3	10.6	109.3	(18.9)	9.6	34.9	12.8
UAP					7.3	(4.3)	(7.2)	23.6
AVE CHANGE	72.1	15.6	0.3	55.6	13.4	(8.9)	5.2	17.3
NO. OF COMPANIES	2	12	13	13	14	14	15	15

Table 1

French Privatisation Returns (Annualised) %
(Capital Gains (Losses) + Dividend Yield)

Source: Datastream

G MEAN AVERAGE	=	14.78% (weighted)
ARITH MEAN AVERAGE	=	21.30 (un-weighted)
		14.88 (weighted)

Notes
(i)   Data adjusted for scrip, rights and consolidation issues.
(ii) Capital gain (or loss) in one year is the average price in year 1 less the average price in year 0.
(iii) Dividend yield is the average dividend for relevant year.

Company	Years since privatisation	Issue price*	Price 30/9/93	Ave. Ann. returns Capital gain (loss) + Dividend Yield
BIMP	6.5	107	240.4	17.5
BTP (LA CIE)	6.5	130	38.0	(5.7)
ALCATEL	6.4	290	727.0	18.6
CRED COMM.	6.5	107	247.5	16.6
CRED LOCALE	1.8	210	422.5	50.5
ELF	7.1	145	397.5	21.6
HAVAS	6.4	237	457.0	12.7
MATRA	5.8	118	383.3	26.5
PARIBAS	6.8	405	465.0	6.8
ST GOBAIN	6.9	355	565.0	10.7
SOGENAL	6.6	125	140.9	6.8
SOC GENERALE	6.3	407	632.0	10.9
SUEZ	6.0	317	342.5	4.5
TV FSE 1	6.3	165	503.2	22.3
UAP	3.5	625	597.0	1.4

Table 2

French Privatisation Returns* %

Source: Datastream

*Adjusted for scrips, rights and consolidation.

Un-weighted Arithmetic Mean   =   14.8%

Weighted Arithmetic Mean   =   13.4%

1980	28.55
1981	-6.45
1982	1.5%
1983	34.9%
1984	46.0%
1985	28.2%
1986	63.9%
1987	14.6%
1988	15.9%
1989	45.4%
1990	5.7%
1991	-1.5%
1992	8.4%
1993*	20.9%

Table 3

Average Returns Achieved on French Bourse 1980-93

Average Annual Returns (Price Changes + Dividend Yield)

Source: Datastream

Averages:	Arithmetic Mean Average	=	21.86%	} 1980-93
	Geometric Mean	=	20.39%	
	Arithmetic Mean	=	22.36%	} 1986-93
	Geometric Mean	=	20.88%	

*to end Setember 19993

358

Company	State Shareholding March 1993 %	Date of Nationalisation
Aérospatiale	73.7	Aug 1936
Air France	99.3	Jun 1945
Banque Hervet	73.5	Feb 1982
BNP	72.9	Dec 1945
Caisse cent. de Réassurance	100.0	Apr 1946
Bull	72.0	Feb 1982
Compagnie Gén. Maritime	100.0	Jul 1933
Crédit Lyonnais	52.5	Dec 1945
Pechiney	55.7	Feb 1982
Renault	79.8	Jan 1945
Rhône-Poulenc	44.0	Feb 1982
AGF	65.5	Apr 1946
GAN	79.4	Apr 1946
UAP	55.9	Apr 1946
Seita	100.0	Jan 1959
Société Mars. de Credit	100.0	Feb 1982
SNECMA	96.9	May 1945
Elf-Aquitaine	50.8	Nov 1941
Thompson	75.8	Feb 1982
Usinor-Sacilor	80.0	Nov 1981
Caisse Nat. de prévoyance	42.5	Jul 1868

Table 4
The New Programme

THE CHANGING PATTERN OF UK PRIVATIZATION

Peter Curwen, Sheffield Business School

Introduction

The present government, which first came to power in 1979, will doubtless be remembered for other things as well, but it is a reasonable assumption that its most lasting legacy will prove to be its programme of privatization, the largest in absolute terms in the world and one which has been extensively copied.

During the period up to the end of the 1980s, the programme consisted essentially of asset sales of various kinds. Initially, these were primarily in the form of council houses, but commencing with the first tranche of British Telecom in 1984, the programme increasingly consisted of the flotation, via a public offer for sale, of corporate assets. However, industrial assets were also disposed of in large numbers via trade sales (to other corporate bodies) and management buy-outs, and altogether there have been roughly two hundred such sales although few have generated any significant net revenue for the government.

A summary of the programme is contained in Table 1. All told, these sales generated roughly £50 billion to be set against government spending at the time. However, the asset sale cupboard is becoming increasingly bare, and apart from its residual holdings in partially privatised companies, the government is left with the likes of the Post Office, railways and coal mines, all difficult to dispose of and unlikely to generate huge sums of revenue.

The government was obviously aware of this situation as the 1980s drew to an end, and accordingly took steps to maintain the momentum of the programme by switching its thrust into new directions, a policy now associated with Mr Major much as asset sales are forever associated with Mrs Thatcher. Broadly speaking, these new directions encompass:

- the contracting-out of services previously performed by central and local government agencies.
- the imposition of *user charges* and fees (for example, for prescriptions or museum entry) in respect of services previously supplied at zero cost to their consumers.

- the introduction of consumer-driven initiatives such as the *Citizen's Charter* in order to simulate market controls on state-owned bodies.
- the introduction of *performance measurement* and payment by results systems into public sector bodies such as the Civil Service.

A useful umbrella term to encompass these initiatives is *privatizing choice*. This term was introduced by Mr Major when addressing the Adam Smith Institute in June 1992. He defined the term as meaning that 'where once socialism nationalised or municipalised personal choice, taking it away from the individual and the family, we will give choice back to them and extend it further.' This, he told the Institute, with arguably a touch of hyperbole, is the 'greatest and most far-reaching' privatisation, and 'the one to which I am most committed.'

The purpose of this paper is to examine the various facets of privatising choice. The position is constantly evolving, and it is very difficult for the well-informed, let alone the interested layman, to keep up to date. Definitive judgements are pending in most cases, and the paper tries to avoid being judgemental since, although the author has a preference for free-market solutions, many readers probably hold opinions to the contrary.

Competitive Tendering in the Local Authorities

It is important to begin by drawing a distinction between *competitive tendering* and *contracting-out*. Contracting-out simply means that an activity previously undertaken in-house is transferred to some other organisation whereas, as the name implies, competitive tendering involves inviting competing offers to supply in accordance with a tender document. Such an offer may be extended to include in-house units, and is frequently known as *market-testing*. However, these terms are often used inter-changeably in the media.

Contracting-out in the local authorities dates back roughly a decade. However, it was initially of little significance, and progress awaited the passing of the Local Government Act 1988 (Carnaghan and Bracewell-Milnes, 1993 pp.27-8). This required all tiers of local government, whether county, district and parish councils, joint boards and committees, New Town authorities and most local police bodies, to adopt competitive tendering for a wide range of services previously supplied by monopoly Direct Service Organisations (DSOs).

In theory, a strong case can be made out to justify the Act. In particular, it can be argued that private concerns are more efficient than their public sector counterparts, and that they have a better understanding of the needs of customers. Furthermore, if they are unsuccessful, they are forced to shut down and cannot expect to be cross-subsidised. In most cases they are subject to the forces of competition, especially when contracts come up for renewal.

However, elements of monopoly do exist in the private sector, and quality is not always satisfactory, so contracting-out is not a panacea for all ills. Nevertheless, competitive tendering should ensure improved efficiency, even if the contract is awarded in-house,

362

provided the tendering process is above-board, although monitoring of quality is obviously of the essence.

The 1988 Act was concerned with refuse collection, building cleaning, street cleaning, grounds maintenance, schools and welfare catering, sports and leisure management and vehicle maintenance. The Act applied to contracts above a specified value, fixed their length and the minimum number of tenders to be achieved, and sought to outlaw anti-competitive practices. It did not forbid the use of DSOs as such, but required them to be operated commercially.

The Local Government Act 1992 extended compulsory competitive tendering to local authority white-collar services, operative, in principle, as from April 1994. An innovation was the proposed introduction of a quality threshold such that low-priced bids below such a threshold could be rejected. This remains controversial because it is not considered to be appropriate for central government to specify quality. On the other hand, if it does not do so then it allows local authorities to bias contracts in favour of their DSOs.

A complicating factor is the existence since 1 July 1993 of the EC Public Service Contracts Directive which may oblige local authorities to put out their largest contracts to tender across the EC (Carnaghan and Bracewell-Milnes, 1993 p.38).

The eventual scale of competitive tendering is accordingly hard to estimate. At the present time tenders worth roughly £2 billion a year are being offered. The private sector has had variable success in winning these contracts. Roughly one in three local authorities have yet to award a single contract to a private company, but those that have offered refuse-collecting contracts have awarded them to private companies in the great majority of cases although the proportion is much lower for all other services.

Just how big a saving has been achieved is hotly disputed, although there can be no doubt that some savings have been forthcoming, and at the very least DSOs have been obliged to examine their working practices if only to hold at bay the pressure for privatization (Carnaghan and Bracewell-Milnes, 1993 chap.4).

Competitive Tendering in the NHS

Compulsory competitive tendering in the NHS was introduced in 1983, and was therefore a fairly early Thatcherite initiative (Carnaghan and Bracewell-Milnes, 1993 pp.116-25). As such, it was inevitably somewhat speculative, and in practice, as noted by the National Audit Office, it has not been a conspicuous success. The explanation for this can be found, in particular, in the discretion allowed to those responsible for the contracts, since they were enabled, for example, to reject low private sector bids on the grounds that an acceptable quality of provision could not be delivered at the tendered price.

They were also in a position to discourage private contractors, for example by the insertion of stiff penalty clauses in contracts. Furthermore, the Department of Health has shown little inclination to insist upon a re-tender, leaving contractors free to bend the rules. Ironically, the change in the law resulted in a reduction in the number of laundry service contracts being awarded externally, and hospital canteens effectively remain a no-go area for private contractors. In any event, where private contractors have won tenders, they have usually taken on the existing workforce, albeit on less-attractive terms than previously. Hence, although savings have been made (Parker and Hartley, 1990), they have undoubtedly been more modest than was anticipated a decade ago.

Market Testing and Civil Service Agencies

Despite its widespread introduction into local authority circles, market-testing met with strong resistance in the corridors of Whitehall. It had its origins in the *Competing for Quality* document (Cm 1730) issued in November 1991. Within a year, a White Paper had been issued by William Waldegrave which contained a hugely ambitious masterplan. Instead of the original £25 million of services to be market-tested in 1992, some £1.5 billion were to be market-tested in 1993. Unfortunately, this plan took insufficient account both of the administrative implications of such a figure and of the absence of the wholehearted support of the affected parties. In spite of this, it was announced in March 1993 that market-testing would be extended to Quangos at the end of the year.

Staff already doing the jobs in question are encouraged to tender for the contracts, either as an in-house team or through a management buy-out. Where they are successful, they are required to meet service specifications and performance agreements, giving details of the standard of work, methods of monitoring and enforcement of the agreement.

Irrespective of whether contracts are won internally, projected savings are expected to be of the order of 25 per cent. Given that the savings achieved in respect of local authority tendering are typically in the 5 to 10 per cent range, this seems a mite optimistic. Certainly, given the labour-intensive nature of most of the services identified for market-testing, such savings can only be forthcoming through redundancies, thereby guaranteeing the wholehearted opposition of most of the civil service.

The increased scale of the market-testing programme brought within its compass a new range of services, to include:

- Professional and specialist services such as accounting, audit, design and project management.
- Executive and clerical operations such as payments of subsidies, payroll and bulk mailing.

- Office services such as data processing, records storage and retrieval and messenger services.
- Estate and construction services, including equipment maintenance and support.

This enhanced programme clearly failed to elicit the desired response since in June 1993 the Prime Minister was called upon to warn a number of Departments about their slow progress. At the time, the DTI, the Department for Education, the Scottish Office and the Department of Transport had failed to complete a single exercise. When the deadline was reached at the end of September 1993, William Waldegrave was obliged to admit that some £800 million of the overall £1.5 billion programme was still outstanding. Furthermore, savings were running at only 14 per cent of the value of the work compared to the 25 per cent predicted, and only £100 million had been saved compared to the target of £375 million.

Waldegrave responded with the claim that considerably more market-testing would shortly be completed, and that delays would be overcome. Arguably the most revealing statistic was, however, that in-house teams had won 57 per cent of the bids by value, and 91 of the 150 contracts awarded where there was a competition between the existing staff and outside contractors. Not surprisingly, private sector contractors alleged that tenders were often framed in such a way that they severely restricted the scope for using innovative ways to achieve savings, and that the tenders were invariably based upon short-term needs rather than longer-term objectives.

As was clearly noted, no private contractor had spare skilled personnel, and it was invariably necessary to transfer most of the existing workforce to the new contractor. These would often be unco-operative because there would be the expectation of subsequent redundancies. Equally, private contractors did not relish the role of taking on staff with a view to firing them, even if the costs were to be borne by the government.

A complicating factor in the above is the European Community *Acquired Rights Directive*. This protects workers' pay and conditions when they change employers, and has been translated into the *Transfer of Undertakings (Protection of Employment)* regulations under UK national law. The government originally claimed that the TUPE regulations applied only to transfers within the private sector, but it has been forced to accept that the European Court of Justice has, through recent rulings, extended the scope of TUPE to cover contracting-out of many, though by no means all, public services. In late-March 1993, a High Court ruling contradicted Home Office legal opinion that TUPE did not apply to the transfer of a prison education service in Manchester.

It is evident that hopes of major savings through market-testing are likely to be confounded if they are unavailable in respect of labour costs, and this has undoubtedly influenced the attitude of prospective private sector contractors. At one point it also appeared to be the case that it would not be possible to offer less favourable pension rights when employees were transferred, in accordance with the provisions of the Employment

Protection (Consolidation) Act 1978, effectively cutting off a further source of savings. However, a test case at the Employment Appeal Tribunal in July 1993 established that pensions were not covered by the Acquired Rights Directive.

This is by no means the only other difficulty to be overcome. Above all others currently looms the *Katsikas v Konstantinidis* judgement in the European Court of Justice, which involved an employee in a German restaurant who refused to transfer to a new owner and successfully claimed compensation from the previous owner. This issue lies outside the specific terms of TUPE, but that does not necessarily preclude a judgement in favour of an employee who is being transferred from a public sector organisation to a private concern. Were such an employee subsequently to make a claim against the relevant public sector redundancy scheme it would obviously discourage public sector bodies from effecting such transfers.

The situation remains ambiguous for the time being. In October 1993 the government issued TUPE guidance notes to local authorities which state that if a local authority obtains legal advice to the effect that TUPE applies, but a tender assumes that it does not, the contractor should be invited to resubmit the bid. If such an invitation is refused, the authority can reject it irrespective of whether it is the cheapest.

In the meantime the reshaping of the civil service proceeds apace. In the quest to introduce the entrepreneurial spirit into the corridors of power, the *Next Steps* initiative was introduced in 1988 in order to create quasi-autonomous executive agencies. In August 1993 there were 91 in existence, each with its own chief executive who has a direct line to the relevant Minister, and a further 20 candidates were identified at that time. The full programme should be identified by January 1994. These agencies, in conjunction with the equivalent bodies within Customs and Excise and the Inland Revenue, will at that time employ roughly two thirds of all civil servants.

Agencies are not fully autonomous since the Treasury and spending departments are understandably reluctant to release their control over such a significant slab of public spending. Civil servants are themselves unhappy about the employment implications of agencies, in particular about the limitations which these may impose upon their careers. Misgivings are also expressed about the limited degree of autonomy that agencies enjoy in practice.

Agencies are heavily involved in market-testing activities. Indeed, some have become so commercially-minded that they operate like private sector concerns. At the end of 1993 the government announced that it intended to privatise as many as possible of the agencies. It is difficult to forecast how far and how fast this will progress in practice, particularly since most are tied so closely to the activities of spending departments. In the meantime, the National Audit Office, in its 1993 Annual Report, has expressed reservations about the effects of civil service reforms on standards of public honesty and accountability.

User Charges

User charges have long been familiar to the general public in the form of prescription charges which have been in continuous use since 1968. During the 1980s these were raised much faster than inflation, and are shortly set to rise again. However, exemptions are wide-ranging and other NHS expenditure has also risen rapidly, so user charges have tended to finance a falling proportion of that expenditure. It is also of interest that health service user charges are in common use throughout the EC, and are applied to a wide range of services. The UK general public accordingly stand more or less alone in their determined resistance to the extension of fees for health services.

Even Mrs Thatcher could do very little to break down this resistance, so it is unsurprising that the government has preferred to switch to softer, but less remunerative alternatives. Some have involved charges to the public, such as entry fees to museums and historical sites, and some to private concerns such as weather forecasts and agricultural testing. Although demand has been discouraged, it has stood up better than might have been expected and the government has been pleased with the amount of revenue raised.

The agency programme has involved the sale of a wide array of services. Some agencies such as the Ordnance Survey, as noted above, have become largely self-financing. A common practice has been the introduction of charges for reproduction of copyright material. Many of these services are sold by one agency to another via a system of internal markets as exemplified by the Property Services Agency. Where an agency is fully self-financing it can be converted into a trading fund similar to the Royal Mint before being subject to a privatization feasibility study. It is of interest that after the successful sale of the Royal Ordnance to British Aerospace the government failed to exploit its success with other similar sales.

Public/Private Co-operative Ventures

Shortly after its election in 1979 the government pondered the thorny question as to how to encourage capital investment without recourse to public expenditure. Its solution was the introduction of the *Ryrie rules* which contained a 'non-additionality' principle such that private funding would replace, rather than be additional to, public spending. Unfortunately, it was also determined that the price tendered by private concerns would have to undercut that fixed by public sector organisations, even though the latter had access to finance at below-market level interest rates. As a result very little was achieved.

Subsequently, the privatization programme served to reduce the Treasury's financing obligations in respect of Associated British Ports, BAA, British Airways and other companies in the transport sector. Nevertheless, with the railways and road building programme remaining a severe drain on public investment funds, the Treasury was obliged to scrap the Ryrie rules in 1989, and this was shortly followed by a Department of Transport document entitled 'New Roads by New Means' which authorised private sector involvement in toll roads.

The 1992 Autumn Statement went further in stating that where private concerns are responsible for government-approved projects and are able to recoup the cost through charges at the point of use, the Treasury will not apply a value-for-money test against a theoretical public sector alternative. However, the problem remains that they must first stand prepared to take responsibility. In the Autumn Statement the government asserted that in principle it was happy to invite private sector participation in joint ventures provided there was a 'sensible' sharing of risks. What was proposed was that the government would specify its contribution in terms of money and risk and invite participation via open competition. However, the private sector would have to accept the risks involved, yet these were often difficult to assess, especially where public funding had previously been the norm, so private concerns were likely to be hesitant.

An interesting illustration relates to the Channel Tunnel rail link. This £2.5 billion project appears to provide an ideal joint venture, since it offers a commercial return. However, the private sector will not meet the full cost, and it was originally accepted that the government could justify investing £1 billion because of the wider benefits, especially to commuters. It has now changed its mind, in apparent contradiction to the *private finance initiative* which ex-Chancellor Lamont referred to in May as 'potentially as important to Britain in the 1990s as privatization was in the 1980s.'

In September 1993, Chancellor Clarke listed 78 joint projects under the initiative. However, 43 of these, including the rail link, are merely proposals, and if the rail link dies the death so may many others. A key difficulty is that if a private contractor devises a desirable project, it must still go out to tender and may end up being built by another company. A recent Treasury paper on competition accordingly promises to reimburse tendering costs in some such circumstances and 'in certain exceptional cases' to relax the requirement for competition.

The government's line on risk is that it must be borne by the private sector but that, provided the project offers value for money, it has no objection to a high rate of profit being earned. Unfortunately, voters may take a less sanguine view and may object very strongly to sizeable tolls which end up in the coffers of private concerns. For this reason the government prefers to move slowly, yet this serves to create a general air of disenchantment among those concerns that are keen to bid, at least for now.

In March 1993, the Environment Minister announced a number of schemes which would involve handing over land for commercial development to private investors who would be able to use profits from property development to help pay for infrastructure investments.

Alternatively, local authority capital receipts could be used as a subsidy, or monies from other agencies. It has been indicated that a private developer of a road tunnel under the Tyne would be allowed to use tolls from the existing tunnel to help pay for its construction. This is a similar arrangement to that used recently for the Dartford Bridge across the Thames.

The Citizen's Charter

In July 1991, the government published a White Paper entitled *The Citizen's Charter* (Cm 1599). It was described as 'the most comprehensive programme ever to raise quality, increase choice, secure better value and extend accountability. It will ensure that quality of service to the public and the new pride it will give to those who work in the public services will be a central theme of government policy for the 1990s.'

In excess of 80 proposals were put forward for improving the quality of public services. Some involved privatization, as in the case of British Rail, while others were concerned with recognising achievement, as in the case of the award of a chartermark. At the heart of the White Paper lay the promise that the public should not merely expect to be kept informed about the kind of service to which they were entitled, but also to be provided with the means to take remedial action should that service not be of an acceptable quality.

The first twenty charters appeared within a year of the publication of the White Paper. In principle, all are equally important. However, the Charter programme will essentially be seen either as success or failure depending upon how it deals with the treatment of parents and schools, rail passengers and NHS patients.

The Parent's Charter is concerned with the provision of information concerning the performance of individual pupils and schools. In November 1992, the initial GCSE exam league tables were published, and were immediately criticised both for inaccuracy and for failing to take account of different pupil capabilities when entering different schools. Information on truancy rates will shortly be forthcoming, and will be followed by information on success in getting pupils into higher and further education.

The arguments about how to interpret the data are unlikely to subside. Undoubtedly, it is unreasonable to expect an inner ciy school to perform as well as one in the suburbs. Nevertheless, in practice some of the most striking discrepancies appear when comparing schools in the same area.

Rail passengers have most to gain directly from the Passenger's Charter since British Rail is obliged to pay compensation where trains fail to meet reliability and punctuality targets. On the other hand, the targets are adjusted to take account of the previous record on a given line, and compensation is not particularly generous when measured against the potential loss which might arise when a journey is seriously delayed. At the beginning of

1993, it was revealed that InterCity routes had a poor record for punctuality, and season ticket holders accordingly received 5 per cent discounts on most routes.

The Patient's Charter promised, in particular, that no one should have to wait more than two years for treatment once they were on a hospital waiting list. In March 1991 there were in excess of 50,000 such patients, but these no longer remained a year later. This was countered by the criticism that the time was only recorded after entering a list, so it could be reduced by delays in so doing, and that all that had happened was an expansion of the queue waiting between one and two years. On the other hand, things had improved somewhat compared to previously.

The publication of a White Paper in November 1992 claimed that roughly 90 per cent of the targets set in July 1991 either had been met or were on course to be met, with British Rail as the main source of failures. There are currently some thirty charters in existence, and the thrust of the initiative has accordingly switched from increasing the number in existence to strengthening those already in operation. This is probably as well since well in excess of £2 million has been paid out in compensation so far.

Conclusion

This necessarily brief overview nevertheless demonstrates that the privatization programme is alive and kicking despite the virtual cessation of asset sales. However, it is evident from the above that it has been no easier to move into the 'privatizing choice' phase of privatization than it was initially to generate asset sales, and recent survey evidence indicates that the general public is as yet unconvinced that they have gained anything substantial from ventures such as the Citizen's Charter.

The government has arguably attached too much importance to the new programme, given the probability of teething problems. Some, in particular the impact of Community directives, could not reasonably have been predicted, but there was unlikely to be much co-operation from those adversely affected, and Mr Major may discover that his epitaph makes little reference to the Charter or other aspects of the new programme.

Bibliography

Carnaghan, R. and Bracewell-Milnes, B. (1993) *Testing the Market. Competitive Tendering for Government Services in Britain and Abroad.* Research Monograph 49 (IEA).

Curwen, P. (1994) *UK Privatization: A Practical Guide* (Ernst & Young).

De Groot, C. (1993) 'The Council Directive in the Safeguarding of Employees' Rights in the Event of Transfers of Undertaking: An Overview of the Case Law', *Common Market Law Review* 331-50.

Domberger, S., Meadowcroft, S. and Thompson, D (1987) 'The Impact of Competitive Tendering on the Costs of Hospital Domestic Services', *Fiscal Studies, 8* (4) 39-54.

Dunsire, A. (1990) 'The Public/Private Debate: Some United Kingdom Evidence', *International Review of Administrative* Sciences, 56 (1) 63-78.

Gormley, J. and Grahl, J. (1988) 'Competition and Efficiency in Refuse Collection: A Critical Comment', *Fiscal Studies, 9* (1) 80-85.

Hartley, K. and Huby, M. (1985) 'Contracting Out in Health and Local Authorities: Prospects, Progress and Pitfalls', *Public Money, 5* (2) 23-6.

Marsh, D. (1991) 'Privatisation Under Mrs Thatcher. A Review of the Literature', *Public Administration, 69* (4) 459-80.

Parker, D. (1990) 'The 1988 Local Government Act and Compulsory Competitive Tendering', *Urban Studies, 27* (5) 653-68.

Parker, D. and Hartley, K. (1990) 'Competitive Tendering: Issues and Evidence', *Public Money and Management* (Autumn) 9-16.

The Citizen's Charter (Cm 1599, July 1991).

Competing For Quality (Cm 1730, November 1991).

The Next Steps Agencies - Review 1992.

	79-81	81-82	82-83	83-84	84-85	85-86	86-87	87-88	88-89	89-90	90-91	91-92	92-93 est[2]
Amersham International plc		64											
Associated British Ports Holdings plc			46		51								
BAA plc								534	689				
British Aerospace plc	43				347								
British Airways plc							435	419					
British Gas plc - sale of shares							1820	1758	1555	4	150		
British Gas - redemption of debt								750	250	800	350		350
British Petroleum plc	276	8		543				863[3]	3030[3]	1363			
British Steel plc									1138	1287			
British Sugar Corporation		44											
British Telecom. plc													
- sale of shares					1358	1246[4]	1081					1666	3520
- loan stock					44	61	53	23	85	92	100	106	
- redemption of preference shares							250	250	250				
Britoil plc			334[5]	293		426							113
BTG												24	
Cable and Wireless plc		181		263		577							
Electricity industries													
- sale of shares (England and Wales)										3134	2329		1457
- sale of shares (Scotland)											1112		825
- redemption of debt											1106		110
Enterprise Oil plc					384								
Forestry Commission			14	21	28	15	16	13	12	15	11	16	14
General Practice Finance Corporation									67				
Harland and Wolff										8			
Insurance Services Group												12	
Land Settlement				2	12	5	2				1		
Motorway Service Area leases			4	1			2	1		2	5	5	5
National Enterprise Board Holdings	120	2			168	30	34						
National Freight Consortium		5[6]											
National Transcommunications Ltd												70	
Northern Ireland Electricity													350
Privatised companies' debt													1337
Professional and Executive Recruitment									5				
Plant Breeding Institute								65[7]					
Rolls-Royce plc								1029	3				
Rover Group plc										150[8]			
Royal Ordinance plc								186					
Short Brothers										30			
Water plcs													
- sale of shares										423	1487	1483	
- redemption of debt										73			
Wytch Farm								18			130		
Miscellaneous[9]	148	189	57	15	4	-2	-4	-2	-13	-23	-22	-6	-81
Total	587[10]	493[10]	455	1139	2050	2706	4458	5140	7069	4226	5346	7923	8000

Table 1

Privatisation proceeds[1], outturn 1979-80 to outturn 1992-93 (£'000,000).

[1] Excludes proceeds from sales of subsidiaries which were retained by the parent industry.

[2] Figures are only given for individual privatizations which have already taken place and for which estimates of the proceeds were available in time for inclusion in this Supplement. Proceeds for other sales are all included under miscellaneous.

[3] Net of the cost of acquiring partly-paid shares under the support arrangements announced by the Chancellor on 29 October 1987.

[4] Includes some third instalments (worth £87 million approx) paid early.

[5] Includes repayments of debentures of £88 million with interest.

[6] £49 million of the £54 million proceeds paid into the pension fund to cover a deficit.

[7] The central government sector received £65 million but only £27 million was paid to the Consolidated Fund.

[8] Does not take into account the cost of deferring payments of consideration.

[9] Includes expenses which could not be netted off the associated sale because they arose in a financial year in which there were no proceeds from that sale. See also footnote 2.

[10] Excludes certain advance oil payments which net out to zero (1979-80: £622 million, 1980-81: minus £49 million and 1981-82: minus £573 million)

Source: Statistical Supplement to the 1992 Autumn Statement, Table 8.4

THE CITIZEN'S CHARTER PROGRAMME: AN EVALUATION, USING HIRSCHMAN'S CONCEPTS OF 'EXIT' and 'VOICE'.

Robert Jones, Sheffield Business School.

Introduction

The literature of administrative thought is now so rich and diverse that there is a veritable Aladdin's cave of perspectives from which to choose on the subject of public sector reform (Lane, 1993). However, in the case of the Citizen's Charter programme, one particular set of ideas seem almost tailor-made for use as an evaluative measure, namely Albert Hirschman's concepts of *exit* and *voice* (Hirschman, 1970). According to official statements, the Charter programme seeks to promote citizen empowerment and public service responsiveness, entailing a shift in power from public service deliverers to public service users. In the words of John Major, "for too long the provider has dominated: now it is the turn of the user" (Citizen's Charter, 1992).

The principal aims of the Charter are to improve quality in public services, to give people more choice, to ensure that citizens know what kind of service they can expect and know what to do when things go wrong. But will the Charter programme lead to significant improvements in the public services, or to the 'empowerment' of public service users? Naturally, each of these questions raises fundamental issues of definition, concerning what is meant by the laudatory concepts of 'empowerment', and 'service improvement'. The ideas developed in Hirschman's seminal work on exit and voice may help us to clarify what is meant by the above terms, and should also provide useful insights into the Charter's prospects of success.

Hirschman's Typology

Hirschman sought to clarify the types of choice available to dissatisfied members or clients of organisations. By *exit* is meant leaving the organisation (if a member) or taking one's

375

custom elsewhere (if a client). By *voice* is meant expressing dissatisfaction with the organisation (with the aim of changing, rather than escaping from it): for a client, this would principally mean complaining about poor service. In classical economic theory, users of services have the option to withdraw from a specific relationship by taking their custom elsewhere. Hirschman argues that there is another possibility, namely that disgruntled customers will express dissatisfaction with the service (that is, will give voice to their complaints). By using this seemingly crude (but in practice very useful) dichotomy, Hirschman examines the range of possibilities available to dissatisfied members or clients. A.H.Birch (1975) and other commentators have elaborated on other possibilities, such as to exit and give voice or to remain and not complain (to suffer in silence).

The latter possibility has frequently been cited as typifying the behaviour of users of many public services. Silent loyalty of this kind can, of course, be interpreted in various ways: for example, it could spring either from strong commitment to the organisation or from a feeling of resignation that exit is impossible and that giving voice is futile.

The exit possibilities of users of services will be determined by a number of factors, such as loyalty; the feasibility of alternatives (taking account of such factors as service quality, price, accessibility and waiting time); the adequacy of information about these alternatives; the search costs involved in investigating the alternatives; clients' assessments of the possibility of improvements in the service; the costs involved in exiting from a specific relationship; and the extent of customer loyalty.

Voice possibilities will also be determined by several factors such as loyalty; the ease of exit; the effectiveness of the formal complaints machinery; and the costs in exercising voice (for example, the possibility of retaliation by the organisation, the time expended or the nervous strain incurred). The effectiveness of voice will also be determined by several factors relating to organisational responsiveness, such as the quality of the complaints machinery and the potential power of complainants (that is, whether or not complaints can result in penalties for poor service, such as compensation or fear of public exposure).

Put bluntly, the extent of exit and voice possibilities determines an individual's (or group's) power relative to an organisation. For the client, the greater the chances of easy exit, and the greater the possibility of effective voice, the better, because the organisation will need to take account of clients' reactions to the services provided. A central assumption of Hirschman's theory is that there is a link between organisational performance and the strength of exit and voice possibilities.

Although the government does not use Hirschman's terminology, the Citizen's Charter programme is, according to official statements, about improving exit possibilities and amplifying voice for the users of public services. The central proposition of this paper is that the Charter programme has not yet led to a genuine and significant improvement in exit and voice for dissatisfied clients of public services. It will be argued that the Charter

376

programme, although the most widely advertised of recent public sector reforms in the UK (which admittedly is not saying much,), could well prove to be one of the least important in terms of its significance.

Exit And Voice Possibilities in the UK Public Services.

A fundamental axiom of free market capitalism is that the discipline of the market provides a major stimulus to organisational efficiency and effectiveness. The organisation will be kept on its toes by the threat of losing customers, or by the threat of adverse comparisons, which could inflict possible damage to its public image. Conversely, the assumption of 'client powerlessness' has been central to the modern critique of public service bureaucracies.

The exit possibilities for clients of many public services are constrained by several crucial factors: first, by the coercive powers of the state, which imposes certain obligations on citizens such as the payment of income tax or of council tax (in practice, there are no exit doors); secondly, by the virtual absence of practicable alternatives as exemplified by the limited availability of school places or of medical services (there are long queues at the exit doors); thirdly, by the cost of pursuing alternatives (such as additional travel costs to a new school, or the time and effort required to identify and pursue alternatives - payments must be made for use of exit doors).

In theory, at least, the voice possibilities available to clients of public services exercising voice have traditionally been stronger than those of exit. There is an elaborate redress of grievance procedure within the public sector, which, although poorly coordinated (and in fact consisting of sets of different grievance procedures) provides dissatisfied clients of public services with access to formal machinery for dealing with complaints. However, as with exit possibilities, voice possibilities are also severely constrained in practice by several factors such as knowledge of (and faith in) the complaints machinery, accessibility and the costs of using the machinery.

The complaints machinery within British public services has traditionally been geared towards settling disputes over entitlements (for example, to social security benefits or to tax exemptions) rather than to complaints about poor service as such (for example, about train delays, dirty compartments, discourteous service or delay in responding to correspondence). There is, of course, an official machinery for voicing complaints about the quality of specific public services, principally through the consumer councils and community health councils. However, these are bodies about which most users of public services have little, if any, knowledge. The effectiveness of this machinery is also generally thought to be very limited, not least because of the limited powers possessed by the 'consumer watchdogs'.

There are also other factors which, in practice, limit the exercise of voice in relation to the public services. First, the scale of the grievance is often too small for most people to go to the trouble of lodging a complaint. Secondly, clients may have a negative perception of the responsiveness of the public service, and therefore a low expectation that the complaint would make much difference. Thirdly, clients often do not have the information on which to base comparative judgements about services. Finally, public services have not generally devoted significant resources to policies designed to encourage and facilitate user 'feedback'.

In short, exit and voice possibilities in the public services have traditionally left much to be desired: but will the Citizen's Charter make much difference?

Background to the Programme.

Although no specific aspect of the Charter programme is new, it has been presented by the current government as a major policy initiative. According to the Minister of Public Services, William Waldegrave, it is "one of the most radical things we have ever tried to do" (*The Independent*, 21 July 1992). It is the only specific policy attributed directly to John Major, and has been dubbed Major's 'big idea' (*Financial Times*, 19 June 1991). Mr Major has affirmed that the programme will remain at the centre of the government's decision-making throughout the 1990s, and will become "an important part of everyday life for everyone" (Citizen's Charter, 1992). There is a Charter Unit within the Cabinet Office, with 27 staff, a budget of £24 million, plus a panel of 10 advisers reporting to the Prime Minister. The fact that the programme has the strong personal support of the Prime Minister may serve to ensure that it will continue to be given a high profile in the government's strategy.

As testament to the fact that the Citizen's Charter is regarded as a good idea in principle, all three main political parties squabble over its paternity, and all published draft Charters prior to the 1992 election. The Charter concept has been traced back by the Labour party to policies adopted by Labour-run local authorities, such as York and Milton Keynes which in the 1980s introduced customer contracts for some services (*The Economist*, 31 October 1992). As early as 1985, Neil Kinnock spoke of the need to set clear targets and standards for local authorities. Liberal-Democrats cite Paddy Ashdown's *Citizen's Britain* book in 1988 as providing a precursory case for a Citizen's Charter. Conservatives point to ideas developed by right-wing think-tanks, such as the Institute of Economic Affairs and the Adam Smith Institute, and to innovatory policies in central government, such as the Inland Revenue's Taxpayers' Charter of Rights (July 1986), and the codification of the rights of tenants against their landlords.

The versions of the Charter offered by the three main parties reflect in some measure wider policy commitments. The Labour and Liberal-Democrat Charters have a stronger commitment to freedom of information and to the legally enforceable rights of citizens than does the Conservatives' Charter. Labour's own Charter, published in 1991, promised a 'quality revolution' in public services and an extension of rights, including consumers' rights, rights to information, a right of equal treatment and Ombudsmen for all public services. However, the Labour document excluded a commitment to competitive tendering. The Liberal-Democrats' Charter, published in 1991, included policies on proportional representation, devolution, freedom of information and a bill of rights and entitlements to housing, health and education.

In the form in which it has been introduced in the UK, the Charter programme is unmistakably a product of the Thatcher years, and is part of the corpus of ideas which has led to the transformation of the British public sector since 1979. It has many identifiable antecedents in reforms of the public sector in the UK and the US in the 1980s. Osborne and Gaebler (1992), and Lan and Rosenbloom (1992), have perceived a major reorientation in American public administration, involving a search for greater public service efficiency and effectiveness, through a shift in organisational culture from 'programme-oriented' to 'mission-driven', 'results-oriented' government . A similar effort to transform the orientation of the public service culture can be observed in the UK, at least if Ministerial pronouncements are taken at their face value. Borrowing terminology from Osborne and Gaebler, William Waldegrave describes recent reforms as being aimed at 'reinventing government' and at introducing an 'entrepreneurial spirit' into the heart of government (*The Independent*, 21 July 1992).

The Citizen's Charter programme is misleadingly named, in that it is not a charter of rights for citizens, but rather for the clients and customers of specific public services. The term 'Client's (or Consumer's) Charter' would therefore be more accurate. The Charters have many features in common, in that they specify performance standards and targets and seek to provide people with indicators of what they should reasonably expect from public services as well as information to improve and extend the range of choice available to citizens. In addition, they commit the organisation's staff to courteous and efficient service and seek to improve means of redress available to aggrieved citizens.

In a general sense, the Charter programme, comprising 150 initiatives to be introduced over 10 years, is about improving the quality of public services and empowering the users of those services. According to William Waldegrave, it puts pressure on public services to "treat customers well, and calls them to account if they do not" (*The Independent*, 21 July 1992). More specifically, it embraces a raft of measures, such as finding more effective ways of delivering services; setting performance targets, with explicit obligations to meet those targets; improving incentives and penalties; making public services more responsive to their users; setting standards and acting swiftly and effectively when things go wrong; and where possible providing compensation to consumers for poor service. The principles of the Charter extend to all public services. They also cover ex-public utilities, such as gas and electricity. By March 1994, 36 Charters had been published, and plans were well advanced to publish more Charters and to extend existing Charters into new areas.

Facilitating Exit and Amplifying Voice?

In this section, an attempt is made to evaluate the prospects of the programme, by examining its implications for the users of public services, from the perspective of exit and voice. Citizens need information upon which to base sound exit or voice decisions. The provision of information should not be regarded as an end in itself, but rather as a means to facilitate impacts. For example, information should encourage users to think about service standards, and should also provide a primary stimulus to improvements in organisational performance. The Charter emphasises that citizens should be better informed about the standards of service they have a right to expect from public organisations, and about the remedies available if standards fall below an acceptable level. However, the extent of public knowledge about the Charter programmes remains very low, as recent surveys by the National Consumer Council and the *Financial Times* have shown (*Financial Times*, 14 March 1994). This may well be because there appears to be no central idea at the heart of the Charter programme, which seems to be comprised largely of recycled public service schemes. The setting up of a Citizen's Charter 'hotline' (*Charterline*) to provide information on the Charters may be a useful measure, but is hardly likely to bridge this yawning gap in public knowledge.

The Charter programme raises a number of fundamental questions about performance evaluation, that is, about what is being evaluated, who is to do the evaluating and what is to be done with the evaluations. Ultimately, the Charter can only be regarded as successful if it results in genuine improvements in the quality of public services. These improvements hinge on several requirements: on the production of performance data of sufficient quantity and quality for users of public services to be able to make reasoned judgements about the quality of those services; on presentation of the data in such a way as to elicit a response from users (that is, do they know or care about specific performance data?); on the service providers being sensitive to information concerning the reactions of service users (that is, does the organisation listen?). In addition to assessing weaknesses in service provision, the organisation must be able to address these weaknesses. For example, knowing what is wrong is of little use unless the organisation possesses both the inclination and the capacity to put things right. None of the Charter measures address this central problem of resource incapacity in relation to the public services.

The Audit Commission has asserted that, by December 1994, local citizens will have a considerable amount of information about the performance of local services, based on national league tables which the Commission will produce. The tables will be based on 152 questions which local authorities, police services and fire services must answer. The league tables will disclose how much each authority spends on education per capitum and so forth.

Even if public service users have comparative performance tables at their disposal, will this data prove to be as valuable an evaluative tool as the architects of the Charter programme appear to think? The first official performance league tables for schools raised many issues relating to the accuracy and fairness of the data. It may be argued that all they revealed is where the middle classes live. This is not, of course, to deny the potential value of such tables, but it is probable that they will always need to be treated with some measure of caution (not least because, far from being mere academic exercises, they are supposed to influence exit and voice decisions). According to William Waldegrave, publication of league tables for schools "gives parents the knowledge to use their power to choose" (Waldegrave, 1994).

A 'badge of excellence' in the delivery of public services, known as a *Charter Mark*, and achieved through open competition, has also been introduced. An advisory panel, currently chaired by Sir James Blyth, Chief Executive of Boots, selects up to 50 winners a year. The winners receive a trophy and the right to use the Charter Mark logo on stationary and publicity material for three years. Winners must have demonstrated measurable improvements in quality of service in the last two years, and have developed plans for a cost-free improvement. The Charter Mark is hardly sufficient proof that the organisation is delivering excellent services 'across the board'. There seems to have been more than an element of arbitrariness, and perhaps even of superficiality, in award decisions so far. Sound decisions concerning exit and voice can hardly be expected to spring from so flimsy a base.

Although the architects of the programme seem keen to play down (or even ignore) the cost implications of the Charter programme, these should not be underestimated. Perhaps the reason why these cost implications can be disregarded is that many of the 'rights' established in the Charters merely codify existing service provisions but, if the programme is to be taken seriously, resources need to be devoted to information gathering, target-setting and self-monitoring activities. Several specific Charter 'rights', such as the right of access to personal files (the Council Tenant's Charter) or to provision for the special needs of disabled passengers, could involve substantial costs. In some cases, compensation costs for failure to meet performance standards are involved, although arguably these have been set far too low to have much impact on the organisation's finances.

It is clear that the Charter programme is expected to be run on the cheap, with its efficiency objectives achieved through downward pressure on costs: for example, performance related-pay schemes are expected to be introduced without adding to budgets.

Implications For Exit.

The exit possibilities enhanced by the Charter may be divided into two main categories. First, there are measures which lead to an increase in the number of exit doors, such as through the liberalisation of rail and postal services or increased competition between schools or hospitals. Secondly, there are measures which lower the costs of exit, thereby expanding the range of effective choice. According to John Redwood, the former Corporate Affairs Minister, the Citizen's Charter is about facilitating "choice in the public services in the market place" (*Financial Times*, 21 June 1991). But are there really greater possibilities of exit? There is no evidence that the Charter has significantly increased choice in any of the public services, and precious little evidence to suggest that it will do so in the future. Only in the provision of information has much progress been made, and we have already noted that this is a necessary, but not a sufficient, condition for exit.

In the vital fields of health, education, welfare or transport the Citizen's Charter programme has made virtually no impact on the range of choice available to citizens. The publication of performance league tables might be said to increase competition between schools, although perhaps more in relation to institutional reputation and image rather than competition for pupils. School places or hospital beds are not, and never will be, equivalent to goods on market stalls, despite the availability of comparative performance data. The Post Office's letter monopoly will be reduced by allowing private firms to compete more directly with the Post Office. British Rail's monopoly is also in the process of being reduced. However, it remains to be seen to what extent choice will thereby be enhanced.

Attempts to widen the range of choice available to clients may well have plausible justification in relation to some public services. However, choice objectives are clearly not relevant to them all. For example, is exit relevant to the ambulance, fire or police services? Madsen Pirie, President of the Adam Smith Institute, has argued that the Charter is not about increasing competition, because most of the public services do not operate in competitive environments. Rather, it is seeking to replicate what the private sector does 'naturally'. In his view it is about enhancing public service performance, and about giving customers better value, through making public services more responsive (*The Independent*, 30 June 1992). In other words, it is about finding ways of achieving levels of efficiency and effectiveness in the public services which are comparable to those achieved by private sector organisations, but by different means, such as targeting and performance-related pay (see below).

There seems scant justification for the official view that the Charter programme will improve choice for users of public services. Whatever its other supposed merits, the Charter, as presently constituted, is most unlikely to increase the number of exit doors significantly, nor will it lower significantly the costs of exit. The credibility of the Charter can only be further damaged by official pronouncements which stress the 'user choice' aspect of the programme.

Amplifying Voice

In the absence of any significant prospect for improving exit possibilities, the best hope for the Charter perhaps rests with the effects it has on voice options. Seeking redress currently has important cost implications for complainants in terms of their time and effort. The White Paper on the Charter said that a complaints task force would be established, to advise on how public access to complaints procedures might be improved. However, the programme does not promise a thorough overhaul of the machinery of redress, nor a Freedom of Information Act, both of which are urgently needed.

The prospect of compensation for poor service could prove to be a powerful incentive to the exercise of voice, and also to enhanced public service responsiveness. According to the Employer's Charter, clients who suffer an actual financial loss as a result of maladministration will be reimbursed. The Rail Passenger's Charter includes references to compensation for failure to meet targets for reliability or punctuality: rail passengers delayed for more than an hour on any leg of their rail journey will normally be offered vouchers to the value of 20 per cent or more of the price paid for that journey. If trains are delayed or cancelled, and as a result passengers decide not to travel, a full refund will be given in return for the ticket.

The compensation aspect of the Charter has received considerable publicity, but so far the results have been disappointing. There are many exemptions and omissions in the Charter's compensation arrangements. In the first year, less than 20,000 BR season ticket holders on 11 of the country's 46 routes qualified for rebates because their services failed to meet punctuality or reliability targets under the Passenger's Charter. British Rail paid out almost £5 million in compensation in 1993 (£3 million in season ticket discounts and £2 million in cash refunds). However, this is similar to the amount being paid prior to the launch of the Charter initiative. Moreover, in many cases, the compensation to be claimed (in the form of discounts on future travel) seems too small to justify the cost in time and effort. For most public services, compensation arrangements still do not exist (a *Financial Times* survey of 15 charters for England found that only 6 had compensation arrangements (*Financial Times*, 14 March 1994).

The Charter seeks a direct link between service standards and remuneration through performance-related pay, the assumption being that officials are far more likely to be kept on their toes, and to take complaints seriously, if they can be penalised for poor performance. At present, performance-related pay schemes have been applied mainly to senior managers (and by no means to all of those). Moreover, the schemes cover only a very small percentage of their total remuneration. In many (perhaps most) cases in the public sector, the principle of performance-related pay will prove to be extremely difficult, or even impossible, to apply on anything other than a token basis.

The Charter programme contains very few measures which amplify voice, or which provide public service users with opportunities to express opinions about public service standards. Moreover citizens are unlikely to avail themselves of opportunities for exercising voice unless they are reasonably confident that their views will be listened to and acted upon. Despite liberal use of the imagery of 'empowerment' in official publications on the Charter, the citizen's traditional role as a passive consumer of public services has not been significantly altered as a result of the programme.

Conclusion

The verdict on the Charter programme so far must be that it has promised far more than it has delivered. It is a good idea in principle, and has stimulated some useful debates about public service objectives and performance. However, it is less revolutionary in conception or impact than its proponents would have us believe, and is no panacea for the problems of the public services. It has not so far led to any significant increase in exit or voice possibilities for public service users and, as presently constituted, seems unlikely to do so. The first three years of the Charter programme hardly justify William Waldegrave's bold claim that the Charter has "begun to change the attitudes and culture of public service organisations" (Waldegrave, 1994). Given that no serious attempt is made in the Charter to address the question of resource inadequacy (the chronic imbalance between objectives and resources in relation to many public services), it is, perhaps, not surprising that it has generated so much public cynicism.

References

Birch, A. H. (1975) 'Economic Models In Political Science: The Case of Exit, Voice and Loyalty', *British Journal Of Political Science* (January) pp.65-82.

Burns, T. (1992), 'Researching Customer Service in the Public Sector', *Journal Of The Market Research Society* (January) pp.53-60.

Citizen's Charter (1992), *First Report* (London: HMSO).

Citizen's Charter (1994), *Second Report* (London: HMSO).

Doern, G. B. (1993) 'The UK Citizen's Charter: Origins and Implementation in Three Agencies', *Policy and Politics, 21* (1).

Hirschman, A. O. (1970) *Exit, Voice & Loyalty* (Cambridge, Mass: Harvard University Press).

Lan, Z. and Rosenbloom, D. (1992) 'Public Administration In Transition?', *Public Administration Review* (November-December) pp.535-7.

Lane, J-E. (1993) *The Public Sector: Concepts, Models and Approaches* (London: Sage Publications).

Osborne, D. and Gaebler, T. (1992) *Reinventing Government* (Reading, Mass: Addison Wesley).

Morley, D. (1992) 'The Citizen's Charter and a Twentieth Century Vision', *Public Money &Management* (January-March) pp.6-7.

Thompson, A. (1992) 'Public Sector Management in a Period of Rapid Change 1979-92', *Public Money & Management* (June-July).

Waldegrave, W. (1994) 'Citizen's Charter - half-way there?, *Financial Times* (17 March).

PRIVATISATION POLICY: A COMPARATIVE ANALYSIS OF THE PUBLIC-TO-PRIVATE PROGRAMME IN THE UK AND BULGARIA

Dimitar Ivanov, Luiz Montanheiro, Sonny Nwankwo and Bill Richardson, Sheffield Business School.

Introduction

In the late 1940s, the UK economy was subjected to a process of nationalisation due, in part, to the powerful arguments put forward in the writings of the 'Keynesian Economics' school. During this period, more far-reaching powers of government intervention into the workings of the market place were advocated. The argument for government's direct involvement in the management of economic infrastructure was based on the need to create a strong welfare state in Britain. By this was meant a more direct government influence on the provision of education, health care, family subsidies and utilities.

The 1980s marked a discernible shift in UK governmental policy towards intervention in economic markets generally and in 'utility' organisations specifically. The Conservative government of that era possessed an ideological commitment to a free- market mechanism and this underpinned a sweeping programme of privatisation of organisations which, prior to that time, had been in public ownership. The rationale behind this programme of privatisation was based on the belief that privately-owned organisations operating in free-market societies produce the following benefits by comparison with publicly-owned organisations:

- improved consumer responsiveness
- improved consumer satisfaction
- greater efficiency in organisational operations

Implicitly, too, the assumption underpinning the privatisation of UK public organisations was that these organisations might be expected to survive and grow based on the assumption that they would be able to compete successfully in their more competitive market places. Additionally, the Thatcher government espoused the merits of wider ownership of assets

389

through the distribution of shares in public organisations amongst the public. By bringing in more individual investors as well as institutions, the economy would hopefully create a progressive pattern of growth. The equity market for organisational stocks and shares was expected to react positively to privatisation flotations and this would in itself act as an impulse to propel the economy forward.

The programme of privatisation did generate some economic expansion in the UK in the latter part of the 1980s. Although the more recent decline in economic performance has raised questions about the validity of the policies of the 1980s, nevertheless Thatcherism has been held up as a model to be emulated by other governments, and Eastern Europe is presently a 'hot-bed' of free-market and privatisation developments. Only some specific public-to-private transitions in the UK can claim to have achieved the above-mentioned objectives.

Attempts to evaluate public-to-private transitionary phases serve a useful purpose if they identify the factors which have been instrumental in the achievement of successful transitions. Although few companies which came into existence through the UK privatisation programme seem able to assume the role of exemplars, one such company, British Telecom (BT), has been acknowledged by a number of commentators as a successful example of privatisation (see, for example, Richardson and Curwen, 1992; Richardson, Nwankwo and Curwen, 1993; Skeel, 1992).

This paper seeks to identify some of the important prerequisites to the British Telecom privatisation programme. A framework of success-generating characteristics might be useful as a means of evaluating the success potential of newer attempts at privatisation. In this paper we use the specific success factors of the BT privatisation case in the role of a more generally applicable model, and use this framework to compare and evaluate the approaches to privatisation being adopted in Bulgaria.

British Telecom: The UK's Privatisation Exemplar

Any government which thinks seriously about implementing a programme of privatisation should consider the overall effects caused by placing some of the utility companies into the hands of private owners. Telecommunications-based businesses, being part of an industry at the forefront of technological change (characterised by changing service availabilities through proliferation), can be very attractive to investors. It is, therefore, also relevant to explore the conditions which applied in the BT privatisation to draw out lessons for today's privatisation analysts and governmental strategists. Material in support of the claims that BT has been successful in terms of its ability to compete, improving operational productivity and customer service is available in the aforementioned references.

390

Factors Underpinning the Success of BT's Privatisation

In what follows we identify six important ingredients in the BT success equation:

1. Personal power and motivation to change existing systems - within a regulatory framework

Person-specific factors played significant roles in the privatisation of BT. In each of the following cases, positions, motivation and personal power were harnessed to achieving changes of the required order:

- Mrs. Thatcher, the then UK Prime Minister, personally propagated the belief that the 'government of business should not be the business of government.' Mrs. Thatcher's position as the primary 'change driver' was bolstered by her political strength (a substantial government majority in Parliament) and tenacious commitment to the goal of privatisation (Winward, 1989; Vickers and Yarrow, 1988).
- The Director-General of the Office of Telecommunications (DGT-OFTEL) and his personal, often proclaimed commitment to create greater market-place competitiveness - with the backing of regulatory powers. The DGT was given wide discretionary powers under the privatisation instrument and these powers were to become instrumental in shaping the change processes and outcomes of BT (see Carsberg, 1990).
- The Chief Executive Office (CEO) of BT (Iain Vallance) displayed considerable skill in and commitment to the creation of a new organisation (see, for example, Caulkin, 1987; Richardson, Nwankwo and Curwen, 1993).

2. A strong strategic position, an attractive market situation and a sound competitive strategy

The privatised BT emerged from a strong, monopolistic position in a market place which has demonstrated strong growth in demand over the years since privatisation (see Richardson and Curwen, 1992). BT's strength derives from its strategic position and corporate strategy - BT has 'stuck to its knitting' (Peters and Waterman, 1982) and concentrated on its stronghold in a growing market situation whereas, for example, some other privatised companies such as British Aerospace emerged from less-advantageous market situations and have diversified into markets which were on the downturn and very competitive.

391

Thus, the simple proposition which emerges from the above analysis is that, when market conditions, competitive strength and corporate strategy are favourable, a privatised organisation is likely to fare successfully.

3. A systematic and incremental process of privatisation

It is perhaps important to note that:

i) public corporations have been privatised, one-by-one except for the Water Companies and generators, in systematic fashion over the past decade in the UK.

ii) at individual organisational level, the move towards full privatisation has been undertaken incrementally, according to a schedule.

Thus, a 'big bang' approach to privatisation has not been attempted in the UK either at national or at organisational level. Rather, privatisations have been developed in a more or less planned way over a period of years.

4. A national culture which incorporates free market principles, structures, systems and behaviours

This point emphasised here is that, while the public corporations in the UK were not operated like privatised companies, they nevertheless operated in a system underpinned by the free market paradigm. Thus a move to the privatised form, although often painful at the individual level, was not a move into the unknown or into an ill-prepared system.

5. Managers required to manage the transition were conversant with, or expert in, the strategic management of competitive organisations

This success prerequisite follows from point 4 above. Existing BT management in the early days of the reorganisation of BT, although not skilled in managing a free market situation, were, nevertheless, aware of what is involved in so doing. A ready supply of skilled managers from outside the organisation has also been available to be recruited into the organisation in order to bolster its skills in commercial and competitive management.

Free-market situations demand free market skills and the UK's competitive market tradition undoubtedly helped the organisation develop and introduce the appropriate calibre of management to facilitate the transition and to manage the newly-competitive BT.

6. A ready supply of politically-acceptable 'owners' with capital available to invest

Each time BT shares have been made available to the public, the offer has been oversubscribed. The vast majority of these shares have gone to most influential institutions and UK-based private investors. Thus, at one and the same time, enough funds have been forthcoming to make the privatisation and the subsequent development of BT financially viable, and the investors making the funds available have been of a political tendency to lend the maximum support to government's ideology. It is unlikely, in the absence of this type of share take-up, that the UK government would have allowed a controlling interest to be acquired by a hostile foreign government.

The above points provide a six-point 'prerequisites of public to private success' which can be used as a checklist against which newer attempts to privatise successfully either in the UK or elsewhere can be evaluated. Competitive advantage (and economic success) is earned at the individual firm level (Porter, 1987). Hence, although the above checklist is most pertinently used in the context of specific organisational change situations, we will nevertheless apply it, in the next half of the paper, to a more general, national approach, namely the Bulgarian approach to privatisation. The aim in doing so is to generate insights into the actual and potential efficaciousness of the policies being adopted in the Bulgarian setting.

Bulgaria: An Insight into the Economic and Political Background

Geographically, Bulgaria is strategically located at the crossroads between Europe, Asia and the Middle East. Viewed against the rigorous excesses of Romania to the north, the fratricidal 1990s violence in Yugoslavia to the west and the confusion in what was formerly the Soviet Union, Bulgaria appears as an oasis of calm and good sense. Bulgaria is widely recognised as one of the more-progressive East European economies, offering opportunities in many important industrial sectors, including information technology, food processing and engineering. Fuelled by foreign credits, it had the fastest-growing economy in the COMECON family during the 1980s and the second-highest GDP. Bulgaria was the only country amongst the old COMECON members to be in a position to 'transform' peacefully. Recently, however, the trade embargo with Serbia, the former Yugoslavia country, has contributed to the general economic uncertainty of Bulgaria.

At the end of 1992, Bulgaria's first non-communist government since the war resigned under very strong parliamentary and national pressure, and at the present time (July 1993) there is a government which is not a coalition but which is under the influence of the

President of the Republic - Dr. Zhelyu Zhelev and the Movement for Freedom and Human Rights.

Bulgaria's record on attracting direct foreign investment has been disappointing thus far. In 1990, direct foreign investment based on balance-of-payments statistics averaged only $1 million per quarter. In 1991 it went up to $16 million per quarter. These investments, though not as large as hoped, have been to some extent instrumental in creating more than 150,000 private firms in Bulgaria since the beginning of the political changes. Most of these organisations are small, with less than 10 working people. Very often, these are family-based companies. Most of them engage in trading activities and offer a limited range of services.

Inflation (120 per cent for 1992 and about 50 per cent for the first six months of 1993) and unemployment (currently about 17.5 per cent) have continued to rise and almost all other economic indicators do not come up to the expectations of international financial organisations such as the International Monetary Fund (IMF) and the World Bank or, indeed, to the aspirations of the Bulgarian Government and its nationals. The Bulgarian economy is also saddled with a large foreign debt of about $1,400-1,500 per capitum.

There is no sign of any recovery in industrial production which, at the end of 1992, was 53-56 per cent below the level of 1990. The political and economic conditions of Bulgaria are, therefore, very controversial and difficult to predict. The implementation of economic reform is proceeding very slowly and western investors are hesitating, with sound reasons, before committing themselves to any level of financial support to Bulgaria.

The Bulgarian Experience of Privatisation

Under strong pressure from the IMF, the Privatisation Law in Bulgaria was passed in March 1992. This established the following rules:

- only workers in firms could buy shares.
- workers could buy shares only in their own firm.
- workers' share purchase capability was restricted to 20 per cent of the total equity of their firm, buyable at a discount of up to 50 per cent but not exceeding the value of one annual salary.
- there was no limit to the stake which institutional investors, banks or firms were able to buy.
- a Privatisation Agency was established to oversee the privatisation process. Six of the Agency's members were selected by Parliament and five by government. Neither these members nor their families were allowed to buy shares.

After some serious difficulties in implementing the above privatisation package together with some resignations from the Agency, a new structure was created for the public-to-private process in Bulgaria through the creation of the National Agency for Privatisation. This agency is a state authority which has among its aims the objective of organising and supervising the privatisation of large state-owned enterprises and the privatisation of several small/medium-sized organisations. The agency is responsible for the privatisation of those state-owned enterprises where the book value of fixed assets exceeds a particular value designated by the state. Enterprises which thus qualify for privatisation account for about 30 per cent of the state sector and employ around 70 per cent of the active labour force within this sector. In the first official declaration of the Agency's Supervisory Board, it was announced that the Agency would vigorously pursue the goal of privatisation and that it aimed to achieve the privatisation of about 25 per cent of the state-owned enterprises by the end of 1995. These plans entail a privatisation of about 20 Bulgarian firms every two months. Even with this schedule it will take ten years to privatise 1,200 enterprises, equivalent to roughly 28-30 per cent of all state-owned firms.

According to the *Transformation and Privatisation of State-Owned and Municipal-Owned Enterprises Act* in Bulgaria, a proposal for a decision to privatise any state-owned or municipally-owned enterprise may have originated from:

- the management bodies of any enterprise which has been transformed into a commercial partnership or of any untransformed enterprise.
- the staff of any commercial partnership or enterprise.
- the Privatisation Agency.

Having provided a sketch of the economic and political situation in Bulgaria, we will now attempt to assess Bulgaria's privatisation programme against our 'prerequisites of public-to-private success' framework.

The 'Prerequisites of Public-to-Private Success' Framework Applied to Bulgaria's Privatisation Approach

1. Personal power and motivation to change existing systems - within a regulatory framework

Although privatisation is a magical word in Eastern Europe where almost everyone after 45 years of collectivism would like to see him/herself as an owner of a business organisation, the privatisation programme seems nevertheless to have stalled because of a widespread belief that the few asset and enterprise transfers that have taken place have not been properly conducted, and that they have largely benefitted those in privileged positions. At the important, grass-roots, manager level, therefore, there is insufficient motivation to privatise.

There is a general consensus amongst all major political parties in Bulgaria over the desirability of extensive privatisation and the formation of a competitive marketplace. However, although the political will exists, the privatisation challenge that confronts Bulgaria is so immense that it is difficult to convert this will into an effective powerful force for change.

As previously stated, the newly-created regulatory body, the Privatisation Agency, has stated its commitment to achieving ongoing privatisation. It remains to be seen how committed and effective the agency will be in practice. Thus, in terms of the first of our prerequisites for successful public-to-private transformations, it seems that existing market conditions make it difficult for those who are strongly committed to privatisation to convert their desires into effective action.

2. A strong strategic position, an attractive market situation and a sound competitive strategy

Under this heading it has to be said that the Bulgarian expectations for the short-term futures of most, if not all of their newly-privatised enterprises are very pessimistic. There are a number of reasons for this pessimism.

- Emerging from the collective, COMECON 'family' system involving, as it did, administrative (rather than market) prices, budget subsidies and closed trade relationships which worked mainly on the barter principle, Bulgarian state enterprises are almost all very inefficient.
- Generally, big debts are owed to the National bank and to other commercial banks.
- Huge orders from the former Soviet Union, other East European economies and some of the markets in the Middle-East have been lost.

Thus, on this 'strategic situation' criterion, the prospects for Bulgarian public-to-private transitionary success look bleak.

3. A systematic and incremental process of privatisation

At the individual organisational level, it seems likely that privatisation will take place in one 'sudden' development. From the national perspective, the commitment is to a high-speed, ten firms per month privatisation. However, neither of these approaches fit with the more orderly and time-consuming approach adopted in the UK, where proportionally, of course, fewer organisations needed to be privatised. One again, therefore, the Bulgarian situation does not measure up well against our 'framework'.

4. A national culture which incorporates free market principles, structures, systems and behaviours

From the economic and political point of view, the issue of privatisation of the East European economies, including that of Bulgaria, is an unprecedented one in history. In most of these economies, the state owns a stake that varies between 80 per cent and 100 per cent in each of their market sectors. Never before has any country made this sort of transformation (Ivanov and Kovachev, 1993a). Indeed, in no country which has experienced privatisation has the share of public sector output in GDP approached that in Eastern Europe (Ivanov and Kovachev, 1993b).

Western countries have the benefit of private markets, stock exchanges, meaningful accounting records, labour markets and personnel accustomed to working and managing in free-market environments. Bulgaria has still to create a unique series of institutional arrangements to facilitate its privatisation aspirations and to make significant changes to its legal, monetary and tax systems in order to ensure the success of the programme and fully to realise the potential benefits of a system of private, entrepreneurial-driven businesses operating in a competitive environment.

The collectivist culture also threatens to reassert itself as public discontent over the failure of the free-market changes to improve the quality of life, thus far, focuses on the comparatively easy-going and secure life which many experienced during the era of socialism. One acute problem is that there is an immense potential for fraud and dishonesty in managing companies' funds. Establishing and enforcing laws in the western economies is relatively easy due to the existence of their extensive private sectors and the concomitant pool of independent investors and managers. Attempting to impose laws in Bulgaria, where virtually all workers and managers are employed by the state, could pose a severe obstacle to the swift transfer of such workers and managers to gainful private sector employment. Here again, the Bulgarian experience is at odds with the prescriptions described in our 'success' framework.

5. Managers required to manage the transition were conversant with or expert in the strategic management of competitive organisations

Bulgaria undoubtedly has many capable and experienced managers. However, their knowledge and skills have been developed under the socialist regime, which means that they lack a basic understanding of the western role and functions of management in private enterprise. The lack of basic education and training is found at all levels of management, but the areas most in need of development are: finance and accounting, treasury and cash management, operations management, marketing, human relations management and strategic management. Neither does Bulgaria have the sort of vibrant economy that is able to offer sufficiently recognisable rewards to attract western-skilled managers. Some western-style management development is being undertaken through western Business School contacts and interactions, but this is a comparatively slow means of technology transfer.

6. A ready supply of politically-acceptable owners with capital available to invest

In the UK, as already stated, most public organisation share offers have been over-subscribed and have attracted significant numbers of individual investors. In poorer societies, less demand exists for share take-up and, as already illustrated, many Bulgarian citizens are reticent about buying into newly-privatised organisations. This opens up the equity market to foreign investors and this, in turn, raises questions about the political acceptability of such trends and the political acceptability of particular foreign investors.

Currently, politically-acceptable western investors are holding back from committing themselves to Bulgarian enterprise-related ventures. Thus, once again, the Bulgarian experience seems not to measure up to the BT-based success indicators.

Conclusion

In this paper we have identified some of the factors which are likely to have been instrumental in helping the BT privatisation process to lead to successful outcomes. We have also used these factors as evaluatory indicators of the success potential of the Bulgarian privatisation programme. The results of this evaluation are not encouraging. On all criteria the Bulgarian approach falls well short of prescribed prerequisite conditions. To the extent that our 'prerequisites of successful public-to-private transitions' framework is generally valid, then the present approach to privatisation in Bulgaria seems to be doomed to fail.

Given this pessimistic assessment, thought needs to be given to how the privatisation movement might be bolstered. Two developments seem to commend themselves. These necessitate attempts to improve the current situation with regard to three of our prerequisites.

The first of these developments involves slowing-up the privatisation programme and a quickening of the installation of the infrastructure which is necessary for the effective functioning of the free-market system. The aim here would be to create a more orderly programme of introducing public sector managers and their organisations to free-market conditions, and would thereby avoid the dismantling, in rapid time, of the traditional, ingrained philosophies and systems with the expectation that managers without experience or infrastructure will, nevertheless, cope. Sudden crises are often necessary to fuel real change, but it might be the case that Eastern Europe has already experienced a big enough 'sudden crisis', and a more orderly approach might now be effectively implemented.

The second strategy is one to be undertaken by those western strategists, of governmental or commercial origins, who wish to see the Eastern European free-market movement succeed. This strategy requires these people to provide or arrange politically-acceptable investments for Bulgarian enterprises in order to maintain and sustain the Bulgarian economy through this difficult transitionary period and to help develop Bulgarian enterprises to play their projected roles as contributors to an extended free-market society.

Finally, we should point out that, although our analysis has, on this occasion, involved Bulgaria, a similar step-by-step assessment might have been undertaken in the context of any other public-to-private developing society (or organisation). We might also add that our pessimistic observations and general strategies for the improvement of failure-prone privatisation systems might also apply to many of the present movements towards privatisation currently underway in Europe, for example, France, Italy and Portugal. The evaluatory framework we have provided here might be used to assess other privatisation contexts and to generate pertinent thought about any further regulatory interventions which might be called for.

References

Carsberg, B. (1990) 'Deregulation and Joint Ventures in International Telecommunications Strategies Regulation: The UK Experience', *Economist Conference*, London (September).

Caulkin, S. (1987) 'Anyone Listening at British Telecom?', *Management Today* (December) pp. 38-44.

Ivanov, D. and Kovachev, I. (1993a) 'Strategies of Transition of East European Economies: The Case of the Balkans', *European Business and Economic Development*, *1* (5).

Ivanov, D. and Kovachev, I. (1993b) 'Models and Reality in the Economic Reform in Eastern Europe', 20th Annual Conference Proceedings, *The Academy of International Business, UK Region*, The University of Glamorgan, 5-6 April, vol. 2.

Porter, M. E. (1987), 'From Competitive Advantage to Corporate Strategy', *Harvard Business Review* (May/June).

Peters, T. J. and Waterman Jr, R. H. (1982) *In Search of Excellence* (New York: Harper and Row).

Richardson, B. and Curwen, P. (1992) 'Competitive Strategy, Competitive Situations and Market Conditions as Determinants of Public Enterprise Success', Conference paper presented at the 22nd International Institute of Administrative Sciences Conference, Vienna (July).

Richardson, B., Nwankwo, S. and Curwen, P. (1993) 'Regulating Consumer Responsiveness in Public-to-Private Organisations in the United Kingdom'. Conference paper presented at the 23rd International Institute of Administrative Sciences Conference, Mexico (July).

Skeel, S. (1992) 'Can Vallance Keep His Balance?', *Management Today* (February) pp. 42-46.

Vickers, J. and Yarrow, G. (1988) *Privatisation: An Economic Analysis*, (London: MIT Press).

Winward, J. (1989) 'The Privatisation Programme and the Consumer Interest', *Energy Policy* (October) pp. 511-517.

SUGARCO AND CIGPRO: CASES IN THE MANAGEMENT OF POLISH STATE OWNED ENTERPRISES FROM STATE CONTROL TO THE MARKET

Beth Kewell, The Buckinghamshire College

Introduction

Since 1989 and the collapse of communism Poland has been through a period of political instability and economic recession. The paper examines the impact recession has had on state owned industry and the kind of industrial structure which has begun to emerge as a result. As Poland begins to pull out of the post-1989 downturn, recent studies by the World Bank (Frydman and Wellisz in Corbo, Corricelli and Bossak, 1991; Corricelli and Revenga, 1992; Pinto, Belka and Krajewski, 1993) have suggested that, despite the lack of effective macroeconomic industrial reform, State Owned Enterprises (SOEs) are responding to market forces and adapting management practices to suit the new environment. Studies by these authors identify the ways in which SOEs are responding to external market changes. These studies do not, however, seek to evaluate the responses of management to internal pressures. This paper therefore examines the ways in which, in two cases at least, the management of Polish SOEs has begun to change from the inside.

The recession of 1990-91 had an impact on both firms examined in the paper. In the case of SugarCo, the business was not threatened by recession but lost crucial state subsidies during 1990 and 1991. Senior management responded to financial pressures with the introduction of market orientated measures and, in particular, new packaging for most of the company's product lines. However, the company's loss-making sweet manufacturing operation has become a real and unchallenged threat to the business.

At CigPro, the recession destroyed a guaranteed export business and left the company in turmoil. The most troublesome area of the business (tobacco processing) was targeted for rationalisation, but this was not enough to improve the factory's operating position. In

401

1991, senior management turned to cigarette production but this diversification soon became a failure.

The paper questions the ability of senior management at both companies to manage enterprise change effectively. Moreover, the attitudes and approach of senior managers observed during research at SugarCo and CigPro reveals a commitment to what the paper concludes (tentatively) to be *management by indifference*.

The paper is divided into two parts. The first section identifies the main economic changes which have effected the industrial behaviour of SOEs since 1989, and the second is based on the case studies of SugarCo and CigPro and focuses on (1) the impact of recession on each firm (2) the management of production and (3) the actions of the senior management at both companies.

The Recession, Industrial Performance and the SOE Environment

The Wider Economy

1989, 1990 and 1991 were particularly difficult years in which the bottom dropped out of the economy[1]. But 1992 and 1993 have brought stabilisation, if not recovery, and recent forecasts suggest that 'Poland is steadily emerging from...deep recession' (EIU, 1993, p.6). However, the recent upturn has done little more than restore 1988 levels of growth[2]. There has also been the addition of high unemployment since 1988[3].

Although the outlook for the economy in 1994 is more promising than in any other year since 1989, the current prospects for industry are less positive than for the economy as a whole and most sectors, (especially those in manufacturing) are still in the grips of recession. The recovery has been fuelled by the expansion of non-industrial sectors. Private retail and service sectors have flourished since 1989 (*Amex Bank Review*, 1993; EIU, 1993; EBRD, 1993a & 1993b). As the following statistical data demonstrate, industry and in particular the SOE sector has yet to recover from recession.

The Industrial Slump of 1990-91

Real levels of industrial production fell dramatically between 1990 and 1991. Table 1 breaks down the amount of output lost in industry between 1989 and 1991. According to Table 1, output fell by an average of 22 percent between 1989 and 1990, and by a further 16.5 percent in the following year. Key industries also fared badly[4]. The causes included credit limits, rising inflation, trade liberalisation and CMEA conversion to hard currency (Murrell, 1993; Pinto, 1993; Slay, 1993b; EBRD, 1993b).

Moreover, falling output and increased producer prices[5] put traditional levels of industrial employment in jeopardy (Lane in Coricelli and Revenga, 1992; ERBD, 1993a; Slay, 1993b). As Tables 2 and 3 illustrate, between 1989 and 1991 there was an increase in the number of firms per sector and a reduction in size by employment in most industries[6]. Despite the slump in industrial output economic forecasts predicted that 'the recovery will...be led by the expansion of the private sector as the state contracts' (*Amex Bank Review*, 1993, p.3). However, growth in the private industrial sector made a persistent but relatively small contribution to the economy between 1989 and 1991[7]. Levels of private sector industrial production increased by around a quarter during this period. Private enterprise thus continued as the minor partner in industry and three quarters of industrial production remained in state hands.

It was the SOE sector which accordingly took the brunt of recession during 1990 and 1991. The 1989-91 period witnessed a decline in industrial output of most SOEs. Furthermore, the slump in output damaged both the productive capacity and size by employment of Polish SOEs (Brunner, 1993; Pinto, Belka and Krajewski, 1993). Hence under such hostile economic circumstances the majority of SOE's have become leaner but not necessarily fitter.

	1989	1990	1991
Coal	89.6	53.8	52.8
Steel	84.8	76.0	51.9
Metal working	109.8	89.7	78.2
Non-ferrous metals	90.5	58.7	29.7
Machine tools	117.4	110.0	84.0
Precision tools	103.2	97.0	75.6
Transport equipment	83.5	62.6	30.0
Electronics	100.6	94.6	75.6
Chemicals	83.9	62.7	50.9
Construction materials	111.2	97.9	88.9
Food	77.3	60.0	67.3
Clothing	122.1	93.6	87.3
Textiles	99.4	52.6	41.6

Table 1:
Output in Industry 1989-1991 (1988=100)

Source: Brunner (1993) p.31

Sector	Total	6-100	101-500	501-1000	1001-
Coal	103	1	12	1	89
Steel	47	10	11	2	2
Metal working	507	126	227	49	55
Non-ferrous metals	33	3	5	7	18
Machine tools	619	121	285	106	107
Precision tools	150	45	68	13	23
Transport equipment	299	51	127	59	62
Electronics	313	59	132	59	63
Chemicals	403	84	208	48	63
Construction	355	94	170	63	28
Textiles & clothing	881	153	454	114	160

Table 2:

Number of Firms and Plants by Size of Employment in 1988

Source: Brunner (1993) p.28.

Sector	Total	6-100	101-500	501-1000	1001-
Coal	85	2	5	2	76
Steel	50	9	13	2	26
Metal working	512	205	230	63	14
Non-ferrous metals	25	1	4	11	9
Machine tools	689	171	351	84	83
Precision tools	162	52	85	11	14
Transport equipment	350	97	157	44	52
Electronics	346	76	177	45	48
Chemicals	460	139	222	45	54
Construction	470	137	276	47	10
Food	1182	248	705	169	60
Textiles & clothing	1099	366	517	126	90

Table 3:

Number of Firms and Plants by Size of Employment in 1991

Source: Brunner (1993) p.28

The Reform of Ownership

The reform of existing state industry has been a top political priority since 1989. Industrial policies have focused on the privatisation of SOEs as a way of generating badly-needed investment and encouraging entrepreneurialism (Brunner, 1993; Slay, 1993a & 1993b).

However, the recession of 1990-91 threw the life expectancy of fast-track reform programmes into doubt and the industrial structure was not subjected to the drastic overall recommended in the Balcerowicz plan[8] (Sachs, 1990; Berg and Sachs, 1992; Slay, 1993a & 1993b).

Industrial policies since the Balcerowicz programme have failed to introduce more than superficial changes to the ownership structure of industry[9]. The current balance of ownership between state and private industry is shown in Table 4. According to Table 4, most new ventures have been small domestic partnerships and the level of foreign participation remains very low[10].

Post-1989 shifts in the ownership structure of industry have fallen well below the initial expectations of some commentators (Berg and Sachs, 1992; Grosfeld, 1990; ERBD, 1993b). Lack of foreign interest has been a contributing factor to what has become 'low capacity of absorption of..foreign capital investment' (Kotowicz-Javor, 1993, p.13). Foreign companies which have invested in Poland have (with a few exceptions) offered advice rather than hard cash (Genco, Taurelli and Viezzoli, 1993; *Financial Times*, 1993; Slay, 1993b).

Alongside what has been a disappointing level of foreign interest in Polish companies, privatisation has since 1990 become 'A contentious issue, and slow progress is to be expected' (EIU, 1993, p.6). There has been a marked change of pace where the privatisation of SOEs is concerned and the number of enterprises intended for privatisation has decreased significantly since 1990[11]. By the last quarter in 1992, only 1,706 of a possible 2,387 state enterprises had transferred into private ownership. Given that there are nearly 10,000 enterprises in Poland's main industries alone[12], the privatisation of such a small number of firms represents a relatively limited change.

As Tables 4 and 5 indicate, both the expansion of the private sector and the process of privatisation have had limited successes. Although the private sector will continue to grow and privatisation is set to continue at a slower pace (EIU,1993), it is unlikely that the balance of ownership will swing in favour of private industry. The future prospects for industry therefore rely heavily on the performance of SOEs and, to a certain extent, the strength of the recovery and the will of the present government to instigate further industrial reform[13].

	Public Sector			
	communal	state	with treasury share	with state legal person share
a)	54	3009	177	277
b)	46	2749	430	255
	Private Sector			
	domestic private partnerships	partnerships with foreign share	cooperatives	foreign small enterprises
a)	9182	2099	2535	656
b)	11335	3463	2565	602

Table 4:

The Ownership Structure of Polish Industry

Notes: a) 31-12-91 b) 31-12-92

Source: Central Statistical Office, Warsaw (1991, 1993).

Number of non-agricultural enterprises allocated to the programme of:	Total	1990 8th-10th month	1991 1st-10th month	1992 1st-12th month
capital privatisation	481	58	250	173
Individual privatisation	298	58	186	54
Successfully privatised via capital & individual programmes	49	6	24	19
Successfully privatised via mass privatisation	183	na	64	119
Enterprises successfully privatised via liquidation	1474	72	878	524

Table 5:

The Privatisation of Non-agricultural SOEs 1989-92

Source: Central Statistical Office, Warsaw (1991, 1993).

The Management of SOEs in the Post-communist Era

The role of Polish enterprise management in the reform of state-run industry has figured heavily in both government reform programmes[14] and western commentary on the progress of industrial restructuring since 1989 (Grosfeld, 1991; Slay, 1993a, & 1993b; Coricelli and Revenga, 1993). In the wake of failed macroeconomic policy there has been a realisation that (if there is to be an industrial upturn) recovery will hail from the state sector. The management of SOEs has therefore become an issue of significance and the spot-light has turned on management action at the microeconomic level. As Pinto, Belka and Krajewski (1993, p.221) recently claimed 'Factors within each firm (such as management action)...are becoming the main determinants of performance'. It has also been argued that hard budget constraints[15] have encouraged pragmatic and, in some cases, entrepreneurial responses from the directors and managers of industrial SOEs (Pinto, Belka and Krajewski, 1993; ERBD, 1993).

This makes the evidence presented by the case material all the more important as the cases of SugarCo and CigPro[16] cast some doubt upon the ability of SOE managers to respond effectively to drastic changes in the economic climate. At both companies there has been a history of under-investment, inefficiency, non-intervention by top management in the internal workings of the firm and an indifference to the management of production. As the case material demonstrates, whereas the managers interviewed at SugarCo and CigPro recognise the external pressures being brought to bear on their respective companies and talk openly about the need for the reform of financial and marketing management, the re-organisation of production is an issue which has yet to be addressed in either firm.

Case 1: SugarCo

SugarCo has been producing refined sugar from locally-grown sugar-beet for over 100 years. This is a simple and continuous operation which is relatively cheap to run and uncomplicated to manage. The processing equipment used at SugarCo is well maintained (if old) and the process has changed little over the past 40 years.

The refining operation is considered something of a success story at the factory and senior management are proud of the fact that in recent years they have gained a competitive advantage of 300 zlotys per kilo of refined sugar over other sugar producers in Poland. According to the plant director "compared with other sugar companies in Poland our sugar is relatively cheap".

SugarCo has survived the recession in comparatively good shape thanks to guaranteed sugar sales in the domestic market. Real sales turnover has been maintained despite rising inflation. In 1990 real sales turnover stood at 234,581 billion zlotys and by 1992 had increased to 294,837 billion zlotys. As a result, only limited changes have been made to the way the sugar business is operated and managed.

For many years government subsidies allowed SugarCo to maintain a surplus of refined sugar at little extra cost. However, by the time the recession had reached its lowest point SugarCo had lost nearly all of the company's direct subsidies from the government, thereby turning the surplus into an expensive luxury. According to the plant director "There were great, great quantities of sugar and we have to get rid of this sugar as soon as possible".

Management decided to re-market existing stocks of surplus sugar in sachets and boxes of cubed sugar. 1 kg bags of sugar were also re-packaged in more attractive western-style bags (which were a major improvement on the old grey paper wrappers previously used in domestic sales). As the company's accountant commented "Sugar was in horrible grey bags five years ago...we have changed the packaging..and these are more popular". Increased domestic sales convinced senior management that their products had potential and, more importantly, that the company's market share could be increased via more sophisticated product marketing. As the plant director commented "Now it's not difficult to produce or to make things..but our marketing policy is definitely the most important aspect to selling these products". Senior management at SugarCo thus became aware that without government subsidies the plant would have to find ways of maintaining the company's existing price advantage over other sugar producers in Poland. Management at the plant have also discovered that when under pressure there is a clear advantage to changing the way products are sold and marketed. Management have since 1991 developed a short-term strategy of intensification to ensure the costs of sugar production remain low. According to the plant's general manager "if the costs are lower the profits will be bigger". This strategy proved to be successful in the past when the market for sugar was far less open. However, the domestic sugar may well become far more competitive over the next few years. If this happens, senior management will be required to look beyond intensification and consider the possibility of rationalising the company.

The following evidence sheds some doubt over the ability of top management to introduce internal cost-orientated changes to the company. To date, very little rationalisation has taken place at SugarCo. A minimal number of seasonal and peripheral workers have been lost. Furthermore, SugarCo is operating a loss-making sweet manufacturing operation and effectively pouring the company's profits down the drain.

The manufacture of sweets began in 1954 as a separate factory housed on the same site as the sugar plant, but under a different management regime. For reasons which are unclear, the sweet business was incorporated into SugarCo during the 1960s. There were great hopes for the sweet making side of the business, and during the 1970s management optimistically predicted that by the mid-1980s they would be making 80,000 tonnes of candy per annum. These targets were never realised and by 1993 SugarCo's sweet operation was only managing to produce a very inefficient 900 tonnes of candy per year.

The rationalisation of sweet production has not been taken seriously by top management. The shop floor manager of sweet production related the ways in which rationalisation had been mishandled by senior management at the plant as follows:

Piotr[17] had been in charge of sugar production from the mid-1980s onwards and taken some of the credit for increasing production levels. He had also been involved with the re-merchandising of sugar packaging. Senior management assumed that Piotr would be able to work similar miracles in sweet production. However, neither the director nor other members of senior management had intervened in the running of the sweet operation for some time and there had been no investment in the operation since the early 1970s. The full extent of the operation's weaknesses were underestimated and senior management proved unable to come up with a strategy to strengthen the operation.

According to Piotr he found "a bigger mess" in sweet production than he had expected, and spent some time looking at the operation's real potential which he estimated to be 1,500 tonnes of candy by the end of 1992, and a daily tonnage of 9 tonnes from then on, at the very maximum. He found even this modest target difficult to achieve in the short term. This has resulted from the fact that "the organisation was so poor...I mean everything was so poor that I am still trying to straighten things".

For example, the materials he had to work with were substandard (especially packaging). It was only when a succession of retail outlets returned the sweets as unsaleable that funds appeared for new materials. "In this situation we needed new packaging but the cost was 300 to 400 million zlotys and we needed a dozen types of these materials; but we didn't have these new packaging materials and so last year shops returned the sweets to us". After some time Piotr received the new packaging materials and commented that "Since we introduced the new packaging no sweets have been returned".

Numerous other difficulties such as a poor product mix and over-staffing plagued the operation. Piotr had tried to deal with some of these problems himself but had neither the resources nor the authority to make changes stick. Piotr explained that "I just want them [employees] to work together and follow me, but some of them do not want to learn anything new and there was no cooperation from my colleagues and I couldn't do everything myself".

The problems associated with sweet production at SugarCo demanded the intervention of management at a senior level and were too serious for one production manager to deal with by himself. The management of sweet production thus became the subject of indifferent treatment from senior management who are unwilling to take responsibility for the chaos that reigned there.

The problem had always been that sweet production was a manufacturing operation which required much more direct intervention from management than sugar production. SugarCo's senior management team had little experience of managing anything other than processing and thus found more complex manufacturing processes hard to manage.

Case 2: CigPro

CigPro is a state owned tobacco processing plant which began operating in 1934. CigPro was badly hit by the domestic recession of 1990 to 1991 and the collapse of the CMEA which left unpaid bills from Russian creditors and lumbered the plant with stocks of unsold tobacco. The fortunes of CigPro have taken a new turn since the beginning of 1992. EuroCig (a multi-national cigarette manufacturer) has contracted CigPro to manufacture EuroCig's *U.S. First*[18] brand of cigarette at the Lublin plant. The presence of a foreign interest at CigPro has been enough to convince the government that CigPro can be reprieved, and state subsidies have continued as a result. It is the presence of EuroCig which has guaranteed the medium-term future of the plant rather than management action.

During the late 1970s CigPro benefited from the relatively low cost of locally-grown tobacco and had profitable home and export markets to rely on. However, export sales fell steadily throughout the 1980s because of poor product quality, and by 1989 senior management were faced with a slump. According to the factory's Planning Manager "In Poland tobacco companies were highly concentrated and we knew that there is much competition around the world and that other companies in other countries can do it cheaper".

In the domestic market, sales of Polish brand cigarettes had fallen off considerably because of increased competition from imported western brands which proved more popular. As a result, the state-run cigarette factories CigPro supplied required less tobacco. According to the company's Planning Manager, Polish cigarette factories "Bought only extra tobacco from us". By 1990, recession had taken hold of the Polish economy, the price of tobacco had risen dramatically and demand had subsequently collapsed. The CMEA was also on the verge of disintegration, and as a result CigPro had few prospective export clients in the pipeline. The quality of the tobacco was also poor, and for this reason had no hope of being sold in hard currency markets.

Thus, by 1991, CigPro's operating position had been seriously undermined and by 1992 sales turnover had fallen to 240 trillion zlotys per annum. The plant's management team were faced with a major crisis and responded to this situation with a simple programme of rationalisation. Output was reduced and the number of workers employed in tobacco processing was also scaled down. Some were given the sack, fewer seasonal workers were taken on and other workers were re-deployed to the brand new cigarette manufacturing operation. The workforce was thus reduced to a total of 635.

Rationalisation did not make any significant difference to the financial position of CigPro. Tobacco processing had been running in excess of capacity for some time and there were already large stockpiles of tobacco at the factory. The drop in output stemmed the flow of surplus but did not provide the whole solution. The work-force had been paid next to nothing and as such the reduction in manpower made little difference to the wage bill.

In the last year losses have continued to mount and senior management have reached the conclusion that "We must get rid of tobacco processing here in Lublin and concentrate on the production of cigarettes". Plant management have come to realise that without a market for the tobacco and capital investment the operation will not be sustainable in the

410

long term. However, no-one from senior management wants to take responsibility for the closure of tobacco processing and the loss of several hundred jobs. Until a suitable axe man is found tobacco processing will continue at CigPro on a limited scale.

Following a trend set by other state run tobacco factories, CigPro turned to the manufacture of cigarettes. By 1991 a substantial amount of investment had been sunk into the project and second-hand *making* and *packing* machines were purchased from Germany. Even before the pilot project had shown whether large-scale production was feasible, CigPro had begun to manufacture three brands of short cigarette. The first brand *Hit* was manufactured from a blend of 30 percent local tobacco and 70 percent imported tobaccos; the second *Hohsur* brand of cigarette contained 60 percent imported tobacco; and the third brand *Polo* was a blend which included 50 percent Polish tobacco. The first two brands *Hit* and *Hohsur* failed Polish government quality tests. According to CigPro's Planning Manager "Last year two of our brands failed and one was successful. So we have turned *Polo* into a longer, cheaper cigarette".

The management of cigarette production was also problematic at shop-floor level. CigPro make cigarettes from scratch and the manufacturing operation has been run and managed by one manager from start to finish. Lasek[19] had been seconded from tobacco processing along with his best workers, and senior management had left him to manage the operation autonomously ever since.

Lasek's style of management involved a low level of intervention on the shop floor, and the workers seemed to be running the machines without much close supervision[20]:

> At the far end of production a case making machine was operated by two workers. The first checked that the fibre was being fed smoothly across two bobbins and into the machine. At the other end of the making machine another operator collected the finished product. Next to the casing machine stand two cigarette filling machines each with four operators working the machinery plus two extra relief workers. The fillers were prone to frequent breakdowns. Across the gangway stood two packing machines. The first packed the cigarettes into boxes of 20 and the second boxes of 20 into packs of 1000. There were a dozen or so workers on each packing machine the operation of which was subject to fits and starts. At the end of the second packer two or three workers put the 1000s into cardboard boxes to be shipped out. There was a lot of work-in-progress and bin after bin of wasted tobacco and cases. The waste seems to be a by-product of the endless stoppages which occurred on the shop-floor.

The cigarette operation now manufactures *Polo* cigarettes exclusively. However, sales of *Polo* cigarettes have been moderate and the operation has become very costly. The company's plan to move into large-scale production has thus been put on hold and the newly-built cigarette hall which has the capacity to mass-produce cigarettes remains derelict.

Moreover, where the production of cigarettes was concerned senior management at CigPro had under-estimated the amount of managerial input needed to diversify into cigarette production. Although the production of cigarettes is a simple process which involves putting paper, filter and tobacco together, the machinery that does the job needs to be carefully maintained and monitored. This in itself required both managerial competence beyond that of senior management at the plant as well as a form of detailed control which has yet to be mastered by shop-floor management. Senior management had no direct control over what the operators did or when they did it. The operators were left to regulate the work themselves and to turn up when they felt like it. Senior management had failed to intervene in the past and were not about to do so in the present. This may have been because they were either unaware of the circumstances or treated under-performance as par for the course. Whatever the case may be, no-one from senior management was monitoring production.

Conclusion

The paper has shown by reference to statistical evidence that SOEs remain the dominant form of industrial enterprise in an economy which has been changed by recession. The industrial structure has not be subjected to the reforms anticipated in 1990 and private enterprise remains the minor partner in industry. Despite the lack of macroeconomic reform, SOEs have showed tentative signs of changing the way the operate in the market place. As the cases of SugarCo and CigPro indicate, SOE managers are beginning to re-think the ways in which products are packaged, sold and marketed. This is due to the fact that both firms are now operating in less-favourable markets with less financial support from the state and fewer guaranteed customers.

The paper has also tried to demonstrate (using what is admittedly tentative evidence) that the internal management of SOEs and, in particular, the management of production has yet to change dramatically. This is in spite of internal pressures within both SugarCo and CigPro to reform the ways in which production is run and operated. From the initial evidence presented by the cases of SugarCo and CigPro, it is evident that production-centred problems have been left to manifest themselves over a number of years. There also seems to be a clear distinction between the approach of line production managers and their counter-parts in senior management. Production management appears to be at the sharp end, but lacks the resources and authority to make changes. However, the real problem in both cases lies with the indifferent attitude of senior managers to production-centred problems and their reluctance to take full responsibility for management weaknesses.

References

Amex Bank Review (1993) 'Central and Eastern Europe: Myths and Realities', *20* (6).

Berg, A. and Sachs. J. (1992) 'Poland', *Economic Policy* (April) pp.118-173.

Brunner, H. (1993) 'The Recreation of Entrepreneurship in Eastern Europe: Neither Magic Nor Mirage', *Paper to EADI VIIth General Conference* (Berlin).

Corbo, V., Coricelli, F. and Bossak, S. (eds) (1991) *Reforming Central and Eastern European Economies: Initial Results and Challenges* (Washington: The World Bank).

Coricelli, F. and Revenga, A. (1992) 'Wage Policy During the Transition to a Market Economy: Poland 1990-91', *World Bank Discussion Paper No.158*.

Economist Intelligence Unit (1993) 'Poland', *Country Forecast Updater* (2nd Quarter 1993).

European Bank For Reconstruction and Development (1993a) 'Current Economic Issues', *ERBD Economic Review* (July).

European Bank For Reconstruction and Development (1993b) 'Annual Economic Outlook', *ERBD Economic Review* (September).

Financial Times (1993) *Poland:Survey* (17th June).

Frydman, R. and Wellisz, S. (1991) 'The Ownership-Control Structure and Behaviour of Polish Enterprises During the 1990 Reforms', in Corbo *et al*, *Reforming Central and Eastern European Economies: Initial Results and Challenges* pp.141-155).

Genco, P., Taurelli, S. and Viezzoli, C. (1993) 'Private Investment in Central and Eastern Europe: Survey Results', *ERBD Working Paper No.7*.

Grosfeld, I. (1991) 'Privatisation of State Enterprises in Eastern Europe: The Search for a Market Environment', *East European Politics and Societies, 5* (1) pp.142-159.

Kotowicz-Jawor, J. (1993) 'Investment in the Transition Period: Case Study of Poland', *Paper to EADI VIIth General Conference* (Berlin).

Murrell, P. (1993) 'What is Shock Therapy ? What Did it Do in Poland and Russia ?', *Post Soviet Affairs, 9* (2) pp.111-140.

Pinto, B. (1992) 'Incomes Policy and Wage Setting Behaviour: Evidence From Polish SOEs During the Economic Transformation Programme, in Coricelli, F. and Revenga, A. (eds) 'Wage Policy During the Transition to a Market Economy: Poland 1990-91', *World Bank Discussion Paper No.158, pp.99-123.*

Pinto, B., Belka, M. and Krajewski, S. (1993) 'Transforming State Enterprises in Poland: Evidence on the Adjustment By Manufacturing Firms', *Brookings Papers on Economic Activity, 1*, pp.213-258.

Sachs, J. (1990) 'Poland's Big Bang: A First Report Card', *The International Economy, V* (1) pp.40-43.

Slay, B. (1993a) 'Evolution of Industrial Policy in Poland Since 1989', *RFE/RL Research Report, 2* (2) pp.21-28.

Slay, B. (1993b) 'The Dilemmas of Economic Liberalism in Poland', *Europe-Asia Studies, 45* (2) pp.237-257.

Endnotes

1. In 1990 and 1991 GDP at constant prices dipped by 18.6 per cent but then recovered by an estimated 3 per cent between 1992 and 1993. This dramatic reduction in levels of GDP indicates that in the early 1990s the economy was considerably weakened by recession.

2. For example, dollar GDP per head is expected to stabilise around 1,879 US $ per head after a period of turbulence. This figure is just below the 1988 threshold of 1,818 US $ per head (See *ERBD Economic Review*, 1993b, p.100).

3. Unemployment went from 0.1 per cent in 1989 to an estimated 16 per cent by the end of 1993, whilst levels of employment have decreased since 1988 by an overall 10.0 per cent (Ibid).

4. Table 1 indicates that over a two-year period (1989-91), output fell in the coal industry to 52 per cent of its 1988 value, while in transport equipment the decrease was 30 per cent and in textiles 41 per cent.

5. Producer prices increased by 212.8 per cent in 1989 and by 622.3 per cent in 1990. For a more detailed analysis of the trend in producer prices see EBRD (1993a, p.162).

6. For example, the number of firms in the machine tool industry which employed between 101-500 employees was 285 in 1989 and a further 106 firms employed between 501-1000 in the same year. By 1991 the composition of machine tool manufacturers had changed as the number of firms employing more than 1001 employees had declined to 83 by 1991.

7. The private industrial sector increased its share of GDP by 13 per cent between 1989 and 1991.

8. The Balcerowicz programme was launched by the first post-communist government in Poland on 1 January 1990. The programme included measures designed to reform industry and through a series of shocks transform Poland into a liberal market economy. The Balcerowicz programme achieved few successes. For more on the subject see Myant, M. (1993) *Transforming Socialist Economies: The Case of Poland and Czechoslovakia* (Edward Elgar) and Murrell, P. (1993) 'What is Shock Therapy? What Did it Do in Russia and Poland?', *Post Soviet Affairs, 9* (2) (pp.110-140).

9. For more on this subject see Slay, B. (1993) 'The Dilemmas of Economic Liberalism in Poland', *Europe-Asia Studies, 45* (2) pp.237-357.

10. A total of 3,463 partnerships involved foreign investors by the end of 1992 as opposed to a total 11, 335 domestic partnerships by the same date.
11. For example, the 1992 total of 1,129 is more or less unchanged on the previous year.
12. In total manufacturing the average number of employees per firm was 710.35 in 1988. For a break-down of employment across industrial sectors see EIU Country Reports for 1993 (various issues) and *International Statistics Year Book* (1989).
13. 1993 has also seen the political pendulum swing back towards former-communists who won a convincing victory in recent parliamentary elections. This may have been a protest vote and a signal of public discontent with the failure of government reform programmes and poor economic performance since 1989.
14. For a more comprehensive explanation of the role of managers in privatisation see Slay, B. (1993) 'Poland: The Role of Managers in Privatisation', *RFE/RL Research Report*, *2* (12) pp.52-56.
15. Hard Budget Constraints were defined as a financial constraint which "induces competition" by the Hungarian economist Kornai, J. (1986) in 'The Soft Budget Constraint', *Kyklos, 39* (1) pp.3-33.
16. The cases of SugarCo and CigPro were originally drafted from notes and interview transcriptions carried out as part of a field research conducted in Lublin Poland.
17. I have changed the name of the sweet production manager for reasons of confidentiality.
18. The name of the brand has been changed.
19. The production manager for cigarette's name has been changed for reasons of confidentiality.
20. The following description of the shop-floor is taken from field notes.

REGULATING CONSUMER RESPONSIVENESS IN PUBLIC-TO-PRIVATE ORGANISATIONS IN THE UNITED KINGDOM

Bill Richardson, Sonny Nwankwo and Peter Curwen
Sheffield Business School

Introduction

The past decade has witnessed a major shift in UK governmental policy towards UK public enterprise organisations. The Conservative government's ideological commitment to privatisation, has required that many utility companies (for example, gas, electricity, water and telecommunications) undertake a 'cultural rite of passage' from the public to the private sector.

However, the perception of market failure characteristics which are seen to apply to the newly privatised utilities has led to the establishment of specially tailored regulatory agencies (for example, OFTEL, OFGAS, OFWAT, OFFER, for the telecommunications, gas, water and electricity industries respectively) to act as proxies for market forces and arbiters of public interests. It has been recognised that a government-to-private ownership change, of itself, is unlikely to promote the necessary change in organisation culture and activity to that state which is seen to represent the ideal, consumer-responsive, free-market response.

The new regulatory bodies have applied a range of strategies designed to improve the reponsiveness of public-to-private utility activity to consumer interests. These strategies have attempted to redress, in favour of the consumer, a perceived imbalance of marketplace power. They have included, for example, the strategies of direct intervention in the organisation's affairs; threat (or fines for persistent failure to provide quality services, for example); exhortation to the organisation, demanding that it changes its ways; the stimulus of greater competitiveness in the marketplace and the provision of useful information to consumers.

Although these change-facilitating strategies may derive theoretical and empirical support from the management and consumer protection literature, there seems to exist a need to provide case examples which contextually evaluate attempts (whether discretionary, induced or forced) at behavioural modification of those 'organisations in transition'. Thus, case-oriented research might lead to a comprehensive explanation of changes which have occurred in organisational attitudes towards consumer responsiveness; the type of changes which have been made to organisation structure, systems and culture; factors which have been instrumental in stimulating these changes; and the success levels achieved in attaining the desired state.

Forces for Change in the UK Telecommunications Industry

* Technology and Market Demand Pressures

Technology and market demand have been crucial in changing the UK telecommunications industry structure. For example, in the context of technological change, the telecom network had developed to a standard where emphasis shifted from building up the network to advancing its quality for meeting diversified needs. Demand characteristics have also changed, with the dividing line between communications and information technology getting thinner and increasingly blurred. The need to respond to these changes, coupled with the rapid advancement in technology, created pressures for reform throughout the industry. Responses at the global level to such pressures have, however, varied, reflecting in part philosophical/ideological arguments and, in part, positions adopted by key decision makers on wider economic and political considerations. For example, one key decision for many governments has been whether the services should be offered by state monopoly or by private regulated companies. Such a fundamental decision, sets in motion a chain of reactions, and an examination of the UK example of privatisation offers an insight into the nature of changes that are likely to be set in motion when such a decision is made.

* Legal Change Mechanisms

Until the early 1980s, a state monopoly provision of telecommunications services in the UK was made available through the British Telecommunications company. Most of British Telecom's activities were protected by statutory monopoly rights. Two broad hypotheses which underpinned the argument for the monopoly provision of telecom services were:
- telecom infrastructure is a natural monopoly; competition would lead to higher cost.

The Director General of Telecoms (DGT) was given wide discretionary powers as a counter-balance to the powers yielded to BT prior to privatisation, including agreement to the 'single entity' privatisation. These powers were to become instrumental in shaping the change processes and outcomes of BT. It is worth making the point that OFTEL's first DGT was as passionately committed to changing the industry as the initiator of the change (Mrs Thatcher). The 'jigsaw' was therefore in place for the radical transformation of the industry which was to unfold.

The regulatory regime imposed on BT contained a lot of conditions to check anti-competitive practices. It prohibits undue preference and discrimination, cross subsidisation, tie-ins, aggregate rebates and so forth. These conditions point to an understanding of the possible distortion a company in BT's position can wreck on the competitive framework - the company was privatised as an inherently powerful single entity.

Two issues, namely, competition and quality of service, provide sources of illustrations of how the DGT and OFTEL have managed to enforce changes in the industry.

Competition

OFTEL's commitment to the competitive mechanism was clearly articulated from the outset. Sir Bryan Carsberg (DGT 1984-1992) saw his role principally as introducing and sustaining competition in the industry. In his first report to the Secretary of State for Trade and Industry he declared:

> I attach high priority to my duty to promote effective competition and I have quickly come to believe that this is one of the most important and urgent of the duties laid upon me by the Act" (OFTEL Report,1984.p.8).

This theme remained consistent in all his reports until 1992 when he relinquished office, viz:

> ...promotion of competition is the most important regulatory weapon and should be seen as complementary to other regulatory approaches...The main thrust of OFTEL's policy continues to be to encourage the development of effective competition as a protection to consumers (OFTEL, various).

The first concrete action by OFTEL towards ensuring fair competition was an endorsement of the duopoly structure of the industry. The reason behind this was based on the assumption that an initial duopoly situation may lead eventually to stronger competition. Too many competitors at the start of the newly-privatised situation might mean weaker competition for BT because each would be vying with the other to win business from BT. The result of this was judged to be that BT would be likely to remain strongly dominant. According to the DGT:

> ...if the doors are thrown wide open, without adequate planning and preparation, the result is likely to be confusion, instability in prices and provision of services, and perhaps a situation in which the original monopolist is able to re-establish its dominance (Carsberg,1987 p.8).

Secondly, OFTEL took away from BT the right to fix entry terms to the network system. In pursuance of his 'duty to promote competition', the regulator became heavily involved as a referee between BT and Mercury Communications (BT's principal competitor) whenever these organisations failed to reach agreement over network system issues. One example of such an intervention was the much orchestrated case of interconnection arrangements wherein OFTEL ruled that BT must allow Mercury unrestricted access to the network. The licence conditions were significantly vague on this issue. That decision to allow the interconnection of Mercury Communications to BT's network system was a very crucial factor in altering the industry's competitive structure. The decision to allow Mercury extensive rights of interconnections at BT's exchanges (in spite of BT's strong protestations) established the ground rules for competition between BT and Mercury. Without such a decision, Mercury's strategy would have collapsed because any Public Telecommunications Operator (PTO) must depend on BT's local circuits to deliver its services. By that decision on interconnections to the network system, OFTEL effectively stopped BT from creating structural barriers to network access and thus entrenching its advantaged position. Thus, the decision created opportunities for bustling competition especially in Value Added Network Systems (VANS) and mobile services. With the recently concluded duopoly review, potential competitors are now lining up to enter the industry as Public Telecommunications Operators.

To ensure that Mercury is not disadvantaged by the sheer size of BT (which has economy of scale advantages resulting from the size of its operations) it was allowed compensatory advantages. It was, for example, exempted from the 'universal service' obligation (including the maintainance of loss-making public pay phones and 999 emergency services), given more freedom to choose the routes on which it would provide its service and the services it would provide. Mercury therefore obtained the advantage of being able to choose low cost areas for its operation while BT has to carry the burden of averaged prices applied across low-cost and high-cost areas.

OFTEL's commitment to competition is summed up in the DGT's speech at the 1990 *Economist* conference:

I adopted a policy of proactive regulation. I said I would not wait in my office for complaints to come in but I would go out looking to ensure that competition was fair. I also said that I would use my strong powers to establish the prospect for financial penalties if I found cases of unfair competition (Carsberg,1990).

The above statement reflects the way in which OFTEL has consolidated its position of power in regulating BT for the purpose of greater consumer responsiveness, and operating efficiency.

Quality of Service

On the issue of quality of service, the DGT declared that:

a change has taken place in the attitudes of people in the industry. They are now thinking more entrepreneurially today. They are thinking up new approaches to business and looking for new kinds of service to offer (Carsberg,1987 p.12).

Up until 1987, BT's quality of service remained a contentious issue. Widespread dissatisfaction was expressed by consumer groups and opinion surveys. For example, a study by the National Consumer Council (NCC,1987) revealed that BT's record on service quality was worse than that of public services in Britain. It is worth noting that 1987 was a particularly difficult year for BT following devastating work stoppages by the striking engineering union.

From 1987, OFTEL undertook a considerable amount of work on the assessment of BT's quality of service. A very important outcome of that exercise was to get BT to publish periodically its quality of service indicators under close observation by OFTEL. To ensure that quality of service does not fall below a certain threshold, OFTEL negotiated an arrangement with BT under which the company will pay compensation to consumers who suffer poor quality of service (see OFTEL Report,1989).

Statistics now available (for example, in OFTEL Reports 1986-1993; BT Annual Reports 1987-1993) point to a continual improvement in quality of service. For instance, in 1992, orders for residential telephones were completed within 10 working days as against 18 in 1987; more than 99 per cent of faults were cleared within two working days compared with 73.9 per cent in 1987; 98 per cent of operator calls (100) were answered in 15 seconds (83.5 per cent in 1987); 92 per cent of directory inquiries were answered in 15 seconds (77 per cent in 1987); fewer than 1 per cent of calls failed due to system outage (2.2 per cent in 1987); and 98 per cent of public pay phones were in good working order (76 per cent in 1987).

It must be mentioned that in spite of the attractive record described by those statistics which indicate improvements in quality of service, there is a growing number of people who do not consider BT's services to provide good value for money (see Table 1). Consideration of Table 1 reveals that in 1992, 86 per cent of consumers surveyed were seemingly satisfied with telephone services provided by BT, and that this was broadly in line with the results of earlier surveys: 83 per cent in 1988, 87 per cent in 1989, and 84 per cent in both 1990 and 1991. However, the percentage of people who think that BT's services represent good/fair value for money has been steadily declining (except in 1992): 67 per cent in 1988, 63 per cent in 1989, 58 per cent in 1990 and 46 per cent in 1991. In other words, between 1988 and 1992, the number of people who considered BT's services to provide positive value for money declined by about 21 per cent. This compares with a 26 per cent increase in the percentage of people who hold a negative perception of the company in terms of a 'value for money' rating.

An explanation for the increasing number of people who regard BT's service as poor value for money might be found in the proactive stance of OFTEL, and especially in its public chastisements of BT. OFTEL has become a very visible regulator. Two factors lend credence to this proposition: (a) the number of representations made to the OFTEL agency (see Table 2) and (b) in 1992, 50 per cent of the people surveyed had heard of OFTEL - this compares with 35 per cent in 1991, 31 per cent in 1990, and 29 per cent in 1989.

* Oftel's Operating Systems and Practices

In terms of harnessing enough power to enforce significant changes and free market type outcomes from BT, cynics originally felt that OFTEL would fall prey to 'agency capture' (Maynes, 1979). The danger of agency capture is seen to be particularly real when the regulatee is the main source of information for the regulator and when systematic contacts do not take place before the regulatory agency and groups having opposing interests. The DGT, however, quickly established procedures for issuing consultative documents on major policy issues, commissioning independent studies and meeting regularly with representative associations dealing with consumer interests. He was also supported by six national and two special interest advisory committees. In addition, the 'Competition and Services Act' of 1992 (under the auspices of the Citizen's Charter) significantly enhanced the DGT's powers for the setting of guaranteed standards of service. These arrangements have created ample barriers against the threat of agency capture.

It is important to note that two factors have helped OFTEL to shore up its power position and thus be better able to speed up the transformation of the telecom industry. First is the cooperation it receives from the government. Although the government has the ultimate political power in determining license conditions in the industry, it has, to date, adopted all recommendations proposed by OFTEL, without exception. The DGT is thus seen as not only having a free hand in administering the regulatory regime but to be able to do so without overt political interference. Consequently, BT has been prevented from forestalling the impact of market liberalisation by 'going behind the DGT's back' direct to the Secretary of State.

A second factor which is very important has to do with the quality of leadership of OFTEL. Professor Carsberg, without doubt, has shown a great deal of acumen in discharging his responsibilities. It may not be an exaggeration to say that the success of OFTEL represents the personal triumph of Professor Carsberg. He has shown an immense zeal and determination in steering the regulatory regime to higher levels of accomplishment. In his own words:

> I have strong powers, power to impose orders which can lead to the imposition of financial penalties following a breach of the rules and powers to initiate procedures to change the rules. I am not debarred from taking an interest in any aspect of the activities of licensees that fall within the telecommunications industry...I bring a great deal of enthusiasm to meeting the challenges that the new regime has established (Carsberg, 1987 pp.12-13).

* Recessionary Conditions

In the 1980s, BT had almost become accustomed to effortless growth in turnover and profits. In the five years before 1992, the company averaged a 9 per cent per annum growth in earnings and enjoyed over 90 per cent of the £13 billion UK telecom market. Although Mercury's entry to the telecom market was expected to result in a decline in BT's overall market share, the company's business continued to grow, partly because the economy as a whole was growing rapidly. It seemed as though the company was insulated from the chill winds of recession which were beginning to bite harder towards the end of the 1980s. By the end of 1991, at a time when many UK companies were repositioning and readjusting for improved customer effectiveness - aimed at stemming the tide of devastatingly decreasing consumer spending - BT had still not shaken off its 'licence to print money' image (Caulkin, 1987).

However, the company suffered a rude awakening in 1992 with a drop in the rate of total market growth, turnover and profits. Earning per share tumbled 38 per cent and pre-tax profit fell by 27.8 per cent in the first quarter of 1992. These reflected what Mr Vallance (BT's Chairman) described as 'the continued pressures of the economy, regulation and competition' (see the *Financial Times* of 30 July, 1992). It became obvious that BT was not recession-proof and that strategic changes would need to be made in line with the general developments in the economy (that is, to take account of the fall in business which reflected the depth of the recession at businesses which were heavy phone users). First, it announced a cost-cutting programme, and in particular a 1 per cent price cut of its basic services.

Secondly, it pushed the 'Release 92' programme which offered attractive terms for voluntary redundancies.

* Organisational Change at BT

The privatisation plan for BT was greeted with a stiff opposition from the Labour Party as well as the trade unions when it was announced in 1982. Considering that the privatisation programme was not simply a landmark in UK's economic history but also a corner-stone of government's policy, the government had to enter some sort of alliance with British Telecom's management to enable it to pull through the privatisation programme.

British Telecom for its part had a set of hidden agenda, which contained three key aspects:
- to avoid a break-up of the company
- to minimise competitive threat
- to secure a light-handed regulatory regime.

Newman (1985) provides a detailed description of how BT acted during the debate on its privatisation bill. For example, the company conducted numerous programmes to brief members of parliament; company representatives were always present at the debates in the parliament, including standing committees. BT even put forward its own amendment to the legislation and very close links were maintained with officials at the DTI. Licence conditions were even negotiated with BT. Despite this unwillingness to change fundamentally, the above-mentioned pressures for change have forced ongoing change on the BT organisation.

Changing an organisation as huge as BT does, however, pose enormous challenges. An early, important, change occurred in 1987 when Mr Iain Vallance succeeded Sir George Jefferson as the Chief Executive Officer of BT. At this time not many people had a kind word for the company. The company did not simply need to shift from a public to private sector culture, but more importantly from a monopoly to a competitive culture. The main challenge rested on turning an introverted organisation into one looking outward towards the customer. Changes since 1987 have been aimed at simplifying management structures, moving closer to markets and customers, changing the attitudes and reducing staff numbers and operating costs compared to sales revenue. These changes reflect strategic moves, which Mr Vallance envisioned as being necessary to get BT into shape to cope with its changing environment, (see Caulkin,1987, and Skeel,1992).

As a recent example of major organisational changes which have been and continue to be implemented, the company, in 1991, launched an ambitious reorganisation programme. Code named *project sovereign*, its thrust was to propel the company towards better service effectiveness and improve organisational efficiency - keeping customers happy and maintaining growth and profitability. Project sovereign is wide-ranging, with several milestones to reach, covering personnel and finance, and all facets of the organisation - all geared towards achieving a slimmer, more efficient and responsive organisation. Although the project is yet to run its full course, it has already resulted in a massive labour lay-off (24,000 lay-offs expected between March 1992 and April 1993), a review of every managerial job description, a review of personnel selection criteria and the launching of an extensive management retraining programme (£260m was spent on training in 1992).

Changes to the organisation's culture were identified by Mr Vallance as the anchor-point of his strategy. In respect of privatisation, it was felt that the company had almost a cultural vacuum:

> with a lot of people from outside, with their own view of how things should be run, and a lot of people from inside, some defending the way in which things had been run before and some wishing to change them (Hill,1989).

Vallance propagated the Total Quality Management (TQM) approach to focus the culture change on customer service - revising a situation where the culture was:

> dominated by engineers, with customers out of sight and out of mind. We didn't even call them customers. We called them subscribers, or 'subs' for short.(Vallance)

The thrust of the company's service orientation is to build a business culture aimed at 'meeting customer requirements first time, every time'. This philosophy was encapsulated in the company's 1987/88 campaign: 'It's you we answer to'. In response to the proactive stance of the regulator and an understanding and awareness of the competitive situation, BT has, under new leadership, taken remarkable strides in its approach to quality of customer service. It now operates a 'customer service guarantee scheme' (code named 'the BT Commitment') which seems to go even beyond what the regulator requires of it. The culture is gradually changing (actively driven from the top) and permeating right through the entire hierarchy of the organisation. To underpin this point, the CEO carries a copy of the 'BT Commitment' in his wallet (and is confident most of his managers do too).

The efficiency/innovation criteria of the privatisation goal seems also to have been largely met. By reshaping the company through restructuring, redundancies and massive investment in manpower training and research and systems development, the company has been able to achieve a sustained growth and profitability (see Tables 3-5). The scope and spread of its activities have also continued to grow, showing an impressive network performance. For example, call failure decreased from 3.6 per cent in 1988 to 0.3 per cent in 1992, and customer lines connected to digital exchanges increased from 9.8 per cent in 1988 to 54.4 per cent in 1992.

However, the road to free market states of greater efficiency and greater customer satisfaction has not been an easy one. A particular problem for the BT management as it has sought to change its organisation to become a modern, competitive force in telecommunications has been the reaction of its people to the impact they perceive these changes as having on their own organisational and personal lifestyles. A series of strikes in the mid-1980s, and the temporary abandonment of the 'operation sovereign' campaign in 1992 are examples of 'quality of working life' problems which have arisen due to the trade-off between this aspect of organisation and the need to improve competitive efficiency.

Further, many people are yet to be convinced that the company is now genuinely customer-driven. The recent revelation about its profit figures attracted widespread condemnation of BT and an investigation by OFTEL. The company was reported to be making in excess of £105-a-second profit. BT's argument, in response to these criticisms, that its prices compare favourably with operations in other countries is, however, not supported by published statistics (see Table 6). On the international telephone circuits, the company's profit figure (see Table 7) has led to a renewed call for unrestricted resale of international telecom services. These events, perhaps, may have contributed to the poor 'value for money' rating of the company, discussed earlier.

Conclusion

This paper has provided a case study approach to describing and explaining the changes which have taken place in the British Telecom organisation during the period since its privatisation in 1984.

Improvements in efficiency and consumer responsiveness - objectives of governmental regulation - have been achieved by BT. This paper has emphasized the role of a number of forces which have influenced organisational activity more closely towards these desired end states. These include:

- A 'champion' politician with the power and will to enforce legal, marketplace and organisational change (in this example, Mrs Thatcher the former Prime Minister of the UK).
- A regulatory regime (OFTEL) headed at the time by a powerful and motivated Director General of Telecoms (Sir Bryan Carsberg) who was actively committed to promoting, in a planned and orderly way, effective competition and higher quality service for consumers in the UK telecommunications market.
- An ambitious UK based competitor (Mercury), keen to take advantage of the more open market opportunities offered.

- Recessionary conditions which have stimulated additional efficiency-seeking organisational changes at BT.
- A chief executive (Iain Vallance) with the power, vision and motivation to change British Telecom's organisation configuration of people, structure, system and culture to achieve continuous improvements in organisational efficiency and customer responsiveness.
- Culture-change-seeking programmes such as project sovereign aimed at improving organisational performance.

Hence, this paper has emphasized how a combined political force for change has harnessed sufficient power and will to regulate the public-to-private BT towards a greater consumer responsiveness. In doing this the paper has identified, for the benefit of other public-to-private politicians, some of the ingredients which might need to be designed into successful privatisation strategies.

References

Beesley, M. (1981) *Liberalisation of the Use of British Telecommunications Network,* (London: HMSO) known as the *Beesley Report.*

Beesley, M. & Littlechild, S. (1983) 'Privatisation: Principles, Policies and Priorities', *Lloyd's Bank Review* (July) pp.1-20.

Carsberg, B. (1987) *The Regulation of Telecommunications Industry* (Edinburgh: The David Hume Institute, Occasional Paper No.6).

Carsberg, B. (1990) 'Deregulation and Joint Ventures in International Telecommunications Strategies Regulation: The UK Experience'. (Speech at the *Economist Conference,* London, September).

Caulkin, S. (1987) 'Anyone Listening at British Telecom', *Management Today* (December) pp.38-44.

Hill, R. (1989) 'The Slow Response To Culture Shock: Ringing the Changes at BT', *The Director* (May) pp.58-61.

Maynes, E. (1979) 'Consumer Protection: Corrective Measures', *Journal of Consumer Policy, 3,* pp.191-212.

Moore, J. (1985) *The Success of Privatisation* (London: HM Treasury. Press Release 107/85).

Newman, K. (1985) *The Selling of British Telecommunications* (Eastbourne: Holt, Rinehart and Wilson).

Skeel, S. (1992) 'Can Vallance Keep His Balance?', *Management Today* (February) pp.42-46.

Vickers, J. & Yarrow, G. (1988) *Privatisation: An Economic Analysis* (London: MIT Press).

Winward, J. (1989) 'The Privatisation Programme and the Consumer Interest', *Energy Policy* (October) pp.511-17.

Level of satisfaction	Percentages				
	1988	1989	1990	1991	1992
Very satisfied	31	35	34	26	31
Fairly satisfied	52	52	50	58	55
Neither satisfied or dissatisfied	3	4	5	5	5
Fairly dissatisfied	10	7	9	7	6
Very dissatisfied	5	2	2	3	2
Don't know	-	-	-	-	-
Value for Money					
Very good value	17	11	11	5	8
Fairly good value	50	52	47	41	45
Neither good nor bad value	10	11	12	13	14
Fairly bad value	18	16	17	24	20
Very bad value	4	4	8	13	7
Don't know	2	6	5	2	5

Table 1
Consumers' Views of BT's Telephone Service

Source: OFTEL 1992

Period	1984/85	1985/86	1986/87	1987/88	1988/89	1989/90	1990/91	1991/92
Number	4559	12100	17947	29740	29423	37028	36940	43351

Table 2
Consumer Representations/Complaints to OFTEL (April-March)

Source: OFTEL Reports 1985-1992

	1992	1991	1990	1989	1988	1987	1986	1985
Turnover (M)	13,337	13,154	12,315	11,071	10,187	9,339	8,317	
Profit after tax (£000,000)	2,074	2,080	1,535	1,579	1,459			
Retained Profit (£000,000)	1,156	1,262	789	930	846			
Profit Margin	23.04	23.38	18.69	22.01	22.50			
Number of Employees	210,500	226,900	247,912	242,723	235,633			
Turnover per Employee	63,359	57,973	49,675	45,612	43,224			

Table 3
Selected (Operating) Statistics

Year	Total Exchange Connections (000s)	Residential Subscribers (000s)	Business Subscribers (000s)
1980	17,353	13,937	3,416
1981	18,174	14,671	3,503
1982	18,727	15,159	3,568
1983	19,186	15,546	3,640
1984	19,812	16,044	3,768
1985	20,528	16,596	3,932
1986	21,261	17,120	4,141
1987	21,908	17,549	4,359
1988	22,857	18,145	4,712
1989	23,946	18,737	5,209
1990	25,013	19,281	5,732
1991	25,488	19,609	5,879

Table 4

Network Utilisation: BT's Exchange Connections by Type of Subscriber 1980-1991

Source: OFTEL Annual Report, 1991

Year	Percentage
1972	42
1980	72
1981	75
1982	76
1983	77
1984	78
1985	81
1986	83
1987	83
1988	85
1989	87
1990	88

Table 5

Telephone Penetration Rates (percentage of households with a telephone in UK, 1980-90)

Source: OFTEL Annual Report, 1991

Country	Profit per £100 of Sales	Profit per Line
British Telecom	£26.50	£79.56
Average US Telecom	£21.80	£46.36
Spain	£37.80	£32.05
Japan	£11.40	£20.62
Italy	£13.90	£8.01

Table 6

International Comparison of Telecom Profitability

Source: *Daily Mirror,* 2 November 1991, p.7

Country	Revenue £m (1987-88)	Profits £m (1987-88)	Profit Margin %
US	192	121	63
W Germany	56	27	48
France	39	17	43
Australia	35	25	70
Japan	29	22	75
Canada	29	20	68
Netherlands	26	14	52
Italy	21	8	36
Switzerland	21	9	44
Spain	20	11	55
S Africa	17	13	76
India	15	11	75
Sweden	15	8	52
Norway	14	9	62
Saudi Arabia	14	8	59
Israel	12	8	69

Table 7

BT's Profit Margins on International Telephone Calls

Source: *Financial Times,* 23 April 1990

Austria	Vienna	73
Belgium	Brussels	76
Canada	Ottawa	84
Denmark	Copenhagen	97
Finland	Helsinki	98
France	Paris	107
Germany	Bonn	85
	Hamburg	94
Italy	Milan	74
Japan	Tokyo	85
Norway	Oslo	97
Spain	Madrid	59
Sweden	Stockholm	133
Switzerland	Berne	98
United States	Washington	173
	New York	74
UK	**London**	**75**

Table 8
Telephone per 100 population in Selected Countries/Cities

Source: OECD

MARKETING AN INDUSTRY IN DECLINE: THE CASE OF THE COAL INDUSTRY

Martin Hall

Introduction

Since the late 1950s, the British Coal Corporation and its predecessor, the National Coal Board, have operated in a mature declining market. The total home market for coal has been dimishing in size and British Coal's share of the available market has declined at an even faster rate.

The NCB was founded in 1947 with the nationalisation of private coal mines in the UK. There were 958 collieries and total production was 200 million tonnes per annum, of which home consumption was nearly 188 million tonnes. There were 718,000 employees and output per employee was 270 tonnes per annum.

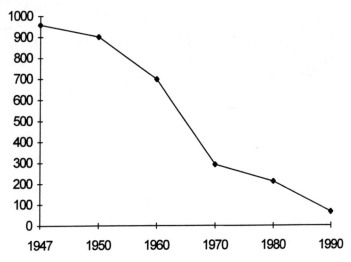

Figure 1
Number of Operating Collieries (NCB/British Coal)

Of the 187 million tonnes used in the UK in 1947, less than one million tonnes were imported (0.4 per cent). Of the 105 million tonnes used in the UK in 1991-92, 20 million tonnes were imported (roughly 19 per cent). The 3 traumatic strikes that rocked the industry in 1972, 1976 and 1984-85 did nothing to help the case for UK coal production and the mining industry. Sympathisers left the cause, including many customers once very loyal to home-produced coal.

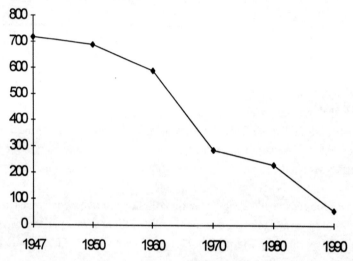

Figure 2
Total Number of Employees (000s)

With the 1979 change of government it become very clear that the industry would not be supported by subsidies and government handouts. It had to make its own way in the market place and become a self-contained viable concern. The government made no secret of its stated desire "to see the largest UK coal industry which is economically sustainable in the longer term".

The Electricity Supply Industry (ESI) Market

Between 1985 and 1991, the price of coal to power stations fell 28 per cent in real terms, and reduced a further 9 per cent in 1992-93. In 1990, 77 per cent of British Coal's total sales were to National Power and PowerGen. Both made it clear during their privatisation process that they intended to diversify their fuel supply sources when the contracts expired in March 1993.

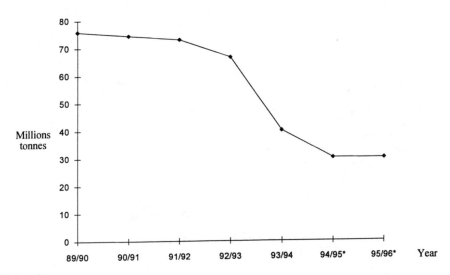

Figure 3
BC Coal Sales to Power Stations

Note: *Projections

The expansion of gas-fired power stations is of concern not only because the long-term contracts on which these are secured will lead to the permanent abandonment of strategic long-term coal reserves, but also because it is doubtful whether the majority of those stations will produce cheaper electricity than the coal-fired power stations they are replacing.

Indeed, if their higher costs can be passed directly on to the consumer, if it is arguable that the "dash for gas" is being precipitated more by a desire to capture a share of a limited and captive market than to benefit the electricity consumer. It is evident that by the latter half of the decade this will lead to significant over-capacity in UK power generation, and the absolute market for coal will shrink - irreversibly - just as British Coal is becoming better placed to win a share of that market.

The Industrial Market

The decline in British Coal's industrial market is very much a long-term one and would not be easy to reverse. The industrial market requires coal of particular qualities and size gradings and as a consequence outputs from different collieries cannot necessarily be substituted for each other. Moreover, only part of a mine's output is of the appropriate grading.

437

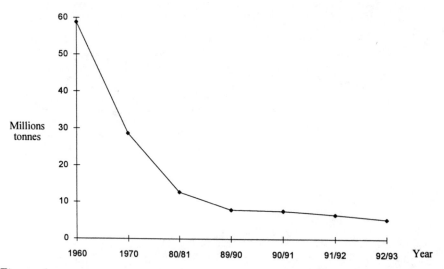

Figure 4
Sales to Industry

Malcolm Edwards, British Coal's Commercial Director until 1991, reported that "British Coal had given up trying to secure other markets because it is convinced that with so many of the UK mines about to be closed, it has no hope of supplying them with British coal".

John T Boyd's mining report (1993) to the government stated that "The industrial market will continue to show a steady decline due to the penetration of gas and the effects of the world-wide recession forcing curtailments in UK industries". In 1991, 7 million tonnes of steam coal were used by industry. The mineral products, chemical, paper and food industries were the largest consumers of coal for non-generation purposes.

In the commercial sector, coal consumption amounted to just over 1 million tonnes in 1991-92. The majority is accounted for by public administration and is used to heat hospitals, schools and a number of offices, but use has declined from over 1.2 million tonnes in 1987 and is likely to continue to do so. Switching to gas has been the main cause of the decline, coal often proving too expensive due to higher delivery, handing and maintenance costs at smaller sites. Furthermore, many local authorities using coal go out to tender for their supplies and only achieve reduced costs by purchasing foreign coal.

The Domestic Market

Domestic coal demand has fallen from 36 million tonnes in 1960 to 5.5 million tonnes in 1991-92 (which includes half a million tonnes of concessionary coal supplied to miners and pensioners). Over the last thirty years, the proportion of homes fitted with central heating

438

has increased significantly. At the same time, natural gas has become available to most households as a result of the extension of the gas transmission system and the continuing development of North Sea Gas supplies. Gas has displaced coal as the dominant domestic fuel for space and water heating. Electricity, and specifically reduced-rate overnight tariffs, has also contributed to coal's declining use.

Total Domestic Consumption	12.7	12.9	9.2	8.4	8.3
British Coal Market Share	10.2	8.9	5.6	4.8	4.2
	80/81	85/86	90/91	91/92	92/93

Table 1
Domestic Sales (Home Heating) (Million tonnes) [1]

Note: [1] Including Coal sold to manufactured fuel plants

Coal also suffers from competition with oil, particularly in rural areas not connected to mains gas. Although domestic oil consumption has declined since the 1970s, the low price of heating oil since 1986 has led to a recent modest resurgence. According to Caminus (1993) the prospects for coal demand in the domestic market are not good. Continued expansion of the gas transmission system will result in further displacement of coal. Domestic gas prices are also falling in real terms due to the British Gas and OFGAS regulatory pricing structure. In the short term, gas for space and water heading will accordingly become more attractive over time and contribute to the expected reduction in coal demand.

More recently BC has been supply constrained, both for domestic quality anthracite and house coal. The decision to close a colliery is ultimately based on its ability to produce low-cost good-quality coal to the power station market. When a colliery is reviewed, little attention, if any, is focused on its performance in the industrial or domestic markets - as a result, good-quality domestic market products are often lost.

Overview of BC's Position

During 1992-93, British Coal maintained its deep mine production strategy of concentrating resources on a smaller number of high-volume coal faces. In addition, by adopting the best mining techniques from around the world and investing in those collieries best suited to meet the needs of the market, major strides were made in improving productivity which advanced nearly 20 per cent on the previous year, and which has risen by 160 per cent in the last 10 years.

In spite of these gains in financial and physical performance, the market conditions confronting the Corporation remain extremely difficult. The depth and duration of the recession has impacted on total energy demand, while the structural changes which are now evident in the market for power station fuels resulted, during 1992-93, in the unwillingness of the two main customers to contract in advance for purchases of more than 40 million tonnes of coal compared with the 65 million tonnes supplied to them in the previous year.

However, the terms of the 5 year supply contracts with the generating companies mean that sales volume has declined by a further 10 million tonnes from the second year of the contracts, and the price British Coal received for the coal, which fell some 20 per cent in 1993, will reduce further in 1994 and each of the next 3 years.

A major challenge facing BC is, therefore, the ability to respond flexibly to meet market opportunities for sales outside the core contracts. However, the extent of the constraints on demand for coal, both from other fuels and from the substantial stocks of coal which customers have built up in recent years, are such that their willingness to purchase substantial additional tonnages in the near future, from whatever source, is likely to be limited.

The structural, organisational and cultural changes which were required to bring the market even closer to the centre of the business needed to anticipate market demands rather than follow them. To this end, external consultants assisted in a major review of the management and overhead structure. The benefits of this have yet to come fully into effect, but British Coal believes this reflects its commitment to the creation of a business which is ever more responsive to the needs of the market.

A 50 per cent reduction in current white collar staffing levels was recommended with the Marketing Department reducing to 190, Finance to 120 and almost all the 310 jobs in Information Technology were under scrutiny as the case for outsourcing services was examined.

Productivity

	1947	1960	70/71	80/81	90/91	92/93
Output per Man Year:	267	310	471	479	1080	1611
Output per Man Shift; - Production - Overall	- 1.09	- - 1.42	2.24	9.09 2.32	20.52 4.32	30.39 6.34

Table 2
Productivity (Tonnes)

Source: British Coal Corporation Report and Accounts 1992/93

440

Deep mines, on average, improved productivity by 19.4 per cent in 1992-93, raising the output per manshift from 5.31 tonnes in 1991-92 to 6.34 in 1992-93. This was in spite of the fact that, throughout the year, the industry was operating in an uncertain environment. At many collieries, achievements far above this average were recorded, a particular example being the productivity of 13.67 tonnes per manshift achieved by the Selby Complex. Altogether, deep-mined output for the year ending in March 1993 was 61.8 million tonnes.

The Coal Review

Imported Coal	-	Low world prices
	-	Readily available
	-	Some of better quality
	-	Some of lower sulphur content
Gas	-	Estimated 93 per cent availability
	-	Aggressive marketing
Oil	-	Price stability continues
Electricity		
Nuclear	-	Reduced social concern
	-	Government support
Wind/wave technologies	-	Wind farms could displace some of the power station requirement
Recession	-	Further reduced UK manufacturing and heavy industry
Clean Air Acts and emissions legislation		
Social factors/demographics -		Few young people use solid fuel
Low proportion of new homes have chimneys		
Licensed Mines		
Generators' import facilities -		May be used to service other markets

Table 3
Market Threats

In December 1992, British Coal submitted written evidence to the DTI Coal Review. The evidence gave an illustrative fuelling balance for England and Wales without policy changes. British Coal said that a number of actions could be taken by government to increase the black fuel market. These measures included:

i)   Not extending the licences of Magnox nuclear power stations.
ii)   Deferring the commissioning of Sizewell B nuclear power station.
iii) Reducing gas burn at combined cycle gas turbine plants (CCGTs).

iv)   Refraining from the construction of further CCGTs.

v)   Eliminating net imports of electricity through the interconnector with France.

These measures could lead to a total potential increase in the market for coal of 20 million tonnes. British Coal said that the government might consider further policy initiatives to prevent the market for coal being eroded further by 1997-98, including refusal to grant permission for further burning of orimulsion.

It was realised that it might not prove practicable for the government to take action resulting in an increased market of as much as 20 million tonnes of coal a year. A further illustrative modified fuelling balance was prepared to show the effect of more prudent assumptions. Under this scenario, the black fuels market in 1997-98 increased by 17 million tonnes and within that the market for British Coal increased by 14 million tonnes. In the event, the White Paper proposals led BC to the view that the additional tonnages available to UK coal producers in 1993-94 would be unlikely to exceed the maximum 10 million tonnes to be imported for electricity generation.

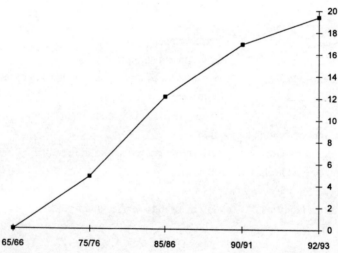

Figure 5

Imported Coal (Million Tonnes)

The seven recommendations which, in the Trade and Industry Committee's view, would secure an increased market were:

i)   The displacement of imported coal or oil through subsidies.

ii)   Removal of the non-leviable status of electricity imported from France and possibly restricting baseload supplies.

iii) Requiring flue gas desulphurisation (FGD) for stations burning orimulsion.

iv) Restricting CCGTs from operating permanently on baseload.

v) The generators to maintain higher-than-planning stock levels.

vi) A consequential increase in sales to non-generation markets as a result of keeping open more pits.

vii) A reduction in opencast output.

In considering the conclusions of the Coal Review White Paper, the government was able to take into account reports by the four consultancy firms appointed by the DTI. British Coal's view was that the report's main thrust was in line with the Corporation's operational philosophy and current strategy.

Their analysis of the market situation which led to the closure announcements of October 1992, and the economic basis on which collieries were selected for closure, broadly confined British Coal's assessments. At the same time, the reports reinforced the conclusion that radical market changes were needed if a substantial, sustainable, competitive and profitable business was to be secured. They also made plain the need for term contracts with the major customers so that progressive efficiency and cost-cutting measures could continue.

Aftermath of the Coal Review

Improved performances by the nuclear power stations and increased use of gas mean that coal burn in power stations this year looks like being seven million tonnes lower than anticipated at the time of British Coal's evidence to the Coal Review in December 1992 - at around 57 million tonnes compared with 64 million.

Power stations which in 1992-93 took over 65 million tonnes, are in 1993-94 contracted to purchase 40 million tonnes - and from April 1994 this will reduce to 30 million tonnes. Coal consumption at power stations has fallen by 20 per cent because electricity generated from other sources of energy has increased.

Latest figures show that nuclear output is up 12 per cent on a year ago. That is equivalent to about three million tonnes of coal. New combined cycle gas turbine stations have been introduced faster and have attained higher levels of output than anticipated. By March 1994, they are expected to have contributed the equivalent of 14 million tonnes of coal - four million more than predicted in British Coal's evidence to the Coal Review.

Coal is being pushed to the margin. Both generators have declined offers of additional coal purchases, and while British coal continues to explore the market, the likelihood of additional sales is remote. The lack of additional demand, coupled with maintenance of production at collieries previously proposed for closure, has resulted in pithead stocks rising through the summer at the rate of 200,000 tonnes a week. In November of 1993, they stood at 17 million tonnes.

On current trends, stocks will increase to over 20 million tonnes by the end of the financial year. This is physically and financially unsustainable and damaging to the prospects for long-life collieries. There is about 45 million tonnes of coal in stock at pitheads and power stations, almost sufficient for the anticipated coal consumption for the whole of next year. Stocks at this level will act as a serious destabilising factor in the coal market in the future. To protect the long-life collieries, it is critical that action is taken to prevent the level of stocks increasing further and to begin to reduce them.

In order to illustrate the ever-increasing problem faced by British Coal, a few selected lines from a press release issued by British Coal when the closure of Bentley Colliery was announced are appropriate:

> The 87 year old colliery is an unfortunate victim of the reduced demand for British coal in a highly competitive market place ... Around three quarters of Bentley's 20,000 tonnes average weekly output is being put to stock because British Coal has been unable to find a market for it ... Despite good operational performances, it is clear that there is no prospect of obtaining any additional sales for Bentley ...
>
> To continue stocking at pits like Bentley will pose a threat to other potentially long life collieries if no action is taken. On this basis, and with no criticism whatsoever of the workforce, British Coal have regretfully concluded that they can see no justification for its continued operation and have therefore decided on its closure.

Conclusion

British Coal traditionally enjoyed a position of strength, operating as a monopoly producer. It failed to react to the changing market circumstances and requirements of the late 1950s and 1960s which accelerated into the situation we see today. It currently competes in two very fierce and excess capacity industries, namely coal and energy.

Many consider the market place to be "unfair", but little has been done to correct this. Indeed, the whole situation was summed up by Cecil Parkinson, a former Conservative Energy Minister, who stated that "The behaviour of the miners in the 1970s and 1980s made it inevitable that the UK could not be totally dependent on coal. They made the argument for diversification to other sources of fuel".

Although British Coal has made major strides in recent years in quality control, productivity, and virtually no days lost through strikes or absenteeism, it has all been "too little too late". Surveys of customers of all categories have shown time and time again that they want:

- More competitive prices
- Continuity of supply
- Consistent quality

444

British Coal has persistently failed to meet these requirements. The circles are now decreasing at an every faster rate. Given the likely further restructuring and re-organisation, the privatisation of only 8 to 12 collieries is a very realistic, and by no means overly-pessimistic scenario.

Bibliography

Boyd, John T and Co (1993), *Independent Analysis of 21 Closure Review Collieries, British Coal Corporation. Executive Summary* (Pittsburgh)

British Coal Corporation (1991) *Report and Accounts* 1990/91

British Coal Corporation (1992) *Report and Accounts* 1991/92

British Coal Corporation (1993) *Report and Accounts* 1992/93

Caminus Energy Limited (1993) *Markets for Coal* (London: DTI)

Consensus Research International (1992) *Industrial Customer Service Report*

DTI (1993) *British Energy Policy and the Market for Coal.* Trade and Industry Committee (First Report). (London: HMSO)

Hall M (1993) *British Coal - Towards the Market Challenges of the 1990's* (Sheffield Business School).